So Much to Lose

SO MUCH TO LOSE

JOHN F. KENNEDY AND AMERICAN POLICY IN LAOS

WILLIAM J. RUST

 UNIVERSITY PRESS OF KENTUCKY

Published by the University Press of Kentucky

Scholarly publisher for the Commonwealth,
serving Bellarmine University, Berea College, Centre College of Kentucky, Eastern
Kentucky University, The Filson Historical Society, Georgetown College, Kentucky
Historical Society, Kentucky State University, Morehead State University, Murray
State University, Northern Kentucky University, Transylvania University, University of
Kentucky, University of Louisville, and Western Kentucky University.
All rights reserved.

Editorial and Sales Offices: The University Press of Kentucky
663 South Limestone Street, Lexington, Kentucky 40508-4008
www.kentuckypress.com

Maps by Richard A. Gilbreath, University of Kentucky Cartography Lab

Library of Congress Cataloging-in-Publication Data

Rust, William J.
  So much to lose : John F. Kennedy and American policy in Laos / William J. Rust.
     pages cm. — (Studies in conflict, diplomacy and peace)
  Includes bibliographical references and index.
  ISBN 978-0-8131-4476-4 (hardcover : alk. paper) — ISBN 978-0-8131-4478-8 (pdf) —
  ISBN 978-0-8131-4477-1 (epub)
  1. United States—Foreign relations—Laos. 2. Laos—Foreign relations—United
States. 3. United States—Foreign relations—1961-1963. 4. Kennedy, John F. (John
Fitzgerald), 1917-1963. I. Title. II. Title: John F. Kennedy and American policy in
Laos.
  E183.8.L3R88 2014
  327.730594090'46—dc23   2013045089

This book is printed on acid-free paper meeting the requirements of the American
National Standard for Permanence in Paper for Printed Library Materials.

Manufactured in the United States of America.

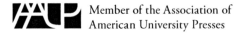 Member of the Association of
American University Presses

Contents

Illustrations follow page 172

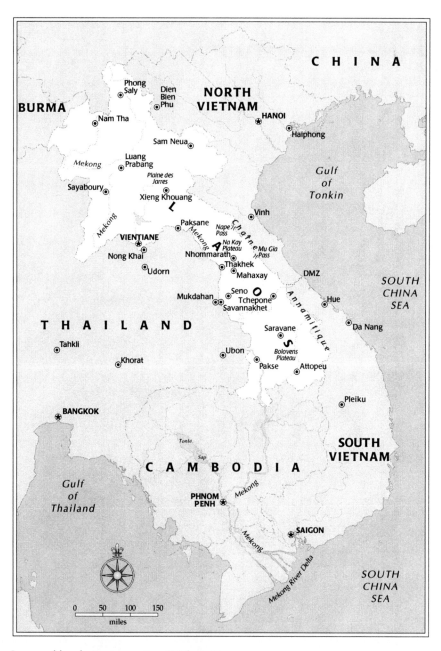

Laos and bordering countries, 1954–1975

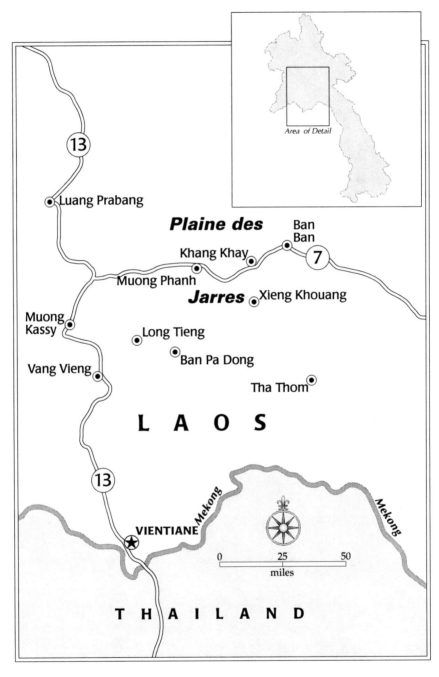

Plaine des Jarres region

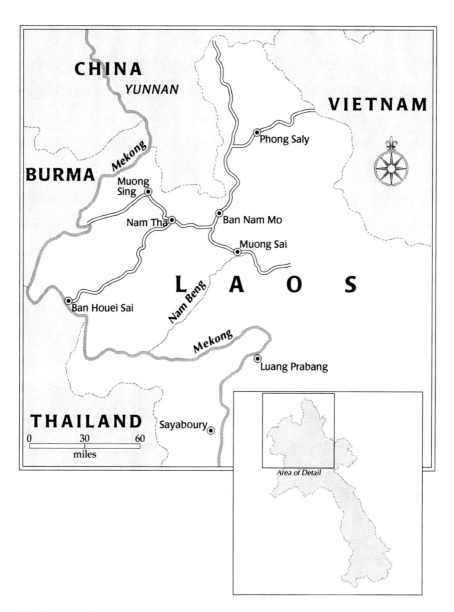

Northwestern Laos

Abbreviations

AID	Agency for International Development
ARVN	Army of the Republic of (South) Vietnam
BI	Bataillon d'infanterie
BP	Bataillon de parachutistes
CI	Counterinsurgency
CIA	Central Intelligence Agency
CDNI	Committee for the Defense of National Interests
CINCPAC	Commander-in-Chief, Pacific
CNO	Chief of Naval Operations
COMINT	Communications Intelligence
DCI	Director of Central Intelligence
DEFCON	Defense Readiness Condition
DNC	Directorate of National Coordination
DRV	Democratic Republic of (North) Vietnam
ECCOIL	Eastern Construction Company in Laos
ELINT	Electronic Intelligence
FAR	Force Armée Royale
FMM	French Military Mission
GM	Groupement Mobile
JCS	Joint Chiefs of Staff
ICC	International Commission for Supervision and Control
INR	Intelligence and Research
LPP	Lao People's Party
MAAG	Military Assistance Advisory Group
MACV	Military Assistance Command Vietnam
NATO	North Atlantic Treaty Organization
NLHS	Neo Lao Hak Sat
NSA	National Security Agency
NSAM	National Security Action Memorandum

NSC	National Security Council
NVA	North Vietnamese Army
NVN	North Vietnam
OB	Order of Battle
OCI	Office of Current Intelligence
ONE	Office of National Estimates
OPLAN	Operation Plan
OSS	Office of Strategic Services
PARU	Police Aerial Reinforcement Unit
PAVN	People's Army of (North) Vietnam
PDJ	Plaine des Jarres
PEO	Programs Evaluation Office
PL	Pathet Lao
PLAF	People's Liberation Armed Forces
PRC	People's Republic of China
RLAF	Royal Lao Air Force
RLG	Royal Lao Government
RO	Requirements Office
RVN	Republic of (South) Vietnam
SEAD	South East Asia Department
SEATO	Southeast Asia Treaty Organization
SIGINT	Signals Intelligence
SNIE	Special National Intelligence Estimate
SOG	Special Operations Group
SVN	South Vietnam
UN	United Nations
USAF	United States Air Force
USG	United States Government
USIB	United States Intelligence Board
VC	Viet Cong (PLAF)

Introduction

We've Got So Much to Lose
if That Thing Goes Sour

President John F. Kennedy began the telephone call with an ironic jab: "Am I talking to the architect of the Geneva Accords?"[1]

W. Averell Harriman, under secretary of state for political affairs and the chief US negotiator at Geneva, replied with good humor that the characterization was accurate. As both men knew well, Harriman had single-mindedly pursued a negotiated settlement of the civil war in Laos. The result was an international agreement that achieved Kennedy's goal of preventing a communist victory without committing American combat troops. There had, however, been skepticism in and out of the US government about the willingness of the communist signatories to comply with the agreement, which recognized a neutral coalition government and prohibited the use of Lao territory to interfere in the affairs of neighboring countries. If the accords went "down," said Harriman, he would "take the blame." The president, who appreciated Harriman's efforts on his behalf, admitted: "I have a piece of it."[2]

The date of the phone call was April 21, 1963. Laos, an impoverished, landlocked Southeast Asian country that was geopolitically significant only because it bordered more powerful communist and anticommunist nations, was one of Kennedy's earliest and most persistent foreign-policy problems. For the third successive spring the country was flaring up into an international crisis. The accords, signed in Geneva the previous July, had removed Laos as a point of direct conflict between the United States and the Soviet Union, yet leaders of the kingdom's competing political factions thought the agreement bore "no relation to political realities within Laos."[3] Renewed fighting broke out on the Plaine des Jarres, the strategic plateau named by the French for its clusters of ancient stone jars. The parts of Laos controlled by the communist-led Pathet Lao, including the infiltration routes from the Democratic Republic of (North) Vietnam (DRV) into the Republic of (South) Vietnam (RVN), remained closed to conservative and neutral officials. And Kennedy and his advisers were once again considering military measures to convince the Pathet Lao, the DRV, the People's Republic of China (PRC), and, above all, the Soviet Union that the United States would not permit a communist takeover in Laos.

In his phone call with Kennedy, Harriman declared that now was "the moment to talk" with Soviet premier Nikita S. Khrushchev: "We have every right to demand that he live up to his agreement."[4] Harriman's comment referred to two understandings between the United States and the Soviet Union. The first was achieved at an otherwise rancorous 1961 summit meeting in Vienna, where Kennedy and Khrushchev agreed that Laos had no strategic significance for either of their countries and that the two superpowers should work for a neutral settlement there. Harriman subsequently reached a second, more specific agreement with Georgi M. Pushkin, Soviet deputy foreign minister for Southeast Asian affairs and his counterpart at Geneva: the Soviet Union would "police the commitments made by the Communist signatories not to interfere in the internal affairs of Laos nor to use Laos as a corridor into South Viet-Nam." Harriman considered this Soviet obligation the "single most important" outcome of the Geneva conference.[5]

With Kennedy's authorization, Harriman traveled to Moscow in April 1963, but his démarche to Khrushchev was unsuccessful. In his report to the president, Harriman observed that Khrushchev "is fed up with the subject [Laos] and wishes it would go away." Whether the Soviet premier had the ability or will to influence the Pathet Lao was a question that remained "unanswered." It was Harriman's "impression" that Khrushchev "probably would like to live up to his Vienna agreement." The Soviet premier, however, was having "difficulty" honoring that commitment because of the more militant views of the PRC and DRV.[6]

Kennedy, unhappy with the failure of the Geneva agreement and with unfulfilled Soviet promises to ensure the compliance of communist signatories, reluctantly explored overt military options to prevent a Pathet Lao victory and to end DRV support for the insurgents. Even before Harriman's meeting with Khrushchev, Kennedy requested a Pentagon study of feasible "military action we could take against Hanoi" that would demonstrate US determination in Laos. The Joint Chiefs of Staff (JCS) returned with proposals for air attacks against ports, bridges, airfields, fuel storage facilities, and industrial plants in both Laos and the DRV.[7] Later that spring Secretary of State Dean Rusk and Secretary of Defense Robert S. McNamara proposed an escalating, three-phase program of pressure in Laos that culminated "in the initiation of military action against North Vietnam."[8]

Kennedy, expressing skepticism about the military effectiveness and the political acceptability of overt attacks against the DRV, approved the program's initial steps, which included increasing covert military support to friendly tribal groups in Laos and South Vietnam (SVN); delivering heavy weapons to right-wing and neutralist forces; and expanding the use of CIA-controlled Thai paramilitary units, South Vietnamese Special Forces, and other third-country "volunteers."[9] In the summer and fall of 1963, the crisis in Laos abated as the rainy season reduced the scale and intensity of military operations. Kennedy continued to urge the Soviets to honor their Geneva commitments, while simultaneously worrying that US-supported military activities might "disturb the quiet" in Laos.[10]

In the final months of his presidency, Laos receded as a significant area of policy interest to Kennedy, who was preoccupied with defeating the communist-led insurgency in South Vietnam. The conflict had appeared to be going relatively well since the infusion of US assistance and military advisers, which he had approved in November 1961. Some two years later, the Buddhist crisis, the overthrow of President Ngo Dinh Diem, reports of military deterioration in the countryside, and the ineptitude of the new junta shattered the illusion of progress in the war. Vietnam was now at the forefront of regional policy concerns, where it remained until the fall of Saigon in 1975.

At the time of Kennedy's death, US policy in Laos was confused and contradictory. On the one hand, the president had approved a gradually escalating program of military pressure to demonstrate US resolve in Laos. On the other hand, his basic policy guidance was that the "US should not take [the] initiative in military escalation."[11] This inconsistency reflected the dilemma Kennedy faced after the collapse of the Soviet-backed Geneva solution. Bereft of a plausible strategy for a united Laos, Kennedy maneuvered tactically to avoid hard choices between intervening overtly with US combat troops and accepting the "loss" of the country to communism. To his successor, Lyndon B. Johnson, Kennedy bequeathed not only an incoherent Lao policy but also military plans for taking the war to North Vietnam.

So Much to Lose continues the story of the US experience in Laos that began with *Before the Quagmire: American Intervention in Laos, 1954–1961*. There is a certain symmetry in the different policy directions that presidents Eisenhower and Kennedy pursued to prevent a communist victory in Laos. Eisenhower supported an aspiring anticommunist dictator, General Phoumi Nosavan, while undermining neutralist leader Souvanna Phouma. Kennedy, reversing course, backed Souvanna, while coercing Phoumi to participate in a coalition government. That both presidents achieved far less than they had hoped suggests the inadequacy of cold war ideology for coping with the complicated historical and political forces at work in Laos.

The first half or so of *So Much to Lose* provides an intimate look at the diplomacy, intelligence operations, and military actions that led to the Geneva accords, ratified by fourteen nations on July 23, 1962.[12] The rest of the book examines the rapid breakdown of that agreement, the response of the Kennedy administration to the collapse of the Geneva solution, and the consequences of that response not only for Laos but also for Vietnam. A central purpose of *So Much to Lose* is examining closely the almost immediate resumption of fighting in Laos after Geneva and the relationship of that conflict to the war in neighboring Vietnam.

The failure of the Geneva accords, Dean Rusk observed long after the Vietnam War had ended, "was a bitter disappointment for John Kennedy. Its impact on him has been greatly underestimated." Four months after Harriman's unsuccessful April 1963 démarche to Khrushchev, President Kennedy told Rusk to warn Soviet officials that if the situation in Laos "continues to deteriorate," the United States would "have to take some [military] action" on behalf of the beleaguered neutral government. The Soviet Union's "hands-off attitude" toward its Geneva obligations, Kennedy said, "removed any right they have to react to that action."[13]

Such comments and the planning Kennedy authorized for military operations against the DRV indicate the seriousness of the crisis in Laos during the last year of his presidency. They do not, however, provide a confident basis for predicting how he would have reacted to the problems in Southeast Asia faced by his successor. Ambivalent about the US commitments in Vietnam and Laos, Kennedy was, on the one hand, a cold warrior who sought to contain communist expansion. On the other hand, he repeatedly resisted recommendations to achieve that goal by intervening in Southeast Asia with US combat troops. Unlike President Lyndon B. Johnson, Kennedy was never forced by circumstances to choose between a communist victory and an overt US military commitment to South Vietnam.

Although the decisions Kennedy might have made about escalation or disengagement in Southeast Asia are unknowable, one can safely assume that he did not view the neutral settlement in Laos as a model for Vietnam. On September 3, 1963, less than three months before his assassination, Kennedy dismissed a vague public statement by French president Charles de Gaulle encouraging a unified, independent, and presumably neutral Vietnam. In a comment captured by his White House taping system, Kennedy observed that the neutralization of Laos was "not working" and declared that the communists "are doing [in Laos] what they would do in Vietnam." Sarcastically referring to columnist Walter Lippmann's endorsement of a neutralized Vietnam as "a great solution," Kennedy said: "I don't think we ought to let this get built up as a possibility of a reasonable outcome."[14]

Kennedy's most far-reaching response to the failure of the Geneva agreement was settling for a de facto partition of Laos based on the territory held by the country's right, left, and center factions. This informal arrangement generally divided the country along a north-south axis, with the center-right coalition controlling the population and agricultural centers of the Mekong River Valley and the Pathet Lao dominating the mountainous jungle region bordering Vietnam. Neutralist prime minister Souvanna Phouma remained in nominal charge of an ostensibly integrated government, and the fighting between the center-right coalition and the

Pathet Lao was "secret"—at least to the extent that neither the United States nor the DRV publicly admitted its own role in the conflict. This fragile equilibrium established a pattern of combat in Laos that grew in intensity during the Johnson and Nixon administrations.

The Pathet Lao and the North Vietnamese tacitly accepted the de facto partition of Laos. Despite a number of military advantages, they refrained from any meaningful attempts to seize the towns of the Mekong River Valley. Such a move would have posed a direct threat to Thailand and almost certainly triggered large-scale intervention by US combat troops. Instead, the Vietnamese communists pursued their principal goal in Laos: improving a network of infiltration trails into South Vietnam that a historian for the National Security Agency called "one of the great achievements in military engineering of the twentieth century."[15]

The Truong Son Strategic Supply Route, known to Americans as the Ho Chi Minh Trail, was initially a simple set of footpaths and mountain trails that allowed anticolonial forces in the First Indochina War to move from northern Vietnam into the country's central and southern regions. At that time, the arduous trip through jungle-covered mountains could take as long as three months. One of the DRV's first decisions of the Second Indochina War was to improve the trails in Laos and Cambodia leading into South Vietnam. By 1961 North Vietnamese combat engineers had constructed an eighty-mile road in east-central Laos, which in dry weather allowed trucks to drive from the DRV to an infiltration hub at Tchepone, Laos. Apart from this road, virtually all traffic on the trails in the early 1960s was by foot.[16]

During Kennedy's presidency, US officials had an imprecise understanding of both overland and maritime infiltration from North Vietnam into South Vietnam. The number of infiltrators who traveled along the Ho Chi Minh Trail was small, estimated at hundreds per month, rather than the thousands and even tens of thousands per month later in the 1960s.[17] In fact, historian Christopher E. Goscha, citing DRV sources, argues that maritime infiltration along South Vietnam's nearly fifteen hundred miles of coastline "was probably more important than the overland [trails] up to and including 1965." The consensus view of Kennedy's national security bureaucracy was that overland infiltration was a problem for South Vietnam, but opinions differed on just how serious that problem was. In December 1962, Deputy Under Secretary of State U. Alexis

Johnson, a diplomat with long experience in Far East political-military affairs, returned from a visit to Southeast Asia impressed by the difficulty of evaluating "the level and relative importance of present infiltration through Laos."[18]

The Kennedy administration's two most voluble counterinsurgency theorists, Roger Hilsman and Walt W. Rostow, held strong opposing views on the significance of infiltration through Laos for the war in South Vietnam. Hilsman, director of intelligence and research at the State Department before becoming assistant secretary of state for far eastern affairs, declared that infiltration was "only of secondary importance" compared with the village-level struggle with insurgents.[19] Rostow, who initially served Kennedy as deputy national security adviser and then moved to the State Department to lead its policy planning council, argued that infiltration was "capable of prolonging the war for a long time."[20] In contrast to Hilsman's emphasis on more effective village-level pacification in South Vietnam, Rostow proposed a political-military "scenario" that would "impose on North Vietnam limited appropriate damage, by air and sea action, if infiltration does not cease."[21]

Rostow later judged the president harshly for not following his advice to bomb North Vietnam: "Kennedy's failure to move promptly and decisively to deal with the violation of the Laos Accords was the greatest single error in American policy of the 1960s."[22] For a decade replete with policy errors associated with Southeast Asia—including a misguided faith in the persuasive power of limited air attacks against North Vietnam—this verdict seems extreme. Yet Rostow's conclusion, however dubious, raises an important question about Kennedy's relatively muted responses to communist violations of the Geneva agreement: Why would he appear to accept an unsatisfactory settlement in Laos, which, at the very least, complicated the counterinsurgency effort in South Vietnam?

Perhaps Kennedy was persuaded by Hilsman's theory that infiltration was an insignificant factor in the village-level struggle. If that was the case, Kennedy ignored not only Rostow's analysis but also persistent US military concerns about infiltration from Laos and Cambodia. Although the president doubted the judgment of many military leaders,[23] senior officers Kennedy did respect, including JCS chairman General Maxwell D. Taylor and intelligence operative Brigadier General Edward G. Lansdale, warned him of the risks posed by infiltration. Moreover, if Kennedy thought that infiltration did not matter much, why did he repeatedly discuss its dangers with advisers, allies, and adversaries?

The explanation for Kennedy's acceptance of a Lao partition allowing communist control of infiltration routes is that he was gambling for time—time to help Diem's government defeat the insurgency in South Vietnam. In April 1961 national security adviser McGeorge Bundy wrote to the president: "If we succeed in Vietnam the erosion in Laos might, in time, be sealed off."[24] Roger Hilsman expressed this idea more forcefully to Pentagon planners two years later. "The key to success in Southeast Asia," he said, was "holding a cease fire line in Laos established by the Geneva Agreement until such time that definite victory in SVN is apparent."[25] Leonard S. Unger, the US ambassador to Laos from 1962 to 1964, told the Joint Chiefs of Staff that North Vietnamese "interest in Laos would slacken if we are successful in South Vietnam."[26]

Based on the generally optimistic official reports Kennedy received in 1962 and much of 1963, victory in South Vietnam seemed a hopeful possibility within two or three years. But in the final months of his presidency, when senior US officials began to question progress in the war, the notion of buying time in Laos while waiting for victory in South Vietnam was stood on its head. Two days before Kennedy's assassination, his senior advisers agreed that covert military operations in the Laos panhandle would contribute to success in South Vietnam.[27]

A symptom of Kennedy's disjointed Laos policy was his tendency to compartment the US responses to the twin crises in Southeast Asia. Laos, he concluded, was essentially a diplomatic problem from which he sought to disengage without suffering an obvious defeat. The president assigned principal responsibility for Laos to the State Department, with Harriman serving as his executive agent and the American ambassador in Vientiane playing the leading role in security decisions affecting that country. Although willing to settle for a cold war "tie" in a neutralized Laos, Kennedy sought to help the South Vietnamese government "win" its struggle against the communist-led insurgency. He relied on the Pentagon for leadership in that conflict, with McNamara in charge of the effort and a four-star general directing US military assistance. In contrast to Kennedy's—and later Johnson's—unhelpful compartmenting of the former states of Indochina, the DRV saw Laos, Cambodia, and South Vietnam as a single battlefield for an integrated campaign of political-military operations.

Although he did not live long enough to face the consequences of his equivocal, disconnected policy in Southeast Asia, President Kennedy could not have been encouraged by reports from the region during the final weeks of his life. In South Vietnam, the nationwide Strategic Hamlet pacification program was deemed counterproductive, and the new military leaders in Saigon seemed politically and organizationally disorganized. The situation in Laos, though less acute, was also worrisome. A "special report" prepared by the CIA concluded that "the long-term prognosis for [Souvanna's] coalition appears dim" and that the right- and left-wing forces were "strengthening their positions in strategically important areas."[28] Shortly before Kennedy's assassination, Michael V. Forrestal, the National Security Council (NSC) staff member responsible for the Far East, warned of the coming "combat season" in Laos and the possibility of "another annual spring crisis."[29]

For President Kennedy, who once commented on the neutral solution in Laos by observing, "We've got so much to lose if that thing goes sour,"[30] his gamble at Geneva must have looked like a very long shot.

When he became president on January 20, 1961, John F. Kennedy inherited a crisis in Laos that included covert US military advisers participating in combat operations, a Soviet airlift to support the Pathet Lao and neutralist forces, and ominous-sounding diplomatic exchanges between Washington and Moscow. Unlike Berlin, Cuba, and other cold war battlefields, Laos was an active combat zone with US and Soviet military personnel in close proximity to one another. It was a dangerous East-West confrontation that had been many years in the making.

After the 1954 Geneva conference ended the First Indochina War, President Eisenhower authorized direct US military and economic assistance to South Vietnam, Laos, and Cambodia to strengthen their ability to resist communism. In Laos, a newly independent country with a small French-educated leadership class divided by personal, family, and regional rivalries, the US government underwrote the country's entire military budget and established an economic aid program that became notorious for its ineffectiveness.[31] Because the Geneva agreement prohibited foreign military forces in Laos, with the exception of a small French presence, the Pentagon hired retired and reserve military personnel to oversee the use of US materiel and to advise the American ambassador on the needs of the

Force Armée Royale (FAR).[32] The failure of the US and French advisory efforts prompted a 1959 decision by the Eisenhower administration to dispatch covert US Army Special Forces teams to Laos to provide training for the FAR.

Through overt diplomacy and covert political action, the US government exerted a pervasive influence on the internal political affairs of Laos, a constitutional monarchy with a weak parliamentary form of government inherited from the French. Between 1954 and 1960, the Eisenhower administration supported Lao leaders based on the strength of their anticommunist convictions, rather than their competence, honesty, or popular support. The embassy and the CIA station in Vientiane, the administrative capital of Laos, sought to prevent the establishment of a coalition government led by Souvanna Phouma, whose neutralist stance during the cold war most closely reflected national aspirations.

The US government, opposed to Souvanna and dissatisfied with the older generation of Lao noncommunist leaders, authorized the CIA to help establish the Committee for the Defense of National Interests (CDNI), a political front group of military and civilian "young Turks." In the summer of 1958 the CDNI was the means by which Eisenhower and his senior advisers "engineered the collapse of Souvanna's cabinet" and prevented Souvanna from resuming his position as prime minister. The following year CIA protégé Phoumi Nosavan overthrew Souvanna's conservative but not particularly dynamic successor, Prime Minister Phoui Sananikone.[33]

American intervention in Lao political life had a destabilizing impact on the ability of the country's fragile noncommunist base to resist the Pathet Lao, a political-military movement whose name dated back to August 13, 1950. On that day, 150 anti-French Lao associated with communist revolutionary Ho Chi Minh, the prime minister and president of the DRV, issued a communiqué establishing a provisional government in Laos. The document was signed "Pathet Lao," literally translated as "Lao state." The resistance movement included aristocrats and colonial administrators who had split off from Lao Issara, a short-lived, post–World War II independence movement. A second founding segment of the Pathet Lao consisted of revolutionaries with humbler origins but closer ties to Ho Chi Minh.[34]

During the First Indochina War, the Pathet Lao had limited popular support, mobilizing only three thousand troops to fight the French. After the 1954 Geneva conference, the influence of the Pathet Lao was largely confined to Sam Neua and Phong Saly, two northern provinces adjacent to North Vietnam. Controlled by the semiclandestine Lao People's Party (LPP), formally established in 1955, the Pathet Lao and its political arm, the Neo Lao Hak Sat (NLHS), expanded into central Laos and the southern panhandle through a combination of propaganda, elections, intimidation, and small-scale military operations. "The Pathet Lao draws much of its support from non-Lao ethnic minorities," CIA analysts observed. "Constituting almost half the Laotian population, these groups have for centuries been treated as inferiors, and have been isolated from the Lao of the Mekong River Valley."[35]

Exacerbating the political and military instability in Laos was an August 1960 coup d'état led by Kong Le, a twenty-six-year-old FAR paratroop captain who denounced foreign intervention in Lao affairs. The Eisenhower administration's response to the coup and to the subsequent neutral government, led by Souvanna Phouma, was undermined by contradictory policies proposed and actions pursued by the State Department, Pentagon, and CIA. After months of wavering support for both Souvanna's government *and* General Phoumi's effort to overthrow it, the US government committed itself to deposing the prime minister. In December 1960 Phoumi's forces, assisted by US military advisers and CIA-controlled Thai paramilitary forces, captured Vientiane. Souvanna fled to Cambodia, and Kong Le's forces retreated to the Plaine des Jarres, where the neutralists and Pathet Lao received supplies from a Soviet airlift.[36]

President Eisenhower and his advisers, anticipating communist retaliation for Phoumi's seizure of Vientiane, received reports from Laos that "sizeable aggression" from North Vietnam had probably occurred. The status of US contingency forces in the Pacific was increased to DEFCON-2, an alert condition just short of maximum military readiness and imminent war. Eisenhower authorized the American ambassador in Moscow "to tell Khrushchev that we view the situation with grave concern, that we are moving the positions of our forces to assure, if necessary, that the legitimate government will not be destroyed, and that in the event of a major war we will not be caught napping." Although high-altitude U-2 photo reconnaissance refuted claims of a North Vietnamese invasion, the combined military forces of Kong Le and the Pathet Lao posed a serious threat to the new Royal Lao Government (RLG). At a White House meeting with Kennedy the day before his inauguration, Eisenhower warned that the "loss of Laos" would be "the beginning of the loss of most of the Far East."[37]

Kennedy's firsthand experience with Indochinese affairs began in 1951, when as a thirty-four-year-old member of the US House of Representatives (D-MA) he traveled to the Middle East and Far East on a seven-week fact-finding mission. The First Indochina War was in its fifth year, with France attempting to reestablish colonial control in Vietnam by defeating Ho Chi Minh's forces. At that time, the US government was financing 40 percent of the French war effort. Kennedy, who admired the courage of the French fighting men, deplored the colonial implications of Truman administration policy: "In Indo-China, we have allied ourselves to the desperate effort of a French regime to hang onto the remnants of an empire."[38]

Three years later, when he was a US senator, when the Eisenhower administration was underwriting 80 percent of the French war, and when the beleaguered garrison at Dien Bien Phu was on the brink of annihilation, Kennedy conditionally supported "united action" by western allies against Ho's forces if France granted political independence to Vietnam, Laos, and Cambodia.[39] Kennedy's willingness to somehow transform France's failing colonial war into a successful western-supported fight against communism was essentially the same position as President Eisenhower's. The United Kingdom, however, had no interest in military intervention in Indochina, and France appeared unwilling to explicitly grant full independence to Vietnam, Laos, and Cambodia.

After the 1954 Geneva conference, Kennedy supported US military assistance to anticommunist South Vietnam and the collective defense treaty establishing the Southeast Asia Treaty Organization (SEATO), ratified by the US Senate by a vote of 82–1.* South Vietnam, Laos, and Cambodia could not join the alliance without violating the Geneva accords, but a separate SEATO protocol extended the treaty's protection to them.

---

*The eight members of the alliance were: Australia, France, New Zealand, Pakistan, the Philippines, Thailand, the United Kingdom, and the United States.

In a speech to the American Friends of Vietnam, a group to which he belonged, Kennedy declared: "Vietnam represents the cornerstone of the Free World in Southeast Asia, the keystone to the arch, the finger in the dike." He added: "This is our offspring—we cannot abandon it, we cannot ignore its needs. And if it falls victim to any of the perils that threaten its existence—Communism, political anarchy, poverty and the rest—then the United States, with some justification, will be held responsible; and our prestige in Asia will sink to a new low."[40]

With the exception of an occasional reference to the Eisenhower administration allowing Laos to "slip behind the Iron Curtain,"[41] Kennedy rarely mentioned the geographically and politically remote nations of Southeast Asia in his 1960 presidential campaign. Laos did not become a full-blown cold war crisis until after the election, when General Phoumi captured Vientiane and the Soviet Union began its airlift to the Pathet Lao and Kong Le's forces. At his pre-inaugural meeting with Eisenhower, Kennedy wanted to know how the outgoing president and his advisers "would deal with Laos." In his own notes of the conversation, Kennedy wrote: "I came away from that meeting feeling that the Eisenhower administration would support intervention—they felt it was preferable to a communist success in Laos."[42]

The new president received very different advice from his senate colleague Mike Mansfield (D-MT), a member of the Committee on Foreign Relations and a Far East expert who first traveled to Indochina in 1953. Critical of the "corrupting and disrupting" effect of the Eisenhower administration's aid program in Laos, Mansfield urged Kennedy to take "a new approach to policy." Mansfield, who sought to limit the US commitment to Laos and to avoid SEATO intervention in the conflict, encouraged Kennedy to make "an active attempt to neutralize" the country. Acknowledging the danger of such an approach, Mansfield warned that the "risks in our present policies seem even greater."[43]

Chapter 1

We Cannot Enforce
What We Would Like

On January 23, 1961, during his first White House meeting devoted to Laos, President Kennedy voiced concerns about the weak military position of the FAR; the reinforcement potential of neighboring China and North Vietnam; and the lack of political support, locally and internationally, for the government of General Phoumi Nosavan, the nominal deputy premier and defense minister, and his front man, Prince Boun Oum. An interagency report prepared for the meeting observed that the military situation was "deteriorating progressively," the British were unwilling to support SEATO intervention, and the French were "working against us" by providing covert support to Kong Le's neutralist forces. Kennedy told his advisers that he couldn't "quite see how the United States alone could solve the problem," and he wondered aloud "how specifically we planned to save Laos."[1]

A neutral Laos was the "optimum," if possibly unattainable, goal for the United States, according to Dean Rusk.[2] Success in negotiating a neutral political settlement would depend on right-wing victories on the battlefield. Kennedy, seeking to strengthen the bargaining position of the RLG, approved a US-backed FAR offensive to retake the Plaine des Jarres, a strategically important region in northern Laos where the kingdom's principal north-south and east-west roads intersected. Kennedy's Laos task force, composed of representatives from the White House, State Department, Pentagon, CIA, and International Cooperation Administration, concluded that Pathet Lao–Kong Le control of the plain threatened both Vientiane and the royal capital of Luang Prabang. Moreover, antigovernment forces could cut the country "in half by a thrust to the Mekong River."[3]

The gap between US aspirations for Phoumi's offensive and the capabilities of his army was considerable. Richard M. Bissell Jr., the CIA's deputy director of plans (operations) and the agency's representative on the Laos task force, recalled a US military briefing for Kennedy on the proposed February offensive. Listening to General Lyman L. Lemnitzer, chairman of the Joint Chiefs of Staff describe the plan, he "could not help but feel that it had very little likelihood of success. In fact, it was impossible. Having recently returned from Vientiane, I was convinced by my brief contact with reality in the field that we were dealing with a situation a million miles from the precision, order, and purposefulness of the Department of Defense."[4]

Bissell did not volunteer his doubts about the FAR offensive to President Kennedy, just as General Lemnitzer and the chiefs "chose to remain silent about their reservations" with the CIA's plan for overthrowing Cuba's Fidel Castro. "This was quite simply the etiquette of bureaucracy," according to Bissell, who apparently was a better judge of Pentagon-supported operations in Laos than his own agency's paramilitary plan for invading Cuba. Phoumi's slow-moving February advance toward the Plaine des Jarres bogged down. Deputy National Security Adviser Walt Rostow informed Kennedy that the FAR had been "stopped by a better organized and better equipped opposition than anyone had calculated." Rostow added that the Lao army was "a relatively weak reed for an offensive against determined and well-armed opposition."[5]

On March 3 the president asked the Pentagon to prepare a plan to seize the Plaine des Jarres—"within the present level of military escalation in Laos."[6] In other words, US assistance to the FAR would be largely clandestine. Six days later, McNamara, Lemnitzer, and Admiral Harry D. Felt, commander of US forces in the Pacific, presented a "concept" for recapturing the plain that would require six to eight weeks to organize and execute. The plan included the use of US helicopters, transport aircraft, and sixteen CIA and US Air Force (USAF) B-26 bombers that were "sanitized"—that is, information identifying the nationality of the aircraft would be disguised or removed. The B-26s, armed with machine guns, rockets, high-explosive bombs, and napalm, would attack antigovernment troop concentrations, supply dumps, and other targets on the plain. CIA-controlled Hmong tribesmen would conduct guerrilla operations against enemy command posts, troop convoys, and supply points.

On D-day more than fourteen battalions of FAR ground troops would attack the plain from the west and south. Five days later, Hmong guerrillas and FAR regulars airlifted by helicopters would conduct harassing and interdiction attacks on enemy lines of communication between the DRV and the plain. In the final assault phase, FAR paratroopers would seize the plain's main airfield, permitting fixed-wing transport aircraft to land follow-up Lao infantry.[7]

President Kennedy, referring to Phoumi's earlier failed attempt to hold the key crossroads on the plain, asked his military advisers why the proposed operation "would be better" than the February offensive. The answer he received was increased US assistance, which this time would include American aircraft and pilots. "We really did not support the earlier plan like we should have," said McNamara.[8] Brigadier General Andrew J. Boyle, commander of the US advisory effort in Laos, and Colonel John S. Wood Jr., Phoumi's closest US military adviser, subsequently attributed the defeat of the February operation to "unobserved artillery fire which fell in the area and scared [the FAR troops] to death." Convinced that the new plan would succeed, Boyle and Wood predicted that the antigovernment forces would "bug out" and "fade into the woods" at the first sign of heavy attack.[9]

Kennedy questioned his military advisers about FAR morale and leadership and the reinforcement capabilities of the communist powers in the region. The generally optimistic answers he received appeared more satisfactory than the civilians' comments about the offensive's political objectives. "What plans [do] we have after winning?" Kennedy asked. The replies from State Department officials, unidentified in the minutes of the meeting, indicated that a military success would trigger "peace seeking" by the communists. The hope was that the situation in Laos could somehow be restored to that of the mid-1950s, when the Pathet Lao was a relatively weak force concentrated in two northern provinces. Kennedy thought that the department's vague aspirations would resolve nothing, leaving the United States "open to continued torture."[10]

Near the end of the meeting, Kennedy asked if there was any disagreement among his advisers about going forward with the Plaine des Jarres plan. No one objected to it. The president, who wanted to meet again before launching the operation, authorized seventeen actions to implement the concept. They included increasing the number of Hmong guerrillas from three thousand to four thousand, negotiating with Thailand to supply the FAR with additional 105-mm howitzers and soldiers to man them, and providing the CIA with US aircraft and "sheep-dipped" crews—that is, US military men who were ostensibly civilians. Information about these actions was assigned the top-secret code word "DISTINCT."[11]

With Pathet Lao military progress moving faster than US and FAR preparations to retake the Plaine des Jarres, J. Graham Parsons, assistant secretary of state for far eastern affairs, proposed a plan to improve the RLG bargaining position while pursuing a negotiated settlement of the conflict. A former ambassador to Laos, Parsons was a career Foreign Service officer closely identified with the Eisenhower policies that had contributed to the crisis Kennedy inherited. In one of his last recommendations as assistant secretary—the new president had appointed him ambassador to Sweden within weeks of assuming office—Parsons proposed a variation of SEATO Plan 5, the alliance's basic concept for defending Laos against communist insurgents. Plan 5 sought to secure Vientiane and other population centers, as well as the lines of communication connecting them. Lao government regulars and paramilitary units would then conduct counterinsurgency operations in the countryside.

Unlike SEATO Plan 5, which included seizing the Plaine des Jarres, Parson's proposal restricted military operations to occupying the major Mekong River Valley towns, still under government control. If France and the United Kingdom refused to participate in the action, then the United States would seek troop contributions from Asian members of SEATO. The total force requirement, according to Pentagon planners, was approximately twenty-five thousand—assuming there was no overt response by the DRV or China. "The troops would go in merely to hold certain key centers for diplomatic bargaining purposes, not to conquer the country," Rostow informed Kennedy. "They would only shoot if shot at."[12]

At a March 21 White House meeting, Dean Rusk discussed the administration's "two-stringed" diplomatic and military approach to Laos. If the Soviet Union stopped the Pathet Lao from conducting offensive operations, then the United States would agree to participate in a fourteen-nation conference on Laos at Geneva, initially proposed by Prince Norodom Sihanouk of Cambodia. This was a significant reversal of policy. US officials had thus far rejected such talks, which would provide an international platform for communist propaganda and for "time-consuming wrangling while the military situation further deteriorates." If the communists refused to observe the ceasefire, then the Pentagon should be prepared for an "emergency landing of US forces in Laos." In an eyes-only message to Llewellyn E. Thompson, the US ambassador to the Soviet Union, the State Department characterized Kennedy's acceptance of the ceasefire-conference formula as the "final attempt to halt [the] present rebel offensive by diplomatic means."[13]

The unilateral US plan to defend mainland Southeast Asia, short of general war, was CINCPAC OPLAN 59–62. Its Lao counterinsurgency operations called for the rapid deployment of some twenty-five thousand ground and air forces. The multilateral plan suggested by Parsons—called CINCPAC OPLAN X-61—included Thai, Philippine, Pakistani, and Australian troops but still required some eighteen thousand Americans. At the March 21 meeting, President Kennedy and his civilian advisers were eager to learn how quickly the United States could deploy its forces to Laos. Admiral Arleigh Burke, the chief of naval operations (CNO) and acting JCS chairman in General Lemnitzer's absence, said that it would take about four days to land ten thousand men. When asked how many troops could land in less time, Burke replied perhaps two thousand to four thousand but noted that it would take at least three days "for any one unit to land and be ready to fight." In a message to Admiral Felt, Burke wrote: "This amount of time [was] accepted reluctantly."[14]

While authorizing further planning for overt unilateral and multilateral military operations in Laos, President Kennedy wanted the Pentagon and CIA to continue clandestine support for the Plaine des Jarres attack, "up to, but short of, the actual commitment of the B-26s and other forces." In his cable to Felt, Burke noted the "great sense of urgency" at the White House meeting: "Covert cover" for military operations in Laos was "getting thin," and US forces "must be ready to move overtly with little warning." Felt increased the readiness status of US forces required for unilateral and multilateral operations in Laos to DEFCON-2.[15]

On March 21 the first four CIA B-26 bombers arrived in Takhli, Thailand, from Taiwan. Preparations for the assault on the Plaine des Jarres, however, continued to move slowly. Major General Thomas J. H. Trapnell, whom the chiefs had ordered to Southeast Asia to appraise the

US plan and other matters, reported that General Phoumi was "regrouping his forces." Phoumi estimated that the regrouping would be completed in two weeks and that he could seize the plain before May 1. Trapnell, who commanded the XVIII Airborne Corps and had led the US advisory mission in Indochina in the early 1950s, considered the timetable "unrealistic": "Phoumi cannot retake the Plaine Des Jarres before June without bombing [by US B-26s]," Trapnell cabled General Lemnitzer and Admiral Felt. "It is not certain that Phoumi can retake the PDJ [Plaine des Jarres] before June even with bombing."[16]

As part of his diplomatic-military response to the crisis in Laos, President Kennedy held a dramatic, nationally televised press conference in the State Department auditorium on March 23. Standing next to three large maps indicating communist progress in Laos since August 1960, Kennedy denounced the Soviet airlift and the North Vietnamese "combat specialists" assisting the Pathet Lao. The United States, he said, sought "a truly neutral Laos." Supporting international proposals for an immediate ceasefire and prompt negotiations, Kennedy also issued a veiled threat of military intervention: if the Pathet Lao attacks "did not stop, those who support a truly neutral Laos will have to consider their response." Referring to SEATO's "special" responsibilities to defend Laos, Kennedy declared: "No one should doubt our resolution on this point."[17]

On the same day as Kennedy's televised press conference, a USAF C-47 "configured for aerial reconnaissance and communication intercepts" was shot down by antiaircraft artillery over the Plaine des Jarres, killing seven officers and men: Alfons Bankowski, Frederick Garside, Ralph Magee, Glenn Matteson, Leslie Sampson, Edgar Weitkamp, and Oscar Weston. Their names are engraved on the first two lines of the first panel of the Vietnam Veterans Memorial in Washington, DC, which chronologically lists more than fifty-eight thousand Americans who were killed in action during the Second Indochina War. The sole survivor of the shoot-down, Major Lawrence R. Bailey Jr., an assistant military attaché in the Vientiane embassy, was one of the first US POWs of the Vietnam War.[18]

Like his predecessor, President Kennedy wanted any possible military intervention in Laos to be a SEATO operation. But the alliance's European members, the United Kingdom and France, were no more receptive to Kennedy's proposals for SEATO intervention than they had been to Eisenhower's. Notwithstanding the "special relationship" between the United States and United Kingdom, British officials thought that mistakes in US policy, particularly since the Kong Le coup, had aggravated the conflict among the Lao factions. They also feared, in the words of John M. Addis, the UK ambassador to Laos, that the United States "might feel impelled [to] take some military action which would lead to escalation and World War III."[19]

On March 24 the American embassy in London reported that the government of Prime Minister Harold Macmillan was "embarrassed" by Kennedy's request for UK consent to a SEATO operation "without any discussion with [the] U.S. concerning details of military plans or cooperation." In a letter to Kennedy, Macmillan offered unspecified UK support if the United States took military action in Laos but opposed the idea of using "SEATO as the organizer of a military expedition." To US officials, it seemed that Macmillan's letter contained "obscurities and contradictions." And if there were serious differences in UK and US viewpoints, Kennedy wanted to prevent the appearance of SEATO disunity, which could be exploited by Moscow.[20]

Seeking clarification of the UK position, the president made an urgent request to meet with Macmillan, who was in Trinidad as part of a tour of the West Indies. On March 26, at the US Naval Station, Key West, Florida, Kennedy told the prime minister that the United States was "extremely hopeful that the Soviets would accept a cease-fire" in Laos. If they did not, SEATO would have to decide what action to take. Kennedy was troubled by the British preference for unilateral US intervention rather than action by SEATO. In Kennedy's view, an exclusively US operation would undermine collective security arrangements in both Southeast Asia and Europe.[21]

Macmillan, who was sympathetic to aspects of Kennedy's appeal, said that the British, too, hoped the Soviets would accept a ceasefire. There was, however, "a real possibility" they intended to "play it stiff." If the western allies gave in, said Macmillan, they were "sunk, not only with respect to Southeast Asia but with respect to Berlin and the rest." Wondering aloud whether covert action by the CIA might reverse the deterioration in Laos, Macmillan was disturbed by the scale of SEATO Plan 5, which he characterized in his diary as "a ruinous undertaking." To Kennedy, Macmillan said: "A more limited operation would make it possible for the Soviets and Communist Chinese to regard it [intervention in Laos] as an 'incident' and not a war."[22]

Kennedy assured Macmillan that the United States was "considering various kinds of paramilitary actions," but they might not be enough to halt Pathet Lao advances. The two leaders discussed the possibility of "a very much watered down version" of Plan 5, which would mainly involve US forces. Near the end of their meeting, Kennedy pressed Macmillan on UK participation in military intervention: if a communist takeover in Laos were imminent, and if a more limited allied military plan were developed, Kennedy asked, would the United Kingdom respond militarily to a formal request from the Royal Lao Government? According to minutes of the meeting, Macmillan "answered carefully: 'It is my personal judgment that we should. However, I must carry the Cabinet. I think I can.'"[23]

"We must respond," Kennedy replied.

In a cable to Rusk, who was in Bangkok for a meeting of SEATO foreign ministers, the president wrote:

> I had a satisfactory discussion with the British and, while they are extremely reluctant to engage in a SEATO enterprise or indeed any military enterprise in the area, I do believe if there are no other means available to prevent Laos from going Communist they would join us in an effort to maintain bridgeheads in Laos on the Mekong River, including Vientiane. They also agree it is important during these coming days at SEATO that an appearance of unanimity be given and I think they will do everything to maintain that appearance.[24]

Kennedy found the French response to US plans for SEATO intervention "less satisfactory." Upon the president's return to Washington from Key West, Hervé Alphand, the French ambassador to the United States, hand delivered a letter from Charles de Gaulle declaring that France was not prepared to use "SEATO as a possible cover for a direct Western intervention in Laos." De Gaulle wrote that he agreed that the situation was "serious indeed" and that the western powers must "prevent Laos from falling into the hands of the Communist camp." He also reminded Kennedy of longstanding French "reservations and warnings" about US policy in the kingdom.[25]

Recommending political rather than military means to resolve the crisis, De Gaulle wrote that an international conference similar to the 1954 Geneva meeting was the "road" that might lead to an independent and neutral Laos. Essential to a successful conference was international supervision of the ceasefire, the cessation of arms deliveries to rival Lao factions by the United States and Soviet Union, and the formation of a Lao government led by neutralist Souvanna Phouma. De Gaulle concluded his letter to Kennedy by confirming his country's informal status as the most reluctant member of the SEATO alliance: "If the day should come when France deemed it necessary to engage its forces once more in that part of Asia, she would probably have to ask herself if such a framework would be the most appropriate to her own responsibilities."[26]

Kennedy asked Ambassador Alphand what France "would actually do if the situation collapses." Alphand replied that he did not know. The president commented that "he did not see how the Soviets could be persuaded to agree to a cease-fire without the presence of some threat."[27]

The next day, March 27, President Kennedy met with Soviet foreign minister Andrei A. Gromyko, who said that his government was studying the western proposal for a ceasefire and conference. The proposal, said Gromyko, appeared to provide the basis for a settlement in Laos. When Kennedy asked when the Soviet Union intended to provide a definitive reply, Gromyko declined to name a specific date, saying only "in [the] nearest future." Kennedy made no overt threats but "emphasized [that the] US would be concerned if Laos [was] taken over by forces hostile to [the] US." In a message to Rusk, Kennedy wrote: "I stressed the importance of an immediate cessation of hostilities, and I reiterated that as a power whose interests and prestige were at stake, we could not remain inactive if the threat of a military take-over continues."[28]

During the early spring of 1961, the "already dismal military situation" in Laos "deteriorated severely," in the words of Huntington D. Sheldon, the CIA's assistant director for current intelligence. Within days of Kennedy's meetings with Macmillan and Gromyko, antigovernment forces seized the FAR base at Tha Thom, gaining control of the southern approach to the Plaine des Jarres. The withdrawal of Royal Lao troops from the garrison was "completely uncontrolled," according to a JCS situation report. An FAR airborne assault to recapture Muong Kassy, on the western edge of the plain, "ended ignominiously in mid-April with evacuation of the troops after little actual fighting." The operation's collapse, Sheldon informed director of Central Intelligence (DCI) Allen W. Dulles, "was a severe psychological blow to [the RLG]."[29]

US officials were particualarly worried by the Pathet Lao military threat to Thakhek, a provincial capital on the Mekong River in the Laotian panhandle. On April 15 antigovernment troops forced the FAR to abandon the village of Nhommarath, approximately thirty miles northeast of Thakhek. General Boyle reported that the regional FAR commander had been unable to "reestablish control of his demoralized troops" and that these soldiers had become "an ineffective fighting force." Dean Rusk warned SEATO representatives that the fall of Thakhek "would cut Laos in half at its narrow waist and bring Communist forces to the Thai border." UK officials conceded that the Pathet Lao had the "capability to cut Laos in two" but saw no evidence of any such intention.[30]

Although Lao soldiers on all sides exhibited little enthusiasm for killing one another, the RLG continued to suffer military defeats. On April 23 antigovernment forces captured Vang Vieng, a village north of Vientiane surrounded by karst hills. Winthrop G. Brown, the US ambassador to Laos, characterized the maneuver as a "considerable military and psychological success for [the] enemy." Despite a joint UK-Soviet appeal for a ceasefire, Pathet Lao forces routed the FAR at Moung Sai, a village some eighty miles north of Luang Prabang. "I do not see how we can afford to let [the] enemy continue his forward movement toward key centers of Laos beyond a certain point," Brown cabled Washington. He and General Boyle concluded that the only way to stop the antigovernment attacks would be with B-26 air strikes, "probably followed up by U.S. or SEATO troops."[31]

On April 26, only one week after President Kennedy's humiliating defeat at the Bay of Pigs, the US intelligence community concluded: "Communist forces in Laos are now close to complete military victory." Under Secretary of State Chester B. Bowles, the acting secretary while Rusk was in Turkey attending a meeting of Central Treaty Organization foreign ministers, told Kennedy that he faced "two difficult and unpleasant alternatives" in Laos: intervening militarily to hold RLG-controlled areas in the Mekong River Valley or accepting a political solution that would likely lead to Laos becoming "a Communist puppet."[32]

Kennedy, chastened by the Cuban fiasco, sought to appear resolute in Laos at a time when his confidence in the CIA and military had been badly shaken. According to notes of a White House meeting, prepared by National Security Adviser McGeorge Bundy, there was "general agreement" among Kennedy's advisers that US military intervention "would be unjustified, even if the loss of Laos must be accepted." Nonetheless, Bundy explained, "the possibility of a strong American response [was] the only card left to be played in pressing for a cease-fire, and accordingly the President explicitly refused to decide against intervention at this time."[33]

Although he denied Ambassador Brown's request for B-26 air strikes, Kennedy authorized the deployment of US carrier forces associated with SEATO Plan 5 and the movement of amphibious forces to within twelve hours steaming time of Bangkok. Among the postmeeting JCS instructions to CINCPAC was an order to prepare "to take measures to stop Red Chinese intervention, including strikes on intermediate bases in North Viet Nam and, if necessary, on bases in Red China which support operations against Laos." Admiral Felt was further informed of civilian "reluctance to use nuclear weapons initially, and their use [was] still subject to [a] later decision" by the president.[34]

On April 27 Kennedy called congressional leaders to the White House for a briefing on Laos. Admiral Burke made the case for US military intervention. Without it, he warned, "all Southeast Asia will be lost." Pointing out the logistic difficulties of moving US forces into a landlocked country with few airfields, Burke said that military operations would be extremely difficult. The United States, he said, "must be prepared for [a] tough, long, and hard war, which may well involve war with China." The congressional leaders unanimously opposed intervention in Laos but supported the deployment of forces to Thailand and South Vietnam. US naval and air power could be employed more effectively in these two more politically stable countries, with less risk of war with China. Kennedy told the group that he had not yet made up his mind about military intervention in Laos.[35]

The immediate need for a presidential decision on intervention was postponed by a May 3 ceasefire agreed to by the three Lao factions. Nine days later the fourteen-nation "International Conference on the Settlement of the Laotian Question" was convened in Geneva. As in 1954, the United Kingdom and the Soviet Union were cochairs of the conference. At the earlier Geneva meeting, the United States had described its role as "an interested nation" that was "neither a belligerent nor a principal in the negotiation."[36] At the 1961–1962 conference, the US government was a full participant.

The overarching US goal at Geneva was establishing a "neutral, politically independent Laos with a firm international guarantee against external aggression." Negotiating instructions, approved by Kennedy, acknowledged the weakness of the US position in Laos: "We cannot enforce what we would like." A probable but disagreeable outcome of the conference was a coalition government that included Pathet Lao cabinet members and Souvanna Phouma as prime minister. Kennedy, who only later supported Souvanna for prime minister, was initially skeptical of the sincerity of his neutrality. "Souvanna Phouma," Kennedy observed to Charles de Gaulle, "may be the best available solution even though obviously he is not a very good one."[37]

De Gaulle, who told Kennedy that the West should promote neutralism in Southeast Asia, said that the French knew Souvanna "well," an understated reference to his country's longstanding financial, advisory, and intelligence support for the Lao prince. Souvanna should be encouraged, said de Gaulle: "He might be able to establish a government which would make Laos 'more or less neutral.'" At a June 2 meeting with Kennedy, de Gaulle declared that if the United States intervened militarily in Laos, "France would not oppose. On the other hand, France would not intervene herself." He warned Kennedy that Southeast Asia was "a bad terrain militarily, politically, and psychologically to fight a war." Referring to the Geneva conference, de Gaulle said that it would be "best to return to the 1954 accords." Moreover, the French "would not hide their support" for Souvanna Phouma.[38]

The immediate US objective at Geneva was marshaling international support for maintaining the fragile ceasefire in Laos. A particular US concern was fighting at Ban Pa Dong, a small village in the mountains above the Plaine des Jarres and the headquarters for the Hmong guerrilla army. Ban Pa Dong had been under attack since late April by a combined force of Pathet Lao, neutralist, and North Vietnamese soldiers. In early May the first elements of the International Commission for Supervision and Control (ICC), a politically balanced body of anticommunist Canadians, communist Poles, and neutralist Indians, initially established to monitor compliance with the 1954 Geneva agreement, arrived in Laos but were unable to investigate alleged violations of the ceasefire.

The principal impediment to effective ICC supervision of the cease-fire was the insistence of the Soviet Union that any investigation required the "express consent" of both the RLG and the Pathet Lao.[39] Unrestricted ICC freedom to monitor the ceasefire, Soviet officials claimed, would be an infringement of Lao sovereignty. The PRC delegation shared this point of view. To western nations, the sovereignty argument seemed a cynical ploy to allow the Pathet Lao to improve an already strong military position. Yet in Laos, a country with a long history of Thai, Vietnamese, and French hegemony, officials of every political affiliation thought that the "ICC should operate only with [the] consent [of the] Lao government."[40]

At the June 1961 summit meeting in Vienna, where Khrushchev tried to bully Kennedy with military threats and ideological polemics, the president stressed the importance of stopping the fighting in Laos and allowing the ICC to investigate allegations of ceasefire violations. Once an effectively monitored ceasefire was achieved, he said, it would be possible to establish a neutral, independent government of Laos. Kennedy suggested that the United States and the Soviet Union influence their respective Lao clients to permit free movement of the ICC throughout the country. Khrushchev, an energetic and mercurial leader described by one historian as "boisterously clownish, belligerently cloying, aggressively insecure,"[41] blamed the United States for the crisis in Laos and objected to the "ICC's becoming a kind of a supragovernment administering the country." The Soviet premier did, however, agree with Kennedy that Laos was of minimal strategic importance and, therefore, not worth a super-power confrontation. "The Soviet Union is for an independent and neutral Laos," said Khrushchev, who pledged that his country "would exert every effort to achieve a settlement."[42]

In a subsequent conversation with Prime Minister Macmillan, Kennedy said that Khrushchev "did not appear very interested" in Laos. The president, according to Macmillan, was "much concerned and even surprised by the almost brutal frankness and confidence of the Soviet leader," who seemed determined to provoke an international crisis over western access rights to Berlin. While discussing political and military options in Berlin, Macmillan observed that "the simple position" for western nations would be to reaffirm their access rights and to meet any communist attack "with all the force at their command." Kennedy replied: "It was certainly this threat which had stopped Soviet action up to now. Unfortunately, there were some grounds for believing that after recent events in Laos and elsewhere, the West seemed to the Russians to be weaker and Mr. Khrushchev might no longer believe in the West's firmness of purpose."[43]

In a June 11 diary entry, Macmillan concluded that "no progress was made on any issue" during Kennedy's meeting with Khrushchev in Vienna. Acknowledging "some soothing words" about Laos in the Kennedy-Khrushchev communiqué, Macmillan wrote that the Soviet Union had done nothing "to get the cease-fire working." Fatalistic about western prospects in Southeast Asia, he wrote that "the Communists will get Laos— by one means or another—and it is hard to see where we are to make a successful stand. (It may even be better to accept—at some point—all the military dangers and difficulties of intervention now. Certainly if the Conference breaks down altogether, it is hard to see what else we can do.)"[44]

Meeting in Zurich, Switzerland, the so-called three princes—Boun Oum (RLG), Souvanna Phouma (neutralists), and Souphanouvong (Pathet Lao)—reached an agreement in principle to establish a provisional government with representation from each faction. A communiqué signed by the princes on June 22 included the domestic policy goal of unifying the three armed forces into a single national army. Among the agreement's foreign policy declarations were the withdrawal of all foreign troops from Laos, the acceptance of unconditional civilian aid from any country, and a prohibition against the kingdom joining or accepting the protection of a military alliance—an indirect reference to SEATO.[45]

The Soviet Union, PRC, and United Kingdom applauded the Zurich communiqué as a promising step toward ending the civil war. US officials, however, viewed the agreement with considerably less enthusiasm. They were disturbed by the rejection of SEATO and the absence of any reference to international supervision of either the ceasefire or the withdrawal of foreign forces. Although the communiqué did not name a leader for the proposed government, the Pathet Lao and the neutralists wanted Souvanna to serve as prime minister. The left and center factions also wanted two-thirds of the cabinet portfolios, which would make the current, pro-American RLG a minority in the new government.

On June 27 Phoumi told Averell Harriman, then the chief US negotiator in Geneva, that the attitude of Souvanna and Souphanouvong in Zurich had been "one of victor over vanquished." Under current circumstances, the Lao general declared, a negotiated settlement of the war would result "in almost complete capitulation to Souvanna Phouma and the PL [Pathet Lao]." Phoumi said that he had not taken a stronger position in Zurich because of his "uncertainty" about US policy. The only way he could establish a "military equilibrium" and a better basis for negotiations was through "strong support from SEATO or the U.S." Phoumi added that he "did not feel that foreign troops in Laos [would be] mandatory," a judgment with which Ambassador Brown sharply disagreed.[46]

Phoumi Nosavan had been both advancing and undermining US objectives in Laos since the late 1950s, when the CIA boosted his military and political career. In a small, impoverished country, with a limited number of potential leaders, the US government judged him to be "the best instrument through which U.S. military advice and aid can bring about maximum results." CIA operative John F. "Jack" Hasey, Phoumi's case officer, described the Lao general as ambitious, intelligent, unscrupulous, moody, and quick to imitate "western customs." Phoumi made a favorable impression on US military officers both in Laos and Washington, DC. After he briefed Pentagon officials in 1959, a US Army officer noted his "sophistication, self-confidence, frankness and open and friendly manner."[47]

Within the State Department, the enthusiasm for Phoumi was more restrained. Assistant Secretary Parsons observed that Phoumi did not enjoy popular support, even within the FAR. He "was not the kind of fellow who could run Laos" for very long, Parsons warned the JCS in 1960.[48] For policymakers, Phoumi's most troubling characteristic was an unwillingness to subordinate his personal ambition to US objectives. The Lao general's illegal power grabs in 1959 and 1960 undercut American efforts to unify the noncommunist elements of Lao society. Phoumi, however, retained the support of the Eisenhower administration because his right-wing authoritarianism seemed preferable to Souvanna's wobbly-looking neutrality. President Kennedy valued Phoumi's anticommunism, but the general lacked the military capability and political support to prevail over the Pathet Lao and the neutralists.

Invited to Washington to discuss the Zurich communiqué and the situation in Laos more generally, Phoumi began two days of meetings with senior Kennedy administration officials on June 29, 1961. It was a time of policy drift, with the State Department proposing two alternatives framed in terms of US willingness to commit combat troops to Laos: (1) If the United States was not prepared to intervene militarily, Harriman should attempt to negotiate the best possible settlement in Geneva, where the communist delegations had shown little flexibility. "This would probably mean accepting a Communist-dominated government of national union under Souvanna and ineffective ICC controls," according to a talking paper prepared for the NSC. "It is also probable that this would result in Communist control of all Laos." (2) If the United States were willing to deploy combat troops to Laos, Harriman could take a tougher stand in Geneva on a wide range of issues and encourage the RLG to reject unreasonable Pathet Lao and neutralist demands. Such a posture would increase the likelihood of a breakdown in negotiations, at which time the United States would "undertake military operations in Laos through SEATO or with those SEATO members prepared to participate, or if necessary, unilaterally."[49]

At the June 29 NSC meeting, Dean Rusk expressed his belief that establishing "a neutralist government in Laos would be difficult, if not impossible." Because of communist intransigence in Geneva and Pathet Lao strength in Laos, he concluded that a decision on US intervention might be required "within 7 to 10 days." Rusk, a soft-spoken Georgian, invariably described by associates as reserved and patient, embodied the post–World War II consensus that confronting aggression early—no more Munichs—was essential to preventing global catastrophe. Although an advocate of "collective security," he supported unilateral US action when faced with communist threats. As secretary of state, Rusk viewed his primary responsibility as providing foreign affairs advice to the president. He was sometimes reluctant to share his policy preferences at large meetings, but on this day he left little doubt about his willingness to intervene militarily in Laos. Linking the US commitment in Southeast Asia to the test of wills with the Soviet Union over Berlin, Rusk said that the United States "had to be firm."[50]

President Kennedy agreed that the situation in Laos might eventually require the introduction of US combat troops, but he was unwilling to identify the specific conditions that would prompt such intervention. At a White House meeting with Phoumi, Kennedy was particularly vague about US intentions: "If negotiations break down, we shall then have to re-examine what measures need be taken." When Phoumi asked the president for his views on a government led by Souvanna, Kennedy said that it would depend on the distribution of cabinet portfolios among the three factions. He added that he "was not sufficiently aware of the different personalities to make a judgment at this distance." According to the minutes of the meeting, Kennedy said that "the British and French look more hopefully on Souvanna to maintain neutrality than do others," an observation indicating the US government's continuing doubts about him. In his summary comments to the general, Kennedy said:

The United States will be influenced by Phoumi's judgment; the objective is an independent and neutral Laos; the United States wants to maintain intimate contact with the General through Ambassador Brown; Ambassador Harriman will return to Geneva to seek to obtain an effective ICC; the makeup of a future government will depend on the General's firmness and judgment; we cannot get everything we want in Laos; in view of the military situation, we do not want to resolve the situation by purely military means; we must therefore seek the best arrangement we can obtain; the evolution of the situation will depend on the General, on the [FAR], and on the King.[51]

Rusk's conversation with Phoumi was also equivocal. On the one hand, Rusk said that the United States was "fully conscious of having undertaken to do its utmost in order to prevent a Communist takeover of Laos," and he flattered Phoumi, praising "the great gallantry with which the General has defended the cause of freedom." On the other hand, Rusk emphasized the "two main reasons" that made direct US military intervention in Laos "difficult": the Kennedy administration's commitment to a negotiated settlement and the risk of triggering "World War III." Speaking "frankly and as a friend," Rusk said that he found "it impossible for the U.S. to state precisely and in advance what might be the circumstances under which the U.S. would find it necessary to intervene militarily."[52]

The ambiguous talks in Washington, which included further discussions at the State Department and Pentagon, allowed Phoumi to interpret US policy in ways that reflected both his anticommunism and his self-interest. He returned to Vientiane "vastly encouraged" and "with [a] feeling that [the] U.S. is now prepared to back him militarily," Brown reported. Because the US government sought an independent, united, and neutral Laos—an outcome Phoumi considered beyond the reach of a Souvanna-led government—the general "concludes that he can count on U.S. support in the military action which will in his view almost certainly be required."[53]

The Joint Chiefs of Staff shared Phoumi's view that US military intervention in Laos would likely be necessary. The chiefs, noting the fall of Ban Pa Dong and attacks against RLG positions, were disturbed that antigovernment forces had been violating the May 3 ceasefire to expand their territory, while the FAR generally restricted its operations to defending areas under government control. In Geneva, the JCS observed, the US negotiating position had been weakened by compromises with the French and British, which were "subject to further dilution" by other conference delegations. The issue that seemed to bother the chiefs most was the US decision to continue participating in the Geneva conference without an effective ceasefire in Laos. In a July 12 memorandum to McNamara, the JCS recommended that the next time antigovernment forces violated the ceasefire, the United States should withdraw its delegation from Geneva and "undertake military operations in Laos." The objective of US intervention: "achieve the necessary military position to permit successful political negotiation for a unified independent and neutral Laos."[54]

The operational plan recommended by the chiefs, "approved at high levels in State and Defense," involved "forces of some SEATO nations as well as the United States." Presumably, the chiefs were referring to one of the variations on SEATO Plan 5. Although Plan 5 and unilateral US concepts for defending Laos provided protection for much of Thailand, there was a growing concern in Washington that they did not include the eastern panhandle region of Laos adjacent to South Vietnam. "The immediate military danger to Viet-Nam as well as to its neighbors derives from the continued infiltration from the North into the Laotian panhandle and over the western border of Vietnam," wrote General Maxwell D. Taylor, a former army chief of staff whom Kennedy had appointed military representative to the president after the Bay of Pigs debacle. "There is no present military plan in existence which is adequate to cope with this threat."[55]

Taylor was a reassuring source of military advice for a president whose confidence in the Joint Chiefs of Staff had been undermined by their advice on Cuba and Laos the previous spring. Kennedy blamed the chiefs for not warning him about the military deficiencies of the CIA's Cuba plan, and he found their counsel on Laos divided and too muscular. During the spring Laotian crisis, Admiral Burke, the CNO, had been the leading advocate of intervening with US ground troops, while General Thomas D. White, the air force chief of staff, was "most reluctant to commit US land forces to the mainland of Asia."[56] General George H. Decker, the army chief of staff, said that the United States "cannot win a conventional war in Southeast Asia" and should consider "using nuclear bombs."[57] Rostow later observed: "I never saw the American military less clear in mind, less helpful to a President, than in the first four months of Kennedy's administration."[58]

The absence of any formal contingency plan for defending the Mekong Valley *and* controlling the border region with Vietnam revealed a wide gap between the political options perceived by Washington policymakers and the military realities in Laos. For months, US officials had been proposing a partition of Laos along an east-west axis if a satisfactory political settlement could not be achieved. Southern Laos, a region formally ruled by Boun Oum and his forebears, and the sole source of General Phoumi's limited political support, had been a separate kingdom until the French unified Laos in 1946 under the sovereignty of the royal house in Luang Prabang. The attraction to US policymakers of either a formal or a de facto division of Laos was straightforward: a right-wing southern stronghold would not only prevent communist control of the entire country but also establish a buffer protecting South Vietnam and much of Thailand.

A key problem with the partition scheme, Ambassador Brown reminded the State Department, was that the Pathet Lao already exercised a "very large influence in the panhandle" and controlled the "crucial corridor regions on the South Vietnam border."[59] Brown, a tall, lean, white-haired New Englander, was a career Foreign Service officer whose assignment in Vientiane began only weeks before the Kong Le coup and ended just before the signing of the Geneva accords. During this tumultuous chapter in US-Lao relations, he faithfully executed the instructions of his State Department superiors—but sometimes only after identifying the flaws in their thinking. Senior US military officers, who resented Brown's unsparing assessments of Phoumi's limitations as a leader, urged his recall on many occasions, including General Trapnell's March 1961 visit to Laos.[60]

Brown argued to State Department officials that any partition concept "acceptable to our side would be difficult if not impossible [to] achieve simply by negotiation." The Pathet Lao was, for example, "very strong around Nape," the name of both a village in the panhandle and a nearby pass from the DRV into Laos. Along the border with South Vietnam, the Pathet Lao controlled territory to a depth of twenty to thirty miles inside Laos. "Let us not delude ourselves into thinking that we have a firmly held southern redoubt into which to withdraw," wrote Brown. To stateside colleagues who contemplated a north-south division of Laos without a significant fight, the ambassador warned: "The Communists will want to keep open the Ho Chi Minh trail at all costs."[61]

On July 28, 1961, Kennedy discussed diplomatic-military affairs in Southeast Asia with State Department officials and his White House staff. U. Alexis Johnson, deputy under secretary of state for political affairs, reported that the communists were "very confident about the current military situation" in Laos. Unless the United States did something to change that assessment, there was little chance of reaching a satisfactory agreement in Geneva, defined by Johnson as a strong ICC and a Lao government capable of avoiding communist domination. Without such a settlement, he said, "Laos will pose an increasing threat to South Vietnam." Johnson added that the United States was "on a sort of treadmill" in Vietnam, with the Diem government inflicting significant losses that the insurgents replaced.[62]

Johnson, a career Foreign Service officer and former ambassador to Thailand, played a central role in coordinating diplomatic, military, and intelligence affairs for the US government. He proposed that the United States introduce "a new element" into Southeast Asian affairs that might change the communists' perceptions of the situation: "a plan to take and hold the southern part of Laos with combined forces of the Royal Laotian Government, Thailand, Vietnam, and the United States." In the event of a breakdown in the ceasefire, Johnson explained, the United States would seek not merely to restore the status quo but also to establish a strong, new position in southern Laos. He also suggested "a new way" of responding to significant North Vietnamese intervention in the kingdom. Previous planning had restricted retaliatory military attacks to targets in Laos. The possibility Johnson raised was US naval and air action against Hanoi and Haiphong. No detailed plan for seizing southern Laos had been formulated, but General Taylor was working closely with General Lemnitzer.[63]

President Kennedy was unimpressed by the proposal. Referring to earlier failures to retake the Plaine des Jarres, Kennedy said that optimistic assessments of military plans for Laos "were invariably proven false." He repeated his concerns about the logistical difficulties of fighting in Laos, which had only two large airfields and was nearly beyond the reach of carrier-based aircraft. He also "emphasized the reluctance of the American people and of many distinguished military leaders to see any direct involvement of U.S. troops in that part of the world."[64] (The distinguished military leaders included General of the Army Douglas MacArthur, who had advised Kennedy to avoid committing US ground forces to Southeast Asia.)

Although notes of the meeting do not identify the speaker, there was a reply to the president's objections: "With a proper plan, with outside support, and above all with a clear and open American commitment, the results [in Laos] would be very different from anything that had happened before." No decision was required that day, said Johnson, but it "would be most helpful [for] planning" if the president indicated his thinking on military intervention in Laos. Kennedy, still unwilling to bind future decisions to hypothetical circumstances, indicated that he was "at present very reluctant" to commit US forces to Laos. "Nothing would be worse than an unsuccessful intervention in this area," said Kennedy. Although he did not have confidence in the military proposal submitted to him, Kennedy said that he was "eager to have it studied more carefully."[65]

Kennedy's skepticism about the military plan did not mean that he was optimistic about a negotiated settlement. His "gloomy view" of the Geneva conference was influenced by disagreements among the three princes over the composition of a new government and by the likelihood that Souvanna would lead it "sooner or later." He was also concerned by reports that General Phoumi sought to "break up" the conference and draw the United States "into military action in Laos." Despite unpromising prospects for a settlement, Kennedy urged his advisers to press forward with negotiations in Geneva and the formation of "a satisfactory government."[66]

Chapter 2

A Wide Measure of Discretion

The basic Lao policy choice confronting President Kennedy in early August 1961 was either military intervention to back Phoumi or diplomatic support for Prince Souvanna Phouma as prime minister of a coalition government. Souvanna was, quite simply, the only candidate for the position with any chance of receiving the approval of the kingdom's three political factions and their international supporters. "If we are not prepared [to] use force to avoid him," Ambassador Brown advised, "we should begin to try affirmatively to make the best of him." Averell Harriman agreed with Brown's analysis, observing that a renewal of hostilities was the only alternative to "accepting Souvanna as prime minister."[1]

Born in the royal capital of Luang Prabang in 1901, Souvanna was a French-educated engineer who enjoyed bridge, fine wine, and a good cigar. A leader of the post–World War II Lao Issara independence movement, he served three nonconsecutive terms as prime minister between 1950 and 1960—a record that reflected both his stature within the kingdom and the political instability of the country. The Eisenhower administration viewed Souvanna's neutralism with hostility, undermined his government in the mid-1950s, and helped put his conservative political rivals in power in 1958 and again in 1960.

Many US officials, particularly in the military and the CIA, still distrusted Souvanna for his insufficient appreciation of the threat posed by communism and the Pathet Lao. Admiral Felt declared to the Joint Chiefs of Staff: "There has been more wishful thinking about Souvanna in the free world [than] about any other character except Fidel Castro."[2] Even American officials more sympathetic to Souvanna viewed him as naïve and excessively self-confident in his ability to manage the competing domestic and international forces affecting Laotian neutrality and independence. Souvanna, claiming that communism was incompatible with the Lao national character, was "certain that once outside influences are removed, the Pathet Lao hard-core can be isolated and their sympathizers drawn back into the fold."[3]

Kennedy reluctantly agreed to pursue the "Souvanna solution." Dean Rusk discussed the shift in US policy with French foreign minister Maurice Couve de Murville and the UK foreign secretary, Lord Home, at a meeting in Paris on August 7, 1961. The British and French had long thought that US support for Phoumi and objections to Souvanna were misguided. In the Europeans' view, Phoumi was a dictator who lacked military competence and political support. Souvanna, on the other hand, was a statesman who was friendlier to the West than most Americans believed. "There must be a Laotian government headed by Souvanna," Couve had written Rusk. "We all know that there is no other solution."[4]

In Paris, Rusk made it clear that US support for a coalition government led by Souvanna came with conditions: None of the key cabinet portfolios—foreign affairs, defense, or interior—could go to the NLHS, the political arm of the Pathet Lao. The inclusion of a limited number of NLHS ministers had to be balanced by representation from the Boun Oum–Phoumi faction. And the center group in a Souvanna government could not be restricted to the leftists who had followed him into exile. (Quinim Pholsena, a former RLG minister who had requested Soviet and North Vietnamese assistance for the neutralists after the battle of Vientiane, seemed particularly untrustworthy to the Americans.) The Lao government must be genuinely neutral, Rusk told Couve and Home: the United States would not put its "stamp of approval on a fraud."[5]

US support for Souvanna also required a revitalized ICC capable of monitoring the ceasefire, the withdrawal of foreign troops, and the introduction of foreign military equipment and personnel. After the 1954 Geneva conference, the commission had been hindered in fulfilling a similar role in Indochina by limitations on the movement of ICC inspectors and by a "unanimity principle" that often paralyzed the work of the Canadians, Indians, and Poles. A new agreement in Geneva, US officials insisted, would have to provide freedom of action for the ICC and prevent the Poles from vetoing investigations of Pathet Lao and North Vietnamese violations. French and British officials shared US aspirations for the commission, but Souvanna insisted that its investigations would require the consent of the Lao government. Privately, he was more flexible, indicating that his government would never withhold approval of ICC investigations.[6]

During the Paris meeting of foreign ministers, Harriman said that he "hoped Souvanna would be helped to understand that he must not allow Viet Cong to use Lao territory to attack Viet-Nam." Rusk added that preventing infiltration from North Vietnam into South Vietnam was "in Souvanna's own interest." Should Laos be used as a corridor for infiltration, Souvanna ran the risk of "armed reaction" from the South Vietnamese side of the border. Edward Peck, the UK assistant under secretary of state responsible for the Far East, thought that stopping infiltration should be discussed with Souvanna but that it should not be a condition for US support: "It is most unlikely that Souvanna Phouma could be in a position to control the jungle trail."[7]

The Paris talks led to an agreement among the three foreign ministers on conditions for western support of Souvanna Phouma as the prime minister of a coalition government. The French, because of their close relationship with the Lao leader, met with him first in northern Laos on August 27. Souvanna was optimistic about establishing a neutral government and vague about the ways that government would work. Neither France nor the United Kingdom found any insurmountable difficulties with Souvanna's views. The United States, however, considered his response "unsatisfactory." For example, Souvanna's proposed slate of eight center ministers, all of whom appeared to be leftists, exacerbated US uncertainty about his neutrality. At an August 29 White House meeting, Kennedy said: "Souvanna should be told that we were anxious to get an agreement with respect to a coalition government nailed down, but that we did not think that his candidates were truly neutral."[8]

If the US government could not come to terms with Souvanna, then Harriman suggested "a major effort to disaffect him and get him to quit." Kennedy asked whether "Souvanna could be induced to count himself out." Rusk replied that it might be possible, but the president was skeptical. With the exception of Thailand and South Vietnam, every country at the Geneva conference supported Souvanna for prime minister. According to notes of the meeting prepared by McGeorge Bundy, Kennedy "made clear that we would like nothing better than 'to get out of Laos, if we can.' We have no other objective there other than to reach an acceptable settlement which does not hand the country over to the communists." But without such a settlement, said Kennedy, "we may have to consider military action."[9]

The president then asked General Lemnitzer to present the latest military contingency plans. The JCS chairman outlined an enlarged version of SEATO Plan 5 as the preferred response to a major breakdown of the ceasefire. This operation would seek to secure Mekong population centers from Vientiane to Pakse; to hold Sayaboury Province up to and including Luang Prabang; and to expel antigovernment forces from southern Laos, including the Tchepone area. The result would be a de facto partition of Laos, with the Pathet Lao continuing to control much of northern Laos. The more expansive US military plan required an increased commitment of regular forces from allies, primarily Thailand and South Vietnam. If Pathet Lao ceasefire violations remained ambiguous, US plans called for stiffening FAR units with company-level US Special Forces and Thai advisers. In addition, Thailand and South Vietnam would covertly introduce paramilitary units into southern Laos to help the FAR maintain and perhaps expand areas controlled by the RLG.[10]

U. Alexis Johnson urged immediate talks with US allies about the contingency planning. McNamara, however, suggested that these conversations avoid any commitments to US military action because of the escalating crisis in Berlin, where the communist German Democratic Republic had just erected a barbed-wire barrier that became the Berlin Wall. "We would not want to tie down substantial forces in Laos if these forces were required to deal with the Berlin situation," said McNamara. Kennedy agreed with McNamara, authorizing discussions with allies about an enlarged SEATO Plan 5 without committing the United States to the operation.[11]

The president also agreed to arming and training additional Hmong guerrillas, increasing the total supported by the CIA to eleven thousand; to raising the number of Special Forces trainers to 500, for a total of 802 US military advisers in Laos; and to resuming photo-reconnaissance missions, which had been suspended since the May 3 ceasefire. Stressing the importance of reaching an acceptable agreement with Souvanna, Kennedy said that he "didn't want to take on a war in Laos in a situation where we lacked French and British support and where public interest in the U.S. had greatly declined." Rusk interjected that he did not anticipate a buildup of US ground forces in Laos equivalent to the deployments during the Korean War. Instead, the United States "would fall back and hit the Communists from the sea and from elsewhere outside Laos." According to minutes of the meeting, Kennedy "indicated his agreement."[12]

After the White House meeting, Kennedy telephoned Harriman, the US official selected to meet with Souvanna. The president wanted to make sure that Harriman made "every effort to get an agreement" with the neutralist leader. Said Kennedy: "The alternative to an understanding with Souvanna was not one that he would like to contemplate."[13]

The son of railroad tycoon E. H. Harriman, he was not a typical Kennedy administration political appointee. Although as self-confident and nearly as vigorous as most officials in the New Frontier, Averell Harriman was more than two decades older than the president and most of his closest advisers. For Kennedy, who declared in his inaugural address that "the torch has been passed to a new generation of Americans," Harriman's long record of public service on behalf of Democratic presidents and his association with Winston Churchill, Joseph Stalin, and other world leaders consigned to history were not unqualified assets. An even more formidable barrier to a high-level appointment was Harriman's distant relationship with the new president and his "active dislike" for the Kennedy family patriarch, Joseph P. Kennedy. According to his biographer, Harriman considered Joseph Kennedy an unprincipled speculator who was "determined to buy the [Democratic presidential] nomination for his son."[14]

A former governor of New York who had sought the Democratic nomination for the presidency in the 1950s and who aspired to be secretary of state, Harriman accepted a relatively humble appointment as an ambassador at large for the Kennedy administration. This ill-defined but flexible position suited Harriman's past experience as a troubleshooter for presidents Roosevelt and Truman. He was soon assigned the task of helping achieve President Kennedy's diplomatic objectives in Laos. Rusk was the official leader of the US delegation at the Geneva conference, but after the initial sessions he returned to Washington, and Harriman took over.

Although he had no previous experience in Southeast Asia, Harriman was convinced that the Eisenhower administration had been wrong in supporting the right-wing faction in Laos, against the advice of the French and British. Based on his long experience in Soviet affairs, which included serving as the American ambassador in Moscow during World War II,

Harriman viewed the Kremlin as the key to a diplomatic solution in Laos. At the August 29 White House meeting, it was Harriman who "suggested that it might be important at some point to make a demarche to Khrushchev and to refer to his agreement with the President at Vienna."[15]

In early September Harriman consulted with European allies about expanding SEATO Plan 5 and reaching an understanding with Souvanna. As Kennedy likely anticipated, the United Kingdom and France were unenthusiastic about enlarging the SEATO plan for intervening in Laos. Frederick Warner, head of the South East Asia Department (SEAD) at the UK Foreign Office, said that the US military proposal was not merely an expansion of Plan 5 but a "wholly new conception." Warner, who considered Phoumi duplicitous, thought the Lao general might view the new contingency plan not as a last resort but as an opportunity to precipitate a military clash and thereby "bring [the] plan into action."[16]

French Foreign Ministry officials shared British concerns about Phoumi's reaction to an expanded SEATO Plan 5. Jacques Roux, the head of the French delegation at Geneva, feared that Phoumi would assume the United States intended to pursue a military solution in Laos and would dismiss Harriman's talks with Souvanna as a "pro forma undertaking." Harriman replied that he understood French concerns, but the US government "couldn't give [the] other side [the] impression that they can walk over Laos." Phoumi would be told that the United States was "earnest about negotiations with Souvanna and that he cannot involve [the] US militarily by initiating offensive action on his own." Harriman emphasized to Roux that he was "under very explicit instructions [to] do everything possible [to] get [an] agreement with Souvanna."[17]

In mid-September Harriman had five formal meetings with Souvanna in Rangoon, the capital of Burma, then a neutral republic. Souvanna welcomed the prospect of American support, explaining that he had accepted Soviet assistance "only because [the] US had abandoned him." He said that the Pathet Lao were his opponents, who must be beaten either politically in elections or militarily on the battlefield.[18] Harriman explained to Souvanna the "absolute necessity" of appointing strong moderates—not just his followers who were sympathetic to the Pathet Lao—as neutralist ministers. Harriman said that without a broadly based center group in his cabinet, the United States could not support him. Souvanna replied that this condition would be very diffi-cult, but he would think it over.[19]

During their talks, Harriman and Souvanna agreed on aspects of ICC supervision of the ceasefire, but they failed to find mutually satisfac-tory language to describe the coalition government's influence on inves-tigations. Souvanna shared the "general Lao disenchantment" with the ICC, viewing it as another threat to the country's weak claim of sover-eignty. Even Phoumi resisted a "strong ICC," according to embassy offi-cials in Vientiane. In Geneva, Harriman had tried to persuade Souvanna to accept the commission's right to launch investigations "in cooperation with" the Lao government, rather than the more restrictive qualification "with the agreement of." The diplomat revisited the topic in Rangoon, but Souvanna agreed only "to reexamine the question."[20]

Harriman told Souvanna that "a major US interest was to get [the] Lao government's cooperation in closing [the] Ho Chi Minh Trail and [the] border with South Vietnam." Souvanna replied that once a new gov-ernment and Laotian neutrality were established, "No one will cross Laos from north to south. We will not allow any country to violate our territo-ries." Admitting that the Pathet Lao exhibited "a certain good will toward Viet Cong passage through Laos," Souvanna did not say how he would shut down the infiltration trails into South Vietnam. (Earlier in Septem-ber, the US ambassadors in Laos, South Vietnam, and Thailand had con-cluded that a neutral government, "with a 'strong' ICC, probably could not, even if it wanted to, do much to prohibit or control VC infiltration through its territory, at least during its 'settling down' period.")[21]

In a discussion of SEATO and the indirect reference to it in the Zurich communiqué, Harriman said that the alliance would only respond to a request from a friendly government. When asked to provide his views, Souvanna replied: "Since Geneva recognized [the] neutrality of Laos, it would be better if the SEATO agreement did not mention Laos anymore. If Laos were attacked, it would of course have to appeal to its friends for support." Harriman said it would be "legally impossible" for Presi-dent Kennedy to amend the SEATO treaty, which had been approved by the US Senate. He proposed that the new Lao government simply reject SEATO protection, a suggestion Souvanna found "satisfactory." Harri-man added that it would be a "hard problem" to gain Chinese concur-rence with this compromise. PRC foreign minister Chen Yi and members of the Chinese delegation in Geneva had thus far demanded the abrogation of the SEATO treaty.[22]

In the final Rangoon meeting, Harriman emphasized the "necessity" of including "moderates"—defined by US officials as anticommunists not aligned with Phoumi—among the neutralist cabinet ministers. Souvanna replied that he had already promised to consider the issue, but the United States "must realize that he could not abandon the people who had followed and supported him in exile." When Souvanna said that "it would be hard" to include more than one right-leaning neutralist in the cabinet, Harriman declared: "If this was true, the President would not be able to support him. I regretted [the] necessity of saying this but it was a fact."[23]

In his report to Kennedy, Harriman wrote that with the exception of "Souvanna's utterly unacceptable position" on neutralist ministers, the talks were "more satisfactory than I expected." Souvanna had exhibited undue confidence in his "own strength and capabilities, but took a realistic position on several subjects." A "disquieting" conclusion to the discussions was Souvanna's inaccurate announcement to the press that the United States and its western allies had agreed to his selection as prime minister. Harriman responded to subsequent press queries with a statement that "many subjects were discussed but no attempt was made to reach a decision on any specific matter."[24]

Harriman left Rangoon convinced that the United States "could deal with" Souvanna.[25] Less reassuring was the diplomat's September 19 meeting with Phoumi and Prince Boun Oum in Laos. Reporting to them on his meeting with Souvanna, Harriman said that the United States "much preferred" a political settlement over the resumption of hostilities. Moreover, President Kennedy would not support any RLG military action "to move north to recapture lost areas, in view [of the] danger of bringing Chinese Communist forces into Laos and precipitating [a] large-scale war."[26]

Harriman urged Phoumi and Boun Oum "to get down to brass tacks around [the] negotiating table to work out [a] peaceful solution." Phoumi claimed that he had always favored negotiations, but his long-time rival Souvanna was "too much under [the] thumb of Communists to be trusted." Harriman, who doubted the general's commitment to a political settlement, reported to Washington his "strong impression that

Phoumi has no real intention of pursuing serious negotiations." For his part, Phoumi told the RLG cabinet, "Mr. Harriman appeared disappointed at [the] outcome of his talks with Souvanna."[27]

While Harriman pursued a negotiated settlement of the Laotian civil war, officials in the Pentagon, State Department, and White House proposed a range of concepts for military intervention in Southeast Asia. One scheme, characterized as "limited holding actions," sought to contain communist expansion in the region without executing SEATO Plan 5 or similar large-scale deployments of US combat troops. Calling for "step-by-step increases in the scope of current actions in Laos," the concept envisioned enhanced US advisory and logistic support in South Vietnam and Thailand. Proposed military actions included using defoliants and mines on the major access routes to the Ho Chi Minh Trail and increasing "feasible" covert activities in communist-controlled territory, "including North Viet Nam." The Joint Chiefs of Staff, however, opposed this limited concept, which would concede the military initiative to antigovernment forces in Laos and would signal a US intention to merely delay a communist victory there. The proposed holding actions, the chiefs declared, would "seriously undermine our military position in the Far East."[28]

The JCS also dismissed a Rostow-conceived plan to station SEATO troops in South Vietnam along the Laotian border. The immediate military objective of the deployment was to impede infiltration and to release some of Diem's forces for counterinsurgency operations. The more significant political goal was an exercise in brinksmanship with the Soviet Union, leading to negotiations. Rostow's concept included a declaration to the Soviets that the United States "cannot accept [the] destruction of Diem via infiltration." With SEATO troops protecting the frontiers of South Vietnam—a more politically defensible mission for the alliance than intervening in the Laotian civil war—continued infiltration would risk escalation that "would not merely threaten Hanoi with air and naval action, but would threaten Soviet or Chinese Communist involvement." Rostow, who assumed that the Soviet Union did not want a superpower confrontation over South Vietnam, suggested that the United States could then use the withdrawal of the SEATO force as a "bargaining counter in a Vietnamese settlement."[29]

The Joint Chiefs of Staff, however, noted four fundamental military flaws with Rostow's plan:

a. SEATO forces will be deployed over a border of several hundred miles and will be attacked piecemeal or by-passed at the Viet Cong's own choice.

b. It may reduce but cannot stop infiltration of Viet Cong personnel and material.

c. It deploys SEATO forces in the weakest defense points should DRV or [Chinese Communist] forces intervene.

d. It compounds the problems of communications and logistical support.

After demolishing Rostow's SEATO plan, as well an alternative concept to deploy SEATO forces along the South Vietnamese border with North Vietnam, the chiefs reminded civilian officials that Laos was the strategic center of mainland Southeast Asia: "Any concept which deals with the defense of Southeast Asia that does not include all or a substantial portion of Laos is, from a military standpoint, unsound."[30]

Instead of "the spreading out of our forces," the chiefs advocated "a concentrated effort in Laos where a firm stand can be taken saving all or substantially all of Laos which would, at the same time, protect Thailand and protect the borders of South Vietnam." Despite the misgivings of President Kennedy and European allies about large-scale military operations in Laos, the JCS remained convinced that some version of SEATO Plan 5 was "the military minimum commensurate with the situation." In the absence of an acceptable Geneva settlement, there was "no feasible military alternative of less magnitude which will prevent the loss of Laos, South Vietnam and ultimately Southeast Asia."[31]

The chiefs' preferred version of SEATO Plan 5 would be "augmented" with South Vietnamese and additional Thai forces. The latest plan called for 48,100 troops, with the United States contributing about one-third of the force. If North Vietnamese combat units moved into Laos and attacked the SEATO troops, the response would be "air strikes on North Viet-Nam." The UK military adviser to SEATO, who supported the proposed retaliatory attacks, acknowledged that his "military opinion [was] perhaps not acceptable" to the Macmillan government. More important, the UK Joint

Chiefs of Staff did not share the enthusiasm of their US counterparts for the expansion of SEATO Plan 5. In a statement of their "preliminary views" of the concept, which envisioned a commitment of 7,900 troops from the United Kingdom, Australia, and New Zealand, the UK chiefs observed that the expanded SEATO Plan 5 offered no additional protection to Thailand, might require "considerable reinforcements" to achieve its objectives, and increased "the risks of Chinese or DRV intervention."[32]

The US Joint Chiefs of Staff, recognizing that SEATO Plan 5 was probably "a politically unacceptable course of action at this time," unenthusiastically proposed an alternative concept that "could provide a degree of assistance to the Government of South Viet-Nam to regain control of its own territory, and could free certain South Vietnamese forces for offensive actions against the Viet Cong." The scaled-back JCS plan called for 22,800 SEATO troops in South Vietnam. A division-strength force would be deployed to the central highlands, where areas of communist control had been increasing since early 1960. Admitting that this "limited course of action" would neither defend Laos and Thailand nor contribute much to the overall defense of Southeast Asia, the chiefs preferred it to other plans proposed by the national security bureaucracy.[33]

President Kennedy, who continued to resist recommendations to dispatch US combat troops to Southeast Asia, formally asked General Taylor to make a firsthand assessment of the situation in Vietnam and to propose a plan for improving it. As with Laos, the overall US objective in South Vietnam was preventing a communist victory. There were, however, significant differences in policies to achieve that goal. To resolve the Laotian crisis, the United States was participating in an international conference aimed at establishing a neutral coalition government that would include communists. In South Vietnam, the United States was helping the anticommunist government of Ngo Dinh Diem in its effort to defeat the insurgents. Taylor later described the purpose of his mission to South Vietnam as recommending ways the United States could "change a losing game and begin to win."[34]

President Kennedy, in Rusk's words, granted Harriman "a wide measure of discretion" in his talks with the Soviet delegation in Geneva. In "eyes only" instructions to Harriman, the first item on the State Department's list of "crucial issues" to discuss with the Soviets was shrinking and integrating the armies of the three Lao factions into a single military force loyal to the new government. Department officials, acknowledging a lack of agreement among the western allies, or even within the US government, about the best method to achieve this goal, favored an approach they described "as zonal in character." Essentially a regrouping scheme without acknowledging a division of the country, the FAR would continue to hold the Mekong Valley, and the Pathet Lao would retain their control of the northern provinces adjacent to North Vietnam and China. The improbable "crux" of the State Department concept was persuading the communist "bloc [to] tacitly agree that Pathet Lao forces now in [the] panhandle area would be withdrawn."[35]

The second "crucial" objective for Harriman in his talks with the Soviets was to reach an agreement in principle that infiltration from North Vietnam into South Vietnam through Laos would constitute a breach of any agreement that might be reached at Geneva. President Kennedy and Secretary Rusk were particularly interested in probing comments by Georgi Pushkin, leader of the Soviet delegation at the conference, that the Soviet Union "could and would control North Viet-Nam."[36] If the United Kingdom assumed responsibility for compliance by the noncommunist signatories, Pushkin said that the Soviet Union would accept a reciprocal responsibility for the "socialist side." The proposal appeared advantageous to US interests, but officials in Washington wanted to know more about the "specific obligations Soviets would be willing to incur, how these mutual obligations could be formalized, and [the] procedures of implementation."[37]

On October 10 Harriman suggested to Pushkin that his proposal for Soviet and UK commitments to ensure the compliance of their respective allies should be formalized in an agreement between the two cochairs. The Soviet diplomat objected to a written bilateral agreement. He was, however, willing to add a less specific sentence to the conference's final declaration that would make the United Kingdom and Soviet Union responsible for "seeing to [the] observation of obligations" by the signatory states.[38] In a Geneva progress report to the State Department, Harriman characterized the Soviet offer as "perhaps the most constructive and encouraging development of [the] conference thus far," as it provided a basis to "hold the Soviets responsible" for PRC and DRV violations of a final agreement.[39]

Harriman, however, was not certain that the Soviet Union had the ability or the will to police compliance by other communist states.

In August he had told a meeting of US ambassadors in Europe of his "impression that the Russians were able to dictate to the Poles and the other European satellites regarding Laos but not to the Chinese or the [North Vietnamese]."[40] And within days of Pushkin's surprising offer "to take responsibility for the socialist states living up to the agreement," Harriman admitted to Chester L. Cooper, a CIA official who worked closely with him in Geneva, "Of course, the whole deal hinges on whether the Soviets will carry out their obligations in good faith."[41]

The authority and operations of the ICC remained a sticking point for Harriman and Pushkin. Because of US concerns over the use of Laos for infiltration from North Vietnam into South Vietnam, Harriman stressed the need for fixed ICC teams and operating centers in southern Laos. Pushkin disagreed: the United States could not expect the North Vietnamese to sign an agreement that anticipated their violation of it. If the United States insisted on fixed ICC teams in southern Laos, Pushkin declared, the conference might come "to [a] dead end." In a comment indicating the diversity of views within the communist "bloc," not to mention suggesting the limits of Soviet authority, Pushkin said: "The Chinese had shown special concern in opposing fixed teams."[42]

The so-called voting procedures of the ICC appeared to Harriman as one of Pushkin's greatest concerns—probably because of Khrushchev's commitment to the "troika" principle in affairs involving communist, western, and neutral states. Khrushchev had unsuccessfully tried to abolish the office of the UN secretary general in favor of a troika. His proposal sought to extend the veto power of the Security Council's permanent members to the Secretariat, which executes the decisions of the world body. Similarly, the Soviet Union wanted all ICC decisions, except for purely procedural matters, to be unanimous. The United States, however, insisted on the right of individual commissioners to initiate investigations and to file minority reports on their findings. Observing that Pushkin had "been far from cooperative" in this matter and others, Harriman reported that the Soviet diplomat "expects us to give in eighty percent if he offers [a] twenty percent compromise."[43]

There is little doubt that Soviet premier Nikita Khrushchev wanted to avoid a military confrontation with the United States over Laos. After his meeting with Kennedy in Vienna, the Soviet Foreign Ministry instructed its negotiators in Geneva to achieve an agreement guaranteeing "real independence and neutrality" in Laos.[44] But not all communist states approved of bilateral US-Soviet diplomacy as a basis for settling the conflict. Marek Thee, a Polish ICC commissioner and a tenacious advocate of North Vietnamese and Pathet Lao interests, later characterized the superpower diplomacy as out of touch with the "actual conditions" in Laos and the region: "The Soviet leadership's notions about the conflict seemed no less distorted than the Americans. Both focused on power relations and disregarded local forces."[45] Ilya A. Gaiduk, a cold war scholar who has conducted research in the Soviet archives, wrote that Thee's assertion of Soviet ignorance of Laotian affairs "cannot be accepted as completely reliable."[46] It is clear, however, that the Soviet policy of "peaceful coexistence" with the West was at odds with the more militant views of the PRC, DRV, and Pathet Lao.

PRC leaders did not approve of the Soviet "tendency to solve local issues through superpower dialogues." In private conversations between Soviet and Chinese officials, Foreign Minister Chen Yi dismissed the importance of the Kennedy-Khrushchev summit and criticized the United States and Soviet Union "for treating Laos as a bargaining chip in their negotiations."[47] For China, the primary concern at both the 1954 and 1962 Geneva conferences was preventing the United States from establishing a military presence in neighboring Laos. While Soviet diplomats encouraged the North Vietnamese to exercise military restraint to avoid US intervention, the Chinese advised a more aggressive posture. Premier Chou En-lai told Pathet Lao leader Souphanouvong that a coalition government would be "fine," but "the final settlement will be decided by force."[48]

For the DRV, Laos was an integral part of their strategy to absorb South Vietnam into a reunified state ruled by Hanoi. Directing revolutionary activities in Laos, the DRV played an "overwhelming role" in the military and political development of the Pathet Lao, according to historian Christopher Goscha. The influence of North Vietnam, the CIA concluded, was "overriding within the Lao Communist movement," and its leaders made "frequent trips from their headquarters in Sam Neua to Hanoi for consultations."[49]

A special DRV advisory group, established in July 1954, trained regular, regional, and guerrilla forces, as well as political cadres, "to build up the Lao communist structure." Following Hanoi's 1959 authorization of armed insurrection and more aggressive action in South Vietnam, the People's Army of (North) Vietnam (PAVN) created two new combat units, the names of which reflected the month and year of their establishment. Group 559, initially comprising some 500 combat engineers, began to improve the overland logistic route into South Vietnam. A 1971 CIA analysis estimated that Group 559 had 2,000 to 2,500 "logistic personnel operating in the Laotian panhandle" in 1961. For 1970, the agency estimated a total of 40,000 to 50,000 logistic personnel.[50]

Group 959, which maintained a forward command post in Sam Neua, became the "main Vietnamese instrument for coordinating the military operations in Laos." Estimates of the number of PAVN troops serving in Laos in 1961 vary. The highest US estimate for that year, produced by the Military Assistance Advisory Group (MAAG) in Laos, was 6,500. According to historian Ang Cheng Guan, "12,000 North Vietnamese troops were in Laos [in early 1961]."[51] The success of antigovernment forces, the chief DRV military adviser boasted, was entirely attributable to the North Vietnamese army: "All the victories over the Boun Oum armies have been achieved by us. The royal troops [of Prince Souvanna Phouma] and the Pathet Lao armies have served us but a cover, that is, a mask."[52]

Battalion 603, a third DRV military unit established in 1959, had the mission of developing maritime routes to South Vietnam. This program was "dissolved" in 1960 and succeeded by Group 759, which created a "secret 'strategic maritime route' running along the Vietnamese coast between Haiphong and the southern tip of Vietnam." In October 1962, according to Goscha, the Vietnamese communists began "to supply the south with modern Chinese and Soviet weapons via the western side of the South China Sea."[53]

The selection of Prince Souphanouvong, Souvanna's half-brother, as the public face of Pathet Lao leadership reflected the DRV's desire to exploit Lao respect for the royal family. Souphanouvong, however, was outranked by Kaysone Phoumvihan, the general secretary of the LPP. Born in Savannakhet to a Lao mother and a Vietnamese father, Kaysone was educated in Hanoi, where he was "cultivated" by Ho's Indochinese Communist Party.[54] Nouhak Phoumsavan, who was born in Mukdahan Province in Northeast Thailand, a region with strong ethnic and cultural ties to Laos, was the second most powerful member of the LPP.[55] When the Second Indochina War ended in 1975, Kaysone became the first prime minister of the Lao People's Democratic Republic. Nouhak was his deputy prime minister.

In the fall of 1961 experts within the US government had a general, if incomplete, understanding of the divergent interests of communist countries and their relationships with one another. Within a month of President Kennedy's inauguration, the CIA produced one of a series of detailed reports on the dispute between the Soviet Union and China over communist ideology, strategy, and tactics.[56] There was also recognition that the Pathet Lao and the People's Liberation Armed Forces (PLAF) in South Vietnam, more commonly known as the Viet Cong, were directed by the Vietnamese Workers' Party and "look[ed] to Hanoi for guidance and support." Knowledge of the relationship between the Soviet Union and its Asian satellites was less clear. In Laos, US intelligence agencies concluded, it seemed "likely" that the Soviet Union exercised "considerable restraint on DRV or Chinese Communist decisions which would risk the broadening of hostilities and raise the issue of USSR or US participation."[57]

Despite a growing understanding of the diverse national interests within a common communist ideology, Kennedy's policy decisions on Laos were largely based on the cold war stereotype of a monolithic conspiracy, efficiently directed by Moscow and obediently executed by its wholly owned subsidiaries in Beijing and Hanoi. Most senior US officials focused on the global aspirations of Marxist-Leninist ideology, paying scant attention to Southeast Asian history, traditional regional rivalries, and other factors that affected relations among and within nations and that limited the reach of Soviet hegemony. Frank N. Burnet, a Foreign Service officer who served as a staff assistant to Harriman and subsequently worked in the embassy in Vientiane, recalled that the emerging "signs of friction" between the Soviet Union and China had little impact on how policymakers viewed the communist threat. "I don't think that we really understood the long adversarial history behind these two great powers," Burnet said. "The idea of a Sino-Soviet Axis was very deeply imbedded in our world outlook. It was a convenient way of looking at the problem."[58]

Chapter 3

Less Precise Language Than We Desire

A Geneva agreement that provided a "reasonable chance" of establishing a neutral, independent Laos was "almost within our grasp," Averell Harriman informed President Kennedy and Secretary Rusk in a top-secret cable, dated October 26, 1961. Acknowledging a few remaining outstanding issues, including the composition of "an acceptable Souvanna government," Harriman urged Kennedy to continue resisting recommendations to commit US combat troops to Laos. "I fully recognize [the] importance of Laos attached to [the] crisis in South Vietnam," Harriman wrote, but the problems in South Vietnam "can best be solved in SVN, rather than [by] trying to find [a] solution by military action in Laos."[1]

Harriman summarized the key arguments against US intervention in Laos, warning that a US-led SEATO force risked "extremely dangerous escalation" and becoming "bogged down indefinitely." Conversely, he argued, the introduction of US troops into South Vietnam "would not be as dangerous or without terminus and would have [the] possibility of far more world wide approval." Harriman reminded the president of the commitments made by the Soviet Union and Souvanna "to block [the] use of Laos territory" for infiltration into South Vietnam, a point the diplomat qualified with the parenthetical observation, "for what that may accomplish." (With Kennedy and bureaucratic allies, Harriman tended to be candid about the possible limits of Soviet guarantees. To US officials less committed to a neutral settlement, he generally described these assurances in a more definitive manner.) Finally, Harriman echoed the concern of Defense Secretary McNamara that a large-scale troop deployment to Southeast Asia would limit Kennedy's military options in any showdown with the Soviet Union over Berlin.[2]

In a separate telegram to Kennedy and Rusk that same day, Harriman charged that the principal barrier to a peaceful settlement in Laos was General Phoumi, who had "no intention of negotiating in good faith with Souvanna for [the] formation of a government."[3] Harriman, who had earlier suggested to DCI Allen Dulles that the CIA "find [a] substitute general to replace Phoumi if he remains intransigent,"[4] urged Kennedy and Rusk to instruct Ambassador Brown "to use his full authority to tell Phoumi he must undertake negotiations in good faith." Observing that Souvanna had recently given the British the "right answers" to major questions about a settlement, Harriman further recommended that Brown "establish direct and continuous contact" with the presumptive prime minister. It seemed "unrealistic" to Harriman that the UK and French ambassadors traveled regularly to his headquarters on the Plaine des Jarres while US diplomats in Laos appeared "aloof": "We must gain and maintain Souvanna's confidence."[5]

Although Harriman's views on US military intervention, Phoumi, and Souvanna largely reflected those of President Kennedy, senior officials in the State Department—including Deputy Under Secretary Johnson; Walter P. McConaughy, assistant secretary of state for far eastern affairs; and his deputy John Steeves—favored a harder line in Laos. In a cable cleared by McConaughy and approved by Johnson, the department questioned Harriman's assessment of Phoumi's unwillingness to negotiate and judged the Lao general's grim view of Pathet Lao intentions as "essentially accurate." Harriman's nominal superiors also rejected his suggested instructions for the embassy in Vientiane: "We consider [the] question of any demarche to Phoumi best left to Brown's discretion in light [of the] evolving local situation. If negotiations appear to falter due [to] Phoumi's intransigence, Brown has adequate instructions authorizing him [to] urge Phoumi in [the] strongest terms [to] negotiate in good faith." And before acting on Harriman's recommendation for more direct contact with Souvanna, department officials wanted to hear Brown's estimate of its impact on US influence over Phoumi. The United States, according to Washington's instructions to Harriman, "must avoid lending [a] degree of recognition" to Souvanna and the neutralists that they had "not yet achieved at [the] present stage of negotiations."[6]

Officials in the State Department had another, more basic disagreement with Harriman: the "gradual erosion" of the US negotiating position at Geneva.[7] Concessions that weakened the ICC were a particular concern. For example, the draft agreement called for Lao government "concurrence" before the commission initiated investigations into alleged violations. Harriman accepted this written limitation on ICC independence because of Souvanna's oral assurance that his government would "not exercise any power of veto" over the commission's inspection teams. The US diplomat was further persuaded by discussions in Geneva that Lao government concurrence for all ICC investigations would be a legal consequence of signing the agreement. From Washington's perspective, however, the gap between the plain language in the draft accord and Harriman's "oral understandings and assurances" seemed troubling. Many officials wanted, but never received, a more binding declaration of ICC independence.[8]

Another source of conflict between the department and Harriman was the draft accord's ambiguously worded requirement for "agreed reports" on investigations by the ICC. On the one hand, the proposed text stipulated that the commission's conclusions and recommendations would have to be unanimous—a position consistent with the Soviets' commitment to the troika principle. On the other hand, the agreement specified that "differences on particular questions . . . may be appropriately reflected" in ICC reports—a western acknowledgment of both the difficulty of achieving unanimous agreement on significant issues and the importance of creating a record of hard-hitting Canadian views. The concern within the State Department was that the word "agreed" might provide an opportunity for the Polish commissioner to block or delay reports on communist violations.[9]

Harriman, warning the department that the negotiations in Geneva were "getting pretty edgy," thought that the language in the draft agreement provided sufficient authority for prompt minority reports by the Canadians. The Soviets, he argued, had yielded on the troika principle by conceding that ICC reports could include the commissioners' "differences." It was for reasons of "form," he explained, that Pushkin insisted on "less precise language than we desire." Harriman tried to reassure his skeptical Washington colleagues by observing that Pushkin, as well as the delegations from India, Canada, and the United Kingdom, thought the proposed "agreed reports" text would allow the ICC to "operate as well as if [the] language were more precise." The question for the State Department, handwritten in pencil on the back of a Washington copy of Harriman's cable, was: "Can we rely upon [an] oral interpretation by Pushkin and [Indian delegate Arthur] Lall in this crucial matter?"[10]

According to Charles T. Cross, the officer-in-charge of Laos affairs from 1961 to 1963 and one of the few officials in the Bureau of Far Eastern Affairs sympathetic to the Souvanna solution, "Harriman was severely criticized by some of his State Department colleagues for relying too much on occasional appearances of Soviet cooperation." After one Harriman-proposed compromise with the Soviets, John Steeves remarked that the next cable from the US delegation in Geneva would likely be signed "Pushkin."[11] James C. Thomson, then a special assistant to Under Secretary Bowles, commented later: "[That] was pretty close to charging treason. Not a nice thought. So there were a lot of people out to get other people and a lot of people thinking we were giving away the crown jewels."[12]

For his part, Harriman was convinced that his appreciation of the negotiating possibilities in Geneva, not to mention his understanding of the president's wishes, was far better than the department's. On October 30, 1961, Harriman objected to a list of proposed revisions from Washington aimed at strengthening the draft agreement he had laboriously negotiated with allies, adversaries, and neutrals. After expressing polite, if almost certainly insincere, gratitude for the department's "extraordinarily prompt and thoughtful" comments, he dismissed virtually every suggestion: "matter lost already . . . politically impossible [to] reopen matter . . . not believe possible . . . no chance of getting Pushkin and Commie bloc [to] drop this word . . . it is not repeat not possible . . . not worth fighting about . . . if [the] department insists."[13]

The differing views of Harriman and the State Department prompted a suggestion that the diplomat return to Washington to discuss the negotiations in Geneva and related matters, including General Taylor's nearly completed appraisal of South Vietnam and his recommendations for US military assistance. When U. Alexis Johnson telephoned Harriman in Geneva to propose the trip home, Harriman objected, declaring that he had achieved all that was possible with the Soviet Union and that the Chinese were "on the verge of walking out." The conversation was "very emotional," according to Under Secretary of State Chester Bowles. With Rusk in Japan for an economic conference, it was Bowles who sought President Kennedy's guidance in dealing with a "problem with Harriman."[14]

Kennedy, joined by Deputy Under Secretary Johnson, spoke with Harriman by telephone on November 2. The principal topic was whether or not the Polish ICC commissioner could exploit the term "agreed reports" in the draft accord. Harriman explained that under the proposed system a single report would contain the opinion of each commission member. In return for the "substance" of minority reporting demanded by the United States, the Soviet Union required the "facade" of appearing to adhere to the troika principle. Kennedy asked what would happen if the Polish commissioner refused to sign a report or tried to delay its submission. Harriman replied that such acts would be a breach of the agreement, and the other commissioners "would be free to send in their reports without the Pole's signature."[15]

In his memoir, Johnson described the phone call with Harriman as "a vigorous three-way exchange." Characterizing himself as "partial to Phoumi,"[16] Johnson thought that Harriman had conceded too much at Geneva to achieve an agreement. He recalled Harriman telling Kennedy that the US government "could not get a better deal." Holding out for a stronger ICC, said Harriman, would either "tie down or break up the conference." Johnson wrote that he could not challenge Harriman's "on-the-scene assessment, and the President told Averell to proceed" with the negotiations.[17] Later on November 2, Robert H. Johnson, an NSC staffer (and no relation to U. Alexis Johnson), informed Walt Rostow that Harriman had won "a very hotly fought argument" with the State Department.[18]

Harriman sought to reassure his vanquished colleagues of the soundness of the agreement he was negotiating in Geneva. In a November 4 cable to the department, he reiterated that the accord would prohibit the use of Laotian territory for interference in the affairs of its neighbors and that the Soviet Union would assume "responsibility for compliance by the [Communist] Bloc signatories." Addressing widespread doubts about the likely effectiveness of the ICC, Harriman declared: "It will be especially important for the commission, acting on the basis of any reasonably valid information, to send its teams to stay as long as necessary to those areas of Laos now being used as [a] corridor or base for Viet Cong operations in South Vietnam, and to investigate carefully and report on any evidence of any such activity."[19]

The magnitude of Harriman's bureaucratic triumph over the department's hard-liners was not fully apparent until a few weeks later, when

Kennedy appointed him assistant secretary of state for far eastern affairs. Harriman's short-term victory, however, was eventually eclipsed by his misjudgments at Geneva, which had long-term consequences for Kennedy's aspirations for a neutral, independent Laos. Many of the oral understandings and interpretations of language that Harriman relied upon proved to be worthless—Souvanna's coalition government did seek to control ICC investigations; the unanimity principle was more deeply ingrained within the commission itself than US officials imagined; and the Polish commissioner in Laos displayed uncommon deftness in obstructing ICC investigations. Harriman's greatest miscalculation, however, was that high-level diplomacy between the United States and the Soviet Union was the key to establishing peace in Laos and ending infiltration into South Vietnam.

Harriman and other US officials failed to understand that DRV leaders, in the words of historian Pierre Asselin, "were never puppets" of the Soviet Union or the PRC, "and their ability to make autonomous decisions was never seriously compromised."[20] More than two decades after the end of the Vietnam War, Chester Cooper, a CIA officer and Harriman aide in Geneva, traveled to Hanoi to participate in a series of conferences involving US and Vietnamese scholars, policymakers, and military officers. During a discussion of Laos, Cooper talked about the "difficulty" of persuading American policymakers to deal with Souvanna Phouma, the unwillingness of the DRV to abide by the Geneva agreement, and the subsequent realization by Harriman that "perhaps he had failed in this negotiation." Reflecting on the US understandings with the Soviet Union, Cooper told his Vietnamese hosts: "It is clear that we should have dealt with you, not Pushkin."[21]

Maxwell Taylor, the leader of the presidential mission to South Vietnam, was an urbane, multilingual general who appealed to Kennedy's sense of style. More substantively, Taylor's distinguished military career included service as commander of the 101st Airborne Division during World War II, superintendent of West Point, and commander of the Eighth Army during the Korean War. As US Army chief of staff from 1955 to 1959, he privately criticized President Eisenhower's "New Look" defense policy for emphasizing nuclear weapons at the expense of conventional military forces. After retiring from the army, Taylor went public with his views, writing *The Uncertain Trumpet*, published in 1960. Among the book's recommendations was a US military posture of "flexible response," which he defined as a capability "for coping with anything from general atomic war to infiltrations and aggressions such as threaten Laos and Berlin."[22]

Presidential candidate John Kennedy praised Taylor's book as "most persuasive" and helpful in "shap[ing] my own thinking."[23] After the Bay of Pigs, President Kennedy wanted Taylor to replace Allen Dulles as CIA chief. Taylor declined that position, but he did accept a White House staff appointment to the newly created position of military representative to the president. The principal responsibilities of the job were to advise Kennedy on military and intelligence matters—without impinging on the statutory responsibilities of the JCS and the DCI. Immediate tasks for Taylor included serving as Kennedy's representative on the interagency committee overseeing covert intelligence operations and reviewing contingency plans for Berlin and Vietnam. The retired general's new assignment reflected not only Kennedy's dissatisfaction with the military advice of the JCS but also the president's discomfort with senior officers he considered "too formal, traditional, and unimaginative."[24] Taylor later recalled: "I am sure the Joint Chiefs of Staff resented my appointment very deeply because it was plainly a reflection of their recent performance. They had to live with it, however, and live with it they did."[25]

During his 1961 visit to South Vietnam, Taylor found a "double crisis in confidence," with many Vietnamese government officials doubting both US determination "to save Southeast Asia" and Diem's ability to defeat the communists. To reverse the declining morale and the deteriorating military situation, Taylor recommended a deeper US commitment to South Vietnam that he characterized as "limited partnership." His proposals to Kennedy included an increase in the US military assistance program; the introduction of helicopter units and other aircraft; and improvements in military-political intelligence, including surveillance of coastal waters and inland waterways. Taylor's most controversial suggestion was the deployment to South Vietnam of some six thousand to eight thousand US ground troops, who would serve as a tangible sign of the US commitment.[26] Many officials—though often for entirely different reasons—opposed this particular idea, including President Kennedy, whom Taylor described as "instinctively against [the] introduction of US forces."[27]

In his letter of transmittal to the president, Taylor observed that his proposed "emergency program" was not the "final word" on US assistance to South Vietnam. Future action would depend on "the kind of settlement we obtain in Laos and the manner in which Hanoi decides to adjust its conduct to that settlement." Continued infiltration from the DRV and covert support for the PLAF would require a US decision on whether or not "to strike the source of aggression."[28] In an earlier "eyes only" cable to Kennedy, Taylor had declared: "The risks of backing into a major Asian war by way of SVN are present but are not impressive. NVN is extremely vulnerable to conventional bombing, a weakness which should be exploited diplomatically in convincing Hanoi to lay off SVN."[29]

The report of the Taylor mission, totaling some two hundred pages, made several references to Laos. An appendix drafted by Sterling J. Cottrell, a Foreign Service officer who chaired the interagency task force on Vietnam, observed: "[South Vietnamese] officials frankly state that the U.S. has abandoned Laos. They are concerned that the U.S. may abandon [South Vietnam] when the going gets rough. They are keenly aware of the effect of infiltration from Laos and are certain it cannot be stopped by any weak 'neutral' Laotian government nor by an ICC, no matter how effective." The report's "Covert Annex," presumably written by David Smith, the CIA representative on the Taylor mission, concluded: "The most important covert operational effort now needed is the observation and harassment of Viet Cong transiting South Laos in Vietnam. Operations presently directed against this target, while qualitatively well conceived are quantitatively too small in numbers of personnel and striking force available to accomplish more than a small part of the job to be done."[30]

During the Kennedy administration's evaluation of Taylor's recommendations, concerns were raised that increased military support to South Vietnam might adversely affect the president's objectives in Laos. In a November 11 memorandum to Kennedy, which a Defense Department analyst later speculated was "drawn up to the president's specifications," Rusk and McNamara wrote:

> It must be understood that the introduction of American combat forces into Viet-Nam prior to a Laotian settlement would run a considerable risk of stimulating a Communist breach of the cease fire and a resumption of hostilities in Laos. This could present

us with a choice between the use of combat forces in Laos or an abandonment of that country to full Communist control. At the present time, there is at least a chance that a settlement can be reached in Laos on the basis of a weak and unsatisfactory Souvanna Phouma Government.[31]

Rusk and McNamara proposed a program of action in South Vietnam nearly identical to Taylor's concept of limited partnership, though without the commitment of any organized US combat forces. Kennedy approved the program, which in the following two years increased the number of US military advisors in South Vietnam from approximately one thousand to sixteen thousand. As in the spring of 1961, when Kennedy sought a negotiated settlement in Laos while authorizing a small increase in the number of US military advisers in South Vietnam, the policy decisions in the fall of 1961 reflected a determination to hold the line in South Vietnam against communist expansion. In his recommendation to Kennedy, McGeorge Bundy described Laos as "a bad bargain." The United States, he wrote, should "give the game promptly to Souvanna and hope for the best, meanwhile holding hard to our new course in South Vietnam."[32]

To Harriman, Phoumi remained the primary obstacle to achieving a settlement in Geneva. The Lao general, unwilling to negotiate in good faith with Souvanna about the composition of a coalition government, refused to travel to the Plaine des Jarres for a meeting of the three princes. Phoumi's ostensible reason was concern for his personal safety—the same stalling tactic he had effectively used in 1960 when plotting Souvanna's overthrow. Commenting on Phoumi's behavior, Harriman cabled Kennedy and Rusk on November 6: "Phoumi, either from inertia or by adroit, deliberate action is leading [the] US to war in Laos." The exasperated diplomat added, "It is fantastic that General Phoumi, who is entirely [a] US creation, should be permitted to continue to dictate American policy."[33]

UK officials shared Harriman's dim view of Phoumi. Ambassador David Ormsby-Gore, an acquaintance of the president and a close friend of his brother Robert, was instructed by the Macmillan government to meet with Rusk "to express British concern over the recent developments in Laos." Phoumi's reluctance to negotiate with Souvanna, said Ormsby-Gore, was preventing the formation of a coalition government and "contributing to a dangerous situation." If the ceasefire collapsed under such circumstances, the "UK would have difficulty in intervening militarily and presumes that the US would also." Rusk explained that the United States was "pressing Phoumi hard to negotiate." He also stressed the importance of reaching an agreement that would likely lead to a genuinely neutral cabinet rather than a government dominated by leftists. Should Phoumi "merely surrender at this point?" Rusk asked. When Ormsby-Gore mentioned the Soviet Union's desire to avoid hostilities in Laos, Rusk observed that because of the West's unwillingness to act in the spring of 1961, "the Soviets probably [were] not overafraid of US intervention."[34]

In Vientiane, Brown urged Phoumi to go to the Plaine des Jarres to meet with Souvanna and the Pathet Lao, warning the general that his reluctance to negotiate was creating a "crisis" in his relations with the United States.[35] The US government, he said, would "not allow its policy to be determined" by Phoumi's intransigence. Brown, who had tried to influence the Lao general's behavior since becoming ambassador in July 1960, realized that tough talk "would not impress Phoumi." The only "effective leverage," Brown wrote the State Department, would be the withdrawal of US military and financial support to the RLG, an act that would have the undesirable consequence of undermining "our bargaining position with Souvanna."[36]

To help strengthen Brown's hand, Rusk instructed the ambassador to deliver to Phoumi a "personal message from me": if Phoumi or Boun Oum failed to attend a meeting of the three princes on the Plaine des Jarres, US officials "would be forced [to] consider whether we have any further useful role to play in Laotian affairs." Perhaps recognizing that such a threat was not entirely credible, Rusk proposed an appeal to Boun Oum's and Phoumi's common sense: "It must be obvious to [the] RLG that [the] breakdown of negotiations on [the] issue of [the] location of [a] meeting would make it impossible to get international sympathy and support for [the] RLG."[37]

On November 14 Brown delivered Rusk's message to Phoumi, who listened "attentively without comment," according to the ambassador's report of the meeting. Phoumi asked for a written text of the message to discuss at a restricted meeting of the RLG cabinet. After his meeting with Brown, Phoumi called in CIA officer Hasey, a highly decorated World War II veteran who had established a soldierly camaraderie with the Lao general. Phoumi asked if Rusk's "threat" was serious. Hasey, whose voice was a raspy half-whisper from wounds to his throat and jaw, replied that the US government expected either Phoumi or Boun Oum to go to the Plaine des Jarres. The following day Phoumi provided his official response to Brown: neither he nor Boun Oum would travel to the plain, but their refusal "in no way constituted a breaking off of the negotiations."[38]

While the three princes argued over the site of their next meeting, US officials considered the "potentially explosive issue of Phoumi's personal position" in a coalition government. He insisted on being named either minister of defense or minister of the interior, cabinet positions that controlled the Lao military and police organizations. Ambassador Brown dismissed the possibility that the Pathet Lao and Souvanna would allow Phoumi to lead a ministry capable of overthrowing a coalition government. Other members of the US mission, however, urged the Kennedy administration to demand the appointment of the Lao general as defense minister. To General Boyle, the Military Assistance Advisory Group (MAAG) commander in Laos, and Gordon L. Jorgensen, the CIA chief of station, a communist takeover seemed inevitable if Phoumi did not control the Lao military. Boyle and Jorgensen, recognizing that the NLHS would strongly resist their proposal, thought the "risk of war" was preferable to the "communization of Laos."[39]

State Department officials, who were more intent on keeping the NLHS out of critical ministries than on securing a particular cabinet post for Phoumi, agreed with Brown. They wanted Phoumi to yield on taking either the ministry of defense or interior if such concessions produced an otherwise satisfactory Lao government. Noting the dissenting views of Boyle and Jorgensen, the department declared to Brown: "In these delicate negotiations [the] US team must speak as one." The instruction was an indirect reference to the destructive conflict between the embassy and the CIA station in 1959, when Ambassador Horace H. Smith supported Prime Minister Phoui Sananikone and Chief of Station Henry Hecksher funded and advised the "young Turks," including Phoumi, who successfully sought the prime minister's ouster. This self-defeating "dichotomy" in US policy split the Laotian anticommunists, according to a State

Department analysis. Ambassador Brown, who had a harmonious working relationship with Jorgensen, cabled Washington: "Department may rest fully assured that all elements [of the] U.S. mission here will speak as one."[40]

Phoumi had many supporters at CIA headquarters and the Pentagon, but they lacked the bureaucratic influence of his most powerful opponent: Averell Harriman, who viewed the Lao general as "an inadequate instrument to further US policy in a government of national unity." Doubting whether Phoumi could "ever be induced to negotiate in good faith," Harriman cabled Brown on December 9: "We must be prepared [to] consider drastic steps such as bringing about Phoumi's departure from Gov[ernmen]t." In this telegram, Harriman defined the US "problem" in Laos as finding a "solution which would not involve on the one hand putting in US forces or on the other allowing Laos to be overrun in the absence of these forces." US policy, he added, must "avoid facing the President with either of these extreme alternatives."[41]

Brown replied that the only way to avoid such a choice was to "go for a coalition government, even if it is less satisfactory than we would wish, and will in all probability be a weaker instrument than we would like." Reviewing the recent history of US-Lao relations, Brown observed that the United States had been unsuccessful in persuading Phoumi and Souvanna to work together: "The pattern of failure is so consistent as to suggest that the obstacles to [the] success of their marriage are fairly fundamental." Nonetheless, Brown concluded that the US government might be able to "force" an "unwilling" Phoumi into participating in a coalition government. "We must, and I will, push this solution for all it is worth."[42]

Phoumi resisted the concessions sought by the United States—particularly the demand to yield the defense and interior portfolios to the neutralists. Although he maintained a friendly attitude with Ambassador Brown, Phoumi was blunt in expressing his disappointment to Hasey. The Lao general complained that the United States was "treating [the] RLG like a small child" and that the policy proposed by the ambassador led "completely downhill into communism." When Phoumi predicted that he would be unable to "swing" the RLG cabinet to the US point of view, Hasey urged him to do his best. Warning Phoumi of "drastic" instructions the ambassador had received from Washington, Hasey told the general that he risked losing US economic and military aid if he did not follow Brown's advice. Phoumi said that he was aware of the risk but "really didn't see much use in US support if all it meant was giving in to the enemy."[43]

Phoumi's principal scheme for resisting the "Souvanna solution" was advocating a government led by Savang Vatthana, the king of Laos. The idea was superficially plausible. The monarchy, along with Buddhism, was one of the few unifying institutions in Laos. Moreover, the US government had frequently, if unsuccessfully, urged the king to play a leadership role in times of political crisis. "If the three princes so requested," Phoumi told Hasey, "the King would head a government."[44]

There was, however, virtually no chance that the three princes would make that request. Souphanouvong and his party superiors would never agree to such a resolute anticommunist leading the government. Souvanna disliked the king for political and personal reasons, which included the monarch's obvious preference for Phoumi. Boun Oum, who also disliked Savang, had resented the royal family's treatment of him since 1946, when he gave up his claim to rule southern Laos as part of France's unification of three separate principalities. "The king," Boun Oum told Hasey, "wants the three princes to come to him on their knees and give him a King's government on a silver tray. This is not possible."[45]

Perhaps the most formidable barrier to a government led by Savang was the monarch himself. The king, then fifty-one, embraced the constitutional limits of his power and removed himself from the day-to-day struggles of Laos. By adopting this posture, he hoped to maintain the standing of the royal family while avoiding the enmity of the factions fighting for control of his kingdom. Savang's unwillingness to exercise leadership in unifying the noncommunists frustrated officials in both the Eisenhower and Kennedy administrations. "There was the most naive conviction, wishful thinking, in Washington that somehow or other the King could intervene and right the situation," Brown recalled.[46]

At a meeting with the king on December 26, 1961, Ambassador Brown said that he had "heard much talk around town [about] the possibility of a gov[ernmen]t with his majesty as prime minister." Savang, looking "morose," replied that he had recently spoken with Soviet ambassador Aleksandr N. Abramov, who had made the same suggestion. The king told Abramov that, as a constitutional monarch, he could play no such political role. And if the constitutional institutions of Laos broke down, Savang said, the country "would be destroyed." Brown, committed to the policy of bringing about a Souvanna government, said that he "very much shared" his majesty's viewpoint: it was "much better" if someone other than the king was prime minister.[47]

As usual, the king's enthusiasm for the Laotian constitution did not preclude royal criticism of his country's leading politicians. "Souvanna would fail" if he became prime minister, Savang declared. The reason was neither his "neutrality policy" nor his "personal weaknesses." It was because of the deep divisions between northern and southern Laos. Souvanna, who Savang claimed was disliked and mistrusted in southern Laos, had made too many commitments to his northern followers: "Therefore he could not govern satisfactorily." Observing that a successful government must represent both regions, the king added that Boun Oum "had erred" by including too many southerners and members of his family in the government.[48]

Having found fault with the leaders of the center and right factions—his contempt for Souphanouvong went without saying—the king expressed his disapproval of actions by the international community. The Geneva conference, he admitted, "had produced some good results" in the international aspects of the conflict. But interference in the formation of a national government was an intolerable violation of Lao sovereignty. "Foreign powers," said Savang, "had made a great mistake" in negotiating with the three princes, who "did not represent any Lao but themselves and were tools of outside powers." Despite his unhappiness with the process for resolving the political crisis, the king hoped that the three princes would reach an agreement on a new government. If they did, he said, he would approve it and ask the Boun Oum–Phoumi government to resign.[49]

In a cable to the State Department, Brown concluded that his meeting with Savang "was not very satisfactory." The king was "obviously annoyed" at the foreign pressure to bring about a Souvanna government. The ambassador reported that he "did not warn [the] king more vigorously against a gov[ernmen]t under his leadership," given Savang's own opposition to the idea. In an interview years later, Brown doubted that the king would have accomplished anything by stepping into the political arena: "He probably served a greater purpose for his country in the long run, and for all of us in the long run, by staying on the throne even though he didn't do a damn thing."[50]

Threatening Phoumi with the loss of US economic and military aid was easy, but withdrawing that support without undermining US objectives was more difficult. A decision by Kennedy to cease all aid to the RLG might trigger a desperate act by the general—for example, a large-scale attack against the Pathet Lao aimed at provoking communist retaliation, which in turn would lead to intervention by US combat troops. Or Phoumi might abandon Vientiane and withdraw with his loyalists to Savannakhet in southern Laos, as he did after the Kong Le coup and the investiture of Souvanna's government. Even the more limited sanction of pulling out US military advisers from forward areas would demoralize their Lao trainees and deny the United States first-hand intelligence. In a January 1, 1962, telegram to the State Department, Brown observed: "The hard fact is that the sanctions we have available to us are somewhat like the atom bomb—too big to use without causing us almost as much harm as [the RLG.]"[51]

Recognizing that modest actions might not be sufficiently persuasive and that stronger ones might weaken the FAR, Brown recommended a gradual cut-off of economic aid and military supplies to the RLG.[52] Although State Department officials were not yet willing to fully endorse the ambassador's program of escalating pressure, Rusk did authorize a temporary withholding of the US cash grant to the RLG for the month of January. When informing the Lao finance minister of the US decision to suspend the three-million-dollar grant, Ambassador Brown expressed disappointment about positions taken by Boun Oum and Phoumi. The United States, said Brown, "was re-examining its entire economic, financial, and military aid program for Laos." Withholding the grant had little immediate impact on Phoumi, but its economic consequences were prompt and significant: the central bank suspended the convertibility of Lao kip to dollars and francs; private exchange rates reduced the value of the kip by nearly half; and the price of food increased 25 percent.[53]

More drastic measures for dealing with Phoumi's stubbornness were discussed at the January 5 meeting of the Special Group, the interagency committee that approved and monitored covert operations. A paper submitted to the group, which included the DCI, the deputy secretaries of defense and state, and the president's national security adviser, proposed covert means either to persuade Phoumi "to play ball" or to "get rid" of him. One possible method suggested to the group was "staging a coup d'etat" to overthrow the general. A coup, however, had a number of disadvantages, which included a long period of preparation and a high risk of dividing the FAR. A more promising course of action was the possibility that "Phoumi might be bribed into resigning or acquiescing in the Western position." The amount of money would be "substantial" and enable the general to "take care of" his loyal followers.[54]

At a White House meeting the following day, Kennedy met with his advisers to decide on next steps in Laos. According to notes of the meeting prepared by McGeorge Bundy, the president "expressed sympathy with the notion of a private high-level offer of financial support to Phoumi for his own needs and those of his followers." In his summary of Kennedy's views, Bundy wrote: "Subject to agreement between the Department of State and the CIA, the President authorized a high-level 'dicker' with Phoumi."[55] John A. McCone, who had replaced Allen Dulles as DCI on November 29, summed up Kennedy's decision this way: "[The] Agency should instruct their people in Laos to discuss the proposal outlined in the memorandum for the Special Group of 5 January 1962." Because parts of McCone's notes remain classified, and because of the obfuscation and euphemisms typical of written records of presidential discussions of covert action, it is difficult to reconstruct the entire White House conversation about Phoumi. For example, a redacted section in McCone's notes refers to a covert sanction that would force the general "to capitulate." This still-classified action would also have the undesirable effect of convincing allied leaders in Southeast Asia that "the United States was not to be trusted."[56]

McCone, a Republican who had served as chairman of the Atomic Energy Commission during the Eisenhower administration, reported the intelligence community's doubts about a Souvanna government with neutralists leading the defense and interior ministries. Based on Souvanna's past actions, the new CIA chief said, Laos would likely become "an open roadstead from North Vietnam to South Vietnam." The Lao prime minister would deny the existence of infiltration and "would do nothing to interdict it," McCone predicted.[57]

Harriman, according to Bundy's notes, "responded very firmly and clearly in defense of the 'Souvanna solution.'" This policy, Harriman said, had been decided the previous August: "The current issue was quite simply whether Phoumi or the President of the United States was to run U.S. foreign policy." Harriman agreed with McCone on the importance of closing the border between Laos and South Vietnam and reminded the group of the Soviet commitment to prevent infiltration. The diplomat said he believed that the "Russians did not want fighting." They wanted "a reasonable agreement." The only alternative to a Geneva accord was war, said Harriman, repeating General Omar Bradley's characterization of enlarging the Korean conflict: Laos would be "the wrong war in the wrong place at the wrong time."[58]

President Kennedy, who valued consensus in national security policy-making, did not explicitly endorse either McCone's or Harriman's analysis. He did, however, make "it clear that he did not want a resumption of fighting." To Bundy, the "clear inference" of the president's comments was a reaffirmation of Harriman's views. In a meeting with Bundy and Rusk the previous evening, Kennedy had "strongly back[ed]" the State Department's "insistence that Phoumi must not take [the] initiative to break [the] cease-fire." The president wanted Ambassador Brown to ensure that the Lao general understood a basic premise of US policy: "[A] resumption of hostilities by [the] RLG under present circumstances would create [a] situation in which [the] RLG would have no support either militarily or in terms of world or American opinion."[59]

While McCone and Harriman disagreed over the Souvanna solution, Defense Secretary McNamara, JCS Chairman Lemnitzer, and General Taylor remained silent, according to McCone's account of the meeting. The reticence of the military men presumably reflected a shared knowledge that the president had made up his mind about this issue some months ago. Silence, however, did not necessarily mean concurrence, particularly in the case of General Lemnitzer, who had submitted to McNamara a JCS memorandum suggesting a "Reassessment of US Policy in Laos."[60]

The paper was a carefully worded dissent from the president's Laos policy. Hedged with qualifiers such as "appears," "seems," and "probably," the memo often lacked the chiefs' typical directness of expression and reflected their uneasy relationship with a commander in chief who had rejected their advice for military intervention in Laos. In addition to feeling unfairly blamed for the CIA failure at the Bay of Pigs, the JCS—

General Lemnitzer, in particular—did not share Kennedy's keen interest in new doctrine and approaches to defeating "wars of national liberation." At a meeting with the chiefs on December 4, 1961, Kennedy "directed that we 'make [South Vietnam] a laboratory, both for training our people, and for learning the things we need to know to successfully compete in this area.'" The chiefs, all senior officers during World War II and the Korean War, were likely appalled by Kennedy's observation that, "as far as he knew, only [Brigadier] General [Edward] Lansdale was an authority on the subject [of guerrilla and counterguerrilla warfare]."[61]

In their January 1962 critique of Kennedy's Laos policy, the chiefs pointed out that the US military assistance and diplomatic programs had been operating "at cross-purposes in some respects." On the one hand, they observed, American materiel and advisers were designed to strengthen the bargaining position of the RLG in achieving "an acceptable agreement on a neutral Laos." On the other hand, US diplomatic efforts had emphasized both restraint on "military counteractions" by the RLG and pressure on its leaders to make concessions with Souvanna. These actions, "though well intended," had undermined the RLG and its army to the point where "the legal government may soon have no tenable position from which to negotiate."[62]

The chiefs observed that the inconsistency in Laos policy was "probably" caused by the "basic difference in outlook" between diplomats and the military—an understated characterization of the sharp conflicts between the State Department and Pentagon over Laos policy since the late 1950s. More to the point, the JCS declared that the apparent pursuit of "a peaceful settlement at all costs" was unnecessary because the balance of power in Laos was shifting toward the government forces. Since the May ceasefire, the FAR had made improvements in tactics, leadership, and combat performance; the Hmong and other tribal groups had demonstrated their willingness to organize local resistance movements; and the RLG's superior airlift capabilities could be exploited in the rainy season. In sum, the chiefs wrote, the RLG "can, and should, negotiate from a position of strength."[63]

Taking a forthright position on the composition of a coalition government, the JCS advocated that the ministries of defense and interior remain in the hands of "the present RLG." Suspicious of Souvanna, the chiefs predicted: "A so-called neutral Defense Minister would almost certainly bar

Western-oriented Laotian officers from positions of high command. The diversion of American-supplied weapons and military equipment from the present RLG forces to Kong Le and Pathet Lao troops also could be expected." Noting the US policy of "strong pressure" on the RLG—that is, Phoumi—to yield the ministries of defense and interior, the JCS suggested that American diplomacy place a greater emphasis on "encouragement and full assurance of continued US support."[64]

The chiefs' optimistic view of the shifting balance of power in Laos was confirmed by a Special National Intelligence Estimate (SNIE) on the capabilities of the opposing military forces: "Both government and antigovernment forces have increased their strength and improved their capabilities during the cease-fire. The government forces, which in May were defeated, demoralized, and near collapse, have made relatively greater improvement." The FAR, the estimate noted, had increased its armed strength; had received extensive support from US, Thai, and Filipino technical personnel; and had benefited from the "stiffening and tactical guidance" of US Army Special Forces assigned to selected battalions.[65]

The estimate was intended to help policymakers resolve differing opinions on FAR and Pathet Lao capabilities that had surfaced at the January 6 meeting with the president. Drafted by the CIA's Office of National Estimates with participation by other relevant government agencies, the estimate was a "rush job" finished in five days. (A typical estimate took six to eight weeks to prepare.)[66] The conclusions of the estimate reflected the views of Admiral Felt, MAAG commander Boyle, and CIA station chief Jorgensen. Harriman, however, objected to the diplomatic implications of both the SNIE and the recently expressed political views of the Joint Chiefs of Staff. "I want to record that we have taken no action in Geneva or in discussions regarding a government of national union based on the strength or weakness of the FAR," Harriman wrote to Rusk. "I mention this as, in connection with these reappraisals, there seems to be an implication that we are now in a better position to negotiate a settlement in Laos because of this change. This is not the case. Insofar as military strength has influenced negotiations, it is the threat of possible U.S. military intervention with or without SEATO."[67]

Official judgments of improvements in the FAR and in the overall military balance were short-lived. In the last three weeks of January, Phoumi's forces suffered several defeats in central and northern Laos that

General Boyle characterized as "complete routs." In each clash, the FAR had been "forced to withdraw," according to a new SNIE on the capabilities of the military forces in Laos. Issued only twenty days after the original, the new version admitted that the earlier document had been "too optimistic" in estimating that the FAR "would have a slight edge" in fighting antigovernment forces: "In particular, we believe that the FAR is unable to deal with any substantial number of North Vietnamese forces, whom they greatly fear."[68]

Chapter 4

A Disagreeable, Hard, and Dangerous Fact

The western edge of the Ho Chi Minh trail ran through the Nhommarath-Mahaxay region of the Laotian panhandle. North of this area, the trail passed from Laos across the rugged Annamite Mountains into the DRV. To the south, the trail led to Tchepone and South Vietnam. Pathet Lao forces in Nhommarath-Mahaxay had been strengthened in late 1961 by the addition of artillery, armored vehicles, and an estimated two North Vietnamese battalions. To the RLG, the enemy buildup seemed a threat to Thakhek, a Mekong River town and the headquarters of FAR Groupement Mobile (GM) 14.[1]

In January 1962 the Eighth Bataillon d'infanterie (BI) of GM 14 conducted a "defensive sweep" south of Nhommarath-Mahaxay, while the Twenty-fourth BI of GM 12 probed to the north. One goal of these flanking maneuvers was to improve the FAR position should antigovernment forces attack Thakhek. Another objective, ordered by Phoumi for this and similar operations nationwide, was "to pressure [the] enemy."[2] On January 17 a reconnaissance patrol of the Eighth BI engaged the Pathet Lao in a fight that included air strikes by three T-6s from the Royal Lao Air Force (RLAF). Slow, single-prop training aircraft, the T-6s had been configured with wing-mounted .30-caliber machine guns, five-inch rockets, and a rack under each wing for a bomb weighing no more than one hundred pounds.

The next day the Eighth BI attacked Mahaxay, but antigovernment forces counterattacked with elements of one PAVN battalion, two 105-mm howitzer batteries, and three armored cars. "The FAR troops made what appeared to be only a token resistance and then withdrew," General Boyle reported to CINCPAC. Antigovernment troops also forced the Twenty-fourth BI to withdraw. While the Eighth BI regrouped, the FAR

Ninth BI and the Eleventh Bataillon de parachutistes (BP) were committed to the fight, but both units "apparently stopped short of their objective without making contact with the enemy."[3]

The FAR suffered similar defeats in northwestern Laos. In the Nam Beng Valley, a sweep by elements of GM 11 in early January encountered "stiff enemy resistance" near Muong Sai, a Pathet Lao stronghold and supply depot. A North Vietnamese–Pathet Lao counterattack forced the FAR units "to withdraw hastily towards the Mekong River." According to the leader of a US Army Special Forces training team, the commanding officer of the Third BI of GM 11 was a politically influential major who "was frightened and stayed drunk for several days."[4]

A more strategically significant FAR debacle began to unfold in Nam Tha, a remote provincial capital near the border with Burma and China. The headquarters of GM 11, Nam Tha and its airfield were critical to supplying FAR forces in northwestern Laos. On January 21 antigovernment forces, estimated at two companies, overran two FAR defensive positions nineteen miles east of Nam Tha, forcing the First BI to withdraw into the town. The Second BI, conducting a defensive sweep nearby, was also driven back into Nam Tha. PAVN and Pathet Lao forces advanced toward the town, placing artillery in the hills east of the airfield. "Enemy intentions at this point are not clear," Admiral Felt informed the JCS. "However, there is little doubt that he could seize the garrison if he chooses to do so."[5]

The Pathet Lao and DRV told the Soviets "that their operations in Nam Tha Province were designed to compel Phoumi Nosavan to the negotiating table." Kremlin officials were skeptical, fearing that these actions would stiffen Phoumi's resistance to a political settlement and risk a resumption of fighting. Khrushchev invited Souphanouvong to Moscow for a meeting in late January. According to researchers Aleksander Fursenko and Timothy Naftali, the purpose of the "summit" was to send a message to the PRC: "The USA and the USSR did not intend to go to war in Laos in the name of China." Although Souphanouvong was confident that the FAR garrison at Nam Tha could be seized in a "few hours," he subsequently assured Aleksandr Abramov, the Soviet ambassador to Laos, that the Pathet Lao would not "give any cause for provocation."[6]

In a January 25 message to CINCPAC, General Boyle expressed his "concern" at the "failure" of FAR operations in central and northwestern Laos.

He reported that there had recently been a "marked build-up" of North Vietnamese forces in the kingdom and that Phoumi, despite warnings from his American advisers, had ordered the FAR to pressure the enemy across the country. Some of these probes and sweeps had triggered sharp enemy reactions, resulting in "complete routs of FAR forces and [the] loss of much equipment." Boyle concluded that despite improvements in the FAR since the May ceasefire, the Lao army continued to have serious weaknesses, especially in "leadership and motivation."[7]

Poor FAR leadership and inadequate military training were long-standing problems for Laos, France, and the United States. Under the terms of the 1954 Geneva accords, only France could provide military training for the FAR. (Limited numbers of US military advisers were, however, permitted in South Vietnam and Cambodia.) The transition from command to advice in Laos was difficult for the French Military Mission (FMM). The precipitous displacement of French small-unit commanders in favor of "totally unqualified Laotians" had a discouraging impact on the FMM, according to the US Army attaché in Vientiane.[8] A US military advisory team visiting Laos in December 1954 concluded: "Even those [French] officers who are assigned as advisors and instructors are giving—by their own admission—only nominal assistance to the Laotian commanders."[9]

Although prohibited from military training in Laos, the United States financed 100 percent of the RLG's defense budget and provided its armed forces with weapons and other materiel. A small, semiclandestine, and largely ineffectual Programs Evaluation Office (PEO), staffed by retired and reserve military personnel, monitored the use of US equipment, advised the ambassador on defense affairs, and reported to CINCPAC and the Pentagon on purely military matters. The first PEO chief, Brigadier General Rothwell H. Brown (retired), found fault with the quality of the French training and the competence of the Lao army: "Individual training is grossly inadequate in the [FAR]. Unit commanders are not sufficiently qualified to develop their men." Brown also observed that one of the factors that most undermined morale in the Lao army was "the assignment to command positions of officers with political influence."[10]

The Eisenhower administration, frustrated by Pathet Lao political and military successes, the poor state of Lao military training, and the limitations on US military assistance, introduced covert Special Forces training teams into Laos in July 1959. The plan for US tactical training teams had provoked sharp protests from the French government, which agreed, reluctantly, to a watered-down version of the initial concept and wanted the teams removed after one year. Between August 1960 and June 1962, as US military support to Laos both increased and became more overt, the French opposed American training policy and had little contact with the FAR.

The US Army Special Forces teams, first named Hotfoot, then White Star in 1961, were trained to operate autonomously in remote areas with indigenous forces. They were not, however, prepared for the limited professionalism of most FAR officers. In the words of one team leader, they lacked "the necessary military background to command or direct simple military operations."[11] Moreover, many Lao officers were unwilling to lose face by participating in training or following advice, particularly when it came from lower-ranking American officers. A US Army adviser returning from Laos observed: "We were teaching too many subordinates over there when we should have been teaching their superiors."[12]

Many American officials attributed the FAR's poor combat performance to the Laotians' inherent pacifism and Buddhist beliefs. Such stereotypical notions inspired ridicule about the fighting ability of an entire country's people. John Kenneth Galbraith, Kennedy's ambassador to India, wrote to the president: "As a military ally the entire Laos nation is clearly inferior to a battalion of conscientious objectors from World War I."[13] This condescending witticism ignored the military achievements of the few well-trained units with capable leaders. The Second BP, which defeated Pathet Lao forces before the August 1960 coup and Phoumi's troops after the putsch, had benefited from a CIA paramilitary adviser and US Special Forces assigned to the unit. And Kong Le, the battalion's commander, had received training at the CIA-sponsored scout and ranger school in the Philippines. "Laotian soldiers are tough and devoted when they have leaders who are worthy of them," observed Lieutenant Colonel Hugh Toye, the UK military attaché in Laos.[14]

The Laotians' toughness and devotion faced their most strenuous test in encounters with PAVN forces. The Vietnamese had been a traditional Lao enemy at least since the late fifteenth century, when they invaded the kingdom of Lan Xang ("a million elephants"), the cultural predecessor of modern Laos. The DRV's victory over France, a European power and the colonial protector of Laos, greatly enhanced the reputation of the Vietnamese for military prowess. To Boyle, it seemed as if FAR officers and enlisted men had "an almost pathological fear" of the Vietnamese. On many occasions, Boyle recalled, the mere presence of PAVN units near a potential battlefield was enough to prompt FAR troops to "just pick up and leave."[15]

The increasing number of North Vietnamese troops in Laos had altered "the equation of the contest," in Admiral Felt's words, with the military balance favoring the antigovernment forces. The revised January 31 SNIE estimated an overall total of some nine thousand North Vietnamese troops in Laos, an 80 percent increase from the figure of five thousand in the SNIE issued only three weeks earlier. Foreshadowing problems with order-of-battle (OB) estimates in South Vietnam, the new SNIE explained that two North Vietnamese battalions, approximately one thousand men, "may have entered Laos in recent weeks." The balance of the discrepancy—three thousand North Vietnamese troops, or 75 percent of the increase—was "attributable to a reassessment of indications previously available and to new evidence." (The nature of the "new evidence" was unstated, presumably to avoid mentioning "sources and methods" of gathering intelligence.) Admitting that estimates of PAVN strength in Laos were "highly tenuous," the SNIE warned: OB figures could change quickly, as units were moved "easily to and fro across the Laotian–North Vietnamese border."[16]

The US intelligence community faced a number of barriers in estimating the total number of PAVN forces in Laos, which included regular battalions; mixed Pathet Lao–North Vietnamese units; and various military advisers, technicians, and engineers. Although CIA officers worked with the Hmong in northern Laos, and US military advisers served with FAR battalions in RLG-controlled areas, much of the intelligence on enemy strength came from Lao and South Vietnamese sources of questionable reliability. The thick jungle canopy over most of Laos limited the usefulness of much aerial reconnaissance. Communications intelligence (COMINT), however, provided some insights into the enemy order of battle. By 1961 US cryptanalysts had made progress in breaking North Vietnamese codes and ciphers. A top-secret annex to a February 1962 SNIE, restricted to select officials cleared for COMINT, discussed North Vietnamese military communication networks in Laos and South Vietnam. The document, parts of which still remain classified, identified PAVN communications networks that "clarifie[d] troop dispositions" in Laos: "In general, these PAVN units are strategically located astride the significant routes between Laos and South Vietnam."[17]

The FAR defeats of January 1962 had immediate political and diplomatic repercussions. In Washington, State Department officials were "disturbed" to learn that Phoumi had ordered the FAR "to push on several fronts in various parts of Laos."[18] The president had specifically sought to avoid a resumption of fighting, and Harriman had assured Souvanna that US advisers "had [the] strictest orders to prevent any offensive" action by Phoumi's forces. Although Brown had informed Washington that the US mission was doing "everything possible to discourage Phoumi [from] taking actions which could be condemned as violations of the cease-fire," the ambassador also reported that the United States was encouraging the Lao general "to counteract all PL encroachments."[19]

In early January Brown cabled that this "delicate balance of pushing with one hand while holding with the other has been effective." By the end of the month, however, the State Department was scolding the US mission for failing to stop FAR operations: "Our instructions were explicit that Phoumi should be restrained from provocative actions even to [the] extent of withdrawing our support if necessary." Department officials declared that MAAG officers assigned to FAR units "must play [an] effective role in this respect." An unclear, poorly drafted concluding sentence seemed to charge the US mission, particularly the military advisory command, with failing to inform Washington about the planning and approval of such "dangerously provocative" actions.[20]

Ambassador Brown conceded that "perhaps" not all of the FAR sweeps and probes had been "soundly conceived from a military viewpoint," but he characterized them as "essentially defensive in [the] face [of a] heavy enemy buildup." In Brown's view, the problem in the Nhommarath–Mahaxay region was the concentration of Pathet Lao–Kong Le–North Vietnamese forces, which included artillery and armor. Although they had not attacked, the enemy forces near Thakhek had caused "justifiable anxiety to the Royal Lao Government and ourselves." Brown informed Washington that Boyle and he had approved the reinforcement of Nam Tha with the Thirtieth BI, which had just returned from six weeks of US-sponsored training in Thailand: "This action [is] obviously necessary to protect Nam Tha from [an] enemy offensive."[21]

The ambassador did not, however, attempt to justify the bombing at Mahaxay by RLAF T-6s. The embassy exercised strict control over bombs and fuses, releasing them to the RLAF only for counterattacks of clear violations of the ceasefire. The bombs dropped at Mahaxay were a secret gift to the RLAF from Marshal Sarit Thanarat, the prime minister of Thailand. Brown told Phoumi that he was "very unhappy" about the bombing sorties, which risked "blowing up" the Geneva conference. The ambassador ordered US air advisers and technicians in Vientiane to "make every effort to ground" the Lao T-6s if the bombing continued.[22]

The Nhommarath-Mahaxay operation also put Brown on the defensive with British Ambassador John Addis, who thought that the FAR maneuvers had been provocative, at the very least, and possibly a violation of the ceasefire. A China expert who became ambassador about the same time Brown did, Addis thought that his American counterpart "was strongly prejudiced in favor of Phoumi and against Souvanna."[23] Although an accurate assessment of the views of the US military and the CIA, Addis's judgment did not reflect Brown's efforts to encourage the formation of a Souvanna-led government.

According to a report from Brown, Addis and his embassy colleagues considered almost any FAR movements into areas held by the Pathet Lao on May 3, 1961, the date of the ceasefire, as violations of the agreement: "Addis appeared [to] believe that Phoumi's activities around Mahaxay had no other objective than to provoke [an] attack by [the] enemy which would justify him in calling for help from Thailand or the US." Brown found it "discouraging" that the British ambassador ignored the "increasing military threat and [the] provocations of the other side." Conceding that the Lao general had been "outrageously obstructive" in the formation of a new government and that some of his military actions were "injudicious" and "even provocative," Brown wrote: the UK's "almost pathologic personal opposition to and distrust of Phoumi" made dispassionate discussion of the military realities in Laos "difficult."[24]

The combination of Phoumi's military weakness and his "self-seeking stubbornness" in negotiations prompted Harriman and the president himself to conclude that a "final showdown" with the Lao general could "no longer be deferred." In a January 25 phone call with Kennedy, Harriman said the US government should "make it very plain to Phoumi, unless he plays ball, [this] is his last chance." Two days later, Kennedy approved a Harriman-proposed cable to Brown that declared: "Since Phoumi patently cannot win militarily, his only hope for [his] own future lies in [the] early formation of [a] Souvanna Government and in his participating in and cooperating fully with it. If he does, we will continue to befriend him." If Phoumi refused to negotiate in good faith or insisted on keeping the defense and interior ministries for the right wing, the US government would "immediately break off all contact with him." The king, Boun Oum, and other RLG officials would be informed of the break, with the objective of triggering a "reorganization of [the] RLG to permit continued negotiations for [the] formation [of a] new government."[25]

In his reply to the State Department, and indirectly to the president, Brown "respectfully suggested" that his instructions would either accomplish little or be counterproductive. The likely outcome of ending personal contact with Phoumi, while simultaneously continuing to provide US support to the RLG and the army, would be to deny the United States "most real knowledge of what is going on without hurting Phoumi." To Brown, it seemed "unrealistic" to make a distinction between the Lao general and the government he led: "The other members of [the] RLG, aside from those who are wholeheartedly supporting Phoumi in his present position, are afraid of him and have no influence with him." Brown, who had jawboned Phoumi for eighteen months with limited effectiveness, wrote: "We must, in my opinion, be prepared to back up any ultimatum by decisive action in the field of sanctions"—for example, suspension of military supplies or the withdrawal of Special Forces from forward combat units.[26]

The State Department response, approved by Harriman, dismissed Brown's concerns, defended the idea of an ultimatum to Phoumi, and assured the ambassador of Washington's careful consideration of "various carrot and stick combinations." The telegram urged Brown to point out to Lao political and military leaders the "tragic consequences [of] their continuing [to] blindly support Phoumi," which "could be quickly and effectively averted by new leadership taking over." Brown continued to resist the instruction, observing that Phoumi would promptly go public with any US ultimatum. The United States could justify stopping aid to a regime with which it disagreed, Brown wrote. But a more difficult diplomatic problem would be a "true accusation" by Phoumi, a minister in a sovereign government, of US threats to oust him by influencing his king, cabinet colleagues, and military associates. "I would appreciate guidance on this point," wrote Brown.[27]

The State Department replied that any repudiation of Phoumi would be made public and could be defended in terms of both Laotian and US national interests: "Public disavowal of an individual by [the] USG is [a] drastic form of sanction and we believe [it] cannot fail but make [a] strong impression on [a] country so totally dependent upon US aid as Laos."[28] Despite their frustration with Phoumi, Harriman and Kennedy temporarily abandoned the idea of shunning him. Brown's opposition undoubtedly influenced Washington's thinking, but there was another reason for postponing a public showdown—leverage with Souvanna. Without an agreement on the composition of a coalition government, the United States was unwilling to take actions against Phoumi that might weaken the FAR. In an effort to seize the initiative, department officials informed Brown that the time had come for "direct negotiation with Souvanna." If he proposed a satisfactory cabinet, then the United States would support that government. Phoumi's participation, according to Harriman, "would be invited but would not be necessary."[29]

While the US government sought to influence the formation of a new Lao government, Phoumi reinforced Nam Tha, and the Pathet Lao and North Vietnamese sporadically shelled the town and its airfield. On February 10 Phoumi asked MAAG to provide C-46 transport planes to airdrop FAR paratroopers from southern Laos into Nam Tha. US officials considered further reinforcement of the garrison a politically undesirable, militarily dubious operation that would likely send "FAR troops into [a] trap." Ambassador Brown, with General Boyle's concurrence, refused the airlift request. The MAAG commander reiterated to Phoumi the "military inadvisability [of] reinforcing Nam Tha." Undeterred by US disapproval, the Lao general proceeded with the airdrop using available FAR aircraft.[30]

In Washington, State Department officials remained "seriously concerned over Phoumi's unwillingness" to follow US military advice. In Bangkok, Prime Minister Sarit declared that communist military activity since the January attack at Nam Tha jeopardized Thai security. He ordered army units to the border area in northeast Thailand. "While Sarit's action is largely a gesture for domestic consumption, it could have a significant impact on the situation in Laos," the CIA warned policymakers. "Phoumi may be further encouraged to pursue his preferred military solution rather than agree to a coalition arrangement."[31]

At a February 21, 1962, off-the-record meeting at the White House, President Kennedy and top national security officials briefed leading members of Congress on administration policy in Laos. Rusk defined the US objective as establishing a Lao government "that had a reasonable chance of remaining neutral and independent." If "the big power blocs" could agree on the neutralization of Laos and on effective enforcement "machinery," then the kingdom could be kept from becoming a base for communist "action" against other Southeast Asian countries. In Geneva, Rusk said, the international community had "gone about as far as it [could] go" in resolving the conflict. Now it was up to the three princes to establish a Lao government: "We do not know whether the negotiations will succeed or not."[32]

Rusk reported the administration's belief that the Soviet Union wanted a negotiated settlement in Laos. Harriman, confirming the apparent desire of the Soviet delegation in Geneva to reach an agreement, said that Pushkin had made concessions "in spite of the pressure of the Chinese Reds." It seemed to Harriman that Khrushchev "was actually trying to make good" on his commitment to Kennedy to work toward the neutralization of the Laos. Harriman expressed his hope that the Soviets "would do their best" to ensure communist compliance with any agreement reached in Geneva and that "infiltration via Laos into South Viet-Nam will end." He added that forming a coalition government was very difficult and that the United States could not predict "with certainty" the outcome of Souvanna's negotiations with the right- and left-wing factions.[33]

President Kennedy provided the congressional leaders with a broad view of US options in Laos. Reviewing the crisis of the previous spring, and a similar White House meeting with the legislative leadership, the president reaffirmed his commitment to a negotiated settlement. "The only alternative" to a neutral government in Laos, he observed, was "possible intervention by the U.S. and others." It was for this reason, Kennedy said, that he wanted General Lemnitzer to review the military operation for intervention in Laos: SEATO Plan 5.[34]

Lemnitzer, who reviewed the military situation in Laos, said that the basic concept of the plan was to secure the major Mekong River towns with SEATO forces. This would release FAR units from defensive positions and allow them to "clear the country of the opposing Communist forces." Like Admiral Burke at the April 1961 meeting with congressional leaders, Lemnitzer discussed the communications and logistic difficulties associated with military operations in Laos. Later in the briefing, Kennedy noted a basic weakness of SEATO Plan 5: the recent buildup of North Vietnamese units in Laos meant that the antigovernment troops "would defeat the RLG forces if they went out into the country."[35]

If, as seems likely, Kennedy intended to convince the congressional leadership that overt military intervention in Laos remained a bad idea, he was successful. Senator Mansfield, who had succeeded Lyndon B. Johnson as majority leader, observed: "If we get involved in Laos, it might be far worse than when we got involved in Korea." J. William Fulbright (D-AR), chairman of the Senate Committee on Foreign Relations, said that he shared Mansfield's misgivings about US military intervention in Laos. Both senators, however, expressed their approval of Kennedy's recent increase in advisory support for South Vietnam. John W. McCormack (D-MA), speaker of the House of the Representatives, said that he "assumed" South Vietnam "was very important" to US national security, but Laos "was another story."[36]

Senator Everett M. Dirksen (R-IL), the minority leader, said, "The Republicans fully supported the President's position." During the meeting, Dirksen and Leverett Saltonstall (R-MA), who chaired the Senate Republican Conference, posed questions about the relationship between Laos and Vietnam. Dirksen asked who, if anyone, would police the three-hundred-mile Laotian border with South Vietnam. Harriman replied that the draft Geneva accord made no provisions for troops along the border. The Soviets, however, had "agreed that they would see to it that the North Vietnamese would stay behind their own border." McNamara, perhaps seeking to allay any congressional anxiety about infiltration, a topic that troubled him greatly later in the 1960s, observed that "only a small percentage" of PLAF reinforcements and weapons came through the "trails and roads in Laos."[37]

In light of debates during and after the Vietnam War about interdicting the Ho Chi Minh trail with US ground forces, one of the more interesting comments at the meeting was made by General Lemnitzer, who declared: "The holding of a line across the southern part of Laos (roughly around the 17th Parallel) won't stop the infiltration from North Viet-Nam into South Viet-Nam. The forces would have to occupy all of southern Laos right up to the northernmost point of the North Viet-Nam border." Less than four months later, Lemnitzer and the chiefs revised their thinking on "seal[ing] off all the infiltration routes," concluding that an amphibious landing in North Vietnam would be a preferable operation.[38]

Ambassador Brown and Washington policymakers continued to disagree over the most effective way of inducing Phoumi to cooperate in the formation of a Souvanna-led government. The United States had stopped economic aid to the RLG in February, but this particular sanction would take many months to have a meaningful impact on the Lao general. Brown argued that only the "most extreme pressure"—that is, suspending US military support and withdrawing US advisers—had any chance of influencing Phoumi. The ambassador acknowledged that military sanctions would have an "adverse effect" on FAR operations, would eliminate a useful source of intelligence, and would reduce US control of the RLG army. Despite these risks, Brown, Boyle, and Jorgensen had concluded that less drastic measures "would have no chance at all to succeed."[39]

Harriman and other officials in Washington, however, thought that the ambassador's plan "move[d] too rapidly into sanctions" with dangerous consequences. The State Department reminded Brown that the US goal was "to obtain Phoumi's cooperation or displace him," while preserving sufficient anticommunist political and military strength to offset NLHS–Pathet Lao power in a coalition government. Before taking steps that would weaken the FAR, department officials sought an "intensive coordinated effort, using all covert and overt means you have at your disposal, with other Lao political and military leaders to build up [an] individual or group willing to support [a] Souvanna coalition." In a veiled reference to the Kennedy-approved bribe for the Lao general, the State Department suggested that Brown "urgently reconsider using the various carrot proposals we have made." The ambassador was also urged to take another look at Washington's suggestion for "isolating Phoumi by no longer dealing with him personally."[40]

Brown, characterizing his instructions as ineffective "half-measures," responded sharply to Washington: "Apparently we in [the] field and officers in [the] Department have [a] widely different appraisal of [the] possibilities of influencing Phoumi to fit into our program." The ambassador repeated his conviction, shared by top US officials in Vientiane, the western diplomatic corps, and most Lao, that Phoumi would not accept a Souvanna government except "under most drastic duress." Even then the general might not capitulate: "This [was a] disagreeable, hard and dangerous fact," which Washington seemed unwilling to face. Brown also repeated his opposition to breaking off all communication with Phoumi, a gesture that would preclude any possibility of influencing the general: "I still feel that cutting all contact with him will hurt us more than it will hurt him."[41]

Harriman replied that he, too, was "impressed" by the differing perspectives of officials in Washington and Vientiane. Since it was "imperative" that the ambassador "have a complete and accurate picture" of administration policy, Harriman wrote that Foreign Service officer William H. Sullivan and NSC staffer Michael Forrestal were on their way to Vientiane to explain Washington's reasoning and to assist Brown "in achieving [the] solution we are all seeking."[42] Despite the helpful-sounding language, the hastily arranged visit to Vientiane by two trusted Harriman associates suggested something less than complete confidence in the ambassador and the senior members of the US mission. "There was not only a concern about the Lao," Sullivan said later, "but also about the direction of our mission out there." Brown, recalling the reaction of his country team—that is, the leaders of the US agencies in Laos—to the visit by Sullivan and Forrestal, said: "All my boys were very upset about it. They were very mad, and they said, 'Damn it, if they don't have any trust in the Ambassador and the country team, why then they ought to remove you. This is terrible.'"[43]

The relative youth of Sullivan and Forrestal and their comparatively modest positions in the bureaucratic hierarchy belied their influence in Lao affairs. Sullivan, then thirty-nine and nominally a UN adviser in the State Department's Bureau of Far Eastern Affairs, had leapfrogged many more senior diplomats to become Harriman's deputy at Geneva. His predecessor, John Steeves, characterized Sullivan as a "brilliant" and "brash" Foreign Service officer.[44] Forrestal, thirty-four, was a partner in a New York law firm who joined the NSC staff after the November 1961

"Thanksgiving Day massacre," an administration shakeup in personnel that included Harriman's appointment as assistant secretary of state and Rostow's transfer to the Policy Planning Council. Forrestal, the son of the first secretary of defense and a family friend and protégé of Harriman, had experience in European affairs but claimed no expertise in his area of responsibility for the NSC, the Far East. He later described one part of his job as ensuring that presidential decisions "were carried out by the various departments of the government."[45]

What Kennedy wanted carried out in Laos—and a key message that Sullivan and Forrestal delivered to Ambassador Brown—was the establishment of a Souvanna-led coalition government with sufficient "right-wing political and military strength" to resist a communist takeover and preserve Laotian neutrality. In instructions to Sullivan and Forrestal, approved by the president at Harriman's request, Brown was granted "full authority" to impose any sanctions necessary to secure Phoumi's cooperation—"except those measures which would destroy the FAR." If Phoumi did not support a Souvanna solution, Brown was authorized to use "all overt and covert means at his disposal" to build support for Souvanna among Lao political and military leaders. In Harriman's words, "the President's objective [was] to undermine Phoumi and get someone else" who would "play the Souvanna coalition game."[46]

Sullivan and Forrestal, in addition to conferring with Brown and other members of the US mission, met with leading Lao politicians and military officers to persuade them that a Souvanna government was the "best prospect for them and their country." After several days of proselytizing, Brown reported that the Lao responses to US appeals were "spotty and not very encouraging." FAR commanders were "almost completely negative" in their reactions, observing that Souvanna had been unable to handle the Pathet Lao in the fall of 1960. Phoui Sananikone, a former prime minister and conservative rival of Phoumi, offered a different explanation for the military commanders' resistance to Souvanna: "If the war stopped their opportunities for advancement would be curtailed."[47]

The responses of civilian leaders to US entreaties were more diverse than the military's. Some civilian supporters of the Boun Oum–Phoumi government simply distrusted Souvanna. Their preferred political outcome was a government led by the king, who would preside over six "councils," each responsible for a major government function. The politicians inclined to support a coalition government seemed unwilling "to take any action to bring about [a] Souvanna settlement." Many of them feared that backing Souvanna would invite retribution from Phoumi and the chief of his secret police, Colonel Siho Lamphoutacoul. Phoui Sananikone, whose prescience about Lao reactions to US appeals impressed Brown and the visiting Americans, said: "There were no Lao who had any influence over Phoumi; certainly none who dared argue against him."[48]

While Forrestal and Sullivan overtly advocated for a Souvanna-led government, the CIA covertly offered Phoumi a substantial financial "carrot" to cooperate with its formation.[49] On March 6, 1962, Gordon Jorgensen and Jack Hasey met with Phoumi at the Lao embassy in Bangkok. The general had traveled to Thailand on February 28 to recover from headaches and generally poor health. The CIA officers delivered a personal message from President Kennedy: with a Geneva agreement now within reach, the three Lao factions must form a government of national union at the earliest possible date. The message declared that Phoumi had great responsibilities and much to contribute to Laos. With only a hint of threat, Kennedy's message expressed the "hope" that Phoumi would "make it possible" for the United States to work with him toward maintaining the kingdom's independence and sovereignty: "I assure you that as long as you do so, you will have my unfailing support and friendship."[50]

Adding a blunt postscript to the presidential message, Jorgensen and Hasey explained that if Phoumi blocked the formation of a coalition government, the United States would neither support him militarily nor come to his assistance if the "other side attacked." The Lao general did not doubt the authenticity of the message from Kennedy—he said that he had just heard the same communication from Ambassador Brown and Admiral Felt, who also met with Phoumi at the Lao embassy in Bangkok. According to White House instructions to the CIA station in Vientiane, the unified message from the ambassador, the military, and the agency was intended to leave "no doubt whatever that all branches of the U.S. Government are at one in [the] execution of policy set by President."[51]

What distinguished Phoumi's meeting with the CIA officers from his earlier conversation with Brown and Felt was an offer of "financial support if he would enter a Souvanna government." Jorgensen and Hasey explained that with covert US funding, even a minor cabinet post offered "great possibilities" for anticommunist work. According to a summary of the conversation, the CIA officers said that the only alternative to their "proposition"—the word "bribe" was scrupulously avoided—was "the U.S. completely withdrawing its support[,] which would have disastrous results." The CIA officers asked Phoumi to keep the conversation "strictly to himself," with the possible exception of Prime Minister Sarit.[52]

Phoumi, whose manner throughout the meeting was subdued but courteous and friendly, did not accept the US offer, saying that perhaps Jorgensen and Hasey "should try this on someone else." He added: "I don't think I can go along with a Souvanna Phouma government and I may retire to Thailand." The CIA officers said that they would seek a more definitive answer from Phoumi when he returned to Vientiane: "If necessary we would talk later about retiring." A report of the meeting was dispatched to CIA headquarters that same day. Richard Helms, the agency's deputy director for operations, immediately forwarded the cable to McGeorge Bundy and Harriman.[53]

Prince Boun Oum proved to be a more tractable target for CIA enticements. Described by the State Department as "an informal, gregarious, and likeable man who generally presents an unkempt rumpled appearance," Boun Oum had been a guerrilla leader during World War II and led commando forces against the Viet Minh invasion of 1954. Anticommunist and pro-French, he was popular in southern Laos, where he was related to most of the region's leaders by blood or marriage. He advocated moral behavior but was "known to be corrupt even by Lao standards, being deeply involved in opium trade and heavily in debt," according to a State Department biographic sketch. Ambassador Brown told President Kennedy that Boun Oum was "a Lao Falstaff" and "a figurehead" who was neither "very intelligent [nor] very decisive."[54]

On March 7, as Boun Oum and Hasey awaited Phoumi's arrival from Bangkok at the Vientiane airport, the CIA officer summarized the previous day's appeal to the general. Flattering the prince, Hasey said that he was "the leading personality in Laos" and "had a leading role to play" in bringing peace to the kingdom. What the United States "required" was Boun Oum's assistance "to help Phoumi convince other cabinet members that the right course of action" was to compromise and participate in a Souvanna-led coalition government. The US government, said Hasey, "felt so strongly about this" and about Boun Oum's "capability of fulfilling this mission" that it was prepared not only to continue supporting the prince's current anticommunist activities but also "to help him out personally, financially, in order that he might continue his work even though he was outside the government."[55]

Boun Oum, listening intently, said that he wanted to think about the offer and asked Hasey to visit him later that day. The CIA officer agreed, saying their discussions should remain "a private matter for the time being." When Hasey arrived at the prince's residence, Boun Oum said that he had spoken briefly with Phoumi, who reported his conversation with Thai officials but did not mention his meeting with Jorgensen and Hasey. After the CIA officer repeated the US position, Boun Oum asked "what he honestly thought." Hasey replied that Souvanna's participation in a coalition government "was the only possible peaceful solution." Boun Oum, expressing appreciation for "the offer of personal support," said that he would try to persuade Phoumi. The prince added that Hasey "could count on his entire collaboration."[56]

Chapter 5

A Severe Loss of Face

Field Marshal Sarit Thanarat, the prime minister of Thailand and a cousin once removed of Phoumi's, played a significant role both in the Eisenhower administration's efforts to overthrow Souvanna *and* in the Kennedy administration's attempt to establish a government led by him. Sarit, called "uncle" by Phoumi out of respect, was perhaps the only person capable of influencing the headstrong Lao general. Personally and politically close, both men believed that developing countries were better served by authoritarian executive power than by parliamentary democracy. Sarit, who overthrew the military government of Prime Minister Phibun Songkhram in 1957, consolidated his "revolution" the next year, abolishing the constitution, legislature, and free press. The State Department characterized his rule as a "benevolent military dictatorship."[1]

Sarit, who suppressed the small indigenous communist movement in Thailand, worried about an NLHS victory in neighboring Laos and the likelihood of infiltration across the one-thousand-mile Thai-Lao border. "The Thai leaders," US intelligence analysts observed, "are fearful of a possible repetition in Thailand of the kind of guerrilla war the Communists have waged in Laos and South Vietnam." Sarit and his military colleagues viewed Souvanna with particular contempt: "Thailand has no faith whatsoever in Souvanna Phouma's ability or integrity. It believes he would pave the way for *de facto* communist control of Laos."[2]

Thailand, "the hub of US security interests in Southeast Asia" since the early 1950s, hosted a broad range of American military and intelligence facilities targeting the insurgencies in Laos and South Vietnam. These bases, which the US government deemed "essential to stopping further communist inroads in Southeast Asia," included training camps for FAR regulars and Hmong guerrillas, bases for USAF photo reconnaissance and CIA intelligence operations, storage depots for ammunition and other military supplies, and a site for intercepting signals intelligence.[3]

Despite receiving substantial amounts of US military assistance for more than a decade, Thai leaders had lost confidence in the Americans' preferred method of defense against a communist attack: SEATO. French and British opposition to SEATO intervention in the Laotian crises of 1959 and 1960–1961 had particularly disturbed the Thai prime minister and his cabinet. According to Pote Sarasin, a Thai diplomat and the secretary general of SEATO, Sarit foresaw a day when France and the UK would react similarly to threats to Thailand and prevent the United States from honoring its military commitment.[4]

At a February 26, 1962, meeting in Bangkok, Sarit and his top military commanders forcefully denounced SEATO to a US official whose name is redacted in the official record of the discussion. (The American was undoubtedly Robert J. "Red" Jantzen, the CIA chief of station in Bangkok, who had developed an especially close relationship with Sarit.) "We are not threatening to get out of SEATO," said Sarit, "we *are* getting out." The US official replied that such a move would "play directly into the hand of the Communists[,] whose aim is to destroy SEATO." When Sarit and his generals attacked US policy in Laos, the American replied that President Kennedy had decided that "a supreme effort to have a truly neutral Laos" should be made and that "it was absolutely essential" for Thailand to provide Souvanna with "whole-hearted support." After much "heated discussion," including a US suggestion that Sarit "should whip Phoumi into line," the Thai prime minister threw up his hands, saying: "You win."[5]

To reach a common understanding with the United States on SEATO and Laos, Thai foreign minister Thanat Khoman accepted an invitation from Dean Rusk to visit Washington. A former Thai ambassador to the United States, Thanat was an accomplished diplomat who spoke English and French fluently. He could also be "blunt, stubborn, and emotional," according to US officials.[6] At a March 2 meeting at the State Department, Thanat told Rusk that Thailand's faith in SEATO had been "shaken" and that Sarit's government could not "continue to delude the Thai people regarding the effectiveness of the SEATO organization."[7]

Thanat said that Thailand "preferred" a bilateral mutual defense treaty similar to the US agreement with the Philippines. Such a pact, he said, would eliminate the "problem" caused by SEATO's "former colonial powers," France and the United Kingdom, which "tarnish[ed] the luster" of the alliance. Rusk replied that a bilateral defense treaty with Thailand "would create domestic problems" for the United States. "We already have a Senate-approved [SEATO] agreement linking us together," said Rusk, "and the Congress would almost certainly question the need for a separate treaty." Although opposed to a bilateral defense pact, Rusk had earlier expressed his willingness to discuss "a suitable" public declaration of US obligations to Thailand. Thanat, aware of the likely limits of American guarantees, gave Rusk a letter from Sarit requesting a high-level "US security assurance" that could be published in Thailand.[8]

This assurance was announced on March 6, when Rusk and Thanat issued a joint communiqué affirming US recognition of both a "collective" and an "individual" obligation to defend Thailand from aggression. The Rusk-Thanat communiqué also declared that both the United States and Thailand agreed on the necessity of "a free, independent and truly neutral Laos." A State Department history of the agreement described it as "the price the United States had to pay to keep Thailand from boycotting SEATO's operations and to persuade the Thai government to agree to the neutrality formula for Laos prescribed by the Geneva Conference of 1961–1962."[9]

During his visit to Washington, Thanat spoke with Harriman about the Thai role in influencing Phoumi to cooperate in the formation of a coalition government. Thailand, said Thanat, "had reluctantly agreed that a political settlement [in Laos] should be worked out." Although doubtful of Souvanna's ability to lead "a truly independent government," he told Harriman that Thailand was "seriously trying" to persuade Phoumi to follow US policy. "Phoumi listens to Prime Minister Sarit on some issues, but not on others," said Thanat. Harriman declared that the US objective of a free, neutral, and independent Laos under a Souvanna-led coalition government remained unchanged. The United States, Harriman said, was willing to support Phoumi in an "important" government position—if he cooperated. "If not, [the] US will have to eliminate him."[10]

When Thanat spoke with the president, Kennedy "emphasized that he did not want Phoumi to throw in the sponge." Despite the general's political weakness, military limitations, and infuriating stubbornness, Kennedy had concluded that Phoumi represented the only military and political strength with any chance of counterbalancing the Pathet Lao. "If he refused to participate [in a coalition government]," said Kennedy, "it would throw the whole picture into imbalance." The president hoped that Sarit "would try to persuade Phoumi not to quit but to cooperate in all our best interests." Thanat said that he was quite sure that the prime minister "would follow the president's desires."[11]

In mid-March 1962 Harriman accepted an invitation from the Thai government to discuss Laos with Prime Minister Sarit in Bangkok. Harriman had already planned to travel to the Far East for meetings with US allies and for a regional conference of American ambassadors. At that conference, held in Baguio, the summer capital of the Philippines, Harriman's review of far eastern affairs included a partisan analysis of recent US history in the region. The Far East, he declared, had been "neglected" by the Eisenhower administration. Mirroring Republican attacks against Democrats for "losing China," Harriman said that it had been "a mistake not to have held on to North Viet-Nam" during the First Indochina War: "This threw out all the advantages we had gained in Korea." (The conventional Republican politicization of the cold war blamed the Truman administration for the Korean War—a stalemate "we were not allowed to win.")[12]

Harriman told the assembled ambassadors that President Kennedy's policy was to support South Vietnam. "The President recognizes that there is the possibility that it may escalate," he said. "If so, the President is prepared to face that contingency. He is determined to see that Viet-Nam is not overrun." In Laos, Harriman declared, the Eisenhower administration "had started a civil war by pushing Phoumi. But the Republicans would have killed the Democrats if the [Kennedy administration] had intervened with U.S. troops." Harriman said he was convinced that the Soviets "want to see a neutral Laos," but it remained to be seen "whether they could carry out their commitments to police" their allies. Characterizing Phoumi "as a U.S. creature and as the big obstacle" to a coalition government, Harriman said: "The President will not permit this puppet to dictate US policy." He added: "The next few weeks would tell the story."[13]

Harriman's acceptance of the Thai invitation to Bangkok was based on Sarit's willingness to join him in pressuring Phoumi to cooperate with American policy. The Thai prime minister, gratified by the Rusk-Thanat communiqué, at least for the time being, indicated to the American embassy in Bangkok that he understood what the US government expected of him. Phoumi, when he learned of Harriman's intention to visit the region, initially said that he welcomed the opportunity meet with him. At a March 17 dinner at the general's home, Michael Forrestal warned Phoumi, "It would be most dangerous to meet with Harriman without having previously come to a sincere conclusion to realign his policy more closely with ours." Phoumi reiterated his readiness to speak with Harriman in Bangkok.[14]

The Lao general, who had backed out of disagreeable commitments to the United States during his 1960 "revolution" against Souvanna's government, changed his mind about the rendezvous. On March 19 he asked Hasey to come to the Vientiane airport, where he informed the CIA officer of his inability to meet with Harriman in Bangkok. Phoumi offered a variety of dubious excuses, which included a previous commitment, the objections of his fellow cabinet ministers, and an unwillingness to have a "clandestine meeting" in Bangkok. Hasey called the decision "a grave error" and "a serious affront." He appealed to Phoumi to reconsider, but the general refused. At the end of the conversation, Phoumi said that if Hasey had any messages to deliver, he could be reached in Savannakhet, his hometown and headquarters in southern Laos. In his report of the conversation, Hasey noted somewhat ominously that a Thai "liaison" officer who had served with Phoumi in the fall of 1960 accompanied the general to Savannakhet.[15]

The reaction in Washington to Phoumi's insult, particularly among Harriman's subordinates in the Bureau of Far Eastern Affairs, was outrage. "Phoumi has thrown down the gauntlet," a department telegram declared to the embassies in Vientiane and Bangkok. Kenneth T. Young, the US ambassador to Thailand, was instructed to "insist that Sarit make every effort [to] get Phoumi to Bangkok for [a] meeting with Harriman." In addition, the Thai government should be informed that the general's failure to see Harriman would "amount to [Phoumi's] breaking" relations with the United States. Ambassador Brown was asked to consider delivering a similar message to the king of Laos. "We assume you and [the country team] have emergency plans for personnel protection in case Phoumi turns against us or if we decide [to] take action against him," department officials wrote. They also reminded the embassy and MAAG to exercise the "greatest vigilance" in case Phoumi launched any "military moves."[16]

On March 20 Ambassador Young spoke with Sarit, Thanat, and Lieutenant General Wallop Rochanwsisut about Phoumi's refusal to meet with Harriman in Bangkok. To Young, Sarit and Thanat appeared "frightened as well as concerned over [the] implications [of] Phoumi's resistance." Both officials expressed a sincere desire to bring about a Harriman-Phoumi meeting, to dispel any lingering doubts about secret Thai "double dealing" with the Lao general, and to facilitate a "reasonable compromise" between the US government and the RLG as soon as possible. When Young mentioned allegations of Sarit covertly encouraging Phoumi's intransigence, the prime minister "bellowed a vehement denial."[17]

Sarit, telling Young that he wanted "to put all his cards on the table," asked Thanat to translate a recent telegram from Phoumi. The cable repeated his questionable explanations to Hasey for avoiding a meeting with Harriman. Sarit, who characterized the situation as "dangerous," said that Phoumi must be handled skillfully because "face" was involved. The Thai prime minister ordered General Wallop, his chief of intelligence and personal intermediary with Phoumi, to travel immediately to Savannakhet to "press" the Lao general to meet with Harriman in Thailand. Young provided Wallop's transportation—presumably an aircraft furnished by Air America, the airline secretly owned by the CIA. Wallop, who had accompanied Thanat to Washington and attended meetings with the president and other US officials, predicted that Phoumi would see Harriman "if we dealt with the question of face."[18]

Wallop was unable to persuade Phoumi to travel to Bangkok. It was the first time the Lao general had declined such an invitation from Sarit. Phoumi did, however, indicate some flexibility about holding talks with Harriman. He said that the RLG, as a sovereign government, could not "accept [a] summons from various American emissaries to meet outside [the] country" for the purpose of "unconditional surrender." Declaring his willingness to negotiate with Souvanna about a coalition government, Phoumi asked that Harriman come to Vientiane for discussions with the RLG. Such an arrangement might permit follow-up talks somewhere in Thailand. Wallop was sure that Phoumi sought a face-saving solution "satisfactory to all three parties concerned."[19]

Harriman agreed with the State Department that Phoumi had "thrown down [the] gauntlet." He was particularly disturbed by a Phoumi comment to Sullivan and Forrestal indicating that his obstructionism sought to discourage Souvanna and persuade him to renounce his royal mandate to form a government. Harriman, despite Washington's earlier reluctance to take steps that might weaken the FAR, requested authority to impose limited military sanctions. Such action, Harriman wrote, might be required "to make [Phoumi] understand [that] he cannot defy the US and expect continuing US support." Harriman added that he would only resort to military pressure in extreme circumstances. The State Department replied that the president was "very reluctant to authorize a decision at this time to invoke military sanctions against Phoumi." Concerned by the appearance of the United States undercutting an ally resisting communism, Kennedy did not want to apply this form of pressure "until further efforts have been made to obtain cooperation by Phoumi."[20]

The CIA confirmed the president's fears about the impact of military sanctions. The Office of National Estimates, responding to a request from Michael Forrestal, concluded that a withdrawal of US training teams, military advisers, and logistic support "would have an immediate demoralizing effect upon the Laotian government and armed forces." Perhaps even more disturbing to Kennedy was the agency's estimate of a less-than-even chance that military sanctions would persuade Boun Oum and Phoumi "to join a coalition government headed by Souvanna Phouma." And even if they did agree to participate, Boun Oum and Phoumi would "probably seek to undercut" Souvanna and his followers. A second CIA paper requested by Forrestal, on "methods the US might employ to replace Phoumi with a new right-wing political figure," is still classified.[21]

Top Pentagon officials unanimously opposed the removal of US military advisers as a form of pressure on Phoumi. At a meeting at CINCPAC headquarters, General Lemnitzer said that this sanction would "hand the country over to the communists and have a devastating psychological impact on Thailand." Lemnitzer, who thought "a showdown in Laos was approaching," doubted that a coalition government would be formed. He was also skeptical that President Kennedy would authorize intervention with US or SEATO combat troops. Urging continued support for Phoumi, "even if he could only hold southern Laos," Lemnitzer suggested that the FAR regroup to form a defensive line across the panhandle, from

Thakhek to Tchepone. According to a JCS history of the Laotian crises, McNamara ended the meeting by concluding that the United States should not remove its military advisers from Laos.[22]

Kennedy, who received McNamara's recommendations by phone, still wanted Harriman to speak with Phoumi if a meeting could be arranged "in a dignified manner satisfactory to Harriman." After another conversation between Wallop and Phoumi, Harriman finally met with the Lao general and Sarit on March 24 at the home of the provincial governor of Nong Khai, Thailand, just across the Mekong from Vientiane. The location of the talks, a compromise between the US preference for Bangkok and Phoumi's choice of Vientiane, allowed Sarit to take a leading role in advocating US-Thai policy toward Laos. Speaking softly, according to the minutes of the meeting, Sarit emphasized that the United States and Thailand would support Phoumi in a coalition government and would come to his aid "should a Souvanna solution go sour." If Phoumi did not accept the proposed neutral settlement, Sarit warned, both the United States and Thailand would "wash their hands" of him.[23]

Phoumi, speaking in a calm, soft-spoken manner, stood his ground. He said that the United States and he had always agreed on a policy of anticommunism, but now there was a misunderstanding about the internal affairs of Laos. "Souvanna is not the man to solve the Lao problem," he said. "Souvanna depends too much on Souphanouvong." He added: "Souvanna no longer has any force or influence in Laos."[24]

Harriman spoke next. Without directly addressing Phoumi's comments, Harriman said that he "wholeheartedly" agreed with Sarit's statements and point of view. He then listed the three steps necessary for establishing an independent Laos: the formation of a neutral government, the withdrawal of foreign forces, and the integration of the three factions' armies. "This third step," said Harriman, "might not take place for some time, perhaps even not for several years." The United States and Thailand would support the noncommunist Lao forces, but Souvanna must be the prime minister of the coalition government. Acknowledging "Souvanna's weaknesses," Harriman said: "The Prince has no intention whatsoever of turning Laos over to the communists."

Harriman challenged Phoumi's statement that the United States had always agreed with him in the past. After the Kong Le coup, the Lao general had ignored Ambassador Brown's advice to join a government led by Souvanna. Instead, Phoumi had formed a revolutionary committee and fought a war that he had lost despite help from the United States. When Harriman mentioned the "lost" war, Phoumi "for a fleeting moment [looked] as if he had been hit across the face with a baseball bat," according to minutes of the meeting.[25]

Phoumi objected to Souvanna's proposed slate of cabinet ministers, some of whom were "the next thing to being communist." He was unwilling to recognize the former paratroop captain Kong Le as a general, which would suggest that he accepted the outcome of the August 1960 coup. And he did not want the neutralists to have the defense and interior portfolios in a coalition government. Harriman replied that "such a stand amounted to Phoumi dictating to the rest of the world." The Lao general responded that he was merely giving his opinion: "The United States was doing far more dictating than he was." The general added that he wanted to have discussions with Souvanna and representatives of other countries but "he did not want to be made to accept ultimatums."[26]

Conceding nothing to the Thais or Americans, Phoumi continued his talks with Harriman in Vientiane at the Ministry of National Security the next morning. Speaking before an audience of senior Lao and US mission officials, Phoumi observed that the RLG agreed with the United States on the need for a peaceful solution and a coalition government. The two countries disagreed, however, on Souvanna Phouma's appointment as prime minister. Phoumi said that he hoped that a "mutual examination of these problems would lead to an agreement within the framework of traditional Lao/US collaboration."[27]

Harriman, echoing Phoumi's conciliatory introduction, began by telling the RLG officials that he "came here as a friend." Providing a detailed analysis of US negotiations with the Soviets in Vienna and Geneva, Harriman acknowledged that there were no guarantees that they would honor their commitments in Laos. But any breach of the Geneva agreement, he said, would be "easy to detect." Noting the "many other important" international problems the two superpowers sought to resolve peacefully, Harriman said there "seemed good reason to hope" for Soviet cooperation in Laos. "The most important thing," he said, "was to get the [North Vietnamese] out of Laos."[28]

Harriman reviewed the commitments made by the United States

and by the RLG to establish a coalition government—one with "major strength in the center" and "with modest participation from the RLG and the PL." Limiting Pathet Lao influence in the cabinet, said Harriman, required an equivalent reduction in the number of RLG ministers: "The center must be the dominating force in the new government and it was therefore inconceivable that the center should not hold the two key positions of Defense and Interior." He said that he understood RLG suspicions, but representatives of every nation at the Geneva conference had concluded that Souvanna was "the only alternative" to lead "a truly neutral government."[29]

Harriman told the RLG leaders that Souvanna had always wanted "strong help" from the conservatives "to make a common front against the PL." Moreover, Phoumi would be "a very important person" in the new government's fight against the communists. Warning that the Pathet Lao would continue to try to take over the country, Harriman defended the concept of a coalition government in Laos. "Some people thought that if you got into bed with communists you would also get infected," he said. "This had been true only in countries where the Red Army had been in control." Harriman pledged that if the Geneva agreement broke down, "you will have not only the U.S. as a friend and ally but also other countries, both those that are neighbors and those further away."[30]

Phoumi thanked Harriman for his "exposition" of US policy but was unmoved by it. A Souvanna solution, he declared, was "unrealizable."[31]

Sisouk Na Champassak, the RLG's acting foreign minister and an experienced negotiator, spoke next. Emphasizing inconsistencies in US policy, he observed that the US government had "expressed serious reservations, even violent opposition" to the inclusion of Pathet Lao ministers in Souvanna's coalition government of 1957–1958. Sisouk also recalled the "active U.S. collaboration and advice" in establishing the CDNI, the CIA-supported political front. Overstating the role of French and British complicity in blocking Souvanna's reappointment as prime minister in 1958, he declared that "the Western powers threw Souvanna out because of his weakness in the face of the PL." Sisouk, noting the recent disagreements among the western allies, particularly since the Kong Le coup, asked how the United States could expect the Lao "to look with assurance on the future."[32]

Harriman, who subsequently characterized his own comments as patient, careful, and affirmative, addressed the issues and questions raised by RLG officials. The Souvanna solution, he admitted, had advantages and disadvantages. "The only question was what was the alternative?" Harriman asked. "No one had anything to suggest, except war." Phoumi again thanked Harriman for his comments but did not agree with them: "The RLG had never accepted Souvanna as Prime Minister."

Having failed to persuade Phoumi and his colleagues, Harriman announced that he was leaving Vientiane later that day. He thought that the RLG was "making a great mistake." Pointing in turn to each Lao official, Harriman said:

> Looking at you all one by one—you, you, you, you, you, you, and you—you are driving your country to disaster. In the name of the President I ask you to reconsider, to consult others, and not to take the responsibility which you have done. If you have no taste for the battle ahead, then the honest thing to do is resign and let others take over who can lead the negotiations to a successful end and avoid disaster. If you do reconsider, you will retain the friendship and support of the United States.[33]

Harriman's report of the meeting suggested that his comments to Phoumi and his colleagues were tinged with regret rather than anger. Other accounts indicated that Harriman lived up to his nickname the "crocodile," which he had earned for suddenly snapping at officials he deemed obtuse. "He was pretty hard on Phoumi and pretty hard on several others and shook his fingers at them," recalled William Sullivan, who was present at the meeting. "There was a great deal of underlying resentment and wrath and annoyance." Embassy political officer Philip H. Chadbourn Jr., who also attended the talks, told a British official: "Harriman spoke with a directness and even brutality that was beyond anything he had previously experienced in diplomacy."[34]

Harriman's tough language appeared to be a counterproductive means of achieving Kennedy's goals. Sullivan reported that RLG cabinet ministers had found Harriman's method of speaking offensive, strengthening their determination to resist "naked coercion by foreigners." Colonel Donald V. Smart, the US Army military attaché in Vientiane, confirmed that Harriman's comments had caused "a severe loss of face," prompting

RLG officials "to stand fast and unite." At a March 28 meeting with Sullivan, Phoumi "remained completely impervious" to US arguments for supporting Souvanna and "expressed resentment against [the] firm stand taken by Harriman."[35]

Harriman and Forrestal returned to Washington at the end of March, but Sullivan remained in Laos to speak with Souvanna in Khang Khay, a small town on the Plaine des Jarres where the neutralists shared a headquarters with the Pathet Lao in a former French Foreign Legion barracks. "Roads miserable, quarters crude, and airstrips primitive," Sullivan observed to the State Department. Kong Le's troops were the predominant force, with some Pathet Lao soldiers and a few Soviets in civilian clothing in the town. Sullivan characterized Khang Khay as a Hemingwayesque "guerrilla camp, peopled by hard eyed little soldiers wearing [an] odd mixture [of] US, French, Soviet, and Chinese type uniforms, with [a] variety [of] businesslike weapons casually slung, but always at hand."[36]

The primary purpose of Sullivan's visit to Khang Khay was to "dissuade Souvanna from throwing in his hand" and to inform him of US and Thai efforts to persuade Phoumi to cooperate in establishing a coalition government. In a series of meetings with Souvanna, Souphanouvong, and others, Sullivan sought assurances that the neutralists and Pathet Lao would not "exploit" any US military sanctions to pressure Phoumi. Souvanna, insisting he had no desire to "starve Phoumi troops or create wholesale mutinies," declared that there would be no attacks "from his side." Souphanouvong, however, said that the Pathet Lao would have to clean out areas the FAR had occupied after the May 3 ceasefire. Sullivan charged Souphanouvong with constructing fictitious boundaries that did not reflect "military realities" in Laos. "He and I had two long and rather explosive arguments on these matters," reported Sullivan, who described Souphanouvong as "a cocky little scrapper who smells victory."[37]

The "only encouraging" result of his visit to Khang Khay, Sullivan wrote, was general agreement on a way of resolving the impasse with Phoumi over the defense and interior portfolios. Instead of a single faction leading one or both ministries, Souvanna, Souphanouvong, and Phoumi would have joint responsibility for overseeing them. The arrangement would be temporary—perhaps two or three months, while the coalition integrated the armies of the three factions and established new local government administration. After this transition period, the defense and interior portfolios would revert to Souvanna. Until then, all major decisions would require the unanimous consent of the triumvirate. Even Phoumi had earlier expressed interest in the idea, indicating that it "would be helpful."[38]

In Washington, Kennedy and his advisers continued to seek ways of increasing pressure on Phoumi without weakening the FAR. The president still hoped that the "cold shoulder treatment" might have some beneficial effect on the general. To shun Phoumi, Harriman proposed the recall of one or more of the three US officials who maintained close contact with him: General Boyle, Ambassador Brown, and CIA officer Hasey.[39] Once again, Washington had offered suggestions that made little sense in Vientiane. Removing General Boyle while "continuing to provide military support [to the FAR] would have little or no effect," Brown concluded. Sullivan wrote that the ambassador had been "Phoumi's albatross" since August 1960: "We shouldn't take him off Phoumi's neck." The personnel move over which Sullivan and Brown disagreed was Hasey's recall. Sullivan, while acknowledging the CIA officer's skill and loyalty, thought that Hasey "should quietly disappear from Vientiane." Brown, however, was convinced that the CIA officer's recall "would deprive us of one of our best, if not the best, sources of information on RLG plans and reactions."[40]

Harriman accepted the recommendations to keep Brown and Boyle in Laos, but he told the CIA to remove Hasey, despite objections from agency headquarters. Hasey's recall reflected not only Kennedy's "cold shoulder treatment" but also Harriman's mistrust of the CIA. He had long suspected the agency and MAAG of undercutting the president's objectives, despite "confident" assurances from Brown that the "vast majority" of embassy, military, and CIA personnel were "adhering strictly to policy."[41] Harriman, Brown later recalled, "was convinced that Hasey had been peddling the old CIA line"—that is, support for Phoumi and opposition to Souvanna.[42]

Hasey did, in fact, personally sympathize with Phoumi's point of view, as did CIA chief of station Gordon Jorgensen. According to Thomas Ahern's history of the agency in Laos, officers in the CIA station in Vientiane admitted that Phoumi was "dishonest, cruel, and . . . a man of limited experience and sensitivity." Yet he was also a gambler "who believes he is now playing for very high stakes which included not only his own

fate but also that of King, country, and . . . his political and military followers."[43] Despite the CIA's advocacy on behalf of Phoumi, Ambassador
Brown saw no evidence of disloyalty from Hasey or the chief of station in
executing his instructions. "I think Harriman was wrong [about Hasey],"
Brown said, "and I think I've a lot better basis for judgment than Harriman had on that situation."[44]

The ambassador, who irritated Harriman by delaying Hasey's recall,
concluded that the most effective means of pressuring Phoumi, while
simultaneously minimizing the damage to right-wing military strength,
was a progressive withdrawal of White Star training teams from FAR field
units. In his analysis of various military sanctions, which included cutting
off imported military supplies and suspending US air transport within
Laos, Brown listed the advantages of removing the Special Forces teams:
it would be a "politically practical" response to a government that refused
to follow US advice; it would satisfy Souvanna and the western allies,
who had specifically requested this sanction; and it would have minimal
impact on the "physical ability of the FAR to fight on its own." Brown
recognized that this last aspect of the proposed sanction also weakened
its effect on Phoumi. He and his commanders, the ambassador observed,
would rather "go it alone without our advice than without our supplies."
And absent any military pressure from the Pathet Lao, Phoumi could
rule "indefinitely" without US advice and would "certainly" transform
the withdrawal of the foreign White Star teams into "a patriotic virtue."[45]

Brown's proposed military sanction appealed to State Department officials and White House staff. In an April 6 memorandum to McGeorge
Bundy, Michael Forrestal observed that "milder forms of persuasion and
pressure have been virtually exhausted." The suspension of US economic
aid since February had taken a toll "on the economy of Laos and on the
morale of the Lao people, including Phoumi's supporters." But continuing
to withhold US financial support risked "destroy[ing] the structure of the
RLG" and its ability to compete politically with the NLHS in a coalition
government. "Military sanctions are the next logical step," wrote Forrestal.
He added: "Whether military sanctions combined with other pressures will
be enough to bring Phoumi around is, of course, the great unknown."[46]

To help policymakers make a more informed decision about this particular unknown, the director of Central Intelligence submitted an SNIE on

April 11 on the likely responses of Phoumi and Boun Oum to a halt in
US financial and military assistance to the RLG. The conclusions of the
SNIE, a product of the entire US intelligence community, echoed the
earlier estimate requested by Forrestal and produced solely by the CIA:
withdrawing US financial and military assistance "would probably not
persuade Phoumi and Boun Oum to participate in a Souvanna coalition
government." Phoumi "would almost certainly not accept" any government role other than a dominant military or police position. And even
if he did join a coalition government, Phoumi would undoubtedly "seek
to undercut Souvanna and his followers." Intelligence officials from the
CIA, the Department of Defense, the army, the navy, the air force, and
the Joint Chiefs of Staff approved the SNIE. But in a lengthy, virtually
unprecedented dissent, Roger Hilsman, the director of the State Department's Bureau of Intelligence and Research (INR), objected to the entire
estimate.[47]

In Hilsman's view, the fundamental premise of the SNIE—an abrupt,
total termination of US economic and military support to the RLG—
was flawed, producing "overly simplified" conclusions. The estimate,
he wrote, did not reflect the "actual complexities of the total context in
which Phoumi and Boun Oum must act." Hilsman faulted the paper for
omitting assessments of Phoumi's intentions and ignoring such factors as
"a serious Thai effort to persuade him" to cooperate. The estimate's failure
to account for these and other possibilities, Hilsman argued, precluded a
judgment that economic and military sanctions would probably be ineffective in persuading Phoumi to participate in a coalition government.[48]

Among the notoriously self-confident men of Kennedy's New Frontier, Hilsman, then forty-two, stood out for his brashness. His combination of brains and physical courage appealed to Kennedy. A graduate
of West Point's class of 1943, which suffered more casualties than any
other in the academy's history, Hilsman served with Merrill's Maraud-
ers in Burma and with the OSS in Burma and China. After the war, he
earned a PhD in international politics at Yale University and worked at
the Legislative Reference Service of the Library of Congress, first as chief
of the Foreign Affairs and Defense Division, then as deputy director for
research. As director of the State Department's intelligence bureau, Hilsman was "a very energetic activist" and "determined to put INR on the
map," according to his deputy, Thomas L. Hughes.[49]

Limited access to sensitive documents and meetings hampered Hilsman's initial efforts to increase INR's influence within the intelligence community. On November 4, 1961, he wrote an emotional note to U. Alexis Johnson about his "humiliating" exclusion from a meeting that day—perhaps related to General Taylor's return from South Vietnam or to the Kennedy administration's new effort to "get rid of" Fidel Castro, Operation Mongoose. To Hilsman, this "incident" was, in effect, "a public announcement to White House, Defense, and CIA officials that they need not concern themselves with the Head of the State Department's Intelligence." He added: "As it happens I was offered the Chair of International Relations at Yale University yesterday. Perhaps it would be better for all concerned if I considered taking it."[50]

Hilsman's threat to resign eventually reached President Kennedy, who met with him for twenty-five minutes on January 10, 1962. During a discussion of the "problems and role" of INR and other matters, Kennedy convinced Hilsman that he could "really be of effective service by remaining in the State Department." Based on Hilsman's experience as a guerrilla leader and INR's work on the political aspects of subversive insurgency, Kennedy asked him to make an inspection tour of South Vietnam and to report back to him and General Taylor. Hilsman's February 2 report, "A Strategic Concept for South Vietnam," concluded that the war was "essentially a battle for control of the villages" and that the central task was providing the people with "protection and physical security."[51]

The report downplayed the significance of infiltration from North to South Vietnam, claiming that it was "only of secondary importance" compared with cutting "the Viet Cong off from their local sources" of supplies and recruits. In a conversation with Walt Rostow, Hilsman charged that the US military and other "American agencies" considered infiltration the "sole problem" in Vietnam. The "dramatic" purpose of his report, he said, was to indicate that building "a wall fifty miles high along the infiltration routes" would not defeat the insurgency in South Vietnam. He added that "relatively simple measures—i.e., the use of ranger companies acting as guerrillas themselves along the infiltration routes—would effectively close the borders."[52]

White House expressions of confidence contributed to Hilsman's fearlessness in challenging military judgments and to his assertiveness as a member of the United States Intelligence Board (USIB), which comprised the leaders of the US civilian and military intelligence agencies. In his dissent from the SNIE on Phoumi's likely response to US sanctions, Hilsman addressed the paper's methodological limitations. But policy preferences—that is, the near certainty that Kennedy would eventually authorize military sanctions—influenced his dissent. During the drafting of the estimate, Hilsman indicated that the paper was "not only irrelevant, but perhaps offensive to the President," according to Sherman Kent, chief of the CIA's Office of National Estimates from 1952 to 1967. Hilsman suggested, "rather abruptly," that the paper be withdrawn. Failing to persuade Lieutenant General Marshall S. Carter, DCI McCone's deputy and the acting chair of the USIB, Hilsman declared that he would "get a presidential order to withdraw the estimate," wrote Kent. "General Carter said, 'Roger, why don't you put that sword back in the scabbard?'" Carter told Hilsman that he could dissent from the whole paper if he wished, but the estimate requested by policymakers would be submitted to them.[53]

Kennedy, reluctant to risk damaging anticommunist forces in Laos, inched toward authorizing military sanctions against Phoumi, an issue that continued to divide the president's civilian and military advisers. As late as April 17, 1962, Kennedy had still not made a final decision about imposing military sanctions. What persuaded him to move toward them was Phoumi's attempt to establish a government with the king serving as prime minister. The latest version of this scheme called for the Lao National Assembly to vote full power to Savang, who had reportedly agreed to lead a government with the three princes serving as deputy prime ministers.

Although the king's actual intentions were a "mystery," according to Ambassador Brown, State Department officials feared that Phoumi's political maneuver "could have [the] effect of revoking Souvanna's mandate or otherwise driving him from scene." Kennedy approved the withdrawal of selected White Star teams from forward positions to the rear—but only if Phoumi did not abandon his king's government plan by May 7, which was four days before the National Assembly convened. Until then, the State Department cabled, Ambassador Young should urge Thai officials to "make [a] more vigorous effort" to convince Phoumi to cooperate in the formation of a Souvanna-led government.[54]

Prime Minister Sarit, informed of US intentions to impose military sanctions if Phoumi tried to establish a king's government, met with the Lao general and other RLG leaders during the last week of April. The Lao officials had embarked on a "goodwill tour" to secure support from anti-communist Asian governments. The Thai pressure to "compromise with Souvanna came as a great shock" to the RLG leaders, according to Sarit. "They returned speechless to [the] guest house and could not eat lunch. Phoumi wept." After more "persuasion, pressure, and even threats of a vague kind," Ambassador Young reported, Sarit said that he had obtained an "unbreakable" pledge from Phoumi "to go along" with the US position on a coalition government.[55]

At an April 30 farewell dinner for General Boyle, whose tour as MAAG chief was ending, Phoumi appeared "quiet and rational" to Brown. In a long conversation with the ambassador, Phoumi largely refrained from his usual criticisms of Souvanna, who had left Laos in early April for an indefinite stay in Paris. Phoumi's comments to Brown about the defense and interior ministries in a coalition government focused on protecting the "legitimate interests" of conservatives, rather than denying the port-folios to the neutralists. When pressed by the ambassador, Phoumi said that he was abandoning the idea of a king's government, at least for the time being.[56]

Claiming his communication codes were insecure, Phoumi asked Brown for US assistance in delivering an oral message to Souvanna, who had indicated a willingness to return to Laos if the prospects for a nego-tiated settlement seemed promising. The US government, said Phoumi, should communicate the sincere desire of RLG leaders "to remove mis-understandings which existed between them and Souvanna." Brown, in his report of the conversation with the Lao general, wrote: "Evident [that] Phoumi is concerned about his bad relations with [the] U.S. and wishes to improve them. Also evident that he is concerned as to how he can do this without too great [a] loss of face."[57]

To Washington officials, the apparent change in Phoumi's attitude was an encouraging, though hardly conclusive, sign of progress. His com-ments to Brown, the State Department concluded, "fulfilled on [the] sur-face at least [the] minimum conditions we gave [the] Thais" and provided a sufficient basis to hold "in abeyance" US military sanctions. The resump-tion of economic aid, however, would depend on the seriousness of Phou-mi's negotiations with Souvanna. The department informed Brown that the financial "carrots" the CIA had offered Phoumi were "still available if he acts in good faith." What worried American officials were the long-standing military, financial, and personal ties between Sarit and Phoumi, as well as the rocky US relationship with the Lao general. "Phoumi can be expected to throw a monkey wrench into the negotiations at any stage if we are not alert," Forrestal warned Kennedy.[58]

Although moving in a more promising political direction, Phoumi still ignored US military advice by continuing to reinforce Nam Tha in northwestern Laos. During the last week of April, Phoumi began moving the Eleventh BP into the town, despite the FAR's numeric superiority in the area. (One of Phoumi's limitations as a military leader was his emphasis on weight of numbers over leadership and training.) With antigovernment forces occupying the high ground around Nam Tha, General Boyle was convinced that the "FAR was asking for shellacking." After conferring with Ambassador Brown, who also opposed moving more Lao troops to Nam Tha, Boyle ordered the withdrawal of White Star training teams, with the exception of two senior advisers and support personnel.[59]

Phoumi, justifying the deployment of the Eleventh BP, told the Americans that he could not afford to lose such an important base in northern Laos. State Department officials, who considered the reinforcements both "an unwise utilization of troops badly needed elsewhere" and a provocation that might end badly for the FAR, suspected that the Lao general had a more devious motive: "[to] provoke Communist action which can provide another pretext for avoiding negotiations or even draw us in." General Boyle arrived at a similar conclusion: "It appeared that Phoumi, as a last desperate effort, was deliberately creating a situation which he hoped would call for intervention by the United States Forces."[60]

Chapter 6

A Very Hazardous Course

After weeks of intensifying skirmishing, the battle of Nam Tha began in earnest at 3:00 A.M., May 6, 1962, when antigovernment artillery began bombarding the FAR command post and a 105-mm howitzer battery on the outskirts of town. Pathet Lao and PAVN infantry, estimated at four or more battalions, attacked the town from three directions. The main force approached from the northwest on the trail from Muong Sing, a small town five miles from the border with China. Machine-gun fire from antigovernment troops in the high ground above Nam Tha covered the valley. Initially, the defending FAR units did a "creditable job in [the] face [of a] well-coordinated attack," according to the senior MAAG adviser at the garrison. The outnumbered First BP delayed the enemy advance from Muong Sing, and FAR artillery continued to fire despite accurate counterbattery shelling from 75- and 85-mm enemy guns.[1]

With the attackers clearly intent on seizing Nam Tha, Major General Bounleut Sanichanh, the ranking FAR officer and a devoted Phoumi loyalist, left the garrison by helicopter at 7:00 A.M. Other FAR officers soon followed Bounleut's example, fleeing by jeeps, trucks, or any other form of transportation at hand. They abandoned some forty-five hundred soldiers—five infantry and three parachute battalions, plus supporting artillery—without a plan or leadership to execute an orderly withdrawal under fire. The FAR artillerymen spiked at least some of their guns and destroyed an unknown quantity of ammunition, but by 10:00 A.M. some of the RLG's best military units had become a disorganized mob heading southwest, eventually crossing the Mekong into Thailand.[2]

In Washington, the first sketchy reports about Nam Tha prompted a range of reactions, including exasperation with Phoumi for provoking the debacle, indignation with the communists for attacking the town while the United States was pressuring the Lao general, and scorn for the fighting ability of the FAR. "The boys have their track shoes on," Under Secretary of State George Ball reported to McGeorge Bundy.[3] Among the first State Department responses to the incident was an instruction to Ambassador Thompson in Moscow to protest the "flagrant violation" of the ceasefire, which endangered a Geneva agreement and risked the "resumption [of] full-scale hostilities."[4]

At a White House meeting, Kennedy asked his advisers about US options if the Pathet Lao pressed their military advantage nationwide. General Lemnitzer, standing before a map of Laos, outlined US contingency plans for holding southern Laos up to the seventeenth parallel, just above the dividing line between North and South Vietnam. Roger Hilsman, who was now playing a significant role in Vietnamese and Lao affairs, objected to Lemnitzer's plan. Walking up to the map, he declared that seizing the entire Laotian panhandle, particularly the infiltration hub at Tchepone, would likely trigger Chinese and North Vietnamese intervention. As an alternative, Hilsman suggested that the US military should occupy only those areas of Laos held by the RLG. Controlling the population centers along the Mekong and securing the main north-south road along the river could "manage the problem presented by the infiltration routes through [Tchepone]," said Hilsman.[5]

In his own record of the meeting, Hilsman observed: "I have no doubt that Lemnitzer did not appreciate a rival strategic analysis." Michael Forrestal, who attended the meeting, recalled that Lemnitzer "stepped back and watched with absolute amazement while this brash civilian from the State Department just moved in on his briefing." Defense Secretary McNamara, according to Hilsman, was also probably "annoyed" by his "presumptuous" observation that the FAR "could at least cope, after training and reorganization and better leadership, with guerrilla warfare." McNamara commented that the US mission in Laos was in a better position to judge FAR capabilities than officials in Washington. This meeting, said Forrestal, "was the beginning of Roger's problems with the military."[6]

In Moscow, Ambassador Thompson and Soviet foreign minister Gromyko accused each other's country of failing to control its Lao client. Thompson reminded the Soviet diplomat of a statement he had made to Rusk that the Pathet Lao would not "exploit" US efforts to pressure Phoumi. Gromyko, who denounced the Lao general's military and political provocations, said: "Boun Oum and Phoumi were allowed to do whatever they liked to prevent [a] coalition government in Laos." Although the diplomatic sparring between Thompson and Gromyko was inconclusive, the latter repeatedly referred to the agreement on Laotian neutrality that Kennedy and Khrushchev had reached at Vienna. The Soviets, said Gromyko, "still wanted [a] neutral Laos and were ready to sign" the nearly finished Geneva agreement.[7]

The Soviets may have wanted a negotiated neutral settlement, but they also acquiesced in the planning for the attack on Nam Tha. In early March, there had been a conference in Hanoi to review the situation in Laos, attended by representatives of the Soviet Union, PRC, DRV, and Pathet Lao. Kaysone Phoumvihan, the general secretary of the LPP, led the Pathet Lao delegation. The conference participants, Polish ICC commissioner Marek Thee later wrote, "decided that the situation was not yet ripe for the formation of a coalition government." Among the Pathet Lao's "most important tasks" was expanding "its military and political forces." The PRC delegates "especially emphasized the need to develop military strength and to solidify positions in the countryside."[8] Fursenko and Naftali, citing Soviet sources, wrote that "the Soviet representative agreed to turn a blind eye to the ongoing military preparations in northern Laos."[9]

On March 20 Souphanouvong told Soviet ambassador Abramov about Pathet Lao intentions "to pursue a policy of 'active defense' that involved attacks on enemy strongholds in the 'liberated areas' of Laos." These operations, Souphanouvong said, would be conducted "reasonably, so as not to cause a widening of the conflict."[10] Abramov, who had recently returned from Moscow, delivered a letter to Ho Chi Minh the following day. A key message in the Soviet letter, which Abramov showed to Thee, was that "comrades" in China, Vietnam, and Laos were more knowledgeable about "local conditions" and better judges of "what practical steps should be taken in the near future." Thee characterized the letter, a copy of which was delivered to the communist parties in China and Laos, as "a clear statement of [Soviet] disengagement as far as internal Laotian developments were concerned."[11]

In the weeks that followed, the PRC provided logistic support to Pathet Lao and PAVN forces at Nam Tha, but they did not participate in the attack. Historian Qiang Zhai wrote that Chinese leaders promptly responded to a Pathet Lao request for "material assistance" and "directed the Kunming Military Region to implement the aid program." The Chinese military "dispatched 2,149 soldiers, 1,772 civilian workers, 203 trucks, and 639 horses and mules to collect and transport military supplies to the Path Lao." Although Phoumi claimed that Chinese combat troops participated in the Nam Tha attack, Zhai's research confirmed earlier US intelligence assessments that the PRC restricted its military assistance to logistic support.[12]

The rout at Nam Tha jeopardized President Kennedy's hope of resolving the Laotian crisis without having to choose between abandoning the kingdom to communism or intervening with US combat troops. Pathet Lao and DRV forces had virtually eliminated RLG authority in northern Laos and could now seize the major towns on the Mekong in two weeks or less. The attack at Nam Tha also threatened to create domestic political problems for Kennedy. Representative Gerald R. Ford (R-MI), for example, had recently attacked the "administration's vacillation, indecision, [and] uncertainty in world affairs" on network television. Ford also indicated that he would have preferred sending US combat troops to Laos instead of pursuing a neutral solution.[13] Kennedy, when he first heard about the attack at Nam Tha, observed: "There will be a lot of people yelling for us to do one thing or another."[14]

At a May 9 press conference, a reporter asked Kennedy whether a failure to reestablish the ceasefire in Laos would prompt a reexamination of US policy. The president, unwilling to directly answer this hypothetical question or to publicly tip his hand, expressed his "concern about the break in the ceasefire." After summarizing the administration's diplomatic actions, he observed: "The longer this rather frayed ceasefire continues, the more chance we will have of the kind of incidents we've had in the past few days." Kennedy indirectly placed some of the blame for Nam Tha on Phoumi, remarking that "some groups" had made the situation more dangerous by avoiding talks to establish a new Lao government. Stressing the importance of reaching a prompt political agreement in Laos, Kennedy acknowledged that negotiations were "a very hazardous course, but introducing American forces which is the other one—let's not think there is some great third course—that also is a hazardous course."[15]

Kennedy's public assessment of the situation in Laos reflected a grim intelligence estimate of the implications of the Nam Tha attack. Without an effective military response or significant progress toward a coalition government, the US intelligence community concluded, Pathet Lao and North Vietnamese forces would likely undertake similar offensive operations in Laos. The finding that may have disturbed Kennedy most was the erosion of the US capability for deterring aggressive antigovernment behavior: "Events of the past year have almost certainly convinced the Communist side that the risk of US intervention has lessened significantly and that they can increase the level of military operations in seeking to achieve their intermediate objectives—a negotiated 'neutralist' coalition government in Laos which they could soon dominate, or the disintegration of the Royal Laotian Government and Army."[16]

To "reinvigorate the US deterrent," Roger Hilsman proposed two threatening military actions: moving elements of the Seventh Fleet to the Gulf of Thailand, as Kennedy had done during the 1961 Laotian crisis; and sending units from the US Army First Battle Group, Twenty-seventh Infantry Regiment, already in Thailand for a SEATO exercise, to Nong Khai, just across the Mekong from Vientiane. On the diplomatic front, simultaneous messages to the Soviet Union, Souphanouvong, and Souvanna would declare that the United States remained committed to a negotiated settlement but could not "tolerate unilateral Communist military advances." These military and diplomatic steps were intended to demonstrate US determination "to defend that portion of Laos now held by the RLG." The overall objective of the plan was restoring the ceasefire, a prerequisite to establishing either a government of national union or a de facto partition of the kingdom.[17]

At a May 10 White House meeting, Kennedy acknowledged that the United States must take some action to demonstrate the seriousness of the US commitment to a neutral Laos. One problem facing the president was that almost any American military response would appear to be support for Phoumi, whom State Department officials now wanted to eliminate "entirely from [the] Laotian scene."[18] After Kennedy and his advisers discussed Hilsman's plan, the president ordered two carrier task forces to sail for the Gulf of Thailand, "purely as a preparatory move."[19] With McNamara and General Lemnitzer in Southeast Asia, Kennedy wanted to defer any further military decisions until their return to Washington.

A more immediate decision made by Kennedy was dispatching John McCone and Michael Forrestal to the Gettysburg farm of former president Eisenhower to brief him on the latest developments in Laos. Earlier that day, at a press conference arranged by Republican congressional leaders, Eisenhower had supported Kennedy's increased assistance to South Vietnam but expressed reservations about a coalition government in Laos. "That is how we lost China," he said.[20] Eisenhower's comments to McCone and Forrestal echoed his advice to president-elect Kennedy sixteen months earlier: if Laos fell to the communists, both South Vietnam and Thailand would be outflanked. And if Southeast Asia was "lost, nothing would stop the southward movement of Communism through Indonesia, and this would have the effect of cutting the world in half." Eisenhower declared that the threat to South Vietnam and Thailand justified the "most extreme measures, including the commitment of US forces to combat in Laos." He added that he would follow up US troop deployments "with whatever support was necessary to achieve the objectives of their mission, including—if necessary—the use of tactical nuclear weapons."[21]

While president, Eisenhower did not deploy US forces to Laos during the crises of 1959 and 1960. He was also ambiguous about the circumstances under which he would authorize unilateral US military intervention. The records and recollections of participants at his January 19, 1960, meeting with Kennedy reveal conflicting perceptions of Eisenhower's recommendations about unilateral military intervention in Laos.[22] What seems clearer is that if he had made a decision to intervene militarily in Indochina, Eisenhower would have probably chosen more aggressive action than either Kennedy contemplated or President Johnson authorized. At the end of his presidency, when it appeared that regular PAVN battalions were entering the Laotian civil war and US intervention seemed likely, Eisenhower was unimpressed when General Lemnitzer outlined SEATO contingency plans that called for seizing the population centers of the Mekong Valley. According to the minutes of a White House meeting, Eisenhower said: "The one thing he had learned in his life was that, if one finds it necessary to use force, one should use enough force to insure that this situation is cured. It is important not to leave a running sore or to fight under self-imposed limitations as we had in Korea."[23]

President Kennedy, after learning of Eisenhower's recommendations to McCone and Forrestal, was concerned that the former president might publicly advocate US intervention in Laos, fueling political pressure for war. Eisenhower, who had thus far been unwilling to publicly criticize

Kennedy's decisions in international affairs, had recently told him that he might dissent from administration foreign policy "under some conditions." At a time when Kennedy defined the "problem" in Laos as staying "out of there," a recommendation by Eisenhower for military intervention would put the administration, in Kennedy's words, "in a tough position."[24]

Within the government, the Joint Chiefs of Staff voiced concerns similar to Eisenhower's, concluding: "A reappraisal of the US policy in Laos is urgently required." The attack at Nam Tha, the JCS observed, had been a major departure from the "communist strategy of limited but constant encroachment" of RLG-held territory. The consequences of the rout included the "disintegration" of the security situation in northern Laos, a threat to Thailand, and diminished FAR morale and capabilities. The chiefs recommended a variety of diplomatic and military actions below the threshold of overt US intervention—for example, demanding an ICC investigation of the attack at Nam Tha, stepping up Hmong guerrilla operations, and requesting the movement of Thai troops to the Lao border. If these limited steps did not lead to an acceptable political solution, the JCS recommended executing SEATO Plan 5, recognizing that Thailand would likely be the only member of the alliance to join the United States in defending the RLG.[25]

Although Souvanna's neutralist forces had not participated in the attack at Nam Tha, the JCS declared that his inability to control the Pathet Lao demonstrated "the futility of relying on him to provide requisite leadership for a neutral Laos." Unlike State Department officials, the chiefs thought it "essential" that Phoumi "remain as head of the pro-Western Laotian forces." They specifically disagreed with the State Department proposal "to undermine Phoumi's prestige and political influence." At a May 11 meeting of State Department and Pentagon officials, Admiral George W. Anderson, chief of naval operations, asked: "Why are we acting so violently against Phoumi instead of against the Communists?" U. Alexis Johnson's reply—that Phoumi was neither "a capable politician nor a capable general"—did not convert the chiefs to the State Department's point of view.[26]

Possible military action in Laos was a major topic of discussion at a 10:30 A.M. White House meeting on Saturday, May 12. McNamara, who had just returned from South Vietnam and from Thailand, where he met with

Ambassador Brown and his country team, reported that Nam Tha was "a military disaster" and that the situation in the Lao "panhandle was very poor militarily." In Thailand, the conditions were "discouraging." Sarit had few forces in the northeast area of the country adjacent to Laos and "very poor intelligence and communications." Despite these grave circumstances, McNamara said there was no need to implement SEATO Plan 5 "at this time." He suggested increasing US military strength in Thailand, including the addition of a marine battalion and two US Air Force squadrons, and moving US ground forces to the Lao border. "If any US action was contemplated in Laos," said McNamara, "we must definitely put forces in South Vietnam to help them against North Vietnam."[27]

The State Department officials attending the meeting commented on political aspects of the proposed military moves. "Whatever we do militarily," said Rusk, "we must do with enough firmness and enough force to convince the Soviets that we really mean business." Harriman and Hilsman wanted to ensure that any US action in Laos or Thailand avoid the appearance of helping Phoumi. They also advocated that US officials "do everything we could to downgrade" Phoumi's leadership. General Lemnitzer, commenting on the paucity of right-wing leaders, asked: "If not Phoumi, who then?"[28]

A topic discussed at the meeting that had made Kennedy "livid" was a *New York Times* story published that morning. It reported that the president, seeking "to salvage a peaceful settlement," would "order a show of United States force in the Southeast Asian waters near landlocked Laos."[29] The implication of the story—that US military moves were a bluff—was an unhelpful message at a time when Kennedy sought to demonstrate resolve. Always worried that Soviet and US miscalculations of each other's intentions might trigger a nuclear war, Kennedy was undoubtedly concerned that the perception of a US bluff in Laos could only lead to one of two undesirable outcomes: a communist victory or the commitment of US combat troops.

The meeting ended inconclusively after nearly two hours, with Kennedy asking his advisers to reconvene at 1:30 P.M. Lemnitzer and Marshall Carter, who attended on behalf of the CIA, "cornered" Harriman after the president left the cabinet room. Visibly upset, they took exception with a Harriman observation at the meeting that "a number of people felt that the President's program [in Laos] had been undermined by the CIA and the military." Although military and agency officials had disagreed with aspects of Kennedy's Laos policy, the accusation that they did not faithfully execute the president's decisions was disturbing. Harriman, a rough bureaucratic infighter and suspicious of CIA and military loyalty to Kennedy, replied disingenuously to Lemnitzer and Carter: he was "merely passing on" information that reporters had discussed with him. Harriman did not identify the reporters but "categorically" denied ever thinking that the CIA or military had undercut Kennedy's Lao policy.[30]

At the afternoon meeting, Kennedy approved the "precautionary dispositions" of US military forces in Thailand that had been recommended by Rusk and McNamara. Pending further authorization by the president on landing US troops, the deployments included offloading a marine battalion landing team and helicopters from the carrier *Valley Forge*, reinforcing the army battle group already in Thailand, and moving a marine fighter squadron and a USAF squadron to Thailand. Kennedy, dissatisfied with the limited amount of intelligence available from Laos, emphasized that he did not want to make a "decision on the actual landing of troops at this time."[31]

In contrast to Washington's conditional orders to the military, the State Department instructions to Ambassador Brown were unequivocal: because of the "debacle" at Nam Tha and the stalled negotiations with Souvanna, the US government had "absolutely no confidence in Phoumi either politically or militarily." The telegram continued: "We believe our best interests would be served if he were eliminated entirely from Laotian scene. If there is any way in which that practicably can be done, we would welcome Embassy suggestions." The message proposed that the CIA "should begin subverting Colonel Siho's [secret police] units in an effort to remove Phoumi's most effective terror weapons over Vientiane politicians."[32]

The State Department, seeking "as complete [a] reorganization of [the] government as possible," instructed Brown to inform "all significant political and military figures in Laos" of the US loss of confidence in Phoumi. Acknowledging that his "immediate elimination" was probably not feasible, the department wanted him removed as a minister in the RLG and returned to the FAR as a full-time military commander. To reduce the likelihood of further military catastrophes, Phoumi should operate "only in accordance with and under direct MAAG guidance." Major General

Reuben H. Tucker III, Boyle's replacement as MAAG chief, should tell Phoumi "in elaborate detail exactly what we believe he did wrong" at Nam Tha. The instructions to Brown emphasized that bringing Phoumi "under wraps" was now an "undeviating policy objective," equivalent to the Kennedy administration's efforts to restore the ceasefire, to establish a coalition government, and to reach and execute a satisfactory Geneva agreement.[33]

In the field of domestic diplomacy, Kennedy once again dispatched emissaries to Gettysburg to brief Eisenhower on the latest events in Southeast Asia. As before, McCone led the delegation. This time, however, he was accompanied by Defense Secretary McNamara and General Lemnitzer, who reported on their trip to Thailand and South Vietnam. The conversation with the former president covered many of the same topics as the previous meeting with Eisenhower, who continued to emphasize the importance of Laos to the overall defense of Southeast Asia.

McCone reported to Kennedy that Eisenhower "now understands the complexity of the situation, the difficulties we have encountered with Phoumi, the extent of the Communist penetration of Laos and the alternative courses of action open to us." Whether Eisenhower was, in fact, more sympathetic to the policy described to him is questionable given his longstanding skepticism of Souvanna and coalition governments that included communists. But whatever his personal beliefs, Eisenhower "made it quite clear he would not at this time privately or publicly urge moving U.S. combat troops into Laos."[34] He also said that he "would try to keep the Republicans in the Senate from becoming Generals and publicly second-guessing and looking over the shoulder of President Kennedy in his conduct of our affairs in Southeast Asia."[35]

On May 14 Kennedy approved the deployment to Thailand of some six thousand US ground and air forces. At a White House meeting the next day, Kennedy and his advisers briefed congressional leaders on Laos and described the troop buildup in Thailand. The president, repeating his fundamental policy objectives, said that his administration "favored a coalition government" in Laos because the FAR was "ineffective" and because "the British and French would not go along with military action." Kennedy observed that the "chances of maintaining an independent Laos were not good." Moreover, he would "not order U.S. military forces into Laos without further exhaustive study and consultation with Congressional leaders." Asked by Senator Everett Dirksen what the United States would do if the situation "caves in Laos," Kennedy replied: "We would then try to hold in Thailand."[36]

The legal basis for the troop deployment to Thailand was a tricky balancing act for Kennedy. On the one hand, the United States was not formally invoking the SEATO treaty for landing US forces, which Rusk described as "a precautionary movement." On the other hand, the president was "personally concerned that [the] U.S. not appear to be acting in Thailand alone." Seeking a "SEATO flavor" for the deployment, the State Department sought token troop contributions from each member of the alliance. Intended as a demonstration of "SEATO solidarity," such contributions would not, however, constitute a "commitment direct or implied to do anything in Laos."[37]

The United Kingdom agreed to return to Thailand a Hawker Hunter fighter squadron that had participated in the recent SEATO exercise. Prime Minister Macmillan considered the deployment "a more or less token force" supporting a bilateral US-Thai enterprise. Australia and New Zealand made troop contributions, too. French officials, however, refused to send any military units to Thailand. Disappointed by the lack of advance consultation, they thought that French participation "would not have a constructive effect" in Southeast Asia and could compromise the future usefulness of the French Military Mission in a neutral Laos.[38]

Ironically, the SEATO ally that caused the most difficulty for the US government was the stated beneficiary of the deployment: Thailand. Prime Minister Sarit and Foreign Minister Thanat readily agreed to the landing of US troops, but they objected to inaccurate statements by the Kennedy administration that Thailand had "requested" the action. Thai officials concurred with the deployment, but they did not ask for it.[39] Another source of friction was the public announcement of the legal basis for landing US forces. Sarit and Thanat were "alarmed and puzzled" by US insistence that the SEATO treaty was the only constitutional basis for sending troops to Thailand. The Thai officials wanted the Rusk-Thanat communiqué to serve as the public justification for the deployment. A third area of disagreement was the Thai government's "far from welcoming" attitude toward troop contributions from other SEATO allies. The State Department instructed Ambassador Young to inform Thanat that the US government considered "it absolutely essential that [the] Thais accept force contributions offered by their SEATO partners."[40]

After US troops had been deployed to Thailand, President Kennedy called Michael Forrestal into the Oval Office to discuss his doubts about the decision: "Mike, do you really think this was a wise thing to do? Don't you think that you people—you, Hilsman, and Harriman—really moved too fast on this one?" In an oral history for the Kennedy Library, Forrestal recalled the president asking, "How am I ever going to get them out? Why did you let me put them in without making it quite clear how we're going to get them out?" In response to Kennedy's questions, Forrestal wrote a memorandum reassuring the president that his decision was "exactly the right thing to do." By demonstrating an ability to move forces quickly into the region, the United States had provided a "real deterrent" to further communist attacks. Once a ceasefire was restored and negotiations were resumed, Forrestal wrote, the withdrawal of US forces might serve as "both a reassurance and a warning to the Soviets and to the Chinese." The White House aide concluded his memorandum by observing: "We are far from out of the woods, but at least we will still have a chance in the area."[41]

General Tucker, acting under instructions from Washington, met with Phoumi in Vientiane at 9:10 a.m, May 13, 1962. Tucker, who had assumed command of MAAG only two weeks earlier, began the conversation by describing the purpose of the US troop movements into Thailand: "establishing conditions" that might lead to a coalition government in Laos. Turning to Nam Tha, Tucker said that the United States had lost "confidence in [Phoumi's] ability as a military leader." He had ignored US advice before the attack at Nam Tha, and after the battle some of the FAR's best units had "lost all semblance of order and control," withdrawing some eighty miles to the southwest into Thailand. Tucker noted "the complete panic" of FAR troops who abandoned Ban Houei Sai, a town on the Lao side of the Mekong.[42] The previous day a US Special Forces team that Tucker had dispatched to Ban Houei Sai found no evidence of enemy activity in the area.

"Rube" Tucker, then fifty-one, was a tough combat leader who had commanded the 504th Parachute Infantry Regiment of the Eighty-second Airborne Division during World War II. Awarded two Distinguished Service Crosses, a Silver Star, and a Purple Heart, Tucker was "probably the best regimental commander of the war," according to his division commander, Lieutenant General James M. Gavin. Tucker was appalled by the incompetence of the FAR, faulting its commanders for having "no idea how many forces they have, or exactly where they are." He informed CINCPAC that "the present combat effectiveness of [the] forces involved in the Nam Tha operation is nil."[43]

Tucker told Phoumi that unless he provided "concrete evidence" of his commitment to reforming the FAR, the US government would not honor his request to transport his vanquished troops in Thailand back to Laos. The first change Tucker sought was the replacement of incompetent commanders with better-qualified officers. Moreover, Tucker wanted MAAG "to have a voice" in these personnel decisions. His second demand was a greater emphasis on developing "a first-class" corps of noncommissioned officers. Among the other changes proposed by Tucker was his own personal approval of any military operation that required a battalion or larger unit. He said that the FAR must accept MAAG advice and allow US advisers to participate "actively in staff planning."[44]

According to Tucker's report of the meeting, Phoumi "agreed that there must be the closest cooperation" between all FAR commanders and their US counterparts. The Lao general acknowledged that Nam Tha had been "a serious blow," but since he had not yet received a complete report on the fight, he was unable to discuss it in detail. Phoumi said that he had ordered guerrilla units into the vicinity of Ban Houei Sai to organize a defense of the area as soon as possible. He had also ordered General Bounleut to return to Vientiane to discuss plans for "the reorganized defense of Laos." Tucker replied: "This was certainly a good first step, but that [Phoumi] would do well to concentrate on the military rather than the political situation."[45]

A key US objective for Phoumi's forces was "to recoup as much of northwest Laos territory" as possible. To the Americans, reestablishing an RLG presence in the region seemed a low-risk activity. US aerial reconnaissance revealed few antigovernment troops in Nam Tha, Ban Houei Sai, or the roads and valleys connecting the towns. Phoumi, however, refused Tucker's pleas to send out patrols to reclaim unoccupied territory or identify the location of enemy forces. The Pathet Lao, the Lao general claimed, would consider such reconnaissance "an aggressive act" and immediately dispatch a superior force that would probably "decimate" the FAR troops. Phoumi also rejected US advice to "clean house in his officer corps." Despite Tucker's observation that General Bounleut "could not lead a squad around a corner," Phoumi would not relieve him.[46]

While Tucker tried to reduce Phoumi's autonomy in military affairs, Ambassador Brown carried out his instructions to discredit him politically. Brown informed influential Laotians that the United Sates had "completely lost confidence in Phoumi's ability and reliability." On May 16 the ambassador reported to the State Department: "Rumors are already circulating in Vientiane that we are supporting [a government] reorganization." The leader preferred by the United States was former prime minister Phoui Sananikone, who in the course of his long political career had managed to alienate many leading Laotians, including Phoumi, Souvanna, Souphanouvong, and the king.[47]

Neither the United Kingdom nor France supported the US plan to reorganize the RLG. Although Phoumi remained a "disgusting, unreliable, and deceptive person," in the words of Malcolm MacDonald, leader of the British delegation at Geneva, the Lao general had agreed both to resuming negotiations with the neutralists and Pathet Lao and to yielding his claim to the defense and interior portfolios. At best, a reorganization of the RLG would further delay negotiations and increase the risk of another major ceasefire violation. UK ambassador Addis warned that additional US intervention in Laotian politics—particularly placing the widely regarded "US stooge" Phoui in a prominent political position—would "violently" arouse the suspicions of the neutralists and Pathet Lao. Jean Brethès, chief of Indochinese affairs at the Quai d'Orsay, told American embassy officials in Paris that the French were "somewhat abashed" by defending Phoumi, their traditional bête noire, to the US government. Nonetheless, the French foreign ministry was convinced that "derailing Phoumi risks trading a known variable pointed in [the] right direction for something unknown which might upset other variables in [the] picture—Souvanna, PL and [the communist] Bloc."[48]

State Department officials were initially undeterred by the opposition of western allies. The department parried objections to an RLG reorganization by observing that the disadvantage of "delay would be more than offset by [the] monkey-wrenches [Phoumi] would throw into each stage of negotiations[,] and his past performance [has been] so bad that we cannot rely on him again." In a conversation with UK officials, who had long denounced the Lao general's duplicity, Harriman "ridiculed the idea that the British were now asking the US to trust Phoumi." The State Department also dismissed concerns about Phoui, including accusations of corruption: "We would have little human material in Laos to work with if we confined ourselves to [the] lily pure."[49]

At a May 18 meeting with Prince Khampan, the Lao ambassador to the United States and a half-brother of the king, Harriman "set forth in [the] clearest terms [the] US loss of confidence in Phoumi[,] citing specific examples of his irresponsible behavior." According to a State Department summary of the conversation, "Harriman expressed [the] hope [that the] RLG would be revamped to include [the] most competent Lao patriots." Asked if the United States would resume providing "material and moral support" to the RLG when negotiations with the Pathet Lao and neutralists resumed, Harriman replied such assistance would be considered, "but only if [the] RLG [was] reorganized." He added that the United States "would give no help to Phoumi."[50]

Ambassador Khampan reported to Vientiane that the US diplomat had demanded a "reshuffling of the Royal Government in which Phoumi would not be included." RLG foreign minister Sisouk, shocked by Khampan's report, called in Ambassador Brown to ask if there had been a change in US policy. Thus far, the US government had said there was an important role for Phoumi in a coalition government. When Harriman learned of the Laotian concerns, he instructed Brown to clarify to the RLG his comments to Khampan. "I made no demand for [the] resignation of [the] cabinet or of Phoumi," Harriman wrote, explaining that he had merely repeated the State Department's guidance to the US mission in Vientiane: a lack of US confidence in Phoumi, the desirability of relegating him to a military role, and the importance of Boun Oum bringing the wisest available advisers into government. "You may tell the King and government," Harriman cabled, "nothing I said to [the] Ambassador differs from positions that you have already taken."[51]

The exact language Harriman used with Khampan is unknown, but reports of their meeting and Harriman's frustration with Phoumi concerned the president. Kennedy, who was well aware of Phoumi's limitations, still regarded the Lao general as virtually the only source of right-wing military strength, however feeble, in an eventual coalition government. According to notes of a White House staff meeting, "McGeorge Bundy stated 'in very soft terms' that he and the President 'were both slightly watchful of Harriman's views on Phoumi.'" In a report to the president about Harriman's conversation with Khampan, Forrestal wrote: "I told Averell this morning after talking with you that I believe you felt that we should ease up on blasting at Phoumi and bear down on getting his cooperation on specific military and political moves."[52]

At a May 24 White House meeting, President Kennedy requested a senior-level review of military contingency plans for US intervention in Laos. A recently established interagency task force, chaired by William Sullivan, had been revising possible US responses to another breakdown of the ceasefire. Concluding that the DRV was the "root cause" of the insurgencies in Laos and South Vietnam, the task force proposed a six-phase program of escalating military action. The first phase called for a further buildup of US forces in Thailand; the final one envisioned amphibious operations in North Vietnam to seal off the main infiltration routes into Laos and South Vietnam.[53]

The interagency planning revealed a basic disagreement between the State Department and Pentagon over a contingency likely to arise in a new crisis: US-SEATO occupation of the major towns in the Mekong River valley with a force of some ten thousand troops in Thailand and eight thousand in Laos. State Department officials, who saw this operation as critical to preempting communist control of population centers, to restoring the ceasefire, and to supporting a neutral political settlement, thought the risk of further escalation was low. Pentagon officials, however, resisted the idea of deploying a relatively small, immobile defensive force, subject to harassing attacks, while the Pathet Lao and North Vietnamese consolidated their position in the rest of Laos. McNamara and the JCS thought that the "minimum" US force for intervention would be thirty thousand troops in Laos, with an additional ten thousand held in reserve in Thailand. Moreover, the defense secretary and the chiefs thought that the occupation of the river towns would "lead quickly to further action" in Laos and possibly North Vietnam.[54]

The State Department and Pentagon also had differing perspectives on the effect of US intervention in Laos on infiltration from North

Vietnam into South Vietnam. The occupation of the towns along the Mekong, concluded Roger Hilsman, "would not prevent the Communists from using the [Laotian] infiltration routes, [but] it would restrict them to a level that we would find manageable." Declaring that North Vietnamese development of the rugged jungle trails of eastern Laos "would be both difficult and costly," Hilsman hypothesized that the presence of US forces along the Mekong and of South Vietnamese troops on the Lao border "would tend to deter the Communists from the large scale effort needed to improve [the trails]."[55] In Hilsman's view, controlling the population centers along the Mekong would mean that "Communist infiltration into South Vietnam would probably be no greater than it has been; very possibly it would be less."[56]

The military had a less equivocal view of the impact of occupying the principal Lao towns on infiltration. "Control of the Mekong Valley would have no effect on infiltration into [South Vietnam]," declared Admiral Felt.[57] A later phase of the interagency contingency plans sought to close the infiltration routes by offensive US action to secure the Laotian panhandle. Yet a closer examination of the formidable logistic difficulties, the large troop requirements, and other factors prompted McNamara to question the wisdom of making the attempt. At a June 2 meeting of civilian and military officials, General Lemnitzer said that the JCS thought a US amphibious operation near Vinh, North Vietnam, was in many ways "less dangerous than the massive occupation of the Laos Panhandle." Characterizing the fighting in Southeast Asia "as very comfortable for the North Vietnamese," Lemnitzer outlined a plan for US forces to drive west across the DRV to the Laos border, sealing off the main infiltration routes into Laos and South Vietnam.[58]

CIA analysts estimated that an amphibious landing in North Vietnam would prompt Hanoi to "take immediate steps to repel the invasion, using its 300,000-man army. Communist China would almost certainly provide additional ground forces if they were needed." The State Department's Bureau of Intelligence and Research concluded: "At a minimum we should expect a large-scale influx of [PRC] troops into the combat situation and probably Soviet warnings of nuclear retaliation."[59] Because a full-scale regional war was hardly what President Kennedy had in mind when responding to a breakdown of the ceasefire in Laos, his advisers quickly dropped Lemnitzer's concept for an amphibious landing in North Vietnam from the contingency planning by the Laos task force.

Ironically, the task force chair, William Sullivan, tried to revive this strategic alternative in December 1965, when he served in Vientiane as the American ambassador to Laos. With regular PAVN units moving down the Ho Chi Minh Trail in increasing numbers, Sullivan was concerned about the impact of infiltration on the Vietnam War but skeptical that US air attacks or cross-border ground operations from South Vietnam could successfully interdict the North Vietnamese. Citing the "obvious military advantages" of sealing off infiltration at the source, Sullivan urged policymakers to give serious consideration to an amphibious operation near Vinh. He did not discount the possibility of Chinese intervention, but he thought it was a risk that the United States would likely have to face "before we finish this business" in Southeast Asia. Like Lemnitzer's original plan, Sullivan's proposal was rejected out of hand by Washington as "politically unacceptable and militarily of uncertain value."[60]

During the spring 1962 Laotian crisis, some of Kennedy's advisers wanted US contingency plans to include air strikes against targets in North Vietnam. CIA chief McCone, echoing Eisenhower's concerns about a communist sanctuary for directing and supplying military operations, told Kennedy that a commitment of US ground forces to Laos "must be coupled with the decision" to launch air attacks against North Vietnamese military concentrations, airfields, supply depots, and transportation and communications facilities—all of which had been photographed by aerial reconnaissance. Walt Rostow, seeking "to impose on North Viet-Nam sufficient costs to make a neutral, independent Laos the most attractive realistic alternative open to the Communists," proposed a "highly selective [air] attack on transport and power facilities." Urging preparation for "any level of escalation," Rostow thought that the balance of power between the United States and the communist world was as favorable as any "we are likely to confront in this decade."[61]

Rostow, an academic by profession, had served in the Office of Strategic Services during World War II and helped identify bombing targets in Germany. An authority on economic development in Third World countries, he memorably characterized communism as "a disease of the transition to modernization." Kennedy, who liked Rostow's erudite anticommunism, appointed him deputy national security advisor. The president, however, also sought crisp summaries of facts and options from his White House aides. He often found Rostow's memoranda long-winded and somewhat remote from immediate problems. McGeorge Bundy later observed: "I've always thought that one of the reasons the President put Walt Rostow in the Department of State was so he wouldn't have to read quite so many papers which he didn't have to decide on."[62]

As in 1961, President Kennedy was not forced to choose among the broad range of military contingency plans his advisers proposed in the spring of 1962. The threat of US intervention had, once again, apparently stopped the advance of antigovernment forces in Laos. On June 11, 1962—a little more than one month after the attack at Nam Tha and a few weeks after the deployment of US troops to Thailand—the three Laotian princes finally reached an agreement on establishing a coalition government.

Chapter 7

A Colossal Booby Trap

Phoumi Nosavan, chastened by US economic, diplomatic, and military pressure, flew to the Plaine des Jarres on Thursday, June 7, 1962, to negotiate with Souvanna and Souphanouvong about the formation of a coalition government. Not entirely confident about his personal security in hostile territory, he startled the neutralist and Pathet Lao leaders by arriving with more than forty western correspondents in tow.[1] Phoumi had assured Ambassador Brown that he would cooperate fully in reaching a political settlement. "It remains to be seen, of course," Brown cabled the State Department, "whether the performance will match the promise." If the Plaine des Jarres talks broke down because of "Phoumi's intransigence," Brown, Ambassador Addis, and French ambassador Pierre-Louis Falaize agreed on the need "to force [the] immediate resignation and/or reorganization of [the] present government coupled with efforts to keep Souvanna in [the] picture."[2]

Phoumi entered the talks with only two demands: (1) All major decisions on domestic and defense matters would require the unanimous approval of the three leaders; and (2) their respective military forces would remain in place until the new government reached an agreement on integrating them into a national army. Souvanna accepted both of Phoumi's basic conditions, and Souphanouvong agreed that each army should remain in place pending a more specific understanding on merging the three forces. The unanimity principle on all major decisions, however, would require more thought, said Souphanouvong. He would provide a reply the next day, presumably after conferring with his Pathet Lao superiors. The horse-trading by the Lao leaders over the distribution of cabinet posts was businesslike, with the proportion of portfolios reserved for left- and right-leaning neutralists the principal area of disagreement. Addis characterized the atmosphere of the talks as "very good," and Brown considered the day's developments "encouraging."[3]

The negotiations resumed at 9:00 A.M. on June 8. Souphanouvong now concurred with Phoumi and Souvanna that major defense and domestic issues should be decided unanimously. The three leaders further agreed that the same principle should apply to foreign relations. There were, however, disagreements over the acceptability of certain individuals for cabinet positions. Souphanouvong, for example, objected to Ngon Sananikone serving as a neutralist minister. The younger brother of former prime minister Phoui Sananikone, Ngon was an anticommunist official whom the State Department described as "a valuable source of information" and "responsive to U.S. suggestions."[4] Phoumi thought that Souvanna's nomination of neutralist general Amkha Soukhavong, locked up in a FAR "reeducation center" since October 1960, was "provocative and improper." According to the draft Geneva accords, prisoner-of-war issues would be a responsibility of the new government. Brown's "main concern" about the potential appointment was what Amkha "might try to do to [the] FAR after being imprisoned by it for so long."[5]

The sharpest disagreement over a cabinet member was prompted by Souvanna's selection of Quinim Pholsena as foreign minister. A representative of the neutralist delegation at Geneva, Quinim was a Laotian of Chinese descent who had struggled for acceptance by the kingdom's class-conscious elites. A protégé of Souvanna's family—he reportedly lodged in the servants' quarters—Quinim had been a civil servant, an elected official, and, at least since 1955, a Pathet Lao sympathizer. Phoumi and his associates believed that "Quinim actually takes orders from the NLHS." US officials shared similar suspicions. According to the State Department, Quinim was "a threat to the U.S. if in any significant cabinet post."[6]

At the Plaine des Jarres meeting, Phoumi declared that Quinim was "unacceptable" as the minister of foreign affairs and proposed right-leaning neutralists as alternatives. Souvanna replied that Phoumi's stance was "impossible" and threatened to "throw in his hand and quit" if the Lao general did not reconsider his position. Phoumi retreated, explaining that he was simply requesting consideration of his idea. He then proposed, and the two princes accepted, a suggestion to adjourn the talks for a weekend of "reflection."[7]

After the meeting, Ambassador Falaize, the foreign diplomat closest to Souvanna, told Brown that the neutralist leader seemed "tired." Souvanna had complained to Falaize about the negotiating behavior of Souphanouvong and Phoumi: "If one side didn't raise difficulties then the other did." To Souvanna's frustration, both men claimed that they would be more flexible in negotiations if they were confident the other wanted to sign an agreement. According to Falaize's report to Brown, Souvanna would not insist on Amkha as a cabinet minister, but he and Souphanouvong were determined to select Quinim as foreign minister. Souvanna, who had "no further proposals to make," repeated an ultimatum to Falaize that he had made earlier to the Geneva cochairs and others: if the three factions did not reach an agreement by June 15, he would quit and return to Paris.[8]

Souvanna's comments and Falaize's report of them to Brown were undoubtedly aimed at encouraging right-wing compromise and hastening the conclusion of the talks. The negotiating maneuver, however, was probably unnecessary. Brown and his State Department superiors swallowed their objections to Quinim, concluding that his appointment as foreign minister "should not become [a] breaking point for negotiations." They rationalized that the unanimity principle in major foreign affairs decisions would limit Quinim's potential for troublemaking in a new government. Moreover, he had thus "far proved amenable to Souvanna's influence."[9] Brown advised Phoumi to yield both on Quinim as foreign minister and on a cabinet portfolio for Ngon. It was "essential," Brown told Phoumi, "that [an] agreement be reached tomorrow [Monday, June 11] if possible."[10]

When the talks resumed on June 11, all outstanding issues were quickly settled, with one exception. Souphanouvong wanted to limit the number of right-leaning neutral cabinet ministers to two; Phoumi sought three. Souvanna sided with Phoumi, observing to his half brother that this demand was "entirely reasonable." Souphanouvong did not budge. The meeting adjourned temporarily, and Souvanna and Souphanouvong engaged in a "violent argument," with the two men pounding tables and kicking furniture. When the talks resumed, Souphanouvong suddenly yielded. "All right," he said, "I agree."[11]

The agreement reached on the Plaine des Jarres selected the people who would serve in a government of national unity and established the coalition's principles of operation. In addition to serving as prime minister, Souvanna would be the kingdom's defense minister. The two deputy premiers, Souphanouvong and Phoumi, were appointed minister of planning and minister of finance, respectively. The agreement's most significant procedural stipulation was that all major decisions required the unanimous approval of Souvanna and his two ideologically opposed deputies. From the US perspective, the chief advantage of the unanimity principle was that it allowed Phoumi to veto any undesirable action proposed by NLHS and neutralist ministers. A disadvantage of the arrangement was the likelihood of perpetual gridlock in managing Lao affairs. "It remains to be seen how a government set up under such provisions will work out in practice, if indeed, it can be made to work at all," wrote Philip Chadbourn, chief of the American embassy's political section. "On the other hand, the new government and its principles of operation appear to be an accurate reflection of the present political realities in Laos, and if these realities tend to work against efficient administration of the country, it is perhaps unfair to blame any resulting inefficiencies on the government."[12]

US officials in Washington viewed the Plaine des Jarres agreement with ambivalence. President Kennedy and Premier Khrushchev exchanged pro-forma public expressions of satisfaction with the accord. Privately, NSC staffer Michael Forrestal observed to McGeorge Bundy that the new cabinet was "not ideal from our point of view."[13] Quinim's appointment as foreign minister still bothered US officials, as did Souphanouvong's role as a spokesperson for the new government. In his first public statement after signing the Plaine des Jarres agreement, Souphanouvong lived up to US officials' low expectations by warning that "American warmongers and their agents" were a threat to the new government.[14]

Committed to "the care and feeding of the Souvanna Government," in Forrestal's words, US officials faced a more immediate challenge in discharging their obligations to Phoumi. Harriman, Brown, and others wanted the United States to resume economic aid to the RLG, suspended since February, for at least one more month. The Lao general, wrote Forrestal, had "behaved more or less like a little soldier" in recent weeks, and US haggling over the "resumption of his monthly allowance" would "wreck the morale of Phoumi, his followers, and his Uncle Sarit."[15] Kennedy, however, initially resisted this line of reasoning. Reacting "negatively" to providing the RLG with a $3 million cash grant, Kennedy wondered to Forrestal "about the political impact" of resuming economic assistance to Phoumi immediately after an agreement on forming a new government led by Souvanna. How could the United States, Kennedy asked, "justify [the] restoration of aid to a dying government with whom we have had so much difficulty?"[16]

An economic reason for the president's reluctance to resume the cash grant was its adverse impact on the balance-of-payments deficit and the gold reserves of the United States. At a time when the dollar was still directly convertible to gold, Kennedy, like Eisenhower before him, worried that surplus dollars in foreign central banks would be redeemed for gold at a rate that threatened the stability of the US economy and the international monetary system. The primary cause of this so-called dollar drain was US defense spending overseas, particularly in Western Europe, where six US Army divisions served as NATO's first line of defense against a possible Soviet attack. Although US economic aid to Laos— about $40 million per year—was small compared with American support for NATO, Kennedy wanted "to limit dollar drain" in the kingdom and to share defense burdens with allies.[17]

At a June 13 White House meeting, Dean Rusk emphasized that the Plaine des Jarres agreement "was just the beginning of a new process to establish a genuinely neutral Laos." With diplomatic details remaining to be worked out in Geneva, and a final international agreement still weeks away, Rusk warned of many opportunities for a communist "double-cross." Particularly worrisome was Souvanna's planned absence from Laos in late June to attend his daughter's wedding in Paris. Rusk, fearing "a colossal booby trap," thought that Souphanouvong might launch a coup while Souvanna was out of the country. Urging the continuation of US military contingency planning, Rusk and other officials at the meeting received assurances from McNamara and Lemnitzer that "such planning was well advanced."[18]

President Kennedy asked about the possibility of establishing a closer relationship between Souvanna and the West. Harriman responded that France would continue to exert a major influence on the new prime minister. "Much of the [US] responsibility" for fostering closer ties with him, said Harriman, "might rest with [the] CIA." He added that "the Agency had some plans to implement this."[19] Although the public record of the

CIA's association with Souvanna is far from complete, case officer R. Campbell James had developed a relationship with him in the late 1950s. A wealthy Yale graduate who spoke with a posh English accent and carried a cane filled with brandy, James mixed well with the older Lao elites. When Souvanna fled the country after the battle of Vientiane, the CIA posted James to Paris, where he maintained contact with him. According to Michael Forrestal, James "was the only American around who knew Souvanna Phouma, and Harriman used him a lot to find out what Souvanna's ideas were on one thing and another."[20]

President Kennedy expressed a particular interest in effective policing of the Geneva accords, a task that posed significant military, intelligence, and diplomatic challenges. One of the agreement's key provisions was the withdrawal from Laos of all foreign military forces (with the exception of a small French Military Mission). At that time, the US government estimated that the total number of North Vietnamese forces in Laos was ten thousand (five thousand organized into ten battalions and another five thousand serving as advisers.) The French government, however, viewed the US order-of-battle estimate with "polite scepticism," according to the American embassy in Paris. A "senior *Defense Nationale* intelligence officer" opined that the number of North Vietnamese military and paramilitary personnel in Laos was "on the order of 2,000."[21]

For their part, DRV officials publicly insisted that there were no North Vietnamese military forces in Laos. Historian Christopher Goscha, citing Vietnamese sources, later wrote that the number of military advisers in Group 959, the principal DRV military organization in Laos, was 3,085 in mid-1962. This total did not include the large number of PAVN troops in Group 559, which improved and defended the Ho Chi Minh Trail, and other North Vietnamese forces. Pierre Asselin, also citing Vietnamese sources, estimated "nearly 10,000 PAVN troops and more than 4,000 militiamen and support personnel from the DRVN in Laos in mid-1962."[22]

Establishing the exact number of US military personnel in Laos in 1962 is a similarly imprecise exercise, hindered by the political sensitivity of the topic at that time and the continuing unwillingness of US agencies to declassify the full record of American involvement in Laos.[23] Aspects of US military assistance to the kingdom had been conducted on a covert basis since the mid-1950s. The widely known presence of American military advisers in Laos was not publicly acknowledged until April 1961, when Kennedy ordered the establishment of a uniformed MAAG. On June 16, 1962—three days after receiving JCS authorization for the planned withdrawal of American military advisers—CINCPAC reported that there were 886 US personnel "assigned to or under the control of MAAG Laos." This number included 444 Special Forces who served in White Star Mobile Training Teams.[24] Excluded from CINCPAC's total were 200 covert Thai military "volunteers" assigned to MAAG (not to be confused with the CIA-controlled Thai paramilitary specialists who trained the Hmong army) and some 450 Philippine civilians who repaired equipment, stored ordnance, and performed similar military support functions for the FAR.

General Tucker subsequently reported that on July 23, 1962—the day the Geneva agreement was signed—"the total MAAG strength was 1190."[25] It seems highly improbable that the US government increased the number of military advisers in Laos by nearly one-third in the final weeks leading up to the Geneva agreement. A more plausible explanation for this and other inconsistencies in US order-of-battle figures was the effort to mask the actual number of American military advisers in Laos. One month after the Geneva agreement, Ambassador Leonard Unger, Brown's successor in Vientiane, urged that US officials "avoid [the] use of numbers" when describing the withdrawal of military advisers: "If queried here, we shall state that at [an] earlier period, when [advisory] activity [was] at its height, there were 700–800 but that number has been somewhat reduced."[26] A subsequent State Department cable to Brown confirmed that Washington officials intended to tell reporters "on background" that the peak number of American advisers in Laos had been 800.[27] Yet according to the notes of an October 1962 telephone conversation, Harriman said that there had been 1,600 US military advisers in Laos.[28] This numbers game reached its misleading conclusion that same month with the US announcement that some 665 US military advisers had withdrawn from Laos in accordance with the Geneva agreement.

A fundamental principle of US planning for an agreement in Geneva was that MAAG advisers—whatever their number—would not be withdrawn from Laos unless the PAVN units there returned to the DRV.[29] To assess North Vietnamese compliance with the Geneva agreement, the US government sought to increase its capability for clandestine intelligence collection in Laos. The CIA, supplementing US aerial reconnaissance and other sources of military intelligence, established "road watch" teams that operated in Pathet Lao territory.

In the northern provinces, the agency recruited Hmong villagers to observe military traffic on roads leading to and from the DRV. The Hmong inhabited the higher altitudes and were viewed with contempt by most ethnic Lao. They were, however, effective guerrilla warriors who had received arms and training from the CIA and the Police Aerial Reinforcement Unit (PARU), an elite Thai paramilitary force "developed and controlled and funded" by the agency.[30] The number of organized Hmong guerrillas grew from approximately 1,000 in early 1961 to 19,500 when the Geneva agreement went into effect.[31] Although the Hmong were temporarily shifting their emphasis from military operations to collecting intelligence, the guerrillas were encouraged to preserve the integrity of their units and to hide their weapons. The CIA would continue airdropping food to them and, if necessary, provide additional obsolete arms "for surrender to the ICC."[32]

With a Geneva agreement on the horizon, the CIA planned to establish a "stay behind headquarters" in Thailand to maintain radio communication with Hmong "intelligence cadres."[33] In southern Laos, a similar program of intelligence operations had been established for the "Kha" tribal people. Kha was a misnomer, meaning slave, for the Lao Theung, the collective name for several ethnic groups who lived at middle altitudes. In late 1961 the CIA and MAAG began to equip and train Lao Theung guerrillas on and around the Bolovens Plateau, "a natural staging area for infiltrators from North Vietnam" to South Vietnam, according to a RAND study of the military geography of Laos.[34]

By combining self-defense measures with economic assistance and propaganda programs, the US mission hoped that the Bolovens initiative would help pacify the area and "interdict [the] movement of foreign troops along [the] Ho Chi Minh Trail."[35] For a variety of reasons—including the withdrawal of US Special Forces training teams, the lack of cohesion among the Lao Theung, and the concentration of antigovernment forces and sympathizers in the region—the Bolovens program did not achieve its lofty ambitions. The CIA did, however, recruit a limited number of

Lao Theung as stay-behind agents who gathered intelligence and reported on infiltration into South Vietnam.[36]

When planning the withdrawal of MAAG advisers and White Star teams, US officials hoped that France would energetically take on the task of training an effective, western-oriented Lao army. The FMM was the only foreign military force in Laos authorized by the 1954 Geneva agreement and the draft 1962 accords. This unique status reflected France's special position as a former colonial power with both a strong cultural influence on the kingdom's elites and a deep aversion to further military intervention in the region. The United States and France had a long record of disagreements over military assistance to Laos, with the former invariably urging more forceful action than the latter thought desirable. By mid-June 1962, the western allies' lack of communication and consultation on Lao military matters had deteriorated to the point where US officials had few insights into French plans to help the new coalition government. "We must find out what the French will do in the way of provision of [military] assistance," U. Alexis Johnson told Pentagon officials.[37]

On June 19, 1962, Deputy Assistant Secretary of Defense William P. Bundy led a US delegation in Paris that continued the tradition of quarreling with French officials over military aid to Laos. The appropriate size of the new government's armed forces was a fundamental area of disagreement. The United States proposed an army of 30,000 (with 10,000 soldiers from each faction) and an 11,000-man gendarmerie. Such a force would be less expensive than Phoumi's 54,000-man regular army, yet still large enough to offer initial resistance against external communist aggression. French officials, arguing that a military establishment of this size would be "provocative" to the communists, suggested a 15,000-man army and a gendarmerie of 3,000. US and French officials also disagreed over the size and scope of the FMM. The Americans sought "an elaborate support and maintenance operation patterned after the MAAG." The French, however, planned to maintain a simple, relatively inexpensive training organization.[38]

Bundy, General Tucker, and other US officials were unable to persuade the French to keep the Filipino technicians who had provided military support to the FAR. Employed by the Eastern Construction Company in Laos (ECCOIL), these civilian technicians were led by veterans of the

Philippine government's successful campaign against the communist-led "Huk" rebels. The company had initially received funding from the CIA to perform paramilitary and military support functions for anticommunist forces in Asia. By 1961 agency funding had been "largely terminated," according to a summary of unconventional warfare resources in Southeast Asia prepared by General Lansdale. In Paris, Bundy and his colleagues argued that the ECCOIL technicians would provide "an additional Western influence" for the new army. The French replied that the Filipinos "were not needed, would be unacceptable to Souvanna, and would provide an excuse for the introduction of [DRV] technicians."[39]

While Pentagon officials encountered resistance from the French government, their counterparts in the State Department sought to defuse an emerging diplomatic crisis in Thailand. Prime Minister Sarit, denouncing the influence of "pro-communists" in the new Souvanna government, indicated to Ambassador Young that Thailand was unwilling to sign the Geneva agreement. State Department officials feared that a Thai refusal to ratify the accord might prompt a similar reaction from the DRV, dooming the conference. In Geneva, William Sullivan observed that virtually "every signature" on the agreement was "dependent on every other signature."[40] In Vientiane, Ambassador Brown declared that Thailand's failure to sign the accord would "arouse Souvanna's suspicions of ultimate Thai intentions toward Laos." And in Washington, Harriman cabled Young that, at the very least, a refusal by Thailand would intensify communist demands for the withdrawal of US troops deployed there in May: "We may thus be faced with [the] alternatives of letting [the] Laos agreement go down the drain or withdrawing our forces [from] Thailand." Acknowledging both the obvious US choice and the communist threat to Thai security, Harriman added: "If Sarit has any sense he will not want us to withdraw at this time."[41]

Ironically, at a time when Harriman warned of the risks of removing US forces from Thailand, President Kennedy decided to make a symbolic withdrawal of troops based on a highly confidential appeal from Khrushchev. On June 18, 1962, Georgi Bolshakov, a Soviet intelligence officer operating under diplomatic cover, met with Attorney General Robert F. Kennedy at the Justice Department. The conversation was one of an ongoing series of meetings between the two men that allowed the American president and Soviet premier to communicate outside of normal diplomatic channels. In his oral history for the Kennedy Library, Robert Kennedy recalled: "I just delivered the messages verbally to my brother, and he'd act on them. I think sometimes he'd tell the State Department—and sometimes he didn't."[42]

At the request of McGeorge Bundy, who disliked personal diplomacy uninformed by government expertise, Robert Kennedy subsequently summarized in writing his meeting with Bolshakov. The Soviet intelligence officer told Kennedy, "Khrushchev personally would be most appreciative if the American Government would pull its troops out of Thailand. He said he understood that the reason the troops had been sent in initially was because of the trouble in Laos and now that that had been settled, it certainly would be a great step toward peace in that area of the world if the troops that had been sent into Thailand were withdrawn." Kennedy replied that he "would take the matter up with the President."[43]

Robert Kennedy delivered his brother's reply to Bolshakov the next day, June 19. "Within ten days we would start to withdraw the troops from Thailand," said Kennedy. Bolshakov asked "if that meant all the troops would be taken out." Robert Kennedy temporized, citing the need for consultation with US allies. He told Bolshakov that he would "keep him advised" on the matter. In his report of the conversation, Kennedy wrote: "I did not make a commitment that they all would be withdrawn although it was clear this was what Georgi was interested in."[44]

President Kennedy initially withheld Khrushchev's message and his reply to it from senior State Department and Pentagon officials. On the same day Robert Kennedy delivered his brother's answer to Bolshakov, National Security Adviser McGeorge Bundy informed Under Secretary of State Ball, then acting secretary while Rusk was in Europe, that the president "was concerned now about unwinding the Thailand thing, now that the weather was good." Bundy added that he wanted the troop withdrawal to avoid appearing as "a sudden White House decision." When Ball replied that the United States should develop a withdrawal plan, Bundy said that the president "wanted to move faster than that. He wants something that will in fact happen if we make progress within the next few weeks."[45]

A few days later White House aide Forrestal told McNamara: "The President really wants us to move the troops out of Thailand." McNamara agreed with Ball that there were many reasons for *not* withdrawing the US forces, including the potentially "disastrous" effect on the Thai government and the appearance of caving in to the PRC, which had denounced the troop deployment. Rusk was perplexed by Kennedy's decision. In an "eyes only" cable to Ball, he wrote that he lacked information on the "full reasoning" behind the proposed withdrawal but requested an immediate briefing upon his return to the United States.[46]

On June 26, one week after his reply to Bolshakov, President Kennedy informed the national security bureaucracy of his decision to withdraw "some portion" of the US combat troops out of Thailand. The number "would be a token affair, amounting to 1,000 of the 3,000 Marines." With an agreement in Geneva still unsigned, Kennedy apparently sought to strike a balance between encouraging Soviet cooperation in Geneva and maintaining a credible threat of US intervention in Laos should the ceasefire break down. According to an administration explanation to the Pentagon, the troop withdrawal was intended "to make it easier for [the Soviets] to carry out their part of the bargain in regard to the Laos settlement."[47]

The initial Thai reaction to the partial withdrawal of the US Marines was one of resignation. "We have no choice," said Sarit, when informed of the US decision by Ambassador Young. "We have jumped into [the] pool with you and we [are] now swimming together."[48] To soften the blow of the withdrawal, the US government chose this moment to offer Sarit a logistic-support program that would provide military and economic benefits to Thailand. The program, initially proposed by McNamara after his May trip to Thailand, included improvements in the country's railroads, pipelines, and airfields. While the US government publicly stressed the economic-development impact of the initiative, a State Department cable to Young explained the program's military purpose: "[to] increase [the] readiness and ability [of] US and allied forces to act promptly and effectively in SEA should [the] need arise."[49]

When the Geneva conference reconvened on Monday, July 2, 1962, there were three relatively minor issues that remained to be resolved, none of which, in Harriman's view, was worth a breakdown in the negotiations. The first concerned the SEATO protocol that extended the alliance's protection to Laos. The PRC initially demanded the abrogation of the entire SEATO treaty. The communist powers then insisted that SEATO formally withdraw its security "umbrella" for Laos. As the conference drew to a close, they sought a specific declaration in the Geneva agreement renouncing SEATO's protection. The US delegation, which had resisted these demands, preferred a more general statement that Laos would not recognize the protection of any alliance. Knowing that Souvanna and the communists would likely not accept this lack of specificity, Harriman sought and received advance authorization to accept language along the following lines: "Laos will not recognize the protection of any military alliance or coalition including SEATO."[50]

The second unresolved issue was ICC supervision of the demobilization and integration of the three factions' armies. The United States had long sought such supervision, which would theoretically ensure that the Pathet Lao demobilized. The communists had claimed that ICC oversight in this matter was an infringement of Lao sovereignty. Souvanna, too, was convinced that the integration of the armies was an internal affair of the new government. The US fallback position was to include a statement in the Geneva agreement calling for the demobilization and integration of the armies. Uncertain whether or not Souvanna would agree to such a declaration, Harriman requested and received authority "to drop the issue if it appears that negotiations will break down on this point."[51]

The third area of disagreement in Geneva was the continued presence of foreign civilians who performed military-support functions. The US government wanted to retain the services of Filipino ECCOIL technicians, whose work for the FAR was valued highly by the Pentagon and CIA. French and British officials, however, supported the prohibition of foreign civilian technicians in Laos. Allowing the Filipinos to remain, the Europeans reasoned, would likely encourage the introduction of similar communist technicians. Harriman, who recommended that the United States concede on this issue, expressed the hope that the French Military Mission would "assume as many of the functions performed by the Filipinos as possible."[52]

Well on his way to resolving outstanding disagreements with adversaries and allies of the United States, Harriman still had unfinished business with the State Department. On July 6 department officials returned to a question that had troubled them in the fall of 1961: ICC independence in initiating investigations of alleged violations of the Geneva agreement. On the one hand, the accord explicitly declared that such investigations required the "concurrence" of the Lao government. On the other hand, the US delegation in Geneva had concluded that the Lao government's signature on the agreement constituted a one-time blanket approval for any investigations sought by the ICC. Department officials wondered—particularly in light of the new government's commitment to the unanimity principle—whether Souvanna shared the US understanding. Unless Harriman thought it "unnecessary or inadvisable," department officials suggested that the US delegation, in concert with the French and British, discuss the subject with the Lao in Geneva.[53]

Harriman, eager to avoid a potentially divisive issue and to conclude the talks promptly, responded that he had "no reason to doubt" the Lao government's shared understanding of the "concurrence" language in the agreement. He noted that all three Lao factions had participated fully in the conference negotiations, and none had objected to the US interpretation.[54] He further referred to his 1961 talks with Souvanna, who said that the ICC would have "his fullest support and cooperation" and that Lao approval for its "investigations would be pro-forma." Exercising his discretion and authority, Harriman declared to the department: "Do not believe it would either be useful or desirable [to] raise this matter again."[55]

Harriman, who considered the commission's terms of reference an improvement over the 1954 accord, warned Rusk against placing "excessive emphasis on [the] ICC as an 'enforcement instrument'" when he discussed the Geneva agreement with the Senate Foreign Relations Committee. (The accord was an executive agreement, not a treaty, which would require ratification by the entire Senate.) India, the chair of the ICC, had not played a forceful role in the past and would likely favor paralyzing unanimity in the commission's work. And Souvanna, despite his pledge to cooperate with the ICC, would undoubtedly have to consider the views of his deputy prime ministers when requesting action by the commission. The "primary responsibility" for communist compliance with the accords, Harriman wrote, "will rest upon obligations undertaken by [the] Soviets."[56]

Harriman had correctly concluded that the Soviet Union shared the US interest in reducing East-West tensions, particularly in a country of such limited strategic importance to either superpower. He had, however, an incomplete understanding of the differing views of Laos among the communist states and the limits of Soviet control over its allies. The Soviet

Union and China, while attempting to maintain an appearance of unity at Geneva, had different conference goals. On the one hand, the Soviets pursued a neutral solution "to eliminate the danger of a global conflict" with the United States. On the other hand, the Chinese "wanted a friendly country on their borders" and "did not regard neutralization as a permanent solution to the Laotian problem."[57]

By the end of the Geneva conference, "friction" between the Soviets and Chinese was "clarion clear" to William Sullivan. As early as August 1961, US officials in Geneva had reported differences between Chinese and Soviet officials, including a "sharp argument" in the delegates' lounge.[58] An indication of the strained relationship between Soviet and Chinese delegates emerged after the plenary session of January 23, 1962, which was notable for a pointed exchange between PRC vice minister of foreign affairs Chang Han-fu and Sullivan. Chang denounced the United States, calling reports of US pressure on Phoumi "a deliberately concocted fairy tale" and dismissing as "absurd" the US proposal for ICC supervision of the integration of the three factions' armies. Sullivan's response included the suggestion that Chang should "tell your leaders that despite their desires and despite their dogma, the United States and the Soviet Union have no intention of fighting a war, on your behalf in Laos. What we intend to do is practice peaceful coexistence there."[59]

Pushkin, exercising his prerogative as cochair, interrupted the order of speakers, stating categorically to Sullivan that Soviet and Chinese views on Laos were "absolutely identical." Any "speculative attempt" by the United States to divide the two countries "was destined to failure," he said. Yet after the plenary session, Pushkin privately told Sullivan that public references by US delegates to Sino-Soviet disagreements "only complicated matters." Speaking "as a friend," Pushkin urged Sullivan to refrain from commenting on any differences between the two communist nations. Years after the conference, Sullivan observed that the divergent Soviet and Chinese perspectives at Geneva undercut "our basic premise, that the Soviets were able to control and to monitor the agreements after the agreements had been made."[60]

A common US misconception was that the Soviet Union and/or China directed Hanoi's foreign policy. Although the DRV depended on economic and military support from both countries, the Vietnamese communists "were remarkably in control of their own decision making," according to historian Ang Cheng Guan. For example, Hanoi's 1959 decision to escalate the struggle against the Diem government was made without the concurrence of Moscow or Beijing.[61] In fact, the independence of DRV policy led to conflict with China. The two countries had a common interest in keeping the United States out of Indochina but differing visions of the region's future. Chinese leaders were "jealous of Hanoi's special ties with the Pathet Lao" and "apprehensive about the Vietnamese tendency to establish hegemony over Laos," according to Qiang Zhai. The competition for influence with the Pathet Lao "constituted one of the reasons for the eventual breakdown of Beijing-Hanoi cooperation."[62]

On Sunday, July 22, 1962, Dean Rusk and Averell Harriman met with Souvanna at the Laotian delegation's villa in Geneva. With the exception of the signing ceremony the next day, the business of the conference had been concluded. Rusk's courtesy call was a prelude to more substantive discussions with the prime minister in Washington the following week. A major goal of the talks in Geneva and Washington was restoring Souvanna's "shaken confidence" in the US government.[63] Rusk, emphasizing the Kennedy administration's "sympathy and support" for Lao neutrality and its determination to work for successful implementation of the agreement, admitted to Souvanna that such statements might be viewed with "a certain skepticism." The Lao prime minister, who bitterly resented the Eisenhower administration's covert efforts to undermine his leadership and to support his conservative enemies, told Rusk of his "complete confidence" both in the Kennedy administration and in the many assurances he had received from Harriman.[64]

Souvanna tried to persuade Rusk and Harriman of his commitment to neutrality, declaring that "he had no intention of presiding over the abandonment of Laos to communism." A less reassuring comment by Souvanna was his uncritical acceptance of a pledge by DRV prime minister Pham Van Dong to "do everything possible to avoid creating internal or external difficulties for the new Royal Lao Government."[65] Souvanna had previously mentioned his conversation with the DRV premier to Harriman, who said that the US government "could hardly be expected to believe Pham Van Dong since he was interfering in South Viet-Nam."[66]

Earlier on July 22, Harriman had argued about Vietnam with DRV foreign minister Ung Van Khiem, a guerrilla leader during the French-

Viet Minh War and a member of the central committee of the Vietnamese Workers' Party. The US government did not recognize North Vietnam, and Harriman's only direct exposure to DRV officials had occurred during official conference sessions and chance encounters at receptions attended by all delegations. A Burmese diplomat helped arrange "a discreet private meeting" between Harriman and Ung in a suite at the Hotel Suisse. With William Sullivan serving as the English-French translator, Harriman and Ung had a relatively cordial conversation about Laos. When Ung observed through his Vietnamese-French translator that the success of the Geneva accords "depended primarily on the United States," Harriman replied: "This was a remarkable coincidence since our Government felt that the success of these agreements depended primarily on the actions of the North Vietnamese."[67]

The tone of the conversation took a more combative turn when the two diplomats discussed Vietnam. Ung said, "The Vietnamese people strongly resented American intervention." The United States, he charged, had undermined the 1954 Geneva agreement on Indochina, preventing reunification of Vietnam "either by federation or elections." US intervention had "grown worse" in recent years, and "Americans were mercilessly killing Vietnamese citizens." Ung said he could not understand how President Kennedy could support a policy of neutrality in Laos and a "policy of military intervention in Vietnam."[68]

Harriman replied in equally uncompromising terms, declaring that "the guerrilla activity and the killing in South Vietnam were directed from the North, and that the guerrillas were led, trained and supplied by the North." President Kennedy, Harriman said, had sent additional forces to help the South Vietnamese "defend themselves against this aggression from the North." The two diplomats continued to exchange charges and countercharges until Harriman declared that further argument would not be "useful." He concluded his remarks by returning to the topic of Laos, observing that the United States and North Vietnam had agreed "to carry out scrupulously all the provisions of the Geneva Agreements." Although neither the United States nor the DRV had any intention of "scrupulously" honoring the accords, Ung concurred with Harriman's statement on Laos and urged him to remember the DRV's objections to "American military intervention in Vietnam."[69]

There was an unbridgeable gap between the DRV's commitment to the reunification of Vietnam and the US goal of preserving an independent, noncommunist South Vietnam. Any political proposal acceptable to one side would have been viewed as surrender by the other. On a number of occasions, Harriman had discussed with Pushkin the possibility of "reaching an understanding which would restore peace between North and South Vietnam." Yet the talks always foundered on their differing perspectives on the conflict, with Harriman denouncing "interference from the North" and Pushkin characterizing Diem as "opposed by the people [of South Vietnam]" and "ruling by terror."[70]

In April 1962 Harriman told Kennedy that he opposed "a neutral solution" in South Vietnam. The president, who said he was eager to reduce the US involvement in South Vietnam at "any favorable moment," did not disagree.[71] In Laos, a more-or-less stable neutral government seemed a hopeful possibility and a reasonable gamble. In South Vietnam, any neutral solution would likely be a transitional step to a reunified Vietnam under communist control. Such an outcome was unacceptable to Kennedy, who viewed the global ideological struggle with communism as a zero-sum game, measured in countries "won" and "lost." Many years after the Vietnam War, McGeorge Bundy described, but no longer defended, the cold war "state of mind," that "every battle lost diminishes you . . . [and] hurts you everywhere."[72]

On July 23, 1962, in the spacious council chamber of the Palais des Nations, the European headquarters of the United Nations, representatives of fourteen nations signed the "Declaration on the Neutrality of Laos" and a protocol for monitoring compliance with that declaration. The Geneva agreement's most reluctant signatories were Thailand and South Vietnam. A high-level Thai legal committee had found the accord "poorly drafted, full of loopholes and dangerous." South Vietnamese president Ngo Dinh Diem feared not only the inability of the new Lao government to control infiltration but also a gradual move by the United States and France to promote a neutral solution in his country. After considerable arm-twisting by American diplomats in Bangkok and Saigon, the two balky allies agreed to sign the accord. Thai foreign minister Thanat, "taciturn" and "depressed," according to Ambassador Young, said: "We will continue to be good boys for you."[73]

President Kennedy, who appreciated Harriman's "great energy and

skill" in securing the agreement, authorized him to join Rusk in signing the accords on behalf of the United States. "I send my very warmest
thanks to you personally for all that you have done in these difficult and
delicate negotiations," Kennedy wrote to Harriman. "I am deeply grateful for this outstanding service." Rusk's own congratulatory telegram to
Harriman was hedged with a note of skepticism: "I hope events will permit it to be said later this proved to be one of your greatest contributions
to your country."[74]

Rusk's doubts about the accords proved to be well founded. In the
initial weeks and months after the Geneva conference, the following provisions were either violated, ignored, or disputed by one or more of the
agreement's signatories:

- The withdrawal from Laos of all foreign troops and military
  personnel
- The withdrawal from Laos of foreign troops and military personnel
  only through designated withdrawal points
- No arms introduced into Laos except those requested by the RLG
- No direct or indirect foreign interference in the internal affairs of
  Laos
- No use of Laotian territory to interfere in the internal affairs of
  other countries
- Observance of the agreement supervised by the Soviet Union and
  the United Kingdom
- The ICC, with the concurrence of the RLG, to supervise and con-
  trol the ceasefire
- The initiation and carrying out of ICC investigations to be decided
  by a majority vote of the commission

In the years following the Geneva conference, Harriman frequently
observed that the North Vietnamese "broke the '62 agreements before the
ink was dry." The statement was an accurate but far from complete summary of the violations and weaknesses of the agreement. The territorial
integrity of Laos "was violated with impunity by both North Vietnam
and the United States, in the name of revolution or freedom, neither of
which had much meaning for the great majority of the Lao people," wrote
historian Martin Stuart-Fox. "What was portrayed by opposing sides as a

heroic struggle against imperialism or communism was a drawn-out misery both for those directly involved, and for those whose only escape was to become refugees."[75]

Harriman and others reached the questionable conclusion that the 1962 Geneva agreement was a "good, bad deal."[76] On the one hand, the weakness of the US negotiating position throughout the conference might justify such a judgment. Moreover, the immediate results of the agreement—an end to overt hostilities and the establishment of a nominally neutral government in Vientiane—support the notion of a "good, bad deal." On the other hand, there seems a stronger case for concluding that the Geneva agreement was, in fact, simply a bad deal. The lack of compliance with the accords led to "secret" warfare in Laos that was far more destructive than the pre-Geneva fighting. And rather than buying time for successfully defeating the insurgency in South Vietnam, as Kennedy hoped, the failed agreement and the de facto partition of Laos facilitated infiltration from North to South Vietnam.

Chapter 8

We Do Not Have
the Power of Decision

Wearing an elegant, lightly colored suit, Prince Souvanna Phouma carried a homburg, a pair of gray gloves, and a gold-tipped umbrella when he stepped out of a USAF plane at Washington National Airport on Thursday, July 26, 1962. Dean Rusk shook his hand and welcomed him to the United States at a brief ceremony at the airport's Military Air Transportation Service terminal. Souvanna, who understood English but spoke it reluctantly, addressed an audience of US officials, foreign diplomats, and reporters in flawless, unaccented French: "I am looking forward to discussing with President Kennedy the question of American help for my country."[1]

At a meeting at the State Department the next day, Rusk and Souvanna resumed the talks they had started in Geneva. After reviewing various ways of providing foreign aid to Laos, Rusk raised a topic that he characterized as "sensitive": the Geneva requirement to withdraw all foreign troops from the kingdom. He noted that the "relatively few" US military advisers were easily identified. But there were several thousand North Vietnamese soldiers, and they appeared "similar to the Lao people." How would it be possible, Rusk asked, to assure "the world that foreign military personnel did in fact leave Laos?"[2]

Souvanna reminded Rusk that they had already discussed this question in Geneva. The prime minister reiterated that his own concerns about the intentions of the North Vietnamese had prompted his June visit to Hanoi. Prime Minister Pham Van Dong had said that all DRV troops would leave Laos by the Geneva deadline and that he would do "nothing to create difficulties for Souvanna within or outside of Laos." Souvanna tried to dispel Rusk's doubts by observing that any North Vietnamese troops who remained in Laos would need food and supplies from villages in the countryside. Westerners might not be able to distinguish the Vietnamese from the various peoples of Laos, Souvanna said, but the villagers could easily recognize their traditional enemy: "Therefore, he was not worried."[3]

Souvanna may not have been concerned about DRV compliance with the Geneva agreement, but US officials were. According to the minutes of a meeting at the Pentagon, McNamara talked to Souvanna about the accords' prohibition against using Lao territory to interfere in the affairs of other countries. "Our particular concern," said McNamara, "was that infiltration from North Vietnam into South Vietnam cease." Souvanna replied that he planned to follow closely the work of the ICC. Without explaining how he would prevent infiltration through Laos, Souvanna said that "he would be responsible for the RLG's fulfillment of its obligations."[4]

At a meeting with DCI McCone and Harriman, Souvanna continued his efforts to allay his hosts' fears about DRV troops in Laos. Once again referring to his visit to Hanoi, Souvanna agreed that the North Vietnamese should leave the kingdom but dismissed their continued presence as "no great problem." He added: "All Lao villagers hated the North Vietnamese. They would keep him informed if the North Vietnamese remained." An unnamed agency note taker observed that Souvanna "did not explain how [the villagers] would communicate with him, and what he would do if North Vietnamese promises were broken."[5]

McCone and his agency colleagues found Souvanna's vague comments about the North Vietnamese in Laos "unsatisfactory." More acceptable to CIA officials was the discussion of the Hmong. Souvanna, who was not informed of US plans to maintain the Hmong guerrilla army "intact with arms hidden" after Geneva, told McCone and Harriman that the United States could continue to air drop rice and nonmilitary supplies to the tribal people. Souvanna naively observed that the establishment of inspection teams, composed of representatives of each Lao political faction, would both prevent the delivery of arms to the Hmong and forestall NLHS complaints about US relief flights. He also gratefully accepted McCone's offer to support the neutralist party's newspaper and to receive regular intelligence briefings. According to notes of the conversation, agency officials believed they had "diminished Souvanna's distrust of the CIA and contributed to his confidence in the intentions of the U.S. Government."[6]

Souvanna met with President Kennedy in the Oval Office at 11:30 A.M. on July 27. Kennedy, sitting in his cushioned rocking chair, said that he was eager to hear how the US government might make the Geneva agreement a success and might assist the prime minister in his work. Dissociating from the Lao policy of his predecessor, Kennedy said, "It was too bad that the United States and other Governments had not supported this policy of neutrality more actively during the late 1950's." He added: "From the beginning his administration had pursued the goal of a neutral and independent Laos." Kennedy's artfully worded expression of support omitted the fact that his decision to back Souvanna as prime minister had been somewhat dilatory.[7]

The president said that his administration and US prestige were committed to the prime minister, to his coalition government, and to his policy of neutrality. When questioning Souvanna about his plans for implementing the Geneva agreement, Kennedy remarked that it would be "a very serious situation" if the accord resulted in "greater infiltration" into South Vietnam rather than "the closing of the corridor" along the border. Souvanna said that he did not think the DRV would use the mountain trails from his country into South Vietnam "since it would be easy to control" such infiltration. The president, after mentioning his intention to withdraw US military advisers from Laos, asked whether there might be "any problem" with the withdrawal of DRV troops. Souvanna replied with his unpersuasive account of his trip to North Vietnam and the promises he had received from Pham Van Dong.[8]

When Kennedy asked how the US government might help Laos in the coming months, Souvanna replied that he intended to make his economic requests through the normal channels in Vientiane. Turning to political matters, Souvanna said that he would be "very happy" if the US government would restrain Thailand "from interference in Lao internal affairs."[9] He blamed Thai rulers for the 1954 assassination of Lao defense minister Kou Voravong, who favored a policy of reconciliation with the Pathet Lao insurgents. And the current Thai prime minister, Marshal Sarit, had helped overthrow Souvanna in 1960 by blocking imports of oil, rice, and other commodities into Laos and by providing critical military and financial assistance to Phoumi. To some US officials, Souvanna seemed "obsessed with his dislike of Sarit."[10] Kennedy, after a pro forma affirmation of the importance of noninterference in another country's affairs, told Souvanna that the US government planned to work closely with both him and Sarit to promote stability in the region.

The meeting in the Oval Office was followed by a luncheon at the White House, with Souvanna as the guest of honor. In a gracious toast, President Kennedy observed that the prime minister and the Lao people likely shared a desire to manage their "own destiny without quite so much interest and attention from so many parts of the world." Fortunately or unfortunately, said Kennedy, Laos and the United States "have been caught up in the stage of history," and the agreement signed in Geneva had implications that extended beyond the Lao borders. "If the Accord at Geneva should turn out to be merely paper," said Kennedy, "then, of course, relations all over the world would become more difficult and the belief in negotiations would be subjected to serious attack."[11]

Souvanna Phouma's visit to Washington was "judged successful" by most US officials. The Kennedy administration had apparently achieved "a measure of mutual trust" with Souvanna and established a foundation for successful collaboration in Laos. Less encouraging was Souvanna's "patently acrimonious attitude" toward Thailand, indicating that Thai-Lao relations would not improve in the near future. Another US concern was the emphasis the Lao prime minister placed on the promises of Pham Van Dong. To William Sullivan, Souvanna's frequent references to them seemed "perhaps a little overdone."[12]

During his visit to Washington, Souvanna had several conversations with Kennedy's advisers about reforming the US economic aid program. He said that he did not want "the country to be flooded with dollars," a reference to the system of cash grants that had financed US military assistance to Laos. Souvanna urged the Americans to support specific economic and social projects that improved living standards for Laotians—for example, the construction of schools, hospitals, and hydroelectric power stations. It was important, he said, that foreign aid be "very concrete so that people could 'see' it."[13]

Kennedy administration officials agreed that US economic aid to Laos was unsatisfactory. Per capita American assistance to the kingdom was about twenty dollars, the highest rate for any country in the world. The US government provided support for health, education, and other development and relief projects in rural villages, but the vast majority of

American economic aid financed the pay of the FAR, which had some seventy-eight thousand regular and irregular forces.[14] (The cost of providing military equipment to the FAR and sponsoring covert paramilitary operations was an additional US expense.)

US economic aid to Laos did not merely provide a low return on investment; the assistance had been counterproductive. Because cash played a small role in a country where 85 percent of the population engaged in subsistence agriculture and used small food surpluses to barter for daily essentials, the US government sought to prevent its financial aid from causing severe inflation in the monetized sector of the economy. To reduce the risk of inflation, dollars were provided to the RLG government, which then sold them to Lao importers for kip, the local currency. In theory, the importation of consumer goods and other commodities would "soak up" the increased purchasing power created by US assistance and raise living standards in the country. Yet as Michael Forrestal observed to President Kennedy, "most of the imports purchased by our aid have been concentrated in the hands of relatively few people, and relatively little has gotten out into the country where it might have done some good."[15] Stripped of bureaucratic euphemism, Forrestal's message to the president was that US economic aid basically financed the importation of luxury goods for urban elites.

There were other problems with cash grants that restricted neither the commodities imported nor their country of origin. In a telegram to the US mission in Vientiane, officials from the State Department and the Agency for International Development (AID) cited "two important domestic considerations" for reforming economic assistance to the kingdom. The first was the sensitivity of Congress and public opinion to US support for a neutral, rather than anticommunist, government. Any transfer of dollars to the Soviet Union or other communist countries for imports "could badly damage [the] reputation and acceptability of AID." The second concern was the US balance of payments: "Unencumbered cash grants, with maximum exposure to a dollar drain, must be strongly discouraged."[16]

The president had a particular interest in France and the United Kingdom providing more economic assistance to Laos. At an August 15, 1962, meeting at the White House, Kennedy observed that the United States "was the only major supplier of external resources" to the kingdom. (At that time, US financial aid constituted 85 percent of total RLG revenues.)[17] He acknowledged that Ngo Dinh Diem's anticommunist government in South Vietnam was "much more" of a US responsibility but declared that the British and the French had "much more" of an obligation to support Souvanna's coalition government. Commenting on the two allies, who had long advocated a neutral solution in Laos, Kennedy said: "Souvanna is their protégé."[18]

Despite his concerns about the cost of US aid to Laos, the president told his advisers that he did not want to be "pound[-foolish], penny-wise." Referring to his administration's gamble on Souvanna's government, Kennedy said: "We've got so much to lose if that thing goes sour." Until the day when communist compliance with the Geneva agreement seemed likely, the US government had, in Harriman's words, "certain interests in maintaining Phoumi's force." To ensure the survival of the kingdom's only anticommunist force, the troubling cash grants that paid for Phoumi's army were an unavoidable necessity for the immediate future. "We don't want to press him too hard until we see a clearer pattern," said Kennedy. "The next six months will be critical."[19]

To help gather intelligence on North Vietnamese compliance with the Geneva agreement, the US Air Force flew high- and low-level reconnaissance missions that Souvanna neither requested nor approved. Between July 23 and November 6, 1962, an "average of three reconnaissance flights daily passed over Laos." The vast majority were high-altitude flights "from Thailand *en route* to missions in South Vietnam," which posed little risk to the aircraft.[20] Missions flown at lower altitudes were another matter. On August 14, 1962, a supersonic F-101 Voodoo fighter, modified for photo reconnaissance, was approximately eight thousand feet above the Plaine des Jarres when hit by Pathet Lao antiaircraft fire. The aircraft's right forward access door was blown off, but the uninjured pilot managed to return to Don Muang Air Base near Bangkok and make a successful emergency landing.[21]

The next day the commanders of the Pathet Lao and the neutralists, generals Singkapo Sikhotchounamaly and Kong Le, respectively, displayed a one-yard-square fragment from the aircraft to Donald Hopson, the new UK ambassador, who was visiting the Plaine des Jarres. When he returned to Vientiane, Hopson informed Leonard Unger, the new American ambassador, that the fragment had a partial USAF insignia on it and a marking that identified the model of the jet. In his report to the State Department, Unger acknowledged that he lacked a "complete picture" of the intelligence operation, but he reminded his superiors that "unauthorized US military flights in Laos" would raise serious questions about the sincerity of the Kennedy administration's commitment to the Geneva accords. Unger acknowledged the importance of gathering intelligence on North Vietnamese troop withdrawals but urged the US government to "discontinue this type of photo reconnaissance flight forthwith."[22]

Unger, then forty-four, was a highly regarded Foreign Service officer and one of the youngest US ambassadors. A Harvard graduate, he began his diplomatic career as an economic officer for Southern European affairs. In addition to serving abroad and at State Department headquarters, he attended the National War College, an institution designed to prepare a select group of military and civilian officials for senior national security positions. As deputy chief of mission in Bangkok from 1958 to 1962, according to a biographic summary prepared for Kennedy, Unger "acquired the deep knowledge and understanding of the Lao situation which ultimately led to his designation as Ambassador to Laos."[23]

Unger was convinced that the Plaine des Jarres incident would raise "acute doubts" in Souvanna's mind about US willingness to work with him and to abandon "covert alternative lines of action." The ambassador, who thought that Souvanna was taking a "truly neutral position" in Lao affairs, requested authorization from the State Department to approach the prime minister on an "informal basis" with the following message: the plane in the August 14 incident was conducting an "observation" mission similar to those requested by the previous Lao government to determine movements of hostile foreign forces. Now that a new government was in power, the incident highlighted the importance of consulting with Souvanna "in all frankness." Unger proposed telling Souvanna that there would be no more US overflights of Laos "without securing RLG permission."[24]

Harriman recommended that the United States stop "all covert flights over Laos." The only permissible flights should be overt relief missions for the Hmong, which had been discussed with Souvanna. Harriman did not, however, agree with Unger's proposed approach to the prime minister. Instead, the State Department instructed the ambassador to dissemble by taking advantage of an inaccurate public report that a US plane had been *shot down* on August 14. If Souvanna asked about the incident, Unger should say that no US aircraft or personnel were missing; therefore, reports that a US plane was shot down were "patently inaccurate." If, as was likely, Souvanna saw through this ruse, the ambassador was instructed to say, "without regard to what has happened in the past," that "no military reconnaissance flights" would be authorized going forward. In an FYI message to Unger, department officials wrote of their "hope" that this evasive explanation "might permit us to weather this particular incident."[25]

On August 16, the same day as the instruction to Unger, the State Department responded to press inquiries about the Plaine des Jarres incident with replies that were narrowly accurate yet wholly misleading. "I have no information about the reported downing of an American plane over Laos," a State Department public affairs official replied to one question. "No US plane is missing in the area." When asked if the US government had "any clue as to what might be involved here," the official replied: "I do not."[26]

Reporters in Washington may have been buying the State Department line, but foreign diplomats, RLG ministers, and ICC officials in Vientiane were not. Ambassador Hopson, who had seen the plane fragment, was "not persuaded" by Unger's insistence that the Plaine des Jarres incident was some sort of "cooked up story." Unger told Canadian ICC commissioner Paul Bridle that the shoot-down report "was just some more propaganda" and questioned the need for an ICC investigation. Souvanna, who was "distressed" by the whole affair, did not press Unger about the nationality of the plane. "We must once and for all put [an] end to [the] mistrust this kind of incident creates," the prime minister said. Unger, undoubtedly relieved, reported to Washington that Souvanna "did not plan [to] make any protest [about] this matter."[27]

Souvanna Phouma's coalition government began to fall apart almost immediately. At an August 17 meeting of the RLG cabinet, a dispute arose over the Geneva provision calling for ICC inspection teams "at all points of withdrawal from Laos." The deadline for establishing these checkpoints was August 22. The NLHS ministers claimed there were no foreign soldiers to be evacuated from the territory they controlled. It was, therefore, unnecessary to propose withdrawal locations in Pathet Lao zones. Only FAR-occupied areas required checkpoints to monitor the withdrawal of American troops.[28]

Phoumi objected to the proposal, charging that "many" North Vietnamese, Chinese, and Soviet forces were present in NLHS- and neutralist-controlled territory. When Souvanna suggested an investigation into this allegation, he received support from the conservative ministers and the right-leaning neutralists in his cabinet. Souphanouvong, however, disagreed. An investigation, he insisted, was unnecessary because there were "no foreign troops" in Pathet Lao areas. Phoumi, threatening to withdraw from the government if the NLHS ministers did not "demonstrate good faith," said: "It would be better if the three groups separated and began fighting as before."[29]

Souphanouvong's statement on ICC checkpoints shocked State Department officials, who thought it "border[ed] on the fantastic." Although the communists had publicly denied the presence of North Vietnamese troops in Laos, US intelligence officials estimated their number at approximately nine thousand.[30] With the Geneva deadline for establishing inspection locations only four days away, the State Department cabled Ambassador Unger: "We find it incomprehensible that at the eleventh hour no check points have been determined and none [are] intended" for North Vietnamese forces.[31]

Unger, whose primary responsibility as ambassador was to make the Geneva agreement work, was instructed by the State Department to impress upon Souvanna and Phoumi the "gravity" of an RLG "failure" to establish a credible group of withdrawal points for foreign forces. The department suggested that Unger point out some of the obvious implications of the cabinet dispute: if there were no North Vietnamese forces in Pathet Lao–controlled areas, Souphanouvong and the other NLHS ministers should welcome a thorough ICC inspection. Conversely, NLHS objections to such an inspection would likely persuade world opinion that communist troops were, in fact, present in the Pathet Lao territories: "[The] absurdity of ICC supervision and control being limited to Phoumi-held areas should be recognized by all parties."[32]

On August 19 Unger informed Souvanna that the US government was "deeply concerned" by the dispute over checkpoints and the threat it posed to the Geneva agreement. Souvanna said that he shared the US con-

cerns, but he believed "a way would be found out of [the] present impasse."
He was meeting with Souphanouvong that same day, and he expected that
they would "ultimately settle on three check points, one for each faction."
This arrangement seemed inadequate to Unger and other US officials, who
wanted at least three withdrawal locations for each faction because foreign
troops were present in the Mekong lowlands, in the panhandle, and in the
northern provinces. Unger made a particular appeal to Souvanna to press
the NLHS for a withdrawal location in Tchepone. Despite his "repeated
urgings," Unger doubted that he had persuaded Souvanna to "insist on
more than one" checkpoint for each faction.[33]

The ambassador then raised another "disturbing" matter with Souvanna: reports that the RLG intended to establish a commission that
would control ICC investigations of alleged violations of the Geneva
agreement. Despite Harriman's understanding that the ICC would receive
Souvanna's full support, the prime minister told Unger that some investigations would be unacceptable because of "considerations of sovereignty."
When Unger observed that the ICC would be stymied if the troika principle governed its work, Souvanna replied that he did not believe there
would be a problem.[34]

Harriman was "deeply disturbed" by Souvanna's ICC pronounce-
ments, characterizing them as not only "clearly at variance" with the
Geneva agreement but also "contrary to his promises." Dismissing Souvanna's sovereignty argument as "specious," Harriman declared: "[The]
basic issue of [a] Communist desire for [a] closed society is involved here."
He urged Unger to emphasize that ICC freedom of movement would
prevent the Pathet Lao from sealing off its territory and would support the prime minister's longstanding goal of Lao "unity and territorial
integrity."[35]

At a meeting with Souvanna on August 22, Unger conveyed Harriman's dismay with the NLHS effort "to upset" the Geneva agreement
and to "render powerless" the ICC. Souvanna, who said that he "heartily
agreed" with the US ambassador, pledged that he would hold out for "at
least one" checkpoint in the Pathet Lao–controlled territory. Apparently
abandoning his confidence in Pham Van Dong's promises, Souvanna
added that Hanoi was the "real obstacle" to progress and that resolution
of the cabinet crisis was unlikely without Soviet pressure on the DRV and
Souphanouvong.[36]

When the checkpoint dispute initially arose, State Department officials thought a formal protest to the Soviet Union as Geneva cochair would be premature. They did, however, instruct the American embassy in Moscow to "express orally and informally our grave concern" to the Soviet foreign ministry. In Washington, Dean Rusk "expressed concern" about the "difficulties" over withdrawal locations to Anatoly F. Dobrynin, the Soviet ambassador to the United States. Protesting Souphanouvong's lack of cooperation, Rusk stressed the Geneva agreement's importance to Khrushchev and Kennedy. "Dobrynin made no comment," according to a report of the meeting.[37]

Frederick Warner, the head of SEAD at the UK Foreign Office, was "not sanguine" about Soviet cooperation in establishing checkpoints in Pathet Lao territory. Nonetheless, he told US embassy officials in London that backing down on the issue would not serve the "best long-run interests" of the West. The dispute over implementing the Geneva agreement was probably just the "first round" of many disagreements in the months ahead, and it "would be foolish [to] give [the] communists [the] impression [that] we [would] likely cave in at every difficulty." The Foreign Office, said Warner, recommended that a formal approach to the Soviets be delayed until the new RLG revealed its intentions more clearly.[38]

On August 23—the day after the Geneva deadline for establishing withdrawal locations for foreign forces—Souvanna Phouma's cabinet decided that there would be one checkpoint for each faction: Vientiane for Phoumi, the Plaine des Jarres for Souvanna, and Nhommarath for Souphanouvong. Nhommarath, located near the center of the panhandle, almost equidistant from the DRV and Thai borders, was the only checkpoint offered by Souphanouvong. US officials, who would have preferred a checkpoint at Tchepone or some other, more significant communist strongpoint, thought that Nhommarath had "limited strategic importance."[39]

The RLG cabinet meeting affirmed that Souvanna's government "would in no way" restrict the "authority or [the] freedom of action [of the] ICC." The cabinet further agreed that RLG officials from any faction could circulate freely in all areas of Laos, a decision prompted by an earlier refusal of Souphanouvong's to allow Souvanna to visit parts of the Pathet Lao zone. In a conversation with Ambassador Unger, Souphanouvong qualified the new freedom-of-movement guarantee with an ominous-sounding observation: until the end of the rainy season, typically mid-October, "many areas will remain inaccessible."[40]

On Friday, August 24, 1962, the Joint Chiefs of Staff and senior State Department officials met at the Pentagon for one of their regular discussions of pressing national security issues. The first topic on the agenda was Laos. Averell Harriman, whose remarks that day combined hardheaded realism, wishful thinking, and bureaucratic dissembling, began his summary of recent developments by reporting that the RLG had selected three checkpoints for the withdrawal of all foreign forces. Although the US government had not yet accepted this decision as "final," Harriman implied that the views of the RLG would almost certainly prevail: "We do not have the power of decision in this matter." He added that any evidence of PAVN forces in Laos would prompt a US demand for an ICC investigation: "We have this right, and we will make use of it." According to detailed notes of the meeting, he neglected to mention that the ICC had the right to ignore US demands. The ICC was obliged to respond to requests for investigations from the RLG, the Geneva cochairs, and a majority of the commissioners, but not from the United States or other conference participants.[41]

Harriman reported "the general view" that the North Vietnamese would "fade out of sight, some leaving Laos and others remaining behind to continue subversive operations." Candid about the enforcement limitations of the ICC, Harriman said he was certain that its investigators would not be allowed to move freely through Pathet Lao–controlled northern Laos, and he admitted that North Vietnamese troops would "be able to scatter" during inspections of specific locations. "They will always have this illusive ability," he said.[42]

Reminding the chiefs and other Pentagon officials of his "direct orders from the president" for US compliance with the Geneva agreement, he said that any violations of the accords must be the result of communist rather than American actions. Should the North Vietnamese or Pathet Lao fail to honor the terms of the accord, President Kennedy would "take up the matter with Khrushchev." Harriman, who recognized the risks associated with the Souvanna solution, emphasized that the US government "must be prepared for a breakdown in the overall situation in

Laos." JCS contingency plans, he said, should be kept current to provide the president with the best possible military advice should action in the region be required.[43]

Harriman speculated that a de facto partition of Laos was a real possibility, with each faction controlling the territory it currently occupied:

> This eventuality would not be too bad for the West. However, we must insure that Laos is not used as a north-south corridor to South Viet Nam by communist forces. We want to watch for any evidence which might show that the Communists are using this route. This will test the good will and intent of the Soviets. The Soviets have said that use of this corridor will not occur. We have a clear-cut understanding with them on this point.[44]

The comments from the chiefs indicated that they were not persuaded by Harriman's presentation. General Curtis E. LeMay, chief of staff of the US Air Force, said that all of the chiefs were skeptical of communist intentions to honor the Geneva agreement. LeMay referred to Pathet Lao resistance to establishing an adequate number of checkpoints and the communist assertions of no North Vietnamese forces in Laos. General Lemnitzer insisted that the United States could not "afford to accept any restrictions" on ICC movements in Laos. "We must blow the whistle on this type of situation before it develops," said Lemnitzer. "We should not accept it."

The chiefs were particularly disturbed by the US decision to suspend unarmed, low-level photo-reconnaissance flights, which had been a key source of intelligence on antigovernment troops for more than a year. The deadline for withdrawing foreign forces from Laos was still six weeks away, and the Soviet Union continued its airlift into the country from Hanoi. Harriman, who had requested the suspension of photo-reconnaissance flights on political grounds, replied with an answer that was less than complete: "The Department of State lawyers have ruled that the reconnaissance flights are in violation of the Agreements." When Lemnitzer persisted in his objections to suspending the flights, Harriman responded that "he could not argue the matter since he was bound to a legal opinion."[45]

Just before noon on Monday, August 27, President Kennedy arrived at Walter Reed Army Hospital to present the Bronze Star for Meritorious

Service to Major Lawrence Bailey, the sole survivor of a US reconnaissance aircraft that had been shot down in Laos seventeen months earlier. The Pathet Lao had released him and four other American prisoners—Special Forces Sergeant Orville R. Ballenger, NBC news photographer Grant Wolfkill, and Air America helicopter crew members Edward Shore Jr. and John McMorrow—three weeks after the signing of the Geneva agreement. Bailey, who had broken his left arm and sustained other injuries while parachuting from the plane, was in solitary confinement for more than a year in a small, dark cell that he later described as "a place without light or life or hope." He lost some sixty pounds—or about one-third of his total body weight—while in captivity. "Kennedy was upset over my condition and the treatment I received from the Pathet Lao," Bailey recalled. Kennedy, with "anger in his voice, his eyes hard," asked: "Did they ever tell you why they treated you like they did?"

"No, sir," Bailey replied. "They did not."[46]

The following day Kennedy met with his foreign policy advisers for a review of post-Geneva developments in Laos. Rusk, who had recently returned from Ottawa, began the White House meeting by discussing his recent conversation with leaders of Canada's Department of External Affairs. He emphasized to the Canadian diplomats the importance of "meticulous conformance" to the Geneva agreement, and he encouraged the ICC to refer infractions to the Geneva cochairs, particularly in the early stages of implementation.[47] After the summary of his talks with the Canadians, Rusk turned to Roger Hilsman for on an update on the withdrawal of DRV troops in Laos.

Hilsman, who had already been asked by the White House to assess communist intentions and to explore their implications for US policy, summarized the findings of his report: there had been no significant withdrawals of North Vietnamese forces, and truck convoys continued to move between North Vietnam and Pathet Lao–controlled areas. The Soviet airlift to supply the Pathet Lao had not stopped, but the number of flights seemed to be declining. On the one hand, Hilsman characterized communist tactics "as consistent with an intention to prevent the formation of a true government of national union." On the other hand, he found no evidence "that the Communists and in particular Moscow are ready to abandon the entire coalition principle." With the deadline for withdrawal of foreign troops some six weeks away, Hilsman concluded that "a definite judgment" about communist intentions was premature.[48]

Discussing the implications of his conclusions, Hilsman mentioned the oft-discussed "fall-back position" should communist actions sabotage Souvanna's government: "a de facto partition under the umbrella of a non-functioning but still visible coalition government."[49] Rusk asked Hilsman to comment on any changes in infiltration since the signing of the Geneva agreement. The request reflected the US concern that at least some of the PAVN forces in Laos might be redeployed to South Vietnam. Hilsman replied with an analysis similar to one he had recently prepared for the secretary: infiltration from North Vietnam into South Vietnam consisted of armed cadres and key officials, rather than organized military units. The infiltrators were well-trained native southerners who had gone north after the 1954 Geneva agreement and who were returning home to provide leadership for an insurgency that relied mainly on the local population for recruits and supplies. In Laos, however, the Vietnamese communists were mostly Tonkinese—that is, native northerners. In Hilsman's view, they were unlikely candidates for deployment to South Vietnam, if for no other reason than their capture would undermine communist propaganda that the insurgency was an exclusively southern affair.[50]

According to the minutes of the meeting, Ray S. Cline, the CIA deputy director responsible for the agency's analytical branch, spoke next, observing that US intelligence agencies had "a number of intercepted messages indicating that the [North Vietnamese] and Pathet Lao are proposing minimum compliance with the Geneva Accords."[51] Cline also mentioned that North Vietnamese and Pathet Lao forces were continuing to fight with the Hmong. When Kennedy asked about US efforts to supply the tribal group, Harriman—who exercised policy control over the CIA's Hmong operation—replied that the US government had permission from Souvanna to provide the Hmong with food and nonmilitary supplies. The next comment, redacted in the declassified minutes of the meeting, likely referred to Harriman's recent authorization of a covert airdrop of ammunition to Hmong guerrillas in the province of Sam Neua. According to Ahern's history of the agency's "surrogate warfare" in Laos, Harriman justified this violation of the Geneva agreement by noting that the Hmong were "clearly being attacked illegally by enemy forces."[52]

With the partition of Laos a looming possibility, Kennedy asked his advisers about current efforts to maintain Phoumi's strength. Harriman replied that the US government continued to pay his troops through the RLG, while "pushing" the Lao general to demobilize less effective elements of his army. Turning to American support for Souvanna, Harriman said that the US government officials were talking to him "about helping his political party."[53] Although additional elaboration of Harriman's comment has been redacted from the minutes of the meeting, Souvanna had earlier agreed to CIA support for publishing his political party's newspaper and for influencing "the youth of Laos to join his movement."[54]

After further conversation on such topics as divisions within the neutralist forces and western economic aid to Laos, President Kennedy concluded the meeting by asking how much of the US intelligence on communist violations of the Geneva agreement could be provided to the ICC. The replies from Hilsman and Cline were, in effect, some but not all. Full disclosure was precluded by the need to protect "sources and methods" for gathering covert intelligence. For example, the ability to intercept North Vietnamese communications mentioned earlier in the meeting by Cline was among the US government's most closely guarded secrets. Hilsman and Cline agreed that the United States could tell the ICC "substantially what was useful although not always in the most convincing way."[55]

General Tucker, the MAAG chief in Laos, saw no evidence that North Vietnamese forces intended to leave the kingdom. By mid-September 1962, only fifteen PAVN "technicians" had officially withdrawn, and Souphanouvong had said that there would be no further evacuations, Tucker cabled CINCPAC. "The communists have tightened security over their area to the point where few if any of our side have been able to penetrate the local 'bamboo curtain,'" he wrote. With enemy attacks continuing, particularly against Hmong outposts, the MAAG chief concluded that the communists "intended by every possible means to retain and expand their present holdings in Laos." Predicting that the North Vietnamese troops would not withdraw by the October 6 deadline, Tucker reported: MAAG Laos, "unless directed otherwise," would leave by that date.[56]

In addition to overseeing the withdrawal of American advisers serving in Laos, Tucker had been responsible for evacuation of some two hundred Thai military "volunteers" assigned to MAAG. US advisers and FAR commanders valued the Thai warriors for their fighting skill and their ability to communicate with Lao soldiers without interpreters. Souvanna, however, viewed all Thai forces in Laos as a violation of the kingdom's sovereignty. Ambassador Unger, who assumed that the US and Thai governments had no intention—"now or ever"—of acknowledging the presence of the Thai soldiers in Laos, feared "some revelation which would be acutely embarrassing." He requested a "black" (secret) evacuation of the Thai troops assigned to MAAG. Within a week of Unger's request, General Tucker reported that the Thai withdrawal across the Mekong River had been completed.[57]

Tucker's MAAG moved across the Mekong, too. Since August 1961 the US military had been stockpiling ammunition, construction materials, and general supplies for the FAR in the Thai towns of Tahkli, Khorat, Udorn, Ubon, and, the capital, Bangkok.[58] When it became clear that an international declaration of Laotian neutrality would be signed in Geneva, Admiral Felt proposed the establishment of a secret "non-resident MAAG Laos" with some eighty US military personnel. Its headquarters would be in Bangkok, with "an advance echelon" in Udorn, some fifty miles south of Vientiane.[59]

General Tucker remained chief of the reduced MAAG Laos but had a new title: deputy chief, Joint US Military Advisory Group, Thailand, or DEPCHJUSMAGTHAI, an acronym that was as misleading as it was ponderous. Tucker's men ostensibly served with the US military assistance program for Thailand, but their real responsibilities were providing advisory support to the FAR and working with both an expanded military attaché office in Vientiane and a new Requirements Office (RO) in the economic aid mission. The primary purpose for increasing the embassy attaché office was to strengthen a US intelligence effort weakened by the withdrawal of MAAG advisers. The RO, staffed by some thirty retired military men with experience in logistic support, was responsible for the supply of legally permissible materiel for the defense of Laos.

The evacuation of the Filipino ECCOIL technicians created a problem for US military assistance to Laos. Because the FAR was incapable of properly maintaining US-provided military equipment—which was in danger of "rapidly turning into junk," according to Tucker—the United States relied on the FMM to provide technicians.[60] The 1962 Geneva agreement permitted a "precisely limited number of French military instructors" to train the armed forces of Laos. This number was unspecified, but there were some two hundred French military personnel in Laos available for training duties.

The FMM, eager to avoid the impression of "merely picking up where [MAAG] left off," did not assume its training responsibilities with the speed and urgency desired by US officials. One barrier to effective FAR training was Phoumi's hostility toward the French for their longstanding support of Souvanna and his policy of neutrality. Ambassador Unger, concerned about French plans to send fifty-six technicians to replace the more than four hundred Filipinos, warned the State Department in September: "We have as yet no assurance that Phoumi is prepared to work with [the] French nor for that matter [that the] French once on [the] scene will be much concerned with effective maintenance [of] US [military] equipment."[61]

More broadly, US objectives in Laos were threatened by France's apparent determination to pursue an independent policy in Southeast Asia. On September 26, 1962, a report from General Gavin, then the American ambassador in Paris, confirmed that France sought to avoid identification with US and UK economic aid programs in Laos and to reduce its role as a "free world spokesman." Gavin observed that France might be seeking greater influence in Indochina, but the region was of "marginal" significance to overall French foreign policy interests. He, therefore, thought it "highly unlikely" that de Gaulle's government would assume the "financial or military obligations which we might consider the corollary of [the] privileged position it seeks."[62]

As the October deadline for withdrawing foreign troops from Laos approached, the US intelligence community concluded that some two thousand PAVN troops and technicians had secretly left but an estimated seven to eight thousand North Vietnamese troops still remained, many disguised as Pathet Lao soldiers. (Subsequent CIA assessments determined that as many as one-half of the estimated nine to ten thousand DRV forces in Laos withdrew to North Vietnam in the three months after Geneva.)[63] At a September 28 White House meeting, Ray Cline of the CIA told the president and his top national security officials: "The Communists will almost certainly seek to retain as many of their North Vietnamese forces and military advisers in Laos as they can do with safety. Souvanna will almost certainly be unable to prevent Communist use of southern Laos as a corridor for assisting the Vietcong effort into South Vietnam."[64]

The question for Kennedy was how to respond to the DRV's apparent intention to violate the Geneva agreement. One option was suspending the withdrawal of MAAG advisers from Laos. In Unger's view, such a decision could be justified as an appropriate response to DRV behavior, which would be supported by South Vietnam, Thailand, and "many quarters" of US public opinion. The disadvantage of this action was that it lacked a legal basis and would likely face objections from the ICC and Souvanna, not to mention the Soviet Union and its allies. Unger recommended that the United States complete the MAAG withdrawal, arguing that it would demonstrate Kennedy's commitment to the Geneva agreement and would permit the ICC to focus exclusively on the North Vietnamese. Public exposure of their violations, Unger hoped, would embarrass the Soviets and "force them to put [the] requisite pressure on North Viet Nam to secure [a] substantial if not total withdrawal."[65]

Although Kennedy approved the withdrawal of the remaining MAAG advisers, the diplomatic and international pressure on the Soviets sought by Unger and other officials would require persuasive evidence of the North Vietnamese presence in Laos. The embassy in Vientiane conceded that it had "no overt intelligence capability whatsoever" in areas where PAVN troops were present.[66] The US government was, however, able to collect clandestine intelligence from road-watch teams operating in Pathet Lao territory, high-altitude photo reconnaissance, and signals intelligence (SIGINT) targeting PAVN communications networks and radars.

President Kennedy asked US intelligence agencies to review ways of providing the ICC with information "without jeopardizing the integrity of intelligence collection."[67] Ambassador Unger received authorization to "sanitize"—that is, to disguise or remove information that might reveal the source of the intelligence—and to "use on the spot all but the most sensitive information about communist violations." Officials in Washington began "to sanitize on a crash basis" sensitive intelligence—for example, SIGINT and high-altitude overhead reconnaissance—for use with Souvanna, Phoumi, and the Canadian member of the ICC.[68] A typical sanitized intelligence report from Washington to Vientiane, intended for release, read: "Lao observers in the Kam Keut area, who have previously

proven reliable, have reported one battalion of North Vietnamese operating with the Pathet Lao a few miles north of Kam Keut in northern
Khamouane Province." The reference to "Lao observers" was intended
to conceal the source of the information, possibly a National Security
Agency (NSA) intercept station in Southeast Asia.[69]

To indicate to the communists that the continued presence of PAVN
troops in Laos risked a direct military confrontation with the United
States, Kennedy "approved the retention of U.S. combat forces in Thailand."[70] The US Army battle group had remained in Thailand since Kennedy's May deployment, but by late July all of the US Marines had been
withdrawn. Sarit, who acquiesced in the withdrawal of the marines, grew
increasingly disturbed by unilateral US actions in Thailand and Laos.
Ambassador Young described the mood of Thai leaders as "one of concern,
reproachfulness, disappointment, defiance, and what I can only describe
as peevishness personally taken out on me sarcastically and bitterly."[71]

On September 28 President Kennedy had a more harmonious encoun-
ter with Pote Sarasin, the Thai secretary general of SEATO, whom Forrestal characterized as "an unusually friendly Thai official and far more
restrained in his views than other Thai."[72] Kennedy asked Sarasin to tell
Sarit of his regret "that there had not been adequate time for full consultations before our Marines were withdrawn." The president added: "It
might be useful to keep the [US Army] Battle Group in Thailand for a
little while until we see what happens in Laos."[73]

The limited steps approved by Kennedy—continuing the MAAG
withdrawal, "sanitizing" clandestine intelligence for release to the ICC
and others, and keeping a small number of US combat troops in Thailand—did not include a diplomatic action recommended by a number of
State Department officials: a direct appeal to the Soviet Union to honor its
Geneva commitments. U. Alexis Johnson suggested to Harriman that the
president "ask for Khrushchev's personal assurance" that all DRV troops
would leave Laos by the Geneva deadline of October 7. Ambassador Unger
recommended that the US government "put the heat on [the] Russians,
pointing out [the] grave consequences to [the] whole neutral solution if
one of its fundamental provisions is flouted by [the DRV]." Harriman,
however, disagreed. He thought that the US government should delay
any formal approach to the Soviet Union until after the Geneva deadline,
when the combined impact of US troop withdrawals and ICC investiga-

tions into North Vietnamese violations would permit more effective diplomatic protests.[74]

Harriman also opposed "a propaganda campaign" aimed at turning world opinion against communist actions in Laos. Michael Forrestal
informed the president that Harriman wanted "to fight this out initially at
the diplomatic level and through the machinery of the Geneva Accords."
Forrestal suspected that Harriman's objection to publicly denouncing
the DRV and Soviet Union was based, in part, on a belief that such a
campaign would have "unfavorable political consequences" in the United
States, further complicating an already difficult diplomatic mission. With
the 1962 midterm elections only weeks away, publicizing communist
bad faith in Laos would inevitably raise questions about the wisdom of
US backing for the coalition government and provide ammunition for
Republican candidates who attacked Democratic irresolution in the face
of communist threats. At that time, Republicans in the US House of Representatives considered the Kennedy administration's ineffectual efforts
against Fidel Castro's Cuba "the biggest Republican asset" in the upcom-
ing election.[75]

Harriman, using a traditional Washington institution to try to influence the press, talked to reporters about Laos "on background" on October 4, 1962. The terms of such briefings allowed the news media to report
the facts and analysis provided by officials, but the information had to
be attributed to unnamed "authoritative United States sources" or some
equivalent obfuscation. Harriman was unhappy with the briefing. The
press, he complained to Donald M. Wilson, deputy director of the US
Information Agency and a former correspondent for *Time,* was inflating
the importance of the October 7 withdrawal deadline and focusing on
problems in implementing the Geneva agreement. With perhaps more
"spin" than conviction, Harriman insisted that there were dozens of other
issues "of equal importance" and "a lot of good news" in Laos: "We don't
want to blow up domestically that Oct[ober] 7 is something of importance." If the situation in Laos falls apart, Harriman said, the cause will
be the resumption of fighting, not an "infringement" of the Geneva agreement. "The real question," he said, "is Khrushchev."[76]

President-elect John F. Kennedy with President Dwight D. Eisenhower, January 19, 1961. (Abbie Rowe/John F. Kennedy Library)

Walt W. Rostow, initially appointed deputy national security adviser, was transferred to the State Department to chair the Policy Planning Council. (Robert McNeill/National Archives and Records Administration)

A Royal Lao artillery battery firing 105-mm howitzers at antigovernment forces, February 1961. (John Dominis/Time Life Pictures/Getty Images)

President Kennedy with Winthrop G. Brown, US ambassador to Laos, 1960–1962. (Abbie Rowe/John F. Kennedy Library)

(Above) Prince Boun Oum, nominal leader of the Lao right-wing faction, addressing villagers in Savannakhet Province on March 1, 1961. (J. C. Cool/National Archives and Records Administration) *(Below)* US secretary of state Dean Rusk, UK prime minister Harold Macmillan, US president John F. Kennedy, and UK foreign secretary Lord Home. (United States Information Agency/National Archives and Records Administration)

(Above) Vienna, 1961, left to right: Llewellyn E. Thompson, US ambassador to the Soviet Union; President Kennedy; Soviet premier Nikita S. Khrushchev; and Soviet foreign minister Andrei A. Gromyko. (United States Information Services/National Archives and Records Administration) *(Below)* Prince Souphanouvong, the public face of the Pathet Lao, speaking with the press in Zurich, June 19, 1961. (Keystone/Getty Images)

Phoumi Nosavan, leader of the Lao right-wing faction, meeting with Secretary of Defense Robert S. McNamara, June 1961. (Department of Defense/National Archives and Records Administration)

The Joint Chiefs of Staff, November 1961: Admiral George W. Anderson Jr., chief of naval operations; General George H. Decker, army chief of staff; General Lyman L. Lemnitzer, chairman, JCS; General Curtis E. LeMay, air force chief of staff; and General David M. Shoup, commandant of the marine corps. (Department of Defense/National Archives and Records Administration)

(Above) President Kennedy shaking hands with Allen W. Dulles, director of Central Intelligence, 1953–1961, at the swearing-in ceremony for his successor, John A. McCone, center. (Abbie Rowe/John F. Kennedy Library) *(Below)* A Soviet armored personnel carrier traveling on Route 7 in northern Laos. (Department of Defense/National Archives and Records Administration)

Secretary of State Dean Rusk and Thai foreign minister Thanat Khoman announcing the Rusk-Thanat communiqué, March 6, 1962. (Jack Lartz/National Archives and Records Administration)

Roger Hilsman, director of intelligence and research at the State Department, was subsequently named assistant secretary of state for far eastern affairs. (Herbert J. Meyle/National Archives and Records Administration)

Kenneth T. Young, US ambassador to Thailand, with Prime Minister Sarit Thanarat. (Department of State/National Archives and Records Administration)

US Marines in Bangkok debarking from the attack transport *Navarro,* May 16, 1962. (Department of Defense/National Archives and Records Administration)

(Above) W. Averell Harriman, the chief US negotiator at the Geneva conference, signing the accords on July 23, 1962. To his left are Dean Rusk and William Sullivan. (Department of State/National Archives and Records Administration) *(Below)* Prime Minister Souvanna Phouma, Dean Rusk, and Foreign Minister Quinim Pholsena on the State Department balcony, July 1962. (George Szabo/National Archives and Records Administration)

Admiral Harry D. Felt, commander in chief of US forces in the Pacific, 1958–1964. (Department of Defense/National Archives and Records Administration)

W. Averell Harriman, ambassador at large, then assistant secretary of state for far eastern affairs, was appointed under secretary of state for political affairs in April 1963. (George Szabo/National Archives and Records Administration)

One of Kong Le's neutralist forces with a submachine gun, stick grenades, and ammunition clips. (Horst Faas/AP)

(Above) Refugees from fighting on the Plaine des Jarres seeking safety in an international relief camp. (United States Information Services/National Archives and Records Administration)

(Right) Savang Vatthana, the king of Laos, leading a royal procession. (Agency for International Development/National Archives and Records Administration)

President Kennedy with his national security adviser, McGeorge Bundy.
(Abbie Rowe/John F. Kennedy Library)

(Right) Leonard S. Unger, US ambassador to Laos, 1962–1964. (Department of State/National Archives and Records Administration)

(Below) Souvanna Phouma meeting with President Kennedy, September 1963. (Abbie Rowe/John F. Kennedy Library)

(Left) Foreign Service officer William H. Sullivan was Averell Harriman's deputy at the Geneva conference and the US ambassador to Laos, 1964–1969. (Robert McNeill/ National Archives and Records Administration)

(Below) General Maxwell D. Taylor, chairman of the Joint Chiefs of Staff, and Robert McNamara reporting to Kennedy after their September 1963 trip to Vietnam. (Abbie Rowe/John F. Kennedy Library)

Chapter 9

Tenuous at Best

After a short flight from his headquarters on the Plaine des Jarres, neutralist commander General Kong Le arrived at Wattay airfield outside of Vientiane on November 5, 1962. Traveling with Prime Minister Souvanna Phouma, Kong Le had not been in Vientiane since December 1960, when General Phoumi's troops, aided by US and Thai military advisers, drove him out of the capital. Kong Le, then a twenty-six-year-old captain and the commander of the elite FAR Second BP, led his outnumbered forces in an orderly retreat that eventually ended in the small town of Khang Khay. His "surprise visit" to Vientiane in late 1962, suggested by US officials, was intended as a "symbolic and potentially important step toward neutralist-conservative reconciliation."[1]

The gesture was immediately ruined by the arrest at the airfield of four of Kong Le's officers, two of whom were members of Souvanna's staff. The arrests were made by representatives of the Directorate of National Coordination (DNC), the FAR intelligence and security organization, which Michael Forrestal called the "local gestapo." General Tucker described the DNC commander, Colonel Siho Lamphoutacoul, as "Phoumi's hatchet man." The American embassy reported that the DNC arrests "drew [an] angry, emotional response from [the] neutralists, who claimed [that] some of [the] detained group [were] seriously beaten." According to French ambassador Falaize, one officer was bound, blindfolded, gagged, and at times "held in a sack." The ostensible reason for the arrests was possession of counterfeit currency, but DNC interrogators appeared far more interested in Kong Le and his plans.[2]

For Souvanna, the arrest of neutralist officers by Phoumi's DNC was both a disturbing reminder of his earlier conflicts with the general and another frustrating example of the unwillingness of the right- and left-wing factions to support a government of national union. Three days before the DNC arrests, Souvanna had complained to Unger about "Phoumi's uncontrolled spending of [government] funds, often for dubious or even unknown purposes." (Left unsaid was Phoumi's "distaste [for] coalition government," which, Unger observed to the State Department, "he has never overcome.") Souvanna, turning to his problems with the leftists, told the American ambassador, "quite categorically," that he could no longer work with Phoumi Vongvichit, the minister of information and a member of the NLHS central committee. Souvanna said that Phoumi Vongvichit's unwillingness to accept his frequently repeated, well-reasoned arguments indicated that the NLHS minister was "not very bright." Unger, who considered Phoumi Vongvichit "quite articulate and self-possessed," replied that perhaps "his ideology and political objectives might better explain [the] impossibility of reasoning with him."[3]

Souvanna went public with his frustrations at a November 7 press conference, announcing his intention to resign if he did not receive better cooperation from his right- and left-wing ministers. "Human patience has its limits," he said. Later that same day, at a diplomatic reception, Souvanna told the Soviet, UK, and US ambassadors of "his complete discouragement, his exhaustion, and his decision to resign if [the] present impasse was not resolved." Characterizing his fellow ministers as "selfish, lacking intelligence and puerile," Souvanna said that he was "up against a wall on both [the] left and right." Unger, who tried to dissuade the prime minister from resigning, reported to Washington that Souvanna "left [the] distinct impression [that] he means what he says."[4]

Policymakers in Washington found these latest developments in Laos troubling. Nearly four months had passed since the signing of the Geneva agreement, yet there was "no real progress" toward unification, according to a report to the president.[5] Should Souvanna's government fail—an increasingly likely prospect—Kennedy administration officials wanted the blame to fall exclusively on the Pathet Lao. But Phoumi's reputation and recent behavior ensured that international opinion would hold the general responsible for the coalition's collapse. Kennedy, who did "not understand how [the] arrest incident could have occurred," wanted Unger to impress upon Phoumi "the adverse [international] reaction to the arrest and detention of the two aides of Prince Souvanna Phouma."[6] US officials "rapped Phoumi's knuckles" for the DNC arrests, but the general defended the action to Unger, stressing the "hostility and nefarious plans" of Kong Le's officers.[7]

Although a personal reconciliation between Phoumi and Kong Le seemed a distant likelihood, the US mission in Vientiane worked to repair its relationship with the volatile neutralist commander. Born to a mixed Lao-Khmu family, and consequently scorned by ethnic Lao elites, Kong Le had demonstrated an aptitude for military leadership in the 1950s and received training in unconventional warfare at the CIA-sponsored scout and ranger school in the Philippines. US officials considered Kong Le a first-rate, pro-American officer—that is, until his August 1960 coup. Opposed to corruption in the government and army and to the presence of foreign troops in Laos, Kong Le was presumed to be under communist control by most Eisenhower administration officials, who suspected he might be "an Asian Castro."[8]

Kennedy administration officials initially held similarly harsh views of Kong Le, whose forces had been allies with the Pathet Lao and had been, "at least at times, under operational control of the PAVN/Pathet Lao headquarters," according to the CIA. Yet the agency also noted that the neutralist forces "appear to be excluded from many operations and areas and in general to be shunted aside."[9] Beyond a common hatred of Phoumi, there was limited ideological affinity between Kong Le's forces and the Pathet Lao. In fact, the US government had observed growing friction between the two groups. Unger reported "many indications" of Kong Le receiving "little help" from the Pathet Lao and "virtually no share" of the Soviet supplies intended for the neutralists.[10] The ambassador, who thought that the US government should help Kong Le, met with the neutralist commander's private secretary on October 29. He told Unger that the Pathet Lao was attempting "to squeeze the neutralist forces out of certain locations" on the Plaine des Jarres.[11]

Unger authorized the delivery of seven hundred blankets and six hundred pounds of medical supplies to Kong Le's troops at Khang Khay.[12] On November 8 President Kennedy confirmed the desirability of such assistance, approving "the provision of supplies and equipment requested by Kong Le amounting to approximately $100,000." In addition to demonstrating support for the neutralists, the aid was intended to advance other policy objectives. Should Souvanna resign, Kennedy and his advisers hoped that a large proportion of Kong Le's troops would "rally to [the] non-communist side." Providing assistance to the neutralist forces would also enable the US mission to reestablish contact with Kong Le. Before his coup, CIA paramilitary specialist Jack F. Mathews and US Special Forces had provided training and equipment for the Second BP. US officials, having had no direct connection with Kong Le in more than two years, sought to assess his personal aims and loyalties, his relationships with subordinates, and his military strength.[13]

Kong Le's forces on the Plaine des Jarres area were in a "parlous state," according to US intelligence reports. If the Pathet Lao chose to attack, a significant percentage of his troops would be "chewed up in quick order." Because Kong Le was the primary source of neutralist military strength,[14] Ambassador Unger was receptive to a request from Souvanna to provide the commander with ammunition for the US-made weapons he already possessed. Unger recognized the risks of military assistance, which included the loss of materiel to the Pathet Lao or its use against the Hmong irregulars, but he wanted to provide tangible support for forces "who wish to resist PL efforts to engulf them."[15]

By mid-November 1962, US officials engaged with Lao affairs thought that the time had come to press the Soviets on honoring their commitments to President Kennedy in Vienna and to Harriman in Geneva. If the Soviet Union lacked the influence to end Pathet Lao obstructionism, Ambassador Unger wrote to the State Department, then this was a fact the US government "should face" sooner rather than later. In Washington, Harriman concluded that the time was ripe "to approach the Russians" about the presence of PAVN troops in Laos and the "use of the Panhandle corridor" for infiltration into South Vietnam. A US appeal to the Soviets, however, was delayed by the ongoing diplomacy to resolve the Cuban missile crisis.[16]

The missile crisis had temporarily relegated Laos and every other foreign policy issue to the periphery of US national security interests. According to transcripts of the meetings of the executive committee of the National Security Council, established to manage the US response to crisis, Kennedy mentioned Laos on October 16—the day he learned that the Soviet Union was secretly placing medium-range nuclear missiles in Cuba. In contrast to Khrushchev's unexpected and dangerous move in Cuba—"it's a goddamned mystery to me," said Kennedy—the president cited the "ceasefire" in Laos as an example of the Soviet Union exhibiting caution and avoiding direct challenges to the United States.[17]

Kennedy made another reference to Laos in a telephone conversation with Prime Minister Macmillan on November 15, when the missile crisis was winding down but no final agreement had been reached on such issues as the removal of Soviet IL-28 bombers from Cuba. Turning to Laos, Kennedy said that the situation there was "coming apart." The president told Macmillan that he did not want to talk about Laos with the Soviet Union "until Cuba is settled," and he suggested a UK approach to Khrushchev, "pointing out that if fighting breaks out and we have partition, everyone will say that no agreement with the Russians will last more than a few months." Discussing Laos in the context of the superpower confrontations in Cuba and Berlin, Kennedy said: "Laos is an example of something negotiated with the Russians. It is the one ornament of the last two years."[18]

The Cuban missile crisis was a serious blow to Khrushchev's leadership—both in the communist world and in the Kremlin. The crisis had intensified the Soviet dispute with China, which criticized Khrushchev for betraying Marxist-Leninist principles and compared his "actions to Neville Chamberlin's efforts to appease Adolph Hitler at Munich." When the Soviet Politburo ousted Khrushchev from power in 1964, its members charged that that the missile crisis "raised the international standing of the United States and damaged the prestige of the Soviet Union and its armed forces."[19]

President Kennedy—aware of China's public denunciation of Khrushchev but not the Politburo's private unhappiness with him—intended to hold the Soviet premier accountable for his commitments in Laos. At a November 29 White House meeting, devoted primarily to Cuba and the causes of the missile crisis, Kennedy raised the issue of Laos with Soviet first deputy chairman Anastas I. Mikoyan, Ambassador Dorbrynin, and other Soviet officials. According to the minutes of the meeting, the president "expressed his concern that even while we are working at getting [an] agreement on Cuba[,] an earlier agreement is falling to pieces because the Soviet Union is not fulfilling its obligations." More specifically, the president declared: "American military advisers have been withdrawn [from Laos] but there are still North Viet Nam troops remaining. The Soviet Union also agreed to use its full influence to prevent Laos from being used as a channel to infiltrate South Viet Nam. Reliable intelligence indicates that approximately 500 Communists infiltrators are reaching South Viet Nam through Laos every month."[20]

Mikoyan replied to Kennedy that he would convey the president's information to the Soviet government. He was "certain," however, that the Soviet Union was "fulfilling its obligations."[21] This was not a persuasive argument with the president, who later in the conversation told Mikoyan that verbal agreements "must be implemented." Kennedy added: "It would be better perhaps if—as in the case of Laos—the Soviet Union would not always insist that it is fulfilling its obligations."[22] At one point in the meeting, Mikoyan tried to shift the conversation from Laos back to Cuba, but Kennedy was not through with the topic. Referring to "extremely important aspects of the Laos question," he said: "There has been agreement on Laos between Chairman Khrushchev and the President at Vienna. If this agreement is not fulfilled, it will appear that no other agreement with the Soviet Union can ever be expected to be successfully implemented."[23]

Around 1:00 P.M., on November 27, 1962, an Air America C-123 transport aircraft loaded with more than twelve thousand pounds of rice was cleared for landing at the main airfield on the Plaine des Jarres. When the plane descended to an altitude of approximately five hundred feet, heavy ground fire hit the cockpit, the right wing, and the right engine. Pilot Frederick J. Riley and copilot Donald C. Heritage were killed while attempting an emergency landing some three and one-half miles from the airport in Pathet Lao territory. The lone survivor, air cargo specialist Charles N. Swain, was rescued by one of Kong Le's pilots, who landed a small, single-engine de Havilland Canada "beaver" near the crash site and flew the injured "kicker" to Vientiane.[24]

Ambassador Unger, after receiving confirmation of the shoot-down, went directly to Souvanna to inform him of the incident. Unger pointed out that, only a few days before, Pathet Lao commander General Singkapo had publicly stated that rice-delivery flights were illegal and that his army would "energetically adopt appropriate measures to deal with future violations" of Pathet Lao airspace. Souvanna, who had authorized the flights to the plain, appeared deeply distressed by the attack. "This threat has been hanging over [my] head for several days," he said. When Unger asked if the Pathet Lao sought to force the neutralists into submission by denying them supplies, Souvanna replied, "No." The Pathet Lao's primary goal, he said, was to end Air America flights in Laos.[25]

Ostensibly a private commercial airline, Air America was secretly owned by the CIA. Air America's overt supply flights for the FAR and its relief missions for the Hmong were based in Vientiane and sponsored by the US economic aid program. "Black" Air America missions that supported CIA operations in Laos were flown out of Thailand. In Laos, a country where covert US intelligence and military personnel had long been a conspicuous presence, the US embassy in Vientiane faced the daunting challenge of convincing Laotians of all political affiliations that Air America was nothing more than a commercial airline with unusually skilled and daring pilots.

NLHS ministers in Souvanna's cabinet repeatedly denounced the overt Air America supply flights as illegal, and Pathet Lao ground fire directed at them "had been [an] accepted fact of life [in] Laos for [a] long time," according to Unger. Between the October 7 deadline for withdrawing foreign forces from Laos and the November 27 attack on the Air America transport, there were seventeen shooting incidents, "most of them minor" and most occurring in remote northern regions of Laos. The downing of the C-123 near the Plaine des Jarres airport, where RLG officials, diplomats, and others routinely landed to meet with neutralists, seemed to Unger an "obvious slap in [the] face to Souvanna" by the Pathet Lao.[26]

Unger amended his conclusion only slightly when he learned that the Air America aircraft had, in fact, been attacked by a "dissident element" among Souvanna's neutralist forces—not the Pathet Lao. After the downing of the plane, Souvanna told the ambassador, neutralist troops loyal to Kong Le engaged in "a major fight" with the dissidents, commanded by Colonel Deuane Sounnarath, and seized the crew of the antiaircraft battery. Souvanna said that Foreign Minister Quinim Pholsena had encouraged Deuane and other neutralists to associate themselves with the Pathet Lao. This particular information probably did not surprise Unger. Like other US officials, the ambassador had long distrusted the leftist minister, who had been "consistently and clearly playing [the] PL game." Earlier on November 29, Unger had denounced the Air America attack to Quinim, who remained "impassive as always." In his report to the State Department, Unger wrote that Quinim's reply was, in effect, "I told you so." This is what happens, he said, when Souvanna sends planes to the Plaine des Jarres without the unanimous consent of his government.[27]

Throughout his conversation with Souvanna, Unger emphasized the importance of taking "decisive action" to restore his authority. Unless the "guilty parties" were "tried and punished," his leadership would be "completely undermined." Souvanna agreed with this analysis, according to the ambassador, but he had "obviously not determined whether he [had the] authority or [the] means" to carry out the recommended action. To Unger, the Pathet Lao–inspired attack, carried out by dissident neutralists, symbolized Souvanna's political isolation. Observing that the prime minister stood "virtually alone" in the struggle between the left and right, Unger informed Washington that Souvanna recognized the Pathet Lao's "unmistakable" intention to "emasculate" the neutralists. There was a "real risk," the ambassador warned, that Souvanna would once again "become deeply discouraged, throw up his hands and resign."[28]

The downing of the Air America plane created an awkward challenge for Kennedy's policy in Laos. The president could not, for example, take direct diplomatic or military action against the Pathet Lao for an attack made by elements of Souvanna's own forces. Unger, in his proposed political response to the shoot-down, recommended that the United States not get bogged down by the details of the case. The byzantine politics of Laos likely persuaded the ambassador that a public discussion of "dissident neutralists," a political grouping unfamiliar to most Americans, would add an unhelpful layer of complexity to an already knotty and controversial policy debate. Whatever his motivation, Unger proposed that the US government emphasize General Singkapo's "inflammatory" threat before the attack and Souvanna's original, though inaccurate, statement after it, which unambiguously blamed the Pathet Lao. "I recommend we leave that record stand as is," Unger cabled the State Department.[29]

In December 1962, two months after the deadline for the withdrawal of foreign troops had passed, there had still been no ICC investigations of—much less reports on—violations of the Geneva agreement. The RLG cabinet ministers, paralyzed by the rule of unanimous consent, could not agree among themselves over the terms of reference for fact-finding missions. The NLHS ministers proposed geographic and time limitations on the investigations that the conservatives found too restrictive. And the

ICC, unwilling to act unilaterally, waited patiently for the outcome of the RLG deliberations. Deputy Under Secretary of State U. Alexis Johnson, who met with Lao leaders in Vientiane on December 5, witnessed "three hundred personnel of the ICC sitting in camp waiting for something to do."[30]

For Johnson, the political atmosphere in Vientiane had an "Alice in Wonderland" quality. Soviet planes shared an airfield with Air America aircraft; doctrinaire left- and right-wing ministers worked in adjacent offices; and planning proceeded for a police force led by a troika of chiefs. "While all the Laos talk glibly of plans and programs for integration of the armed forces, economic and political plans for the whole of the country, etc., it all seemed to have an air of unreality barring an unforeseen and major conversion of Pathet Lao attitudes," Johnson wrote in his trip report. "It was my impression that, barring such a change, the best we can hope for in the foreseeable future is a continuation of the present de facto situation with Souvanna Phouma continuing to hold a leaky but important umbrella over it."[31]

A meeting with Souphanouvong took a through-the-looking-glass turn when Johnson said that the US government was troubled by the presence of North Vietnamese troops in Laos, "particularly from the standpoint of South Vietnam." Souphanouvong, appearing sincere, courteous, and articulate, looked Johnson "straight in the eye" and declared in "impeccable" French: "There are no foreign forces in the zone under my control." His faction, Souphanouvong said, had agreed to inspections of designated villages, but ICC officials wanted "to travel all over a given area." He added: "There was no use in their going into the jungle where they would find nothing."[32]

Speaking with Ngon Sananikone, a pro-American minister, Johnson stressed the importance of getting ICC teams into the field, with or without NLHS restrictions on investigations. The commission's first steps, he said, might have to be small ones that expanded into larger actions: "The important thing is to begin." Ngon countered that an inadequate investigation would not likely find any North Vietnamese troops. This, in turn, would make the right wing vulnerable to charges of "lodging a complaint without foundation." He added that the conservatives did not want a repetition of the "unhappy experience" in 1959, when a United Nations fact-finding team was unable to clearly establish whether North Vietnamese troops had invaded the northern provinces of Laos. Ngon indicated to Johnson that the conservatives would "not be responsible for any break-down in the [Geneva] agreement but will be quick to show that the agreement will not work because of Pathet Lao intransigence."[33]

When Johnson met with Souvanna, the prime minister's views about the ICC were alternately antagonistic and sympathetic to the US position. He disputed the US claim that the RLG had agreed to independent, unrestricted ICC investigations when it signed the Geneva agreement. "RLG approval was required in each case," he said. A less debatable topic was Pathet Lao "foot dragging" in approving investigations. The previous day, Souvanna said, the Pathet Lao had demanded that the ICC restrict its investigations "to certain villages, one at a time and exclusive of the outlying areas." The danger in such an approach was that the Pathet Lao would "pass the word of ICC presence along to the next village." Ambassador Unger suggested that, in light of the NLHS obstructionism and delaying tactics, perhaps it would "be better to get the ICC out to investigate even though conditions were not ideal." Johnson agreed, adding that continued Pathet Lao opposition to ICC action would provide the basis for an appeal to the British and Soviet cochairs of the Geneva agreement.[34]

Despite US encouragement, neither the RLG nor the ICC moved quickly. Right-wing ministers continued to have reservations about Pathet Lao restrictions on investigations. Phoumi appeared to be persuaded by US appeals for action, but Unger was unsure whether the RLG would either "get off the dime" or "find new ways to let [the] matter drift longer." If there were further delays, Unger wanted the Canadian ICC commissioner, Paul Bridle, to take the initiative and propose an investigation of a village in Sam Neua province, which the Pathet Lao had agreed to in principle. "Unfortunately, Bridle seems less than fully prepared to act," Unger informed the State Department. He suggested that the department convey the following message to the Canadian government: "Continued [ICC] inactivity [is] beginning to make [an] internationally sponsored institution look ridiculous."[35]

The Canadians' approach to their ICC responsibilities was a deep disappointment to Kennedy and his advisers, who sought more vigorous action in promoting US policy objectives. Walking a diplomatic tightrope, the Canadians sought to be "alert to the interest of the non-Communist side and ready to defend those interests if necessary," according to Bridle.

Yet the Canadian commissioners were also determined to demonstrate "impartiality in reaching conclusions and in taking necessary actions regardless of which side was in the dock." Canadian diplomats in Vientiane told Ambassador Unger of their reluctance to be too closely identified with US interests: "We don't want to appear as Bulgarians." Yet the Poles, Bridle wrote later, were "fully prepared to subordinate" the objectives of the ICC "to the needs of their Indochinese ideological partners."[36]

The Canadians, at least initially, agreed in principle that ICC operations were best served by unanimity among the commissioners. "It made for a harmonious commission and, in the case of recommendations to the parties, for maximum effect," Bridle recalled. The Indian chair of the ICC, Avtar Singh, was particularly committed to the principle of unanimity. According to Michael Forrestal, Bridle and Singh took "the view that the Commission's ability to function even in a limited way must be preserved at all costs, and that nothing must be done to disturb the delicate balance within the RLG. The result of this thinking is immobility." Forrestal, who visited Laos and South Vietnam with Roger Hilsman in January 1963, reported to the president: "No one believes that the ICC is capable of evicting the [North Vietnamese] from the Pathet Lao territory."[37]

During their 1963 trip to Laos, Forrestal and Hilsman met with General Kong Le at his Khang Khay headquarters. The neutralist commander, a little over five feet tall, was in "good spirits" and grateful for US assistance. He told his visitors, who included embassy officials and the US Army attaché, Colonel William Law, that Foreign Minister Quinim was responsible for the subversion of the dissident neutralists and for the November 27 shoot-down of the Air America plane. Kong Le was confident of his ability to resist the Pathet Lao, claiming that he "controlled all the strong points in the area." Forrestal reported to Kennedy that the neutralist "probably overestimates his own strength." (In a message to the JCS, General Tucker assessed the situation more bluntly: Kong Le was "talking from the jail house," and if the Pathet Lao attacked, it was "doubtful" that his forces "would get out with anything except small arms.") Forrestal recommended that the United States provide Kong Le with "enough military supplies to resist an overt attack by the Pathet Lao for at least long enough to enable the cumbersome Geneva machinery to operate and conceivably to enable Souvanna to call upon FAR or [Hmong] help."[38]

Forrestal's trip included a visit to the new Hmong headquarters in Long Tieng, where he met with Vang Pao, the charismatic commander of the guerrillas. The CIA, which had provided "a carefully selected" subset of the tribesmen with training in intelligence reporting, considered the Hmong cadre "one of the best stay-behind intelligence organizations yet achieved."[39] Despite their prowess in paramilitary and intelligence operations, the Hmong seemed to Forrestal "one of the most difficult residual problems we face in Laos." He recognized a "moral obligation" to people who had largely forsaken agriculture to fight on behalf of the United States and who would be trapped in Pathet Lao territory in any strictly enforced partition scheme. Ambassador Unger and Charles S. Whitehurst, Jorgensen's successor as CIA chief of station, "have started to tackle in detail the possibilities of self-sufficiency and resettlement," wrote Forrestal.[40]

A more immediate problem was the effort to supply the Hmong through Air America. Although the US embassy claimed there was a firm agreement with Souvanna for nonmilitary deliveries to the tribal people, the prime minister had accepted the flights only tacitly and with great reluctance. In fact, Souvanna had stressed to Unger the "absolute necessity" of channeling aid to the Hmong through the RLG because independent Air America missions encouraged the guerrillas to ignore the authority of the central government. With Souvanna under increasing Pathet Lao pressure to halt the flights, Forrestal reported that the prime minister was "rapidly backing away" from his earlier acquiescence. Even Phoumi, who had longstanding ties with the CIA, disliked Air America because its employees "behaved on occasion in an arrogant way even toward right-wing officials in Vientiane." Among all three factions, Forrestal informed Kennedy, Air America was "about the most unpopular institution in Laos."[41]

The Vietnam report to the president by Hilsman and Forrestal was somewhat more optimistic than their Laos paper: "The war in South Vietnam is clearly going better than it was a year ago," when Kennedy increased the US advisory commitment to that country. Noting that "awesome" challenges remained, Hilsman and Forrestal observed that the PLAF was still "aggressive" and "extremely effective." The two officials reported an "ominous" phenomenon that became a consistent feature of enemy strength assessments for years to come. Despite greater military pressure by the

Diem government and reports of large enemy losses, intelligence "estimates credit the Viet Cong with actually increasing their regular forces." An estimated twenty thousand enemy troops were killed in action in 1962, yet the number of regulars in the PLAF increased by more than 25 percent to twenty-three thousand, with "100,000 militia, supported by unknown thousands of sympathizers."[42]

To Hilsman, the principal drafter of the report's analysis of the counterinsurgency program in Vietnam, increasing enemy strength in the face of large military losses suggested that the PLAF was "still able to obtain an adequate supply of recruits and the large quantities of food and other supplies they need from the villagers of South Vietnam itself." Infiltration of men over "the so-called Ho Chi Minh Trails" seemed to be, at most, some three to four thousand over the past year, according to captured documents and POW interrogations. This appeared to be a relatively small number compared to the larger number of replacement troops implied by enemy order-of-battle estimates. The supplies infiltrated over the trails were specialized equipment—for example, radios, medicine, and "perhaps" a few automatic weapons, "although no weapons have yet been captured which could be proved to have been brought in after 1954." To Hilsman, the conclusion seemed "inescapable": The PLAF "could continue the war at the present tempo, or perhaps increase it, even if the infiltration routes were completely closed."[43]

Hilsman's State Department colleague Walt Rostow had reached quite different conclusions about infiltration. In a memorandum to Dean Rusk, he listed three reasons why infiltration was a "very significant" factor in the war in South Vietnam. First, effective counterguerrilla campaigns required at least a fifteen-to-one manpower advantage over the insurgents. This meant that even relatively small numbers of infiltrators created a recruitment burden on the South Vietnamese government that "should not be regarded as trivial." Second, infiltrators from North Vietnam were well-trained cadres who formed "the bone structure of the Viet Cong" and were, "therefore, disproportionately valuable" to the insurgency. Third, the continuing flow of infiltrators, which symbolized North Vietnam's responsibility and support for the Viet Cong, was "an exceedingly important morale factor." Rostow warned that "continued acceptance of the infiltration burden is capable of prolonging the war for a long time." Injecting domestic politics into his argument, Rostow declared:

"The President will face a difficult problem in 1964 if some 10,000 U.S. forces are still engaged in Viet Nam with the end of the war not in sight."[44]

Rostow, like Hilsman, seemed unburdened by self-doubt. Their vigorously expressed opposing views on the relative importance of infiltration reflected each man's preferred approach to the war in South Vietnam. Hilsman, the World War II guerrilla leader, sought to cut off the PLAF's access to the rural Vietnamese population through a nationwide system of defended villages and hamlets. This "strategic concept," which included other civilian and military measures, was intended to win the allegiance of the people to the central government. Rostow, the World War II bombing planner, had great faith in US airpower to compel North Vietnam to stop its direction of and support for the insurgency in the south. Acknowledging the need for political and economic progress in South Vietnam, he sought "to impose on North Vietnam limited appropriate damage, by air and sea action, if infiltration does not cease."[45]

In contrast to Hilsman's and Rostow's strong opinions, the fact base for official judgments about the importance of infiltration was weak. Part of the problem, of course, was that the Pathet Lao had sealed off eastern Laos. A more literal barrier to gathering information about infiltration was the rugged thirteen-hundred-mile border between Laos and Vietnam, a region that had an overall population density of less than one person per square mile. One US official, flying along the border, described the area this way: "Mile after mile of mountains and steep valleys unfold below you. The whole area is covered by impenetrable forest growth. Now and then you see a hut, or a cluster of three of four, in the middle of nowhere. The monotony is broken occasionally by an open plot burned into a hillside for planting."[46]

Questions about the infiltration trails were raised at the January 17, 1963, meeting of the Special Group (CI), whose members included DCI John McCone, Attorney General Robert Kennedy, JCS chairman Maxwell Taylor,* and Deputy Defense Secretary Roswell Gilpatric. The primary mission of this committee was to develop interdepartmental programs to combat subversive insurgency, which the president considered "a major form of politico-military conflict equal in importance to conventional warfare." The group's chair, U. Alexis Johnson, had reported the

---

*Taylor succeeded Lemnitzer as chairman of the JCS on October 1, 1962. The position of military representative to the president was abolished.

difficulty of obtaining "a clear view of the level and relative importance of present infiltration through Laos." On January 18 McCone asked his analysts to prepare a paper on the use of the trails by the North Vietnamese. He instructed them "to describe precisely any limitation on our intelligence on the subject."[47]

Five days later the CIA's Office of Current Intelligence (OCI) delivered to McCone a memorandum with a carefully hedged summary conclusion: infiltration "almost certainly continues, although possibly at a lower rate than last spring and summer." Acknowledging that an "accurate and detailed assessment" of infiltration was "severely handicapped by the lack of reliable intelligence," the OCI analysts wrote that "the only substantive" information since July 1962 came from: (1) two defectors, who had entered South Vietnam in separate groups; and (2) a report of another North Vietnamese unit from "several" sources that were not named in the OCI memorandum. Numerical estimates of infiltration, the analysts admitted, were "tenuous at best," with captured enemy documents and interrogations of infiltrators providing "some basis for assessing movement along the trails." A key difficulty was that South Vietnamese officials, who "had a tendency to exaggerate," were "the only source of infiltration reporting."[48]

Although unable to quantify infiltration with precision, the agency analysts provided a more detailed qualitative description of enemy movements down the trail. By 1961 DRV combat engineers had built an eighty-mile road in eastern Laos near the demilitarized zone, which allowed trucks to drive from North Vietnam to Tchepone in the dry season. The primary limitation of the foot trails was the lack of food, a problem that was being addressed by the establishment of depots about one day's march from each other. These way stations, which also provided guides and limited medical care for infiltrators, were generally commanded by a North Vietnamese noncommissioned officer and fifteen to twenty other personnel, often locally recruited. Depending on the route and weather, the length of the trip from North Vietnam to the south averaged thirty to forty-five days.[49]

Captured or defecting infiltrators were usually PAVN regulars, most often from the 305th and 324th divisions. These infiltrators, who were originally from South and Central Vietnam, had regrouped in North Vietnam after the war with the French. In almost every case, infiltrators from the north returned to serve in the area where they were first recruited to fight the French. The agency estimated that "North Vietnam has a stockpile of about 60,000 to 70,000 regrouped southerners," a figure that was about three times US estimates of total PLAF regulars in South Vietnam.[50]

The DRV, according to CIA analysts, did "not attempt to replace Viet Cong battle casualties" with infiltrators, who were considered an "investment in military growth" and served as "commanders, technicians, and professional cadre for Viet Cong military development." The North Vietnamese expected the PLAF to recruit the bulk of its manpower in the south, to acquire its food locally, and to capture the majority of its weapons from the South Vietnamese army. Infiltrators did not, however, arrive in South Vietnam "empty-handed." They carried "high-priority materiel such as communications and light weapons."[51]

To collect more detailed intelligence on infiltration, CIA officers operating out of Thailand were organizing, training, and equipping Lao trail-watch teams on "a priority basis."[52] A nascent agency project in the panhandle, with the cryptonym "Hardnose," began to monitor North Vietnamese troops who traveled into Laos through two major entry points: the Nape and Mu Gia passes in the Annamite Mountains. Hardnose got off to a slow start. Convincing the trail-watch teams to move deeply into eastern Laos was "always touchy," wrote Richard L. Holm, the CIA case officer who initially ran the project.[53]

On the South Vietnamese side of the border, intelligence operations targeting infiltrators were somewhat more developed but still modest when compared to the size and difficulty of the terrain. In 1959 the governments of Ngo Dinh Diem and Prime Minister Phoui Sananikone signed an agreement that allowed South Vietnamese forces to conduct reconnaissance and harassment operations up to ten kilometers inside the Lao border.[54] Diem suspended these operations a few weeks before the signing of the Geneva agreement. In South Vietnam, the CIA and US Army Special Forces provided weapons and training for a variety of anti-infiltration programs. Hilsman concluded that regular patrolling by US-trained tribal people in Vietnam's Central Highlands "should go far toward choking off the infiltration routes."[55]

This dubious conclusion reflected not only Hilsman's views but also those of General Paul D. Harkins, the perennially optimistic commander of US forces in Vietnam, who had declared that large-scale infiltration "was becoming increasingly difficult" for the North Vietnamese.[56] General Earle G. Wheeler, the US Army chief of staff, had a more skeptical view of the various anti-infiltration programs. After a January 1963 visit to South Vietnam to assess the counterinsurgency effort for the joint chiefs and the secretary of defense, Wheeler concluded that, overall, victory was "a hopeful prospect." The problem of "external assistance for the Viet Cong," however, "must be solved by methods more practicable than surveillance of the country's borders."[57]

Wheeler recommended that the US government "should do something to make the North Vietnamese bleed" for their support of the southern insurgency. Summarizing the range of available military options, he acknowledged that overt US attacks against targets in North Vietnam were a "grave step" and "a far-reaching national decision." He also mentioned the CIA's "minor intelligence and sabotage forays" in North Vietnam but dismissed them as "offering essentially no promise of influencing the progress of the war." Maneuvering between these two extremes, Wheeler suggested that the Military Assistance Command Vietnam (MACV) strengthen the unconventional warfare capabilities of the South Vietnamese and direct them "in a coordinated program of sabotage, destruction, propaganda, and subversive missions against North Vietnam."[58]

In a companion memorandum to its January 23 analysis of infiltration, the CIA's Office of Current Intelligence prepared an assessment of the overall situation in Laos. The report, dated six months to the day after the signing of the Geneva agreement, characterized Souvanna's coalition government as "little more than an uneasy and pro forma association of the opposing Laotian factions." Observing "no real progress" in civilian or military integration, the CIA concluded: "The country essentially remains in a state of de facto partition, roughly along the lines existing at the time hostilities formally ended." Souvanna, Phoumi, and Souphanouvong were "each scheming to turn time to his own advantage," though none of them sought "a deliberate breakup of the coalition at this stage."[59]

The DRV, according to agency analysts, seemed "content with the existing state of affairs." The military situation was "generally quiescent," as it had been for several months. The CIA estimate of PAVN strength in

Laos was two to five thousand, a range 50 to 80 percent lower than earlier post-Geneva order-of-battle estimates. The agency reported that the North Vietnamese and Pathet Lao had apparently abandoned their efforts to "mop up" the Hmong forces in the mountains of the northeastern and central provinces: "Instead, the Communists are trying to starve out these pockets by action against Air America supply aircraft and by political pressure to bring all such aircraft under direct control of the coalition government."[60]

Within the State Department, there was a growing frustration with the weak neutralist and conservative response to the "stepped-up PL offensive against US operations and presence in Laos." Souvanna's continued reluctance to exercise decisive leadership was troubling but not entirely out of character. More puzzling was the unwillingness of Phoumi and other right-wing ministers to "use their veto to block unfavorable actions" by the RLG.[61] (The notion that conservative RLG officials might sometimes be more concerned about Lao sovereignty than cold war ideology rarely occurred to Washington policymakers.) The harshest US judgments, however, were reserved for the Indian and Canadian representatives of the ICC, who were "faltering at every turn." The ICC's "miserable record so far"—two restricted investigations that had found no evidence of DRV troops in Laos—was blamed on Indian chairman Avtar Singh's unnecessary "penchant" for unanimity.[62]

The evenhandedness of the Canadian commissioner, Paul Bridle, "particularly disappointed" State Department officials.[63] An experienced diplomat who had served in Canada's Department of External Affairs since 1945, Bridle had been his country's ICC commissioner in Laos in the mid-1950s and the deputy chief of the Canadian delegation at the Geneva conference in 1961–1962. In the immediate aftermath of Geneva, a classified State Department assessment of other delegations characterized Bridle as "one of the ablest members of the entire Conference, with a fine mind, excellent sense of humor, and remarkable poise and balance in debate and discussion."[64]

Yet the performance of the ICC after Geneva had prompted State Department officials to ask W. Walton Butterworth, the American ambassador in Ottawa, "whether it would be possible or desirable to suggest [Bridle's] replacement" to the Canadian government.[65] Butterworth appreciated the concerns of his department superiors but informed them that Bridle was well respected by leaders of Canada's Department of External Affairs. Moreover, Canadian officials would find it difficult to believe that he was not conscientiously carrying out his instructions: "It would be inadvisable and in fact highly counterproductive [to] attempt [to] suggest [that] Bridle be replaced."[66]

The basic problem with the ICC, in the view of Kennedy administration officials, was that neither Singh nor Bridle seemed to be able to prevent the Polish commissioner, Marek Thee, "from running circles around them." A diplomat and researcher associated with the Polish Institute of International Affairs, Thee was adept at procedural ploys that either delayed or narrowed the scope of investigations in Pathet Lao territory. He requested an ICC investigation into Air America, characterizing the airline as "a paramilitary organization" that violated the Geneva agreement. To the disgust of US officials, Singh and Bridle agreed to the investigation. The US government had taken the position that the overt relief flights of Air America, based in Vientiane, were open to inspection by any and all RLG officials. (The flights out of Thailand supporting covert intelligence operations in Laos were, of course, another matter altogether.) The State Department instructed Unger to inform the ICC that the United States would not cooperate with an investigation of Air America before the commission got "down to serious business on [the] gross communist violations."[67]

The depth of Kennedy's unhappiness with the ICC's performance may be inferred by a State Department telegram to the US ambassadors in Ottawa and New Delhi—a cable that the president himself likely inspired. Noting that the "ICC failure" in Laos had "attracted [the] concern of [the] highest authority [of the] USG," a standard, indirect reference to the president, the telegram began with a sweeping overstatement: "Unless [the] Canadian and Indian members [of the ICC] assume [the] responsibilities which are theirs and theirs alone[,] they will be responsible for [the] dismal failure of [the] Geneva Agreements." Bridle, the cable declared, "should be as vigorous and ruthless for carrying out [the] Agreements as [the] Pole unashamedly is for [the] Communist objective of destroying them." Singh should "oppose with all means available to him [the] communist assaults on [the] integrity of [the] Agreements." After the message was sent, Michael Forrestal delivered to Kennedy a copy of "our response to the Laos-ICC problem."[68]

Near the end of the Vietnam War, Bridle wrote an essay on the Canadian experience with the ICC in Indochina from 1954 to 1972. Discussing the failure of the commission in Laos, Cambodia, and Vietnam, Bridle made the fundamental, but sometimes overlooked, observation that the responsibility for complying with the Geneva agreements belonged to the nations that signed them. The ICC's job was monitoring and reporting on that compliance, a task complicated by the chronic "lack of cooperation" from one government or another. Referring explicitly to his assignment in Laos, Bridle noted both the "noncooperation" of the Poles and the ICC's inability to launch an investigation into Air America because of "a right-wing veto in the tripartite government."[69]

The king of Laos, Savang Vatthana, visited the United States in the last week of February 1963 as part of a global tour of nations that had signed the Geneva agreement. The visit was a largely ceremonial expression of Lao gratitude, with senior officials of the RLG, including Prime Minister Souvanna Phouma, accompanying the king to Washington. Despite the trip's celebratory purpose, Savang retained his harsh views of the multilateral and Laotian efforts to end the conflict. "The King resented the imposition of the new Geneva settlement and the formation of the government of national union including communists," according to a State Department biographic sketch prepared for Savang's visit. "He is severely critical of the entire Lao leadership, particularly of Souvanna, and hence pessimistic as to the future of his kingdom. His own negative stand has alienated many of his people who look to the King as the one real symbol of Lao unity."[70]

In a meeting with President Kennedy, who asked Savang what more the United States could do to help Souvanna's government, the king replied that he "kept outside any partisan politics." He said that it was the prime minister's responsibility "to save the country and to carry out his promises made to the entire world, to the King, and to the people of Laos." In subsequent conversation with Kennedy, Savang declared that Souvanna's coalition government "was not suitable to anyone in Laos" because it was the result of international pressure, rather than a good-faith agreement among the Lao factions. The king was not alone in this sentiment, according to Unger, who reported that, in general, the Lao considered themselves "international pawns." Moreover, they thought that the neutral solution reached at Geneva bore "no relation to political realities within Laos." Savang told the president that Souvanna, even among his own faction, was the country's only "true neutralist."[71]

Savang doubted that the communists would abide by the Geneva agreement, and he dismissed the efforts of the ICC to monitor the accords. The king observed to Kennedy that the problems of Laos and Vietnam "were tied together." Summarizing recent Lao history, Savang reminded the president that the "strife" between the Vietnamese and French had spilled over into Laos during the First Indochina War. Laos had been drawn into the current Vietnamese struggle because it provided "the easiest route of access" from the north to the south. Savang added that despite his country's status as neutral nation, it was "difficult to see a final solution in Laos without one in Viet-Nam."[72]

In contrast to the king, Souvanna provided Kennedy with a more optimistic assessment of the situation, noting that it had "not deteriorated." The atmosphere in Vientiane had improved since the November arrests of the neutralist officers, which almost "led to the break-up of the government." As to the rest of Laos, Souvanna said with typical confidence, there was "no need for alarm." A lack of trust between Phoumi and the Pathet Lao remained, but a solution was possible. Souvanna said that if the Americans used their influence with Phoumi, and if the Soviets put pressure on the Pathet Lao, then "the situation will improve."[73]

President Kennedy and other US officials did not share Souvanna's overall optimism. A State Department background paper prepared in advance of the king's visit reported: "There has been virtually no internal progress in Laos in the seven months since the signing of the Geneva agreements, due primarily to Pathet Lao obstructionism, but also to Prince Souvanna's own inertia." Kennedy, who characterized the current situation as "very dangerous," appeared to agree with the prime minister's assessment of the influence of the Soviet Union. In his final remarks to the Lao officials, the president "stressed the fact that the Russians could play an active role in Laos." He said that the United States had signed the Geneva agreement "in good faith," as peace and neutrality in Laos were "important, not only for peace in Asia, but for the peace of the entire world." He added: "If this effort failed, the efforts of all 14 signatories would then be reduced to nothing, Laos would not be neutral and independent and a very difficult situation would exist for the entire world."[74]

Harriman had delivered a similar message to Soviet ambassador Dobrynin at the State Department earlier in February. Declaring his intention to amplify President Kennedy's remarks to Deputy Chairman Mikoyan the previous November, Harriman reiterated that there were large numbers of North Vietnamese troops in Laos and that the DRV continued to use the kingdom "to interfere in South Vietnam." The ICC had been stymied by RLG restrictions on its investigations, and the Pathet Lao had "made unprovoked attacks on Royal Army units, peaceful tribesmen and even neutralist forces." Emphasizing American and Soviet responsibilities to help unify Laos, Harriman said that the US government was convinced that the withdrawal of North Vietnamese forces would "require Soviet cooperation." Ambassador Dobrynin replied that he did not necessarily agree with all of Harriman's comments but would forward them to Moscow.[75]

Harriman had an even more pointed, adversarial discussion with Lao foreign minister Quinim Pholsena during the king's visit to Washington. Quinim, a nominal neutralist who had collaborated with the Pathet Lao, obstructed ICC investigations, and objected to Air America relief flights, was characterized by State Department officials as "probably the most dangerous individual" in Souvanna's cabinet.[76] Harriman interrogated Quinim, asking who was responsible for the November shoot-down of the Air America flight to the Plaine des Jarres. Why weren't the eastern portions of the country opened up? What was the Pathet Lao concealing? Why was it attempting to starve out Kong Le's forces? Who was responsible for the recent assassination of Colonel Ketsana Vongsanovah, Kong Le's field commander and a Souvanna loyalist? Harriman claimed that he was not making accusations against Quinim but merely quoting Kong Le in hopes of gaining a better understanding of the "extraordinary activities" in the Plaine des Jarres.[77]

Quinim politely thanked Harriman for his "information" and "the sincerity of his expression." Although largely noncommittal in his replies, Quinim assured Harriman that all neutralist forces were loyal to Souvanna. The Lao minister said that it would be "an error" to describe him as a "competitor" to Souvanna; however, his allegiance was to a policy of neutrality, not an individual. He "would only support Souvanna Phouma as long as he remained a neutral." Quinim said that he could not answer why the Pathet Lao and the North Vietnamese acted as they did, but he cautioned against being "absolute in our judgments." As for Kong Le's accusations of his attempt to destroy Souvanna, Quinim said that the neutralist commander "was free to say what he chose."[78]

The Lao policy of the Kennedy administration remained unchanged in mid-March 1963: support for Souvanna's government of national union and implementation of the Geneva agreement. Yet the dysfunction within the RLG, the ineffectiveness of the ICC, and other factors prompted US officials to think more about partitioning Laos. On March 15, 1963, the State Department asked Ambassador Unger to consider the "most advantageous" ways of geographically consolidating the noncommunist parts of Laos. He was also asked to assess the possibility of "extending noncommunist control" into Tchepone and "clearing up the Pakse, Attopeu and Saravane triangle," three towns in southern Laos that were on the periphery of the Bolovens Plateau.[79]

In a telegram notable for its wishful thinking, the department acknowledged that Tchepone and the Bolovens Plateau were "important to [the] communist side particularly in relation to Viet Cong operations in South Vietnam." Yet it seemed to officials in Washington that the noncommunists in Laos enjoyed certain "advantages," including "easy access" to these areas and "probably greater military strength" than the Pathet Lao. Perhaps, the State Department suggested, the neutral government could establish a presence in Tchepone and the Bolovens Plateau through road building and other projects, "without necessarily running the risk of real fighting." The cable from Washington concluded: "We do not of course want to escalate violations of [the] cease fire."[80]

Unger, in his analysis of the merits of partitioning Laos, dismissed the notion that the neutralists and conservatives could establish a presence in eastern and southern Laos without violence: "I see absolutely no possibility [of] extending non-Communist control into [the] Tchepone area if we do not wish [to] run [the] risk of real fighting or of escalating violations of cease-fire." Unger added that, for the DRV, Tchepone was "probably [the] key point" in the Pathet Lao zone, and he could not "conceive of its being yielded without a fight of such proportions as to upset [the] entire settlement." A "complete cleaning out" of the Pakse-Attopeu-Saravane triangle was "also difficult to imagine."[81]

Admiral Felt, who agreed with Unger's overall conclusion, asked

General Tucker for his assessment of the State Department's suggestion to extend noncommunist control into eastern and southern Laos. The MAAG chief replied that he was "convinced that friendly control could not be extended into the Tchepone area. Any such move would certainly generate [an] immediate [Pathet Lao/PAVN] military reaction." Tchepone, he wrote, was the "keystone" to DRV operations in South Vietnam: "A threat to any part of the Ho Chi Minh Trail will mean a fight." Tucker pointed out that before the Geneva agreement, the FAR, at full strength, could not move into these areas. The idea of attempting such an operation while the army was demobilizing seemed "odd" to the general.[82]

Chapter 10

A Piece of War

The assassination of Foreign Minister Quinim Pholsena on April 1, 1963, should have shattered the durable stereotype of Laotian pacifism. Arriving at his home in Vientiane after a diplomatic reception, the minister was killed and his wife wounded by two short bursts from an automatic weapon, fired by one of their household guards. Like all bodyguards assigned to neutralist cabinet ministers, the shooter was one of Kong Le's men. After his arrest, the assassin, a young corporal, claimed to have acted on his own in retaliation for Quinim's divisive activities and for the murder of Colonel Ketsana. The State Department's Bureau of Intelligence and Research, however, quoted a neutralist source who said, "The assassination was carried out in accordance with a Kong Le plan." A report from the CIA station in Vientiane suggested that "the entire Kong Le contingent guarding the house acted in concert. The very quiet undisturbed atmosphere around Quinim's house immediately after the shooting indicates that all Kong Le soldiers were 'working by the numbers.'"[1]

The complexity of Laotian politics invites speculation that there might have been more to Quinim's assassination than divisions among the neutralists. For example, Phoumi, a longstanding enemy of Quinim, exercised tight control over Vientiane through the DNC. At the time of the murder, Phoumi was in the process of reconciling with Kong Le because of their common struggle against the Pathet Lao, which sought to weaken the neutralist commander's forces through subversion, selective violence, and interdiction of food and military supplies. A legitimate question is whether Kong Le conspired with Phoumi to murder Quinim, a suspicion heightened by the notably efficient arrest of the alleged assassin. And if Phoumi was involved in the plot, did he hope that Quinim's assassination might lead to a resumption of fighting and increased military support from the United States?

Many questions surrounding Quinim's murder remain unanswered, but it is clear that his assassination exacerbated the already tense situation on the Plaine des Jarres. Within days of his death, the conflict there escalated into the first large-scale breach of the Geneva agreement, with the Pathet Lao capturing the towns of Khang Khay and Xieng Khouang and forcing Kong Le to move his headquarters to the western edge of the plain. The CIA estimated that only one-half of the three thousand neutralist forces were "effective." The agency, however, judged the three thousand Pathet Lao troops in the area to be "fully effective," largely because of support provided by PAVN units that protected supply lines and intimidated the neutralists by their proximity to the battlefield. "Kong Le is extremely vulnerable," DCI McCone told Kennedy and his advisers. "The morale of his troops is poor."[2]

Souvanna's initial response to the fighting on the Plaine des Jarres was "characteristic indecision," said McCone. "He has alternately censured Kong Le for being too aggressive, urged him to stand firm, and warned against attempting to regain lost territory." Ambassador Unger encouraged Souvanna to establish a permanent ICC presence on the plain and to request an investigation into the presence of DRV troops. Initially noncommittal with Unger, Souvanna was more assertive with the British and Soviet ambassadors, denouncing the "perfidy" of NLHS officials who sought to drive the neutralist forces off of the plain. Appearing "deeply disturbed," he characterized the situation as "extremely grave" and accused the North Vietnamese of providing "cadres" for the Pathet Lao. Souvanna asked the Geneva cochairs to intervene immediately with the DRV and NLHS "to stop their aggressive action."[3]

In the face of increasing Pathet Lao pressure on the neutralists, Kennedy administration officials became even less constrained by what they called the "technicalities" of the Geneva agreement. The US government supplied weapons and ammunition to Kong Le and encouraged General Phoumi and Hmong commander Vang Pao to assist their former neutralist foe. Phoumi placed on alert three paratroop battalions in Savannakhet and six companies of infantry in Vientiane for deployment to the Plaine des Jarres. Agreeing with Ambassador Unger that "as far as possible FAR participation [should] remain secret," Phoumi organized army "volunteers," disguised as neutralists, to help Kong Le.[4]

Some eight thousand Hmong guerrillas in the hills ringing the plain were in the best position to support the neutralist commander. Although neither organized nor equipped for conventional warfare, Hmong fighters could reduce Pathet Lao pressure on Kong Le through "harassing and diversionary tactics," according to McCone. At an April 10 NSC meeting, the CIA chief reported that Phoumi, Vang Pao, and neutralist military officers had met in Vientiane to develop "coordinated plans for covering Kong Le's possible withdrawal to Luang Prabang." Kennedy sought assurances that the neutralist commander was "getting what he thinks he needs from us." Averell Harriman, recently promoted to under secretary of state for political affairs, replied to the president: "We have that on the top priority."[5]

Harriman recommended putting "pressure on the French" to strengthen the forces of Phoumi and Kong Le. The FMM continued to have difficulties training the FAR and disapproved of the increasing US support for Kong Le. Although they did not want the Pathet Lao to "strangle" the neutralist forces, the French found the American supply effort a "to[o] open bear hug," which, in turn, prompted the Pathet Lao to increase its pressure on Kong Le. What disturbed Harriman most about the French was their "rather neutral position" toward the military forces of the three factions and their unwillingness to represent US interests in Laos. Harriman's observation encapsulated a basic post-Geneva disagreement between the United States and France: the former tried to prevent a Pathet Lao victory by encouraging a center-right alliance; the latter sought to maintain a neutral equilibrium by promoting three separate factions.[6]

At 11:15 A.M., April 19, 1963, President Kennedy telephoned Harriman seeking the latest information about Laos for an appearance that day at the annual convention of the American Society of Newspaper Editors. Kennedy, whose prepared remarks focused on domestic economic issues and the budget, anticipated questions about this latest Laotian crisis. In recent days the Pathet Lao had taken control of the northeastern corner of the Plaine des Jarres and had forced Kong Le's neutralist forces to retreat from the main airfield to a fallback airstrip to the west at Muong Phanh. "The situation doesn't look very good, does it?" Kennedy said.[7]

"It looks very bad," said Harriman, who added that the only "good" development was that Souvanna had, for the first time, publicly blamed the Pathet Lao for the fighting: "That gives us a reason for now going directly to Moscow" to confront Khrushchev on the Soviet pledges to ensure communist compliance with the Geneva agreement. Asked explicitly by Kennedy for his opinion on "going to the Russians," Harriman replied that the US government "ought to" approach the Soviets. Moreover, he and Roger Hilsman, the newly appointed assistant secretary of state for far eastern affairs, would likely recommend that Harriman himself should point out to Khrushchev "that this is a really serious situation." Less than an hour after his phone call with the president, Harriman told National Security Adviser McGeorge Bundy that he was "perfectly willing" to go to Moscow "if the president wanted him to."[8]

Meeting with Khrushchev about Laos would not be a mere diplomatic protest. In a memorandum to Kennedy, Michael Forrestal wrote that a Harriman trip to Moscow would seek to "impress the Soviets with the fact that there is real danger of U.S. physical involvement in Laos if the Geneva Accords continue to be flagrantly violated by the Pathet Lao and the [DRV]." Harriman, according to Forrestal, thought that the introduction of US troops into Laos must be "a real possibility" before any meeting with Khrushchev. An analysis by the State Department's Bureau of Intelligence and Research concluded: "United States military deployments in the vicinity of Laos credibly signaling intent to intervene seem the only possible means of stimulating Soviet pressures on Hanoi to desist from further military support for the Pathet Lao."[9]

Kennedy approached the decision to send Harriman to meet with Khrushchev with considerable deliberation. At an April 19 White House meeting attended by top State, Defense, and CIA officials, Kennedy reminded his advisers that they were only discussing "the question of whether Governor Harriman should go to Moscow," not making "a recommendation." Attorney General Robert Kennedy observed that there was an even "more important" question than whether Harriman should meet with Khrushchev: What would he tell the Soviet premier? "You can't just go and say, 'Please, you've got to behave,'" said Robert Kennedy. "We've got to go and say, 'If you don't, this is what we're prepared to do.'"[10]

What the Kennedy administration was prepared to do in Laos was far from clear. Among the military options discussed at the April 19 meeting were sending US ground troops back to Thailand and redeploying White Star Special Forces teams to Laos. Defense Secretary McNamara opposed both measures, a position that reflected the longstanding dispute between the State Department and the Pentagon about the use of military force in Southeast Asia. Some State Department officials, including Roger Hilsman, had concluded that the introduction of US ground troops into Thailand during the 1962 crisis had "made the Communists reassess the levels of overt military aggression they can undertake in Laos without triggering US intervention."[11] Pentagon officials, however, were uncomfortable with using US ground troops merely as a political signal. The US military wanted any further deployments to include a much larger logistic and combat force capable of dealing with any form of escalation, including execution of the "limited nuclear operations" of CINCPAC OPLAN 32–63, the US war plan for defending mainland Southeast Asia.[12]

"If military pressure is to be threatened," said McNamara, the United States should deploy a carrier task force off the coast of North Vietnam or Air Force units to Thailand. Without commenting on McNamara's recommendation, President Kennedy requested an NSC meeting the next day to continue the discussion. He wanted military proposals from the Pentagon—"up to considering some action in the Hanoi area"—that would indicate the "increased concern" of the United States with the situation in Laos. In response to a question from Harriman about "the direction" of his thinking, Kennedy acknowledged that the threat of US intervention had "held the line" in the Lao crises of 1961 and 1962. Yet he also mused about what would happen after the "threat is gone." In other words, what would the United States do if the Pathet Lao continued to attack neutralist forces after he sent carriers or a limited number of ground troops to the region?[13]

Although Kennedy recognized the possible limits of Soviet leverage and interest in Indochina, his comments to his advisers that day indicated a belief that Khrushchev could remove North Vietnamese troops from Laos as easily as he could withdraw Soviet missiles from Cuba. Explicitly linking the cold war battlefields in the Caribbean and Southeast Asia, Kennedy said that Laos and Cuba were "very interrelated" and wondered whether "doing something more intense in Cuba"—for example, low-level reconnaissance over the island—might influence the Soviets and events in Laos: "We can't very well permit them [the communists] to push ahead [in Laos] while we look like we are accepting the situation in Cuba, which is very unsatisfactory to us."[14]

At the April 20 NSC meeting, Kennedy asked his advisers what kind of US "military preparations" might help strengthen any diplomatic approaches to the Soviets by the British, the US ambassador in Moscow, or Harriman. General Taylor recommended that Admiral Felt should visit Vientiane, then Bangkok, to confer with the SEATO military committee. Taylor also suggested that a carrier task force sail from Subic Bay in the Philippines to the Gulf of Tonkin. Both steps would be threatening gestures indicating that the United States was preparing for military intervention in the region.[15]

Rusk proposed the deployment of US ground forces in northern South Vietnam, perhaps in Hue or Danang: "If we have to consider threats against or action against North Vietnam, I think some forces there in that part of the country could be extremely helpful." Taylor, however, responded that he saw no advantage in putting troops ashore in South Vietnam. "It might come up later, but not now," he said. President Kennedy also knocked down Rusk's idea, observing: "You'd have a tough time getting them out of there. I'd rather put them in Thailand than Hue. But anyway we're not going to settle that today."[16]

Shifting the topic to possible military operations against North Vietnam, Kennedy asked his advisers for recommendations should such action be "desirable." One idea that the president mentioned was a CIA proposal to sabotage the port of Haiphong by sinking a ship at the harbor's shallow entrance. Casting about for a plausible military response to the crisis in Laos, Kennedy asked the Pentagon to prepare a study "of exactly what we could do" to North Vietnam. He also expressed skepticism "that bombing even Hanoi would do much compared to the risks it would entail." General Taylor assured the president that there were many military options, ranging from a visible naval presence in international waters off the coast of Vietnam to bombing "selected points" outside of Hanoi. McNamara added that there were "several very vulnerable rail bridges that could be taken out if that seemed desirable."[17]

During a discussion of the administration's various diplomatic initiatives with the Soviet Union, including a nuclear test ban treaty, Kennedy vented his frustration with Moscow's inability or unwillingness to abide by its Geneva commitments: "We're not going to be able to talk [to Soviet officials] about anything if the Geneva Accords are going to blow up." He added that the communist attacks against Kong Le's neutralist forces were "a much more direct assault on the Geneva Accords than we could have anticipated."[18]

As in the previous day's meeting, Kennedy made a dubious connection between Laos and Cuba, a point of view that emphasized the global chess match with Khrushchev over a nuanced understanding of the political and historical forces at work in Southeast Asia. According to minutes of the April 20 meeting, prepared by William E. Colby, chief of the CIA's Far East Division, "The President stated his belief that it was necessary to raise the pressure somewhat in Cuba. He felt that we could hardly continue to carry out a mild policy in Cuba at the time the Communists are carrying out an aggressive policy in Laos." Kennedy approved high-altitude U-2 flights over Cuba, which the Soviets had recently threatened to shoot down, and other covert activities targeting the Castro regime. The president also authorized Harriman to proceed to London and Paris to confer with allies about Laos but still did not decide whether he should go to Moscow.[19]

The next day, Sunday, April 21, Kennedy made his decision. Calling Harriman from Camp David, the presidential retreat in Maryland, Kennedy wryly asked: "Am I talking to the architect of the Geneva Accords?" Harriman told Kennedy that now was "the moment to talk" with Khrushchev. "We have every right to demand that he live up to his agreement." Harriman added that confronting Khrushchev may "not do any good but it won't do any harm." Kennedy concluded the conversation by saying, "I think you ought to do it."[20]

At the time of Kennedy's phone call with Harriman, the fighting between the Pathet Lao and neutralists on the Plaine des Jarres had decreased to sporadic skirmishing and occasional artillery exchanges. As usual, the fighting among the Laotians had not been particularly intense. Between March 31 and April 20, eighty-five neutralist and seventy-one Pathet Lao forces were killed in action. Kong Le, although suffering some defections to the dissident neutralists, had been strengthened by the arrival of the Ninth and Twenty-fourth FAR infantry battalions and specialists in such areas as armor and communications. Hmong guerrilla units near the plain not only harassed Pathet Lao lines of communication but also hand-carried to Kong Le's forces supplies that had been airdropped by Air America. The US mission in Vientiane reported that the neutralists' "once precarious position has been considerably improved."[21]

To stop the fighting on the Plaine des Jarres, Souvanna Phouma traveled to Khang Khay for talks with Pathet Lao leaders Souphanouvong, Nouhak, and Singkapo and with Colonel Deuane, the commander of the dissident neutralist forces. Accompanying Souvanna were the three ICC commissioners in Laos and the ambassadors from the United Kingdom and Soviet Union. The Pathet Lao officials charged that Kong Le had been the aggressor in the recent fighting and that FAR troops had participated in the action. To bolster his allegations, Souphanouvong claimed to have intercepted communications between Kong Le and Phoumi.[22]

Souvanna, acknowledging a request from Kong Le for conservative reinforcements, told the Pathet Lao leaders that he had refused it. According to a report of the meeting by UK ambassador Hopson, Souvanna backed Kong Le's military actions and "made it clear" that the Pathet Lao version of events was "only one side of the story." The prime minister declared: "Past history must now be forgotten and immediate measures [must now be] taken to stop further killing." His proposal for ending the crisis included a ceasefire, a withdrawal of Hmong and FAR forces from the plain, and a settlement between Kong Le and Deuane that Souvanna would decide as an internal neutralist matter.[23]

Ambassador Hopson, reviewing the poor record of past truces and agreements, expressed his doubts that this ceasefire would "last any longer than the others." Declaring that some way must be found to ensure compliance with this latest agreement, Hopson urged the ICC to establish teams on the plain in areas controlled by the Pathet Lao, the neutralists, and, if necessary, the Hmong. Souvanna endorsed this recommendation, but Polish ICC commissioner Thee opposed it. Souvanna, posing the question directly to Souphanouvong, asked if he would accept an ICC team in Khang Khay. After a short consultation with Nouhak, the answer was "no."[24]

Souvanna also received a negative reply when he asked Souphanouvong whether he intended to return to Vientiane. The prime minister reminded his half-brother of his obligations to the government and the king, but Souphanouvong was unmoved. Vientiane, which the US embassy described as "unusually tense" in the weeks after Quinim's assassination, was once again a dangerous place for NLHS officials. In 1959 the government of Phoui Sananikone had jailed Souphanouvong and other NLHS leaders, who escaped the following year and made their way to Sam Neua. On April 16, 1963, a little over two weeks after Quinim's murder, an "unknown gunman" assassinated a police official who was one of the foreign minister's followers. The American embassy reported that Souphanouvong and other leftists were "highly agitated" by this latest political killing.[25]

On April 19 Phoumi Vongvichit, the NLHS minister of information, slipped out of Vientiane. Other leftist officials were rumored to be planning to leave for Pathet Lao–controlled territory. Siho's DNC, tightening its grip on the city, raided Phoumi Vongvichit's premises, confiscated procommunist propaganda, and arrested a printing clerk. In a meeting with Ambassador Unger, Souvanna gave no indication of concern over the exodus of NLHS ministers. He told Unger that Phoumi Vongvichit had asked to go to Sam Neua to work for a peaceful settlement of the conflict. The request seemed to amuse Souvanna, as it confirmed that neither Souphanouvong nor Phoumi Vongvichit could act independently of the LPP. "[The] central committee in Sam Neua obviously calls the shots," said Souvanna. He subsequently asked Phoumi Vongvichit to return to Vientiane, but the appeal was no more successful than the one to Souphanouvong.[26]

Only two relatively insignificant cabinet officials remained in Vientiane as NLHS members of the coalition government. Maintaining the façade of a government of national union, the absent NLHS ministers did not formally resign, and Souvanna did not strip them of their portfolios. Although not fully appreciated at the time, Souvanna's second coalition government was effectively finished, lasting only nine months.

At the April 22 NSC meeting, the third White House discussion of Laos in four days, President Kennedy talked about the dilemma of maintaining the fragile truce on the Plaine des Jarres. If Phoumi withdrew his reinforcements, a prerequisite for any ceasefire, "Kong Le's position is almost hopeless," said Kennedy. Yet the presence of FAR troops provided an excuse for further Pathet Lao attacks on neutralist positions. "I have so little confidence that Phoumi's forces would contribute anything to the fighting," said Kennedy. Perhaps the presence of Phoumi's reinforcements on the plain, he said, was "more harmful than it [was] useful."[27]

Among the first topics discussed at the meeting was a State Department paper on US actions in Laos that, in Rusk's words, "might provide some basis for attacks or charges that we ourselves have been in violation of the [Geneva] ceasefire agreement." The report included a summary of US covert operations in Laos, an unusually sensitive topic for an NSC meeting attended by at least eighteen officials. To maintain "plausible deniability" of the president's knowledge of clandestine intelligence activities, such discussions were generally confined to the smaller Special Group, chaired by McGeorge Bundy. The covert operations in the State Department paper included high- and low-level photo-reconnaissance missions, electronic intelligence (ELINT) overflights to gather information on enemy radars, and ammunition airdrops to the Hmong guerrillas. Since the signing of the Geneva agreement, "eleven covert ammunition resupply drops from Thailand have been made to [Hmong] tribesmen in Laos." Also mentioned in the report were the two CIA case officers at Hmong headquarters and sixty-five Thai PARU forces scattered among the Hmong guerrilla units. Because these and other covert activities were either unknown to the communists or difficult to prove, Rusk told the president that the US government was "in reasonably good shape" to deny charges of violating the Geneva accords.[28]

It is unclear whether Kennedy was reassured by Rusk's questionable conclusion. Since the mid-1950s, the CIA had played a conspicuous role in Laos that inspired suspicion among allies and protests from communists in and out of the kingdom. Kennedy had consistently insisted that any breakdown of the Geneva agreement must be a consequence of overt violations by the communists rather than those of US-backed conservatives and neutralists. At the April 22 NSC meeting, he appeared concerned that US covert activity might be blamed for the collapse of the agreement. Kennedy's immediate response to Rusk's presentation was a question about the CIA's most successful program in Laos: "How much" of the fighting in the Plaine des Jarres was attributable to communist "anxiety" about the Hmong guerrillas? "What is the reason," Kennedy asked, "for the increased attention to Kong Le [by] the Pathet Lao and the dissident neutralists?" Rusk, answering the second part of Kennedy's question but not the first, declared that the "Pathet Lao–oriented neutralists" had long intended to take over Kong Le's forces. Hilsman speculated that the late foreign minister Quinim had "exceeded his instructions" by assassinating Colonel Ketsana, which set in motion a chain of events that "escalated beyond what the communists intended."[29]

When the conversation turned to US military moves in the region, Kennedy asked about the destination of the carrier task force and the marine battalion landing team discussed two days earlier. McNamara replied that naval units were heading toward the Gulf of Tonkin below the demilitarized zone separating North and South Vietnam. The task force included the attack carrier *Ticonderoga*, four destroyers, and the amphibious assault carrier *Princeton*. The positioning of US forces reflected the Pentagon conviction that if military threats—rather than military action—were the president's preferred instrument of policy, then the possibility of carrier-based air attacks against North Vietnam was the least objectionable option among weak alternatives. Kennedy, who shared the State Department view that a limited number of ground forces represented a more credible threat of US intervention in Laos, observed: "The Marine battalion really doesn't seem to me to do much good off South Vietnam if we don't think we would land there. The only place you could conceivably land would be Thailand."[30]

Instructing the Pentagon to move the fleet toward the waters off of Thailand, Kennedy quipped that this decision had already been reported in that day's *New York Times*. The remark drew hearty laughs from his national security team, but Kennedy was hardly amused by the article's claim that he intended to merely "show the flag" in the Gulf of Siam. Echoing a *Times* article from May 1962, reporter Tad Szulc wrote that Kennedy and his advisers would use the US Navy "only as a symbol of force for the time being," implying that any fleet movements were a bluff. Citing unnamed "authoritative sources," Szulc wrote: "The Administration had no plan to send Marine and Army forces to Thailand," undercutting the threat the president hoped to convey to the communists. The article "couldn't have put it in a worse way," Kennedy said to his advisers, adding that the report was "not completely accurate, but it's just enough to make the whole exercise look rather futile."[31]

Near the end of the meeting, Kennedy asked whether the Defense Department had prepared its recommendations for possible military action against North Vietnam. "We're still working on it, Mr. President,"

McNamara replied. The next day the Joint Chiefs of Staff submitted to McNamara military options that might "bring about stability in Laos." To demonstrate US intentions, without using force, the chiefs proposed naval maneuvers off the South Vietnamese coast, high- and low-altitude photo reconnaissance, and the deployment of air units to Thailand. Recommendations for landing ground troops in Thailand, Laos, or South Vietnam were conspicuously absent. The JCS proposals for overt action with "hostile intent" included air attacks against ports, bridges, airfields, fuel storage facilities, and industrial plants in both Laos and North Vietnam. The chiefs, emphasizing the risks of escalation and the consequent need for additional US forces, warned: "If the DRV were bombed, Communist China would consider a strong military reaction."[32]

To Pentagon officials, the options for preventing a communist victory in Laos appeared to be either militarily ineffective or politically unacceptable. The threatening military moves that had halted Pathet Lao advances in 1961 and 1962 seemed to have "worn thin and cannot be relied upon," wrote Stephen A. Loftus Jr., acting director of the Far East Region of International Security Affairs, the Defense Department's policy advisory unit. Moreover, the failure to take military action after an unsuccessful threat would raise serious questions about US steadfastness among allies and adversaries.[33] Military planners were unimpressed with Roger's Hilsman's suggestion to deploy "up to one division" of US combat troops in the Mekong Valley of Laos. In Hilsman's view, a limited commitment of ground troops to support the Geneva agreement would demonstrate to friends and foes "the US intent to maintain stability in Southeast Asia."[34] The Pentagon, however, opposed putting combat units of any size just in Laos. A small force would be vulnerable to communist escalation, and a large one would still not be confronting the source of the problem: North Vietnam. And despite the president's request for proposals for direct action against the DRV, the military solution preferred by the chiefs, Pentagon officials concluded that such attacks were "unpalatable" to the administration.[35]

Before meeting with Khrushchev in Moscow, Averell Harriman traveled to London to discuss Laos with British officials. As Geneva cochair, the United Kingdom had thus far played the leading role in urging the Soviet Union to encourage the communist signatories to comply with the agreement. Edward Peck of the Foreign Office admitted that the UK cochair role was "about played out for now." The next phase, he said, would be Harriman's "testing" of the Khrushchev-Kennedy understanding reached in Vienna. At an April 23 lunch with Foreign Secretary Home, Harriman said that the United States agreed with the British that the "Geneva 'facade' must be maintained intact even if current developments should result in [a] de facto partition of [the] country."[36]

In Moscow, on April 26, Harriman met with Soviet foreign minister Gromyko, who had earlier insisted to British officials that the United States was "to blame for [the] current difficulties" in Laos. Harriman, after an exchange of diplomatic pleasantries with Gromyko, presented the US case: Kennedy and Khrushchev had reached an agreement in Vienna, confirmed at Geneva, which was in danger of breaking down. Although Souvanna Phouma had not been the US choice for prime minister, the Kennedy administration had done its utmost to support him and Laotian neutrality. While the US government welcomed the recent Khang Khay ceasefire agreement, the Pathet Lao refused to permit the stationing of ICC representatives with its forces on the Plaine des Jarres, and Polish commissioner Thee prohibited ICC inspectors from remaining with Kong Le's troops overnight. "The Pole," said Harriman, "has remained completely uncooperative, apparently preferring to follow the orders of the Pathet Lao rather than the dictates of his own conscience." Harriman declared that the first US-Soviet objective should be "giving the ICC full freedom of movement to carry out its responsibilities."[37]

Gromyko, unmoved by Harriman's representations, observed that the situation in Laos could take a dangerous turn. Initiating a testy exchange about the assassination of the Lao foreign minister, Gromyko asked: "Who killed Quinim Pholsena?" The United States, he said, "had reacted in a rather routine fashion to the murder," and Soviet officials were "more than puzzled" by the assassination. Harriman replied that the US government was puzzled by the murder, too. "Only you can know how puzzled you are," the foreign minister responded. Harriman, according to the minutes of the meeting, reacted with "considerable heat" to the implication of US complicity in the assassination. He "challenged Mr. Gromyko to explain this statement," adding that the United States had also denounced the killing. The Soviet foreign minister responded by reaffirming his government's "condemnation of the 'forces' and people behind the murder."[38]

Gromyko said that the Soviet Union had not changed its position of support for a neutral, independent Laos. In the present crisis, he declared, there were two options for the superpowers: "pour fuel on the fire" or demonstrate "coolness and restraint." Gromyko said: "Reports of the 7th Fleet movements, and plans to send military contingents to Thailand are not contributing to caution and restraint." Moreover, he dismissed as "completely absurd" the allegation that North Vietnamese troops remained in Laos. The US might have "suppositions," he said, but there were no facts to back them up. "Gromyko was at his legalistic, pettifogging prime," according to William Sullivan, who had traveled to Moscow with Harriman.[39]

Harriman and Gromyko debated for two and one-half hours, agreeing on virtually nothing about the causes of and remedies for the conflict in Laos. At the end of the meeting, Gromyko did acknowledge that Harriman's remarks had persuaded him of the US government's continuing interest in Laotian neutrality. Harriman, stressing one of Kennedy's principal themes, said that Laos was a symbol of US-Soviet cooperation that "would have an effect on many other questions of greater importance." Harriman subsequently warned Gromyko that if "the neutralists were blotted out," the ensuing confrontation between the right-wing forces and the Pathet Lao "could result in a dangerous situation which might spread far beyond Laos."[40]

At 3:00 P.M., April 26, 1963, Harriman met with Khrushchev in his office in the Kremlin Senate, the same room where the American diplomat had negotiated with Josef Stalin two decades earlier. "Cordial" and even "genial" at times, "Khrushchev looked very tired," Harriman reported to Kennedy,[41] neither of whom knew the extent to which the Soviet premier was losing support among his Kremlin colleagues for his erratic brinksmanship in Berlin and Cuba and for his unilateral management of Soviet affairs. Harriman, after making diplomatic small talk about changes in the office since his earlier visits, handed Khrushchev a letter from President Kennedy that read:

I have become most concerned over recent developments in Laos. As you know, I have always regarded our mutual commitment in Vienna to bring peace to that unhappy country as an impor-

tant milestone in Soviet/American relations. If we could work
successfully together to make Laos neutral, we could, I have
thought, make progress in resolving other matters which are at
issue between us.

It is because of this concern that I have asked Governor Harriman to make a special trip to confer with you as my representative
on this particular aspect of our relations. You and your colleagues
have known him well and I put great hope in the results of his discussions with you. I will be awaiting Governor Harriman's report
with keen interest.[42]

Khrushchev, after hearing a Russian translation of the letter, thanked
Harriman and said that he agreed with its contents. The deteriorating
situation in Laos, said Khrushchev, was "just as unpleasant for the Soviets as it was for anyone else." Commenting on the small number of Soviet
personnel in Laos, Khrushchev claimed that his country had little first-
hand information on events there and a limited ability to influence them.
Declaring Soviet support for the neutral government of national union,
Khrushchev said that the United States apparently wanted "something
different." He commented on US naval movements off the coast of Vietnam and "other indications of the use of military force." What did all this
mean? Khrushchev asked. Was it blackmail? Did the United States really
want war or "only a piece of war"? He added that it was "all right with
him if the United States wanted another outbreak" of fighting in Laos.[43]

Harriman said that what President Kennedy wanted was a restoration of the ceasefire on the Plaine des Jarres. Denouncing the Pathet Lao
for both its attacks on Kong Le and its resistance to establishing an ICC
presence on the plain, Harriman proposed that the United States and
the Soviet Union "develop joint action to install the ICC." Khrushchev
agreed that stationing ICC representatives in the plain seemed "practical"
but declared that such an arrangement was beyond "the competence" of
the two superpowers. This was a decision that could only be made by the
Lao government.

When Harriman observed that the Soviet Union had a "responsibility" to ensure that the "socialist groups behave in accordance with the
Geneva agreement," Khrushchev replied that the diplomat was "very
clever in trying to put such a responsibility on him." Indirectly backing

away from Pushkin's explicit Geneva commitments, the Soviet premier made the risible claim that "the international socialist movement is built on the principle of mutual respect for sovereignty." Later in the conversation, Khrushchev said to Harriman, "very seriously," that he should tell President Kennedy, "We are still true to the word we gave him in Vienna, but the situation is very delicate. Our word is in regard to a third party and this makes for a real problem."[44]

During the three-and-one-half-hour conversation, which included discussions of Cuba, Berlin, and a nuclear test ban, Khrushchev dismissed the importance of Laos. "There is nothing really serious going on in Laos," he said. "It is a country with only two million people. No matter what happens there, there will be no waves created in the river or in the ocean." William Sullivan, who attended the meeting with Harriman, recalled: "Khrushchev obviously didn't want to be pinned down on anything." Michael Forrestal, who was also present, told his colleagues on the NSC staff: "Khrushchev did not have the foggiest notion of the geography of Laos and, when Harriman mentioned a few Laotian personalities, Khrushchev impatiently exclaimed that he did not know all those silly Laotian names or the individuals to whom these names belonged."[45]

Harriman, in his report to the president, wrote that Khrushchev "is fed up with the subject [of Laos] and wishes it would go away." It was Harriman's "impression" that "Khrushchev probably would like to live up to his Vienna agreement." His "difficulty" in keeping the agreement was the more militant attitude of the PRC and DRV. Whether or not Khrushchev had the will or ability to influence the Pathet Lao or even Marek Thee remained "unanswered." In a subsequent conversation with Prime Minister Macmillan, Harriman "expressed doubt as to how much Khrushchev could or would influence the Pathet Lao or [North Vietnamese] actions in Laos."[46]

Belatedly, Harriman requested a State Department assessment of Soviet influence with China and North Vietnam "in the light of continued Communist obstructionism in Laos and against the background of the Sino-Soviet dispute." Thomas Hughes, who succeeded Roger Hilsman as the director of INR, concluded that Moscow could "probably" influence Beijing's support for the Pathet Lao by threatening to renege on the Soviet commitment to defend China if the conflict in Laos escalated. On the topic of Soviet influence over the DRV, Hughes observed: "There is inadequate evidence for assessing Hanoi's present relationship with Moscow." In other words, the State Department's intelligence arm made the astonishing admission that it had little idea of the strength or weakness of Soviet leverage with North Vietnam, the primary sponsor of the Pathet Lao.[47]

To Assistant Secretary Hilsman, the Soviet Union appeared "partly unwilling" and "partly unable" to influence China and the DRV. He concurred with the notion that only a serious threat of US intervention in Southeast Asia would induce the Soviets "to live up to their special commitment" at Geneva. "It is questionable whether the Soviets realize how far we have been pushed towards US military action in the Laos-Viet-Nam area," he wrote to Harriman, adding: "It may be time for us to give them clearer signs of the true situation." Hilsman recommended that the United States maintain public and private pressure on the Soviet Union to follow through on its Geneva promises. Such a policy might have some effect on Soviet efforts to be "helpful" in Laos. If it did not, then the contrast between Soviet obligations and performance might increase international support "for whatever measures we may have to employ in Laos."[48]

An immediate indication of Khrushchev's limited influence on the Pathet Lao occurred on May 3, 1963, when two ICC helicopters came under fire from mortars and automatic weapons shortly after landing on the Plaine des Jarres. On a mission to retrieve the body of a French military advisor killed by a road mine the previous day, the passengers on the helicopters included Indian, Canadian, and Polish ICC representatives, as well as French diplomats and soldiers. Three Frenchmen and one Indian ICC official were wounded. The Pathet Lao blamed the attack on "reactionary forces," a claim few found persuasive. In a conversation with Ambassador Unger, Souvanna said that "he had all but concluded [that the] PL want war sooner or later."[49]

Accounts of "Thee's ridiculous behavior" after the incident particularly disturbed US officials. Before hearing any evidence about the attack, he challenged eyewitness reports of Pathet Lao responsibility and tried to place the blame on FAR forces that were not even in the area. The day after the attack, according to the State Department, "Thee incredibly saw fit to put on [a] silly act of posing for [a] photograph before the damaged helicopters while others were engaged in removing bodies of those killed earlier by [a] Pathet Lao mine."[50]

A more substantive aspect of Thee's obstructionism was his refusal to allow Polish ICC representatives to join their Indian and Canadian colleagues at Kong Le's headquarters to monitor the ceasefire. This failure to abide by an ICC majority decision, the US government charged, constituted a Polish violation of the Geneva agreement. On May 6 William R. Tyler, assistant secretary of state for European affairs, summoned Polish ambassador Edward Drozniak to the State Department to protest this Geneva violation and Thee's "irresponsible behavior" after the attack on the ICC helicopters. Tyler's démarche in Washington was no more effective than Harriman's in Moscow. The Polish government replied that sending the ICC to the plain was "illegal" because the action lacked the unanimous approval of the coalition government. Dean Rusk, expressing his disappointment to Polish foreign minister Adam Rapacki, suggested that the Geneva accords had significance beyond the borders of Laos and that "it would be difficult to predict the serious consequences" of a breakdown in the agreement.[51]

While US diplomacy faltered, contingency planning for air strikes against North Vietnam continued. At a May 6 meeting at CINCPAC headquarters, where senior officials from Washington and Saigon were reviewing programs in South Vietnam, Admiral Felt's staff presented a "plan for overt, gradually escalating operations in North Vietnam" to a restricted group of military and civilian officials. McNamara said that eight targets, recently submitted to President Kennedy by the Joint Chiefs of Staff, should be incorporated into planning for possible US military operations in North Vietnam. General Wheeler explained to the group that the JCS targeting was "designed to convince Ho Chi Minh he should desist from intervention [in Laos]."[52]

Wheeler, after listening to an army concept for covert sabotage and harassment operations in North Vietnam, repeated a conclusion from his Vietnam report earlier in the year: "Ho Chi Minh is fighting a war without making much of an investment." Demonstrating the political sensitivity that characterized his tenure as JCS chairman under Lyndon Johnson (and that frustrated some of his fellow military officers), Wheeler declared that proposals for "offensive action" against the DRV must not place the president in an "intolerable" position in relation to the Geneva agreement. Aware of Kennedy's reluctance to take overt military action against North Vietnam, Wheeler said that recommendations for air attacks "invited a negative presidential decision." He dismissed the CIA's "meager assets" for operations against North Vietnam and repeated his January proposal for MACV direction and guidance of covert attacks conducted by the South Vietnamese. The JCS and CIA chief McCone "were generally in favor of this concept," said Wheeler. Such attacks would not cripple North Vietnam, he said, but they would "levy a cost upon the DRV" for its actions in South Vietnam and Laos.[53]

McNamara, unwilling to comment on proposals for covert military action in North Vietnam before the chiefs reviewed them, shared the overall conclusion of conference participants that there had been "favorable progress" in South Vietnam. The US officials discussed Laos only peripherally and did not appear unduly alarmed by infiltration from North Vietnam, estimated at approximately five hundred men per month. There was speculation that infiltration of personnel and materiel into South Vietnam would increase "as roads through Laos improved." John H. Richardson, the CIA chief of station in Saigon, said that US and South Vietnamese border control programs could hinder but not stop infiltration. At least twice during the meeting, McNamara asked about the source of Viet Cong arms and ammunition. Colonel James M. Winterbottom, MACV's chief of intelligence, estimated that 50 to 60 percent of Viet Cong weapons were US arms captured from the South Vietnamese. The Viet Cong also locally fabricated small arms, grenades, and mines.[54]

The next day at the White House, McNamara briefed President Kennedy on the Honolulu conference. Observing that most Viet Cong recruits and weapons came from South Vietnam, McNamara predicted that the United States would get the war "under control" within two or three years. By then, he hoped that the number of US military advisers in South Vietnam, which in 1963 totaled some sixteen thousand, could be reduced to five hundred to seven hundred. Ironically, only one day before the beginning of the Buddhist crisis, which would destabilize the Diem regime and lead to deepening US involvement in Vietnam, McNamara's principal concern appeared to be the "fantastic" cost of military proposals for assistance to South Vietnam during the presumed postwar years of 1965 through 1967. Referring to the administration's nearly $500-million-per-year military assistance program in South Korea, McNamara commented to Kennedy: "We certainly don't want another Korea to develop in South Vietnam, and we are well on the way to doing that."[55]

To demonstrate progress in the war and to encourage South Vietnamese self-reliance, McNamara repeated a recommendation that he had earlier made to Kennedy: "We ought to think about the possibility of bringing a thousand men home by the end of the year." He informed the president that he had asked the military to begin planning for such a withdrawal, but he had not yet made a final decision about it. Kennedy agreed that it was too soon for a decision. If the war was not "in very good shape," the president said, a withdrawal of US troops would be counterproductive. "Absolutely," McNamara replied, adding: "But on the other hand, if we had two or three victories, this would be just exactly the shot in the arm we have to have."[56]

Chapter 11

We're Going to Have to Take Some Action

The US commitment to Laos entered a new and ambiguous phase in May 1963. The fighting on the Plaine des Jarres, the flight of the NLHS ministers from Vientiane, and the failure of US diplomacy with the Soviet Union meant that the neutral government of national union envisioned by the Geneva agreement was likely finished. In a cable to the State Department, Ambassador Unger observed that in recent years US policy had moved from an unsuccessful military effort to establish a "pro-western conservative" government to a political "contest" among three factions conducted "under conditions of general peace rather than military action. At this point we are somewhere in between." Anticipating further Pathet Lao encroachment across the country, Unger sought "a better understanding" of US military objectives in Laos.[1]

The reply from the State Department reflected the Kennedy administration's uncertainty about next steps: "Role of US and/or SEATO in case [the] Lao situation should deteriorate further is again being studied in Washington along with [a] general updating of contingency plans." Beyond this vague assertion, the department could "only provide general guidance." The most basic US objective was ensuring that the FAR and neutralist forces had sufficient military strength to "hold out" against a Pathet Lao offensive—at least long enough for Washington officials "to focus international attention" on the fighting and to decide "what actions to take."[2] In his history of CIA support for the Hmong, Thomas Ahern observed that the department's reply to Brown "came close to saying that the United States would not know what it wanted until imminent disaster compelled it to act."[3]

The fundamental concept for US military intervention in Laos remained SEATO Plan 5 and its multilateral and unilateral variations. State Department and White House officials considered such sizable deployments of US troops an appropriate response to a large-scale communist offensive but an unimaginative, muscle-bound option for coping with the gradual erosion of neutralist-FAR positions. The planning challenge, according to Forrestal and McGeorge Bundy, was devising "a military course of action as a means of making the Pathet Lao and their allies think twice before going any further."[4]

In a June 17, 1963, memorandum to the president, Rusk and McNamara proposed a three-phase program of "graduated increases in US political and military pressure" to prevent "further expansion of Communist control in Laos." Approved by State Department officials, Pentagon civilians, and the Joint Chiefs of Staff, the paper stressed that the proposed actions were not merely "a contingency response" but "a method of influencing the over-all situation." A significant document in the history of the Vietnam War, the memorandum foreshadowed not only the military planning in Vietnam during the first year of the Johnson administration but also the flawed analyses that emphasized demonstrations of US "determination," threats of "serious consequences" for the DRV, and assurances of control over escalation.[5]

The program's first phase, characterized as "stretching" the Geneva agreement, included proposals for stepping up the delivery of 105-mm howitzers and other heavy weapons to Kong Le and Phoumi and for "expand[ing] the use of highly mobile South Vietnamese border patrols in Laos." The stated objective of this phase was the reconstitution of the government of national union, the withdrawal of North Vietnamese forces from Laos, and the restoration of neutralist territory lost since April 1, 1963. Although "not sanguine" about achieving these ambitious goals, the memorandum's authors were prepared to "settle for establishing an informal but stabilized partition under the facade of a neutralist government." Diplomatic and political actions in this phase would convey "the idea that our patience is growing short; if the Communists will not cooperate under the Geneva Agreements we must take other measures to protect Lao independence and regional peace."[6]

The program's second phase—the need for which was virtually a foregone conclusion—involved "measures overtly outside the Geneva framework." US involvement in them, however, would remain clandestine. Proposed military actions included the expanded use of Thai PARU units and "other specialist teams"; support for third-country special forces ("primarily SVN and Thai 'volunteers'"); and an increase in CIA "sabotage operations" in Laos and North Vietnam. The objectives of this phase remained the same as the first: reconstitution of the national union government under the Geneva agreement or an informal partition. The political message was US willingness to "take extraordinary measures to offset Communist expansionism."[7]

An intelligence estimate of communist reactions to the first two phases of the program conveyed a mixed message to policymakers. On the one hand, there appeared to be "a good chance" that the proposed actions "would lead either to a re-establishment of the Government of National Union or to *de facto* partition." On the other hand, neither phase "would go far to insure lasting stabilization in Laos." The country's internal situation, according to intelligence analysts, "would remain highly vulnerable to the virtually certain continuance of determined Communist efforts at subversion." The Soviet Union, China, DRV, and Pathet Lao were convinced that "they have a good thing going in Laos" and that "the undercutting of the US position" was only a matter of time.[8]

The third phase of the program called for air attacks against the DRV, the mining of approaches to Haiphong harbor, and the commitment of American and SEATO ground troops to operations in Laos and North Vietnam. The overt military action of this phase, according to the proposal, "logically" called for an enlarged objective: the "cessation of DRV subversive activity" in all of Southeast Asia. A possible alternative objective was a Geneva conference to establish a formal partition of Laos that ensured noncommunist control of the Mekong River Valley and the panhandle and, if possible, "a foothold" in the Plaine des Jarres. Intelligence officials informed policymakers that they could not "estimate with any degree of confidence" the communist reaction to phase-three actions.[9]

The sequencing of phase-three military operations revealed lingering disagreements between the State Department and the Pentagon. In a covering memorandum to President Kennedy, Forrestal reported that State Department officials thought it "essential that some U.S. ground forces, if only of a token nature, be introduced into Laos before an air or ground attack upon North Vietnam." The department's goal was "to convince North Vietnam and the ChiComs of the seriousness of U.S. intentions in Laos without running the danger of a rapid escalation." The Pentagon, however, insisted that "no U.S. forces should be introduced into Laos except in connection with a simultaneous operation against North Vietnam," wrote Forrestal. "The military fear that unless our action and our objectives are clearly designed to eliminate the heart of the threat in Hanoi, to introduce troops into Laos would risk long term commitment of U.S. personnel under the most adverse military circumstances."[10]

At a June 19 White House meeting to review the proposed program, President Kennedy sided with the State Department on the sequencing of phase-three military operations, declaring in his opening remarks that he thought that ground troops were "required in Laos prior to air action." Skeptical about the utility of US air attacks, Kennedy said that the "threat of such strikes is influential with the DRV, but that the actual strikes might be less significant." He asked his advisers: "Can air strikes hurt the enemy?" General William F. McKee, vice chief of staff of the air force and acting chairman of the JCS, replied that the Pacific Command had identified more than two hundred targets in the DRV and that attacking them with Navy and USAF aircraft "would seriously hurt" North Vietnam.[11]

Harriman said that the State and Defense departments were seeking approval to proceed with phase one, to plan for phase two, and to consider the possibility of moving to phase three "in the future." Kennedy asked if there were any "tricky items" in phase one, which purportedly only "stretched" the Geneva agreement. Harriman replied that there were very few tricky actions in this phase, which essentially stepped up current US activities. DCI McCone commented that certain proposed CIA operations violated the Geneva agreement and would likely raise suspicions about US involvement in them. Harriman, responding with artful sophistry, said that Souvanna Phouma had already approved "most" of the phase-one proposals and that the US government should rely on the prime minister's authority rather than on the language of the accords.[12]

McNamara, who supported the execution of phase one, observed that the inherent time lag of its military-diplomatic actions would permit detailed planning for phase-two operations. In contrast to his confident, if often mistaken, assessments of the war in Vietnam, McNamara said that he did not have "a firm feeling of the situation" in Laos. He did point out to the assembled officials the pessimistic views of Admiral Felt, who believed that Pathet Lao progress was "moving faster than we realized." In a cable to the JCS, Felt had opined that phases one and two, "while desirable," would not "bear fruit quickly enough to be effective." Implicitly advocating quick escalation to phase three, Felt thought it was "essential" to move ground "forces into Laos concurrently with air strikes in Laos and North Vietnam."[13]

McCone disagreed with Felt's assessment of rapid deterioration in Laos, characterizing the Pathet Lao strategy as "continuous nibbling" that required close US attention. President Kennedy said that he wanted to hear British and French estimates of the situation. Only after learning their views, he said, should US officials "inform them of what we intend to do." Referring to longstanding French criticism of US policy in Laos, Kennedy said that he wanted "the French to be thoroughly involved and consulted at the outset so that they could not later be in a position of saying that the U.S. had unilaterally messed up Laos." When asked whether the program of graduated pressure should be discussed with Thai officials, Kennedy resisted, observing that "whatever we do will be inadequate in Sarit's mind." The president did, however, acknowledge that specific recommendations involving Thai assistance would require further consultation with Sarit's government.[14]

Kennedy approved the execution of phase-one actions and planning for phase two. He directed that the more drastic steps of phase three should "be further refined and reviewed," particularly the unresolved sequencing of ground and air action. At the end of the meeting, Kennedy commented on the domestic political challenges of introducing US combat forces into Laos:

> We have to recognize some facts of life, (1) this course of action at the moment would have a very poor reception in Congress; (2) any such action of this nature will obviously be compared to the situation in Cuba; and (3) that we may have to face this problem and we may have to do it, but it will be extremely difficult to gain complete US support for such action.[15]

The three-phase program of gradually increasing military pressure had been created in Washington without any direct consultation with the US mission in Vientiane. Ambassador Unger, who was on leave and in Paris when the president approved the program's initial actions, felt obliged "to sound the old warning that we should proceed only when we are entirely prepared to assume all the consequences." In a letter to Roger Hilsman, Unger "strongly urge[d] no firm decisions" on a number of planned activities until the two had an opportunity to talk in Washington. Concerned about gaining Souvanna's approval for the program's paramilitary and military operations, Unger indirectly referred to the chaotic fall of 1960, when the US government nominally supported the neutralist prime minister while covertly aiding the anticommunist Phoumi: "We must keep [Souvanna] with us and avoid the emergence again of the appearance of two separate U.S. policies."[16]

A phase-one proposal to establish strategic hamlets in the Mekong River Valley seemed a particularly dubious idea to Unger and his colleagues in Laos. The fortified villages and their related social, economic, and political programs were the principal pacification initiative in South Vietnam. (An analysis by RAND, the military-funded think tank, subsequently concluded that the Diem regime's strategic hamlet program "was poorly administered and its accomplishments were grossly overstated.") Whatever their value in South Vietnam, strategic hamlets seemed to Unger ill adapted to the sparsely populated Lao countryside.[17]

Another questionable Washington decision was the assignment of US military officers to Kong Le's headquarters on the Plaine des Jarres. Although the presence of US combat advisers would undoubtedly increase the competence and morale of neutralist forces, "it would be impossible to persuade [the] French [that] this action [was] appropriate." Anticipating damaged relations with the French ambassador and the FMM officers assisting Kong Le, US officials in Vientiane recommended frequent visits by the embassy's military attaché to Kong Le's headquarters and the possible "special assignment" of a CIA officer to the plain.[18]

The State Department, as instructed by Kennedy, solicited UK and French views of the situation in Laos, while remaining cryptic about US plans. The initial response from the US embassy in London was that the Foreign Office tended to agree that additional actions were required to halt military deterioration in the Plaine des Jarres and elsewhere. David K. E. Bruce, the American ambassador to the United Kingdom, further reported: "[The] British would appreciate more info on specific measures [that the] US [is] contemplating." On June 21 Harriman told the French ambassador, Hervé Alphand, that the United States was "quite ready to discuss developments in Laos fully with the French." When Alphand asked if US plans included "possible military action," Harriman replied: "Nothing was excluded."[19]

Kennedy, like his presidential predecessor and successor, was frustrated by seemingly insufficient UK and French support for US policy in Southeast Asia. (The contrary view, of course, is that the US government simply would not listen to good advice from the Europeans.) On Saturday, June 22, just before boarding Air Force One for a ten-day tour of Europe, Kennedy "erupted again about Laos and asked what our Allies are doing about Laos." UK Ambassador David Ormsby-Gore was summoned to the State Department for a meeting on June 24 "to impress upon him the seriousness" of the US assessment.[20]

Hilsman, during his analysis of the situation in Laos, told Ormsby-Gore that the US government was trying "to act instead of react to various contingencies." He added: "We wished to signal that we meant business." The British diplomat, noting that he was speaking without instructions from his government, said, on the one hand, that "blatant" US violations of the Geneva agreement "would cause concern to the UK." On the other hand, the British government "would approve" discreet efforts to strengthen the Hmong and other noncommunist forces. Hilsman, without going into details, observed that events might "eventually" force the United States "to make moves that would directly violate the Agreements." Harriman, however, emphasized that the initial actions contemplated by the United States fell "within our interpretation of the Geneva Agreements."[21]

What do you want the UK government to do? Ormsby-Gore asked the State Department officials. Harriman replied: join the United States in tripartite meetings with the French here in Washington. The western allies would examine military and economic matters, as well as determine "what steps were possible and advisable if the situation in Laos should become worse." The US government "hoped to stimulate the French into positive thinking and action." Harriman emphasized Kennedy's desire for "inter-allied action so that if something serious happened, all of us would be together and the US not alone, as before." Ormsby-Gore indicated that the United Kingdom was willing to "participate fully" in the proposed meetings.[22]

French officials, preferring bilateral diplomacy, were less eager to join the new group. They were, according to British diplomats, "suspicious that

[the] US is attempting [to] drag [the] French along on courses of action already decided and which may contravene [the] Geneva agreements." Responding to Washington's request for their assessment of the situation, the French reported that the Pathet Lao was capable of expelling the FAR and the neutralists "from all areas outside [of the] Mekong Valley north of Thakhek." Although the FAR and Hmong guerrillas remained a military factor, the neutralist forces "had lost their morale," giving up territory they had shared with the Pathet Lao "without any real combat." Moreover, an "unspecified but certainly not decreased" number of North Vietnamese troops remained in Laos. "Under these circumstances," French officials observed, "it is difficult to define how the neutralist forces could be reinforced within [the] terms of [the] Geneva Agreements."[23]

Despite their prescient skepticism about US intentions, the French agreed to participate in the three-way talks. The first meeting, on July 3, accomplished little more than agreeing to include the Australians in future meetings. The French representatives emphasized that their ongoing participation was "contingent" on the "informal character" of the discussions, and US officials did not reveal their thinking on possible phase-two operations. At a briefing on Southeast Asia for President Kennedy the next day, Hilsman reported that he had met with the allies and that the US government was "moving ahead on the plan" of gradual political-military pressure in Laos. At this meeting, attended only by White House staff and State Department officials, Harriman declared: "I think it's plain that the Russians are trying to disengage" from their Geneva commitments. "Moscow," he said, "is blaming us rather than the communists [in Laos and the DRV] for the trouble."[24]

Kennedy asked no questions and made no comments about Laos at this meeting, which was devoted primarily to the burgeoning Buddhist crisis in South Vietnam. The religious-political protests and Diem's ineffectual response to them were crystalizing noncommunist opposition to his government. Based on reports from Saigon, coup attempts seemed likely in the coming months. "If there is a coup, and/or if Diem is killed, it's hard to say whether it will be a smooth transition or chaos," said Hilsman. "I think we are all agreed that the chances of chaos are much, much less than they were a year ago." Citing the increased tempo of South Vietnamese operations against the PLAF, Hilsman declared: "The war continues to go well in spite of the Buddhist crisis."[25]

Harriman, who had long considered Diem's government "a repressive, dictatorial and unpopular regime," told the president: "I am a little bit more optimistic than Roger" that South Vietnam would "not fall apart if something happens to Diem." Forrestal added that Marine Major General Victor H. Krulak, the JCS special assistant for counterinsurgency and covert operations, had recently toured South Vietnam for two weeks. Krulak concluded, said Forrestal, that US military and economic programs had "stiffen[ed]" South Vietnam to the point where, even if there was "a political upheaval," the country would "probably still hold together in the fight against communism."[26]

Forrestal's characterization of Krulak's trip and conclusions was overstated. The general's visit was one week long, not two, and, more important, his report did not speculate on the impact of a coup on the war. Krulak did, however, comment on the effect of the Buddhist crisis on military operations: "There appeared no evidence that the front line counterinsurgency effort has yet been impeded or decelerated at all by the crisis." Perhaps an unintentional exaggeration, Forrestal's remarks to the president, combined with Hilsman's and Harriman's comments, reinforced the view that the overthrow of Diem would have little adverse effect on the prosecution of the war in South Vietnam.[27]

On the same day as Kennedy's briefing on Southeast Asia, Philip Chadbourn, the chargé d'affaires in Vientiane during Unger's absence, met with Souvanna Phouma. Chadbourn's comments to the prime minister, similar to conversations he held with UK, French, and Australian diplomats, were an incomplete and misleading summary of US plans and actions. The US government, said Chadbourn, was "thinking about possible measures to redress the military situation." He added: "[The] measures we were contemplating were within [the] framework of the Geneva Accords[,] although we might want to put [a] broader interpretation on [the] accords."[28]

Souvanna made a "perceptible nod" when Chadbourn mentioned increasing US support for FAR and neutralist troops. In addition to providing heavy weapons and replacement equipment to Phoumi and Kong Le, Chadbourn said that the US government was considering releasing one-hundred-pound bombs to the RLAF's tiny fleet of aging T-6s. The bombs would be used "to safeguard any important strategic center" under attack, he said. Souvanna commented that "bombs should be supplied only as [a] last extreme measure." When Chadbourn said the United States was thinking about assigning three military advisers to the Plaine des Jarres, Souvanna interrupted, declaring that the US military attaché should coordinate support with neutralist officers in Vientiane. "No American should be established permanently [on the plain]," said Souvanna. The full-time presence of Americans there would allow the communists to charge that he and the United States had violated the Geneva agreement. "It was all right for [the] FMM to be there," he said, "but not for [the] US."[29]

Chadbourn made a similarly incomplete presentation to Phoumi, who smiled broadly, saying that he was "greatly relieved" by US plans. Among the phase-one decisions Chadbourn did *not* mention to either Lao official was "expanding the use of highly mobile South Vietnamese border patrols to interdict [North Vietnamese] entry into South Viet-Nam and to gather intelligence." The current small-scale operations were supported by the CIA and conducted by South Vietnamese special forces and tribal ranger companies. Chadbourn was concerned that the public exposure of expanded intelligence and combat patrols would be deemed a Geneva violation that neither US allies nor Souvanna could defend. Acknowledging their intelligence value for the war in South Vietnam, Chadbourn worried that expanding cross-border operations, which he characterized as the "sting of [a] hornet," would alert the North Vietnamese tiger "prematurely to [a] possible serious effort to interdict [the] use of [the] supply routes."[30]

Ambassador Unger, who was in Washington and preparing to return to Vientiane, remained uncomfortable with the State-Defense program of graduated military pressure. He was, for example, reluctant to accept the phase-one decision to replace RLAF T-6s with more modern T-28s, fearing that their deployment "would represent escalation" and trigger communist retaliation. In a meeting with President Kennedy, Unger warned: "Increased emphasis on military action may tempt people here in Washington, as well as General Phoumi in Laos, to assume a return to the relationships of several years ago and the seeking of a military solution." Kennedy, who agreed with Unger on the importance of continued support for Souvanna and a neutral Laos, did not acknowledge, much less resolve, an emerging contradiction in US policy: appearing to adhere to the Geneva agreement while simultaneously engaging in actions demonstrating determination to prevent a communist takeover.[31]

The president—despite Harriman's observation about Moscow's disengagement from its Geneva commitments and despite a recent intelligence estimate discussing Hanoi's "considerable freedom of action" in Southeast Asia—continued to hope that the Soviet Union might curb communist military activity in Laos. When Kennedy asked Unger about current Soviet influence in the kingdom, the ambassador replied that it was "very little." In Vientiane, Unger said, the Soviet ambassador appeared cooperative but did nothing to restrain the Pathet Lao, the North Vietnamese, or even the Polish ICC commissioner. Kennedy and Unger agreed that the Soviet Union, despite its limited influence, "should be continually reminded" of its Geneva commitments.[32]

Throughout his presidency, Kennedy had said, in public and in private, that a failure by the Soviet Union to observe its Geneva obligations would jeopardize any future agreements with the United States. Despite this rhetoric, Kennedy authorized Harriman to conclude a treaty with the Soviet Union on a topic of far greater global significance: the banning of nuclear tests in the atmosphere, in outer space, and under water. In his final negotiating instructions to Harriman, which covered a wide range of East-West issues, Kennedy "indicated the importance of repeating our dissatisfaction with the present situation [in Laos] and our desire for the Soviets to live up to their commitments." During the conclusion of the negotiations for the partial test-ban treaty, Harriman spoke with Khrushchev about Laos, but the Soviet premier "bluntly" informed him that the responsibilities of the Geneva cochairs had been fulfilled: "The problem in Laos is now an internal one."[33]

Dean Rusk told Kennedy and his advisers that Khrushchev's position on Laos was "very unsatisfactory." The Soviet Union, said Rusk, was "running out from under an obligation in a way we can't accept." National Security Adviser McGeorge Bundy, noting the futility of "simply saying we're really disappointed" by Khrushchev's attitude, suggested the following message to the Soviets: "If they duck out on Laos, then the consequences may well be requirements on us to take further action." Kennedy endorsed this vague threat. He wanted Rusk, who was about to leave for Moscow to sign the test-ban treaty, to indicate that the Soviets' failure to meet their Geneva commitments "really removed any right they have to react" to US military action to support the neutral solution. The president returned to this theme later in the meeting, observing that the United States "had to suggest" to the Soviets that if they maintained their "hands-off attitude," in the face of continuing military deterioration in Laos, then "we're going to have to take some action."[34]

Kennedy's threatening language should not be wholly dismissed as bluffing. At a July 30 meeting, recorded by the White House taping system, the president reviewed the progress of phase-one actions in the State-Defense program of escalating pressure and authorized several carefully selected phase-two activities. A State Department memorandum prepared for the meeting reported increased US military support for the FAR, neutralists, and Hmong guerrillas, including the delivery of more 105-mm howitzers and 4.2-inch and 81-mm mortars to Phoumi and Kong Le. Such phase-one actions fell within the Kennedy administration's definition of "stretching" the Geneva agreement. "On the covert side"—that is, CIA operations that were inarguably violations of the accords but US involvement could be plausibly denied—"South Vietnamese patrol activities in the border area of the Ho Chi-Minh trail are being stepped up to gain intelligence, enlist supporters, and prepare for larger, more concentrated interdiction efforts."[35]

At the July 30 meeting, attended by Rusk, McNamara, Taylor, McCone, Harriman, and other senior advisers, Hilsman made the oral presentation of the State-Defense program and answered virtually all of the questions posed by Kennedy. "Probably the most important thing," Hilsman said, was that State Department officials, as instructed by the president, had consulted with British and French diplomats. "Much to our delight," he reported, the US government had gained their reluctant acquiescence to replacing RLAF T-6 aircraft with T-28s. He added that the western allies had concurred with the overall program of gradually increasing military pressure, "to the extent we revealed it to them."[36]

While discussing the provision of arms to Kong Le's forces, Hilsman admitted there was "one problem." Unfortunately, the next forty-seven seconds of the tape recording of this meeting remain "excised" for reasons of national security.[37] The excised discussion possibly refers to covert methods of supplying the neutralists on the Plaine des Jarres and the "black" Air America supply flights to the Hmong headquarters at Long

Tieng. At the time of this meeting with Kennedy, State Department officials considered the airlift of weapons by US civilian flight crews a "substantive violation" of the Geneva agreement. "To determine whether or
not we wish to continue in violation," the department cabled Vientiane,
"we need to assess the risks of this policy and thoroughly investigate all
possible alternatives."[38]

Turning to political and economic activities, Hilsman said that the
United States sought to engage western and Asian allies in road building, well digging, and similar civilian aid initiatives that would benefit
the rural population. In proposing next steps for the Laos program, the
State Department organized phase-two actions into three categories. The
first category, for which the department sought Kennedy's approval, was
essentially an "extension" of phase-one activities. The proposed actions
included US military "guidance" for FAR operations to clear and hold
strategically significant areas; offensive attacks against the Pathet Lao
with RLAF T-6s and T-28s; and increased use of Thai PARU forces and
South Vietnamese border patrol units.

The last category-one activity was: "Expand sabotage operations
against North Vietnamese bases both in Laos and North Vietnam."[39] This
item referred to CINCPAC's work on what was then called OPLAN 34,
which envisioned the formation of a Special Operations Group (SOG),
under MACV command with CIA participation. This group would support, train, and advise South Vietnamese armed forces for "covert PsyOps
and military actions in NVN." The operations would ostensibly be "sponsored by a Vietnamese 'national liberation movement' non-attributable to
the US or the Government of Vietnam." OPLAN 34, designed to make
the DRV pay a price for its role in both South Vietnam and Laos, exempli-
fied the fungible nature of US covert and overt plans to punish Hanoi.[40]

After Hilsman requested approval for the new activities, Kennedy
asked what was meant by the "selected offensive use" of T-28s. Hilsman
replied: "This would be for attacks on Pathet Lao concentrations for retaliation if, let's say, the Pathet Lao began to build up alarmingly oppo-
site a place called Attopeu in the south, which we regard as significant."
Kennedy, seeking a better understanding of the implications of introducing T-28s, asked a series of follow-up questions: How many T-6s were in
Laos before the Geneva agreement? What's the difference between a T-6
and a T-28? Would the T-28s really have any value? To this last ques-

tion, McNamara replied: "[The T-28s] won't accomplish much militarily, Mr. President. They will indicate some escalation, however, because they are more advanced models." Hilsman, rarely shy about contradicting the defense secretary or any other Pentagon official, defended the military utility of T-28s by observing that obsolete T-6s, armed only with machine guns and rockets, had recently disrupted a Pathet Lao attack in southeastern Laos.[41]

Kennedy, who wanted to know more about the views of the French, asked whether they had agreed with the US program or were simply keeping their objections to themselves. Hilsman said that the French initially had "two grave doubts" about the introduction of T-28s: (1) the new replacement aircraft—although "technically" permitted by the Geneva agreement—would trigger propaganda blasts from the Pathet Lao; and (2) the increase in FAR military capabilities might tempt Phoumi "to seize power" or attempt some other rash action. Hilsman told the president that he had been able to reassure the French on both counts and that they had agreed to the introduction of the new aircraft. "So it [the talks with French] really went very well," he said.[42]

Responding to the president's question about what had "happened in Laos lately," Hilsman replied, "Well, sir, it's not much, as a matter of fact." He added: "It's too early to say whether our activity has communicated itself to the communists or not. The fact remains that for the last five days things have been quiet on the Plaine des Jarres." The dubious implication that the nascent State-Defense program might be having an impact on Pathet Lao operations prompted McCone to comment that the CIA placed "somewhat more importance" on recent heavy rains for the lull in military activity. Hilsman, agreeing that the weather had been more important than the US program, remained confident that the combination of political, economic, and military activities in Laos would "get the message across to the communists."[43]

When Kennedy asked if any of the proposed phase-two military actions would "disturb the quiet" in Laos, Hilsman explained that such considerations were the reason the State and Defense departments were seeking a delegation of presidential authority for the timing of phase-two activities: "We want to be able to play this very much like an orchestra and to call on certain instruments when we need it."[44] The comment reflected a widespread conceit within the US government that the DRV and other communist powers would both recognize and respond to subtly calibrated expressions of American determination.

The next day, July 31, McGeorge Bundy signed NSAM 256, which officially informed the secretary of state, the secretary of defense, the director of Central Intelligence, and the chairman of the Joint Chiefs of Staff that the president had reviewed the progress of phase one of the Laos program, had approved the proposed category-one actions of phase two, and had authorized continued planning for the remaining phase-two activities. This careful military escalation and, more generally, Kennedy administration attention to Laos were soon eclipsed by the deepening crisis in South Vietnam.

A nationwide crackdown on Buddhist pagodas by the Diem government prompted Hilsman, Harriman, and Forrestal to draft State Department telegram 243 to Saigon, the infamous cable of August 24, 1963. Approved by Kennedy on a Saturday, when he was in Hyannis Port, Massachusetts, and Rusk, McNamara, McCone, and Bundy were also out of Washington, the telegram sparked a week of feverish activity by US officials to stimulate a military coup d'état in South Vietnam. The South Vietnamese generals did not act then, but the daily meetings in Washington revealed deep divisions among Kennedy's advisers, with most State Department officials claiming that the war could not be won with Diem, while their Pentagon counterparts were convinced that the war could not be won without him.

Near the end of that last week in August, when the breach between the Diem government and the US mission in Saigon was an open secret, Charles de Gaulle released a vaguely worded statement expressing French willingness to help restore an independent, unified Vietnam. Ambassador Alphand told Dean Rusk: "The statement reiterated the points which General De Gaulle had made in his meeting with the President in the spring of 1961. The French did not feel that a military solution could work."[45]

Most observers interpreted de Gaulle's statement as a proposal for a negotiated neutral settlement in Vietnam, an idea that the influential syndicated columnist Walter Lippmann promptly endorsed. US officials, however, were irritated by the offer from "Nosy Charlie," as McGeorge Bundy referred to de Gaulle in a memorandum to the president. The

French were contributing little economic aid to Southeast Asia, and the FMM had been "most unhelpful" in Laos.[46] At a White House meeting, President Kennedy dismissed the idea of neutralization in Vietnam, observing that it was "not working [in Laos] because the communists, of course, are doing what they would do in Vietnam." He added: "In view of the fact that Walter Lippmann is endorsing General de Gaulle['s proposal] as a great solution, I don't think we ought to let this get built up as a possibility of a reasonable outcome."[47]

It appears that Kennedy's opposition toward neutralization in Vietnam was based not only on the failing agreement in Laos but also on domestic political considerations. A few days earlier, when the president and his advisers were discussing US support for a coup against the Diem regime, Rusk commented on growing congressional unease with the weak South Vietnamese political base for prosecuting the war:

> The feeling is that we are up to our hips in the mud out there. We have no real basis on which we ask our fellows to get shot at in this enterprise. I think the morale of the Congress has gotten very nasty, Mr. President. It's going to get increasingly so if it goes on.

Kennedy, who explicitly referred to the alarmist congressional reaction to Chiang Kai-shek's defeat in China, replied: "I know that everybody is mad about this situation, but I know they'll be madder if South Vietnam goes down the drain."[48]

The neutralization of Vietnam was a topic of conversation between Kennedy and Souvanna later that September, during the prime minister's visit to the United States for the annual opening of the UN General Assembly. Souvanna, who was critical of Diem in private conversations, had endorsed de Gaulle's proposal. Kennedy told Souvanna, "The United States would consider the neutrality of Vietnam if conditions indicated this would be successful." Unfortunately, such conditions did not currently exist. There was no "personality who could lead a united Vietnamese people," Kennedy declared, and "North Vietnam would dominate South Vietnam," intensifying communist pressure on Laos and Cambodia. "General De Gaulle's proposals on Vietnam were fine," the president said, "but for the future."[49]

Souvanna replied with his frequently stated view that solving "the Lao problem depended on a settlement in Vietnam." He told the president that the DRV did not want his government "to extend its authority over the entire country since this would prevent North Vietnam from using Laos to penetrate South Vietnam." Kennedy did not mention the US program of military pressure, but he did emphasize its primary political-diplomatic message: "We would never accept communist control of Laos and are determined to support the Prime Minister's government. We want the PL and the other communists to continue to know this." In a final comment to Souvanna, who planned to visit Moscow before returning to Laos, Kennedy said: "The Soviets had a continuing responsibility to see that the Geneva Agreements work and the Prime Minister should make this clear to Chairman Khrushchev."[50]

In the late summer and early fall of 1963, senior US officials intermittently urged the Soviet Union to honor its Geneva commitments. When Rusk traveled to Moscow to sign the nuclear test-ban treaty, Khrushchev emphatically dismissed the idea of Soviet influence on the behavior of Laotians who "were set on fighting again." He declared that "the Laotian situation had now entered a new stage" and that "the USSR was not going to do anything."[51]

President Kennedy, during a wide-ranging discussion of US-Soviet relations with Ambassador Dobrynin, observed that Laos remained a threat to international peace. "Let's say you have an intensification of the struggle in Laos, when it looks like all of Laos, including the Mekong, is going to go under [Pathet Lao control]," said Kennedy. "And SEATO implements its plan to try to hold the towns along the Mekong. And that causes the Chinese to feel that these are Western troops too close to her boundaries." Alluding to US escalation "to prevent our forces from being driven out" of Laos, Kennedy said that the United States might "have to take some action against the, uh, infrastructure," presumably a euphemistic reference to US air attacks against military targets in southern China and the DRV. Kennedy added that such a dangerous scenario was "certainly within the range of possibility."[52]

After briefly discussing Germany with Dobrynin, Kennedy returned to the topic of Laos. "I wish none of us had ever gotten into Laos," he said. Noting the importance of keeping that country "stabilized to the extent it's possible" and of maintaining Souvanna in power, Kennedy asked:

"Can the Soviets do much about trying to keep this situation [pause] so that we don't have the problems that I talked about? Can you do much now with it or is it pretty much a North Vietnamese operation with the Chinese?"[53] Dobrynin, who had initially chuckled at the idea of Laos representing a threat to world peace, replied: "The Soviet position was well known. The Geneva Agreement had set up Souvanna Phouma and a coalition government had been established. The Soviets did not want to interfere, and they had no troops there and did not intend to send any. In these circumstances, what could they do?"[54]

US messages to the Soviets about Laos varied in their intensity and were invariably mixed in with communications on other East-West issues. In a September 10 conversation with Foreign Minister Gromyko lasting more than an hour, Foy D. Kohler, the American ambassador in Moscow, discussed the United Nations, disarmament, Berlin, joint US-Soviet space projects, and a nonaggression treaty between NATO and the Warsaw Pact. Kohler also raised the topic of Laos, declaring that the United States "continued to be disturbed at [the] way [the] Soviet Union shirked its [Geneva] co-chairman responsibilities." The predictable US protest about Laos prompted an equally predictable reply from Gromyko: "[The] Soviet Union stands for a neutral, independent Laos but [the] dispute between [the] Princes was in [the] Sov[iet] view an exclusively internal Laotian affair in which [the] Sov[iets] did not intend to interfere."[55]

Kennedy, six weeks before his assassination, spoke very briefly about Laos with Gromyko, who was in the United States for the opening of the UN General Assembly. The Soviet foreign minister wanted to discuss ways the Soviet Union and the United States could build on the "good spirit created by the Moscow treaty" partially banning nuclear tests. In a two-hour conversation covering virtually every aspect of US-Soviet relations, Kennedy referred to Laos only once, reminding Gromyko of the Soviet responsibility "to prevent that situation from collapsing."[56]

Perhaps Kennedy's minimal emphasis on Laos with Gromyko reflected a belated realization that this small, poor country was insignificant in the overall scheme of East-West relations. There are, however, other, more likely explanations for the president's reticence. One is his probable conclusion that scolding the Soviets over their Geneva commitments had long passed the point of diminishing returns. Another possible reason for the brevity of Kennedy's comment on Laos was that the military situation in the Plaine des Jarres and other parts of the kingdom remained relatively quiet. Despite intermittent artillery exchanges and small-scale skirmishes, there were few reports of "important positional changes" or material damage on the plain. In southern Laos, according to the CIA, reports of Pathet Lao preparations for military activity were thus far "all smoke and no fire."[57]

With the rainy season still limiting military operations in Laos, the US program of gradually escalating pressure moved forward. An October 12 update on the program reported that additional heavy weapons were being delivered to Phoumi's and Kong Le's forces; that new US military attachés were serving as operational advisers to leaders of the FAR and the neutralist forces; and that air resupply of arms to Kong Le, friendly tribal groups, and FAR outposts in Pathet Lao territory continued "satisfactorily." On a less positive note, the effort to improve intelligence collection in southern Laos was "badly hurt" by the political instability and coup plotting in Vietnam. Some of the South Vietnamese special forces trained for cross-border intelligence operations had been sent to Saigon to defend Diem from some of his own generals. As part of the Kennedy administration's pressure on Diem to reform politically, the CIA suspended its support for the Civilian Airborne Rangers, an oxymoronically named force intended for operations in Laos and North Vietnam and described by the agency as "well trained, flexible, and aggressive."[58]

The aspect of the Laos program that seemed most sensitive to the White House was the use of T-28s. Forrestal informed the State Department that the aircraft should only attack Pathet Lao targets in areas that the FAR and neutralists held prior to April 1, 1963. He specifically opposed T-28 missions to support Hmong operations in Pathet Lao territory. "My sense of the rules of this little war," he wrote, "is that such action is most likely to provoke an escalation, possibly in the form of Chi-Com or DRV air retaliation." Forrestal added that he was "all in favor of using the T-28 in going after artillery positions in the Plain of Jars and to respond to nibbling aggression by the PL as it occurs."[59]

In a cable to Vientiane providing policy guidance on RLAF T-28 missions, the State Department stated that the United States had no intention of taking the "initiative in military escalation in Laos." Authorizing the "carefully limited use" of T-28s, the department approved reprisal attacks for enemy provocations—for example, responding to an artillery bombardment by "strik[ing] the offending PL gun emplacement."[60] To Pentagon officials, such precise limitations on reprisal strikes seemed an "unrealistic requirement." More broadly, they viewed restrictions on T-28 operations as "slowing the momentum of the three phase program approved in July to turn the tide of events in Laos."[61]

On November 1, 1963, a special report from the CIA's Office of Current Intelligence concluded: "Reunification of Laos—the proclaimed goal of the provisional government formed by the opposing factions in July 1962—appears more remote than ever." Observing that the kingdom remained "divided into pro- and anti-Communist camps," agency analysts wrote that neither the Pathet Lao nor Phoumi had shown much interest in the neutral solution, although both seemed "to find the coalition regime a useful tool in their efforts to undermine the governmental fabric." With the rainy season ending, the two sides were "strengthening their positions in strategically important areas."[62]

Policymakers likely paid little immediate attention to the CIA report, which was issued the same day as the coup d'état that toppled the Diem regime. Kennedy privately admitted that the US government "must bear a good deal of responsibility" for the coup and wondered "whether the generals can stay together and build a stable government."[63] Diem's overthrow, although an inflection point in the Vietnam War, had little direct impact on Laos. One policy connection between the coup and Laos was Rostow's unheeded suggestion that the establishment of a new government in Saigon provided an opportunity to explicitly "confront Hanoi" with the choice of ceasing infiltration or "accepting retaliatory damage in the North"—in other words, the bombing program he continued to recommend.[64]

Within a few weeks of seizing power, the ruling South Vietnamese generals decided to contact Phoumi about an "incognito and discreet visit" to Saigon. The generals, who held Phoumi in "high regard," extended the invitation to develop "a collaborative effort along [the] Lao-Vietnam border against Viet Cong lines of supply and communication." Although seeking to avoid "open conflict" in Laos, which might trigger large-scale DRV intervention, the CIA station in Saigon concurred in the "desirability of continuing and stepping up discreetly handled Vietnamese operations" in eastern Laos.[65]

Two days before Kennedy's assassination, virtually all of the senior members of his national security team met in Honolulu with leaders of the US mission in Saigon to discuss ways of both bolstering the new government in South Vietnam and waging the war more effectively. Laos was a peripheral concern. The policy proposal that most directly affected the kingdom was establishing a zone fifty kilometers inside the Lao border, where US-supported South Vietnamese irregulars could conduct intelligence operations without prior approval from the State Department or the Special Group. The responsibility for advising and supporting these operations would shift from the CIA to MACV, which, after the Bay of Pigs fiasco, was assumed to be the better-qualified sponsor of paramilitary operations in Vietnam.[66]

Hilsman, who opposed the delegation of Washington's authority for approving such politically sensitive violations of the Geneva agreement, acknowledged the importance of gathering intelligence on infiltration from North Vietnam. The proposed cross-border operations were also part of the phased program of increasing military pressure in Laos. By the logic of gradual escalation, a buildup of CIA-controlled tribal activities in the panhandle and FAR-ARVN cooperation in southern Laos would permit "active harassment" of infiltrators from North Vietnam: "As strength develops in the corridor, appropriate targets should be attacked aiming toward eventually hitting Tchepone and possibly [a] staging base just inside North Viet-Nam near the Lao border."[67]

One State Department official who resisted the idea of South Vietnamese intelligence operations in Laos was Ambassador Unger, who called them the "most obvious problem area in which our strategies of seeking military victory in Viet-Nam and [the] preservation of [a] neutral and relatively quiescent Laos, threaten to come into conflict." It seemed to Unger that South Vietnamese operations large enough to have a meaningful impact on "halting infiltration" could not remain covert. Although Souvanna was pessimistic about restoring the coalition and critical of DRV activities in Laos, he would not likely approve military actions that would be denounced by the NLHS, the French, and others. South Vietnamese "military operations within Laos would threaten [the] Geneva solution on both [the] domestic and international planes," Unger wrote the State Department. Of course, he added, it was up to officials in Washington to determine whether the threat infiltration posed to US objectives in South

Vietnam "would justify placing in jeopardy [the] entire basis [of] our present position and efforts in Laos."[68]

Unger, traveling to Saigon, presented his views directly to McNamara, who concluded that plans for South Vietnamese operations in Laos would be neither "politically acceptable" nor "militarily effective." The defense secretary concluded that infiltration was a "serious and annoying" problem but a "lower priority" than the ineffectual new government in South Vietnam, the lack of leadership in the US mission in Saigon, and the military progress made by the PLAF, at least since the coup and probably earlier. The president to whom he was reporting these pessimistic findings was no longer John Kennedy but Lyndon Johnson, whose role in Lao affairs as vice president had been even smaller than his minimal influence on Vietnam policy.[69]

Epilogue

An Awful Mess

From the first day of his presidency until the last, Lyndon Johnson viewed Laos as a secondary theater of the conflict in Southeast Asia. Only two days after Kennedy's assassination, Johnson met with Henry Cabot Lodge, the American ambassador in Saigon, to review post-coup developments in Vietnam and to develop guidance for the State Department, Pentagon, and other government agencies. Laos, however, remained "relatively quiet," in Roger Hilsman's words. In a country-by-country summary of Far East crises that might confront the new president, Hilsman urged alertness for renewed dry-season attacks by the Pathet Lao but reported, "There are no problems for decision at this time." Perhaps overstating both the execution and the effectiveness of the program of gradually escalating military pressure, he wrote: "Some months ago we developed and have been pursuing with encouraging results a joint State-Defense-AID-CIA phased plan to strengthen Souvanna's government and forces to enable them to meet further Communist encroachments."[1]

As anticipated, fighting resumed at the end of 1963, with small-scale FAR and neutralist probing operations triggering larger-scale Pathet Lao responses in central Laos and other parts of the country. Backed by North Vietnamese troops, the Pathet Lao drove the FAR and neutralists off of the Na Kay plateau, a victory that simultaneously threatened Thakhek and facilitated infiltration into South Vietnam. In a January 31, 1964, memorandum to General Taylor, Vice Admiral Herbert D. Riley, the director of the Joint Staff, described the situation in Laos as "clearly deteriorating." Observing that Vietnam and other foreign policy issues had diverted official attention from the kingdom, Riley wrote: "We have made the proper noises about seeking our objectives in Laos, but we have continued to do little or nothing in the direction of the accomplishment of those objectives." He added: "I am not sure what our policy is in Laos since I have seen no indication whatever of any serious effort being made to follow any of the agreed courses of action."[2]

On February 12 DCI McCone submitted an SNIE warning that the situation in Laos could "deteriorate rapidly." Intelligence officials estimated that the absence of a "sharp US reaction" to "recent Communist advances may have emboldened Pathet Lao and North Vietnamese leaders."[3] As with previous dry-season crises, Hilsman proposed a series of political, military, and covert actions aimed at "giv[ing] the Communist side reason to believe that we are prepared to escalate the conflict in the area in order to defend our positions there." His first recommendation was to resume the three-phase program of escalating pressure. Specific suggestions included expanding the use of Thai PARU paramilitary forces, enlarging the number of Hmong guerrilla units, and increasing sabotage operations against DRV bases in both Laos and areas of North Vietnam adjacent to the kingdom. Hilsman also revived the idea of cross-border operations into Laos by South Vietnamese forces—an action that Unger and McNamara had recently opposed.[4]

The Joint Chiefs of Staff, who chafed under the US government's "self-imposed restrictions with respect to impeding external aid to the Viet Cong," concurred with the State Department recommendations for Laos. They also proposed an additional military action: the resumption of low-level aerial reconnaissance over Laos. Such missions would seek to collect military intelligence and demonstrate US resolve in Southeast Asia. The reconnaissance flights, the chiefs noted, would be "an overt violation" of the Geneva agreement: "Implementation would require a policy determination to the effect that the U.S. is no longer willing to permit unilateral violation by the Communist side."[5]

When asked to comment on Washington's proposed actions, Ambassador Unger doubted that any of them would have a "decisive effect on [the] course of events [in] Laos." Moreover, he thought that State Department talk about a "solution" in Laos was unrealistic. Under the current "ground rules" of US policy—loosely complying with the Geneva agree-

ment, maintaining the façade of a coalition government, and supporting Souvanna—Unger thought that the best short-term outcome was the
preservation of territory held by the right-wing and neutralist factions. A
unified Laos, responsive to the government in Vientiane, was "certainly
unlikely as long as there is no solution [in] South Viet-Nam."[6]

Any contemplated military action in Laos, wrote Unger, must take
into account the views of Souvanna, whose central objective remained
removing the kingdom from the "field of East-West conflict." Noting
the prime minister's belief in the Lao proverb, "when buffaloes fight, it
is the grass that gets hurt," Unger observed that Souvanna might share
US concerns over the communist threat, but he was unsympathetic to
coordinating American actions in Laos with those in Vietnam. The
ambassador predicted that Souvanna would be "adamantly opposed"
to "launching guerrillas from Laos against North Vietnamese targets in
[the] DRV."[7]

In March 1964 President Johnson's views on Laos reflected the policy contradictions he inherited—simultaneously demonstrating determination and avoiding provocative action. As with Vietnam, he sought to
postpone tough decisions about military escalation in an election year.
In a temporizing message to Ambassador Lodge, whom he viewed as a
potential Republican candidate for president, Johnson wrote: "Additional
actions against Laos and Cambodia should be intensively examined." The
president said that he favored South Vietnamese cross-border operations
into Laos—if Souvanna approved them—and that he would authorize
low-level reconnaissance—if current high-altitude U-2 missions provided
inadequate intelligence. Stating the obvious, Johnson observed that US
participation in air or ground operations in Laos raised "tough diplomatic
issues." He mentioned to Lodge, as a "first thought," the importance of
seeking support from Souvanna and building a stronger case for actions
that "might have only limited military effect and could trigger wider
Communist action in Laos."[8]

During Johnson's presidency, primacy in developing and executing
policy in Laos remained with the State Department. There was, however, an almost immediate shakeup among senior officials responsible for
Southeast Asia. Johnson had disapproved of both US encouragement of
Diem's overthrow and the role of Hilsman and Harriman in promoting the coup. Hilsman, disliked by senior Pentagon officials and lacking

high-level support within the State Department, was dismissed as assistant secretary of state. "I fired Roger Hilsman, with the full approval of Mr. Rusk," George Ball recalled. "He had become very difficult. He was so full of his own omniscience with regard to Vietnam, and he was lecturing the generals on strategy. He became rather a nuisance. So we got rid of him."[9] William Bundy moved from the Pentagon to the State Department to become assistant secretary for the Far East.

The more widely respected Harriman remained at the State Department, but his influence with the White House declined sharply. Around the time of Hilsman's dismissal, Johnson began shifting Harriman's responsibilities from Southeast Asia to Africa, a continent of limited interest to the new president. "Exiled to Africa" was Harriman's characterization of the change.[10] Despite considerable effort, he was unable to gain Johnson's confidence and was eventually named an ambassador at large, his initial position when he joined the Kennedy administration. With Harriman's influence diminished, Dean Rusk became more assertive in the formulation of Lao policy.

In an April 17, 1964, "think piece" for the State Department, Ambassador Unger wrote that the long-term viability of the conservative-neutralist zone in Laos would require new leaders who could rally popular support and reduce the French-educated elites' "throttle-hold on [the] economy." Souvanna, he wrote, would have to be persuaded to focus on international affairs and to permit a "gradual takeover of internal leadership by [a] younger, more vigorous group." Phoumi would have to be eased out of power, "probably earlier rather than later," as there was "no reason [to] believe he would ever voluntarily lend support to or even countenance [the] kind of changes required to put Laos on [a] constructive road." Without such political intervention, Unger saw "a dwindling possibility of retaining at least this zone of the country free from communist domination without resort to strong military action."[11]

A more immediate political problem was the worsening relations between the neutralists and conservatives, which jeopardized "the remaining viability of the Geneva solution." Phoumi's corruption—his illicit business interests included a gambling casino and monopolies in selling pork and importing gold—and the right-wing harassment of neutralists in Vientiane disturbed Souvanna, who threatened to move his faction's civilian and military officials back to the Plaine des Jarres. For his part, Phoumi thought the prime minister too weak to resist further Pathet Lao encroachment and indicated to Ambassador Unger that he would be "happy" if all of the neutralists left Vientiane. More ominously, Phoumi said that he "favored a return to the policy of finding [a] military solution" in Laos.[12] Deepening the country's political divisions was the failure of ongoing tripartite negotiations to neutralize and demilitarize the royal capital of Luang Prabang, then under right-wing control. After a futile summit meeting with Pathet Lao and rightist leaders on April 17 and 18, Souvanna publicly announced his intention to resign as prime minister.

With Ambassador Unger in Saigon, embassy chargé Philip Chadbourn tried to dissuade Souvanna from quitting. The prime minister, who appeared "extremely depressed," reaffirmed his intention to submit his resignation to the king. For two years, Souvanna said, he had tried "to resolve [the] Lao problem and now had to admit failure." Blaming both the left and the right for the impasse, Souvanna said: "The Lao themselves simply do not want a settlement." Chadbourn, urging patience, asked Souvanna to postpone any final decision until Unger returned to Vientiane. Souvanna agreed but gave the diplomat "little reason to believe [that] he will go back on his decision to resign."[13]

With Souvanna apparently headed for retirement, DNC chief Siho and General Kouprasith Abhay, commander of the FAR military region that included Vientiane, launched a coup d'état. At about 4:00 A.M., April 19, intermittent gunfire broke out throughout Vientiane, as coup forces set up roadblocks, secured key government installations, and arrested Souvanna and some five hundred other neutralists. The local radio station broadcast a communiqué announcing the formation of a fifteen-man ruling junta: the Military Revolutionary Committee. An officer conspicuously absent from the list of committee members was Phoumi Nosavan. According to CIA analysts, Phoumi reportedly had planned to take over the government once Souvanna officially resigned, but Siho moved first. Kouprasith, who had opportunistically participated in the overthrow of Souvanna in December 1960, played a similar role in the latest plot.[14]

The State Department, seeking to put "humpty dumpty together again," denounced the coup, reaffirmed its support for the government of national union, and called for the release of all neutralist prisoners.[15]

Ambassador Unger, who immediately returned to Vientiane, told Siho and Kouprasith that the United States could not "accept or support" their coup, and he demanded that they reinstate Souvanna's coalition government. Unger reported to Washington that the two rightists gave the "impression of being badly frightened little boys who now realize they have climbed far out on [a] limb and [are] uncertain how to proceed or whether to draw back."[16]

Despite their fearful appearance, the coup leaders continued to control Vientiane, to maintain martial law, and to enforce a curfew. After what he described as "considerable difficulty," Unger persuaded DNC officials to allow him to visit Souvanna at his residence, where he was temporarily confined to house arrest. With Souvanna standing on a second-floor balcony, Unger conveyed messages of US support from the street below—"diplomatie à la Romeo et Juliette," in the words of the French ambassador.[17] On April 22 Unger and other members of the diplomatic community traveled to Luang Prabang to seek the king's help in restoring the government of national union. Savang was "vastly amused by our statement that we did not wish to interfere in [the] internal affairs of Laos," Unger reported to the State Department. Nonetheless, the king made it "abundantly clear how stupid and destructive he felt [the] coup of April 19 had been."[18]

The revolutionary committee, yielding somewhat to international pressure and royal disapproval, announced its support for an expanded and reorganized government, with Souvanna serving as prime minister and limited participation by the Pathet Lao. After an April 24 cabinet meeting, Souvanna agreed to the arrangement, though the details of the government reorganization required further discussion. "Souvanna obviously does not relish negotiations with [the] revolutionary committee who will be holding most of [the] cards in their hands as well as [a] sword over his head," Unger informed Washington. "Even if we achieve [the] minimum goal of keeping Souvanna and his gov[ermen]t nominally in power and avoid any open break of [the] Geneva and related agreements, we can look forward to strong influence and pressure on him, often of [an] extremist sort, from [the] revolutionary committee."[19]

On May 2 Souvanna announced that the neutralist and conservative factions had merged and that he would direct their combined military affairs. Neither his statement of center-right unity nor his declaration of leadership was entirely persuasive. US military intelligence officials in Vientiane reported, "Situation still potentially very dangerous with no real assurance [that the] Souvanna gov[ernmen]t and Geneva Accords will survive. Bitter military action between 'friendly' factions [is] still entirely possible." Ambassador Unger admitted to the State Department that the US mission was unable to answer a "fundamental question": "Who is in charge of [the] Lao government today?" He observed that Souvanna was "perhaps deceiving himself as to how completely he is in control."[20]

Phoumi, who remained deputy premier, retained the support of many FAR officers, but his control of the country's right wing had been weakened. Marshal Sarit, his closest foreign patron, had died the previous December, and the new military regime in Thailand was no longer a reliable source of personal financial support. (Phoumi had appealed to South Vietnam and Taiwan for "alternative" assistance, according to Souvanna.)[21] Within Laos, the Sananikone family, Phoumi's longstanding political rivals, supported the April 19 coup d'état. The officers of the revolutionary committee—particularly Siho, whom William Bundy characterized as "a real thug"[22]—were both a political and a physical threat to Phoumi. Two weeks after the putsch, Unger reported: "It is now quite apparent that Phoumi's position, perhaps even life, has been precarious."[23]

The Pathet Lao denounced the April 19 coup as an "American-Phoumist" plot. Souphanouvong, unalterably opposed to the revolutionary committee's plan to expand and reorganize the cabinet, told diplomats visiting his Khang Khay headquarters: "Any change of government, however slight, would require consultation with the NLHS." Although the government of national union was an almost completely fictitious polity, Souphanouvong and other NLHS officials "insisted that [the] three factions still existed." Moreover, they viewed the center-right merger as a "trick" that violated the unanimity principle endorsed by the Geneva conference. Despite reports of Pathet Lao military moves if the government of national union were not restored, the NLHS provided vague public assurances that there would be no attacks against neutralist forces on the Plaine des Jarres "for [the] time being at least."[24]

During the last week of April 1964, the US intelligence community concluded that the North Vietnamese and Pathet Lao had been "working steadily to improve their capabilities for expanded and sustained military operations." U-2 reconnaissance missions revealed the expansion of a staging area in the DRV and improvements in road networks and bases in Laos. Reports of truck convoys and other intelligence suggested a significant logistical buildup. CIA officials admitted that they did not know whether the additional forces were intended for Laos or South Vietnam. To obtain more detailed intelligence on communist military movements in Laos, President Johnson's Washington advisers unanimously recommended low-level aerial reconnaissance by US aircraft and cross-border ground operations by South Vietnamese forces.[25]

Before these intelligence operations began, the Pathet Lao launched a mid-May offensive to drive Kong Le's neutralist forces completely off the Plaine des Jarres. With the shattered neutralists retreating to the southwestern edge of the plain, Unger reported to the State Department: "[The] communists may now have just about finished [the] job, well started by [the] conservatives on April 19, of destroying [the] neutralists."[26] Souvanna, outraged by the attacks, told western diplomats that North Vietnam, China, the Soviet Union, and Poland would do nothing to stop the fighting. Only force, he said, would "persuade [the communists] to desist." According to Unger's report of the May 19 conversation, "Souvanna repeatedly made it clear [that] he believed there [was] little to be gained by cranking up [the] Geneva machinery."[27]

That same day in Washington, Ambassador Alphand informed Rusk that France intended to ask the cochairs of the Geneva conference to convene a meeting of the agreement's fourteen signatories. "Since the April 19 coup and the recent violence on the Plaine des Jarres," said Alphand, "the situation has become completely modified; it no longer corresponds to what the French and other nations had in mind when they signed the Geneva Accords." Noting the dissolution of the "vital neutralist center," Alphand said that Laos had evolved into "a confrontation" between the center-right coalition and the Pathet Lao. Rusk replied that it would be "very unfortunate" if France asked to reconvene the Geneva conference without further consultation with the United States and the United Kingdom, which were providing the vast majority of western support to Laos. "The fundamental and inescapable fact," he said, was that the 1962 Geneva agreement called for a unified Laos under the leadership of Prime Minister Souvanna Phouma, yet the Pathet Lao had "not made the slightest movement" toward accepting his authority.[28]

On May 20, the day after Alphand's meeting with Rusk, President de Gaulle announced a French appeal to the Geneva cochairs for an international conference to restore peace and neutrality in Laos. The US government resisted the French proposal, demanding preconditions that the communists would not likely accept—for example, a Pathet Lao withdrawal from areas of the Plaine des Jarres previously occupied by the neutralists. A key US concern was that another international conference on Laos would inevitably introduce the unwelcome topic of neutralizing Vietnam. According to Ambassador Unger, a reluctant warrior who had struggled for nearly two years to make the 1962 Geneva accord work, any new agreement "could only be worse than [the] last," with the United States likely "obliged to beat an even more recalcitrant right wing (and perhaps Souvanna too) into negotiations and concessions to [the] Pathet Lao[,] which we full well know could only benefit [the] latter."[29]

Unger had initially opposed US low-level reconnaissance missions in Laos but withdrew his objections because of Souvanna's "stinging" denunciation of the Pathet Lao for attacking the neutralists and because of his own "growing conviction that it will take [a] concrete showing by U.S. forces to persuade [the] communists [that] we mean business." On May 24 Unger reminded the State Department of the "degree to which we [are] now becoming involved in measures in violation [of] the Geneva Accords." In this message, the ambassador was specifically referring to Air America pilots flying T-28 combat missions over the Plaine des Jarres, an action he characterized as "absolutely necessary if we are to meet [the] urgent requirements in this ugly situation."[30]

Despite the gravity of the most recent crisis in Laos, the "lynch-pin" of US interests in Southeast Asia continued to be South Vietnam, where a weak government led by General Nguyen Khanh was losing the fight against the PLAF. As US officials considered air strikes against the DRV, Rusk thought that communist violations of the 1962 Geneva agreement provided a better legal justification for overt attacks than Hanoi's support for the insurgency in South Vietnam. McNamara and McCone disagreed, declaring that Laos was a less important issue for Americans and that US military operations based on DRV activities there would have little public support. William Bundy, analyzing the "peg for action" against the DRV, agreed: "Before we hit North Viet-Nam, we would wish to justify such action not merely on account of Laos but, perhaps far more, on the basis of the continued North Vietnamese aggression against South Viet-Nam."[31]

On May 25 McGeorge Bundy submitted to President Johnson a "basic recommendation and projected course of action on Southeast Asia," which summarized the thinking of Rusk, McNamara, and other senior officials. The memorandum called for "a Presidential decision that the U.S. will use selected and carefully graduated military force against North Vietnam" if the DRV did not heed an "appropriate diplomatic and political warning." The purpose of the attacks would be "to bring about a major reduction or elimination of North Vietnamese interference in Laos and in South Vietnam." It was the "hope and best estimate" of most of Johnson's advisers that limited air strikes against the DRV would not trigger "a major military reply from Red China."[32]

Johnson was troubled by his advisers' recommendation. He dreaded what he called the "horrible" alternatives of US combat operations in Indochina or withdrawal from the region.[33] On May 27, two days after receiving the recommendation for limited air attacks against North Vietnam, Johnson was casting around for new sources of advice. "I don't want to do anything on the basis of just the information I've got now," he told his friend and former senate colleague Richard Russell (D-GA). When Johnson mentioned Rusk's view that "Laos is crumbling and Vietnam is wobbly," Russell replied: "Oh, Laos, Laos, Laos, hell, it ain't worth a damn."[34]

Johnson, who feared Chinese intervention if the United States attacked North Vietnam, questioned his advisers' assessment of that possibility: "They're kind of like [Douglas] MacArthur in Korea—they don't believe that the Chinese Communists will come into this thing, but they don't know." He also spoke with Russell about the domestic political impact of withdrawing from Southeast Asia: "Well, they'd impeach a President, though, that would run out, wouldn't they?" In a less hyperbolic moment, Johnson observed that the Republicans would "make a political issue out of it [a decision for overt military intervention], every one of them."[35]

During a phone call with McGeorge Bundy that same morning, Johnson said that it seemed as if the Unites States was "getting into another Korea. It just worries the hell out of me." Summarizing his dilemma in Southeast Asia, he said: "I don't think it's worth fighting for and I don't think we can get out. And it's just the biggest damned mess I ever saw."[36] He asked Bundy whether there was anyone else who could advise the administration on US policy in Vietnam and Laos. One can speculate about Johnson's motives for such comments to Bundy and others—for example, creating a record of his willingness to explore every alternative before escalating in Southeast Asia—but it is difficult to avoid the conclusion that Johnson felt trapped by the decision he faced.

Bundy agreed with Johnson that Southeast Asia was "an awful mess." Summing up the president's views as searching "for some means of stiffening this thing" without overt escalation, Bundy said that he, McNamara, and others had explored options short of military intervention and that perhaps there were "some marginal" actions the United States could take. Bundy then suggested that Johnson do something "Kennedy did at least once" during the Laotian crises of his presidency: "Make the threat [of intervention] without having made your own internal decision that you would actually carry it through." Johnson, who apparently had little use for such irresolution in matters of war and peace, cut off Bundy's explication of Kennedy's approach in midsentence. "What does Bill [Bundy] think we ought to do?" Johnson asked.[37]

McGeorge Bundy, abruptly pulled back to the present, replied that his brother thought the United States should "touch" up North Vietnam.

Acknowledgments

So Much to Lose would not have been possible without the assistance of archivists at the John F. Kennedy Library, Boston, MA; the Library of Congress, Washington, DC; the Lyndon B. Johnson Library, Austin, TX; the National Archives and Records Administration, College Park, MD; and the US Army Military History Institute, Carlisle, PA. I am particularly grateful for the help provided by Stanley Fanaras, Jeff Hartley, and Timothy Nenninger at the National Archives; by Stephen Plotkin and Maryrose Grossman at the Kennedy Library; and by Jenna de Graffenried at the Johnson Library.

Timothy Castle, a Southeast Asia historian and the author of *At War in the Shadow of Vietnam* and *One Day Too Long*, read an early draft of the manuscript and made several thoughtful suggestions. Ang Cheng Guan, a diplomatic and international historian and the author of *Vietnamese Communists' Relations with China and the Second Indochina Conflict, 1956–1962*, pointed out a number of useful sources. Two anonymous reviewers selected by the University Press of Kentucky (UPK) provided constructive criticism that was helpful in revising the manuscript. I am delighted to be continuing my association with the UPK; its editorial director, Stephen M. Wrinn; and his team of editors, production specialists, and marketers. I am particularly pleased that *So Much to Lose* is part of UPK's Studies in Conflict, Diplomacy, and Peace because one of the series editors is George C. Herring, a historian whose Vietnam War scholarship I have long admired.

As with *Before the Quagmire: American Intervention in Laos, 1954–1961*, Kristin Coffey assisted with the research and improved my prose with her editorial comments. Despite the help of many people, I am solely responsible for the book's conclusions and analysis and for any errors of commission or omission.

Appendix 1

DECLARATION ON THE NEUTRALITY OF LAOS. SIGNED AT GENEVA, ON 23 JULY 1962

The Governments of the Union of Burma, the Kingdom of Cambodia, Canada, the People's Republic of China, the Democratic Republic of Viet-Nam, the Republic of France, the Republic of India, the Polish People's Republic, the Republic of Viet-Nam, the Kingdom of Thailand, the Union of Soviet Socialist Republics, the United Kingdom of Great Britain and Northern Ireland and the United States of America, whose representatives took part in the International Conference on the Settlement of the Laotian Question, 1961–1962;

Welcoming the presentation of the statement of neutrality by the Royal Government of Laos of July 9, 1962, and taking note of this statement, which is, with the concurrence of the Royal Government of Laos, incorporated in the present Declaration as an integral part thereof, and the text of which is as follows:

The Royal Government of Laos,

Being resolved to follow the path of peace and neutrality in conformity with the interests and aspirations of the Laotian people, as well as the principles of the Joint Communiqué of Zurich dated June 22, 1961, and of the Geneva Agreements of 1954, in order to build a peaceful, neutral, independent, democratic, unified and prosperous Laos,

Solemnly declares that:

(1) It will resolutely apply the five principles of peaceful co-existence in foreign relations, and will develop friendly relations and establish diplomatic relations with all countries, the neighbouring countries first and foremost, on the basis of equality and of respect for the independence and sovereignty of Laos;

(2) It is the will of the Laotian people to protect and ensure respect for the sovereignty, independence, neutrality, unity, and territorial integrity of Laos;

(3) It will not resort to the use or threat of force in any way which might impair the peace of other countries, and will not interfere in the internal affairs of other countries;

(4) It will not enter into any military alliance or into any agreement, whether military or otherwise, which is inconsistent with the neutrality of the Kingdom of Laos; it will not allow the establishment of any foreign military base on Laotian territory, nor allow any country to use Laotian territory for military purposes or for the purposes of interference in the internal affairs of other countries, nor recognise the protection of any alliance or military coalition, including SEATO;

(5) It will not allow any foreign interference in the internal affairs of the Kingdom of Laos in any form whatsoever;

(6) Subject to the provisions of Article 5 of the Protocol, it will require the withdrawal from Laos of all foreign troops and military personnel, and will not allow any foreign troops or military personnel to be introduced into Laos;

(7) It will accept direct and unconditional aid from all countries that wish to help the Kingdom of Laos build up an independent and autonomous national economy on the basis of respect for the sovereignty of Laos;

(8) It will respect the treaties and agreements signed in conformity with the interests of the Laotian people and of the policy of peace and neutrality of the Kingdom, in particular the Geneva Agreements of 1962, and will abrogate all treaties and agreements which are contrary to those principles.

This statement of neutrality by the Royal Government of Laos shall be promulgated constitutionally and shall have the force of law.

The Kingdom of Laos appeals to all the States participating in the International Conference on the Settlement of the Laotian Question, and to all other States, to recognise the sovereignty, independence, neutrality, unity and territorial integrity of Laos, to conform to these principles in all respects, and to refrain from any action inconsistent therewith.

Confirming the principles of respect for the sovereignty, independence, unity and territorial integrity of the Kingdom of Laos and non-interference in its internal affairs which are embodied in the Geneva Agreements of 1954;

Emphasising the principle of respect for the neutrality of the Kingdom of Laos;

Agreeing that the above-mentioned principles constitute a basis for the peaceful settlement of the Laotian question;

Profoundly convinced that the independence and neutrality of the Kingdom of Laos will assist the peaceful democratic development of the Kingdom of Laos and the achievement of national accord and unity in that country, as well as the strengthening of peace and security in South-East Asia;

1. Solemnly declare, in accordance with the will of the Government and people of the Kingdom of Laos, as expressed in the statement of neutrality by the Royal Government of Laos of July 9, 1962, that they recognise and will respect and observe in every way the sovereignty, independence, neutrality, unity and territorial integrity of the Kingdom of Laos.

2. Undertake, in particular, that

   (a) they will not commit or participate in any way in any act which might directly or indirectly impair the sovereignty, independence, neutrality, unity or territorial integrity of the Kingdom of Laos;

   (b) they will not resort to the use or threat of force or any other measure which might impair the peace of the Kingdom of Laos;

   (c) they will refrain from all direct or indirect interference in the internal affairs of the Kingdom of Laos;

   (d) they will not attach conditions of a political nature to any assistance which they may offer or which the Kingdom of Laos may seek;

(e) they will not bring the Kingdom of Laos in any way into any military alliance or any other agreement, whether military or otherwise, which is inconsistent with her neutrality, nor invite or encourage her to enter into any such alliance or to conclude any such agreement;

(f) they will respect the wish of the Kingdom of Laos not to recognise the protection of any alliance or military coalition, including SEATO;

(g) they will not introduce into the Kingdom of Laos foreign troops or military personnel in any form whatsoever, nor will they in any way facilitate or connive at the introduction of any foreign troops or military personnel;

(h) they will not establish nor will they in any way facilitate or connive at the establishment in the Kingdom of Laos of any foreign military base, foreign strong point or other foreign military installation of any kind;

(i) they will not use the territory of the Kingdom of Laos for interference in the internal affairs of other countries;

(j) they will not use the territory of any country, including their own for interference in the internal affairs of the Kingdom of Laos.

3. Appeal to all other States to recognise, respect and observe in every way the sovereignty, independence and neutrality, and also the unity and territorial integrity, of the Kingdom of Laos and to refrain from any action inconsistent with these principles or with other provisions of the present Declaration.

4. Undertake, in the event of a violation or threat of violation of the sovereignty, independence, neutrality, unity or territorial integrity of the Kingdom of Laos, to consult jointly with the Royal Government of Laos and among themselves in order to consider measures which might prove to be necessary to ensure the observance of these principles and the other provisions of the present Declaration.

5. The present Declaration shall enter into force on signature and together with the statement of neutrality by the Royal Government of Laos of July 9, 1962, shall be regarded as constituting an international agreement. The present Declaration shall be depos-

ited in the archives of the Governments of the United Kingdom and the Union of Soviet Socialist Republics, which shall furnish certified copies thereof to the other signatory States and to all the other States of the world.

In witness whereof, the undersigned Plenipotentiaries have signed the present Declaration.

Done in two copies in Geneva this twenty-third day of July one thousand nine hundred and sixty-two in the English, Chinese, French, Laotian and Russian languages, each text being equally authoritative.

For the Union of Burma: U Thi Han
For the Kingdom of Cambodia: Nhiek Tioulong
For Canada: H. C. Green, Chester Ronning
For the People's Republic of China: Chen Yi
For the Democratic Republic of Viet-Nam: Ung-van-Khiem
For the Republic of France: M. Couve de Murville, Jacques Roux
For the Republic of India: V. K. Krishna Menon
For the Polish People's Republic: A. Rapacki
For the Republic of Viet-Nam: Vu van Mau, Thanh
For the Kingdom of Thailand: Direck Jayanâma
For the Union of Soviet Socialist Republics: A. Gromyko
For the United Kingdom of Great Britain and Northern Ireland:
    Home, Malcolm Macdonald
For the United States of America: Dean Rusk, W. Averell Harriman

Source: United Nations, *Treaty Series,* No. 6564, pp. 302–5.

Appendix 2

PROTOCOL TO THE DECLARATION ON THE NEUTRALITY OF LAOS. SIGNED AT GENEVA, ON 23 JULY 1962

The Governments of the Union of Burma, the Kingdom of Cambodia, Canada, the People's Republic of China, the Democratic Republic of Viet-Nam, the Republic of France, the Republic of India, the Kingdom of Laos, the Polish People's Republic, the Republic of Viet-Nam, the Kingdom of Thailand, the Union of Soviet Socialist Republics, the United Kingdom of Great Britain and Northern Ireland and the United States of America;

Having regard to the Declaration on the Neutrality of Laos of July 23, 1962;

Have agreed as follows:

Article 1

For the purposes of this Protocol

(a) the term "foreign military personnel" shall include members of foreign military missions, foreign military advisers, experts, instructors, consultants, technicians, observers and any other foreign military persons, including those serving in any armed forces in Laos, and foreign civilians connected with the supply, maintenance, storing and utilization of war materials;

(b) the term "the Commission" shall mean the International Commission for Supervision and Control in Laos set up by virtue of the Geneva Agreements of 1954 and composed of the representatives of Canada, India and Poland, with the representative of India as Chairman;

(c) the term "the Co-Chairmen" shall mean the Co-Chairmen of the International Conference for the Settlement of the Laotian Question, 1961–1962, and their successors in the offices of Her Britannic Majesty's Principal Secretary of State for Foreign Affairs and Minister for Foreign Affairs of the Union of Soviet Socialist Republics respectively;

(d) the term "the members of the Conference" shall mean the Governments of countries which took part in the International Conference for the Settlement of the Laotian Question, 1961–1962.

Article 2

All foreign regular and irregular troops, foreign para-military formations and foreign military personnel shall be withdrawn from Laos in the shortest time possible and in any case the withdrawal shall be completed not later than thirty days after the Commission has notified the Royal Government of Laos that in accordance with Articles 3 and 10 of this Protocol its inspection teams are present at all points of withdrawal from Laos. These points shall be determined by the Royal Government of Laos in accordance with Article 3 within thirty days after the entry into force of this Protocol. The inspection teams shall be present at these points and the Commission shall notify the Royal Government of Laos thereof within fifteen days after the points have been determined.

Article 3

The withdrawal of foreign regular and irregular troops, foreign paramilitary formations and foreign military personnel shall take place only along such routes and through such points as shall be determined by the Royal Government of Laos in consultation with the Commission. The Commission shall be notified in advance of the point and time of all such withdrawals.

Article 4

The introduction of foreign regular and irregular troops, foreign para-military formations and foreign military personnel into Laos is prohibited.

Article 5

Note is taken that the French and Laotian Governments will conclude as soon as possible an arrangement to transfer the French military installations in Laos to the Royal Government of Laos.

If the Laotian Government considers it necessary, the French Government may as an exception leave in Laos for a limited period of time a precisely limited number of French military instructors for the purpose of training the armed forces of Laos.

The French and Laotian Governments shall inform the members of the Conference, through the Co-Chairmen, of their agreement on the question of the transfer of the French military installations in Laos and of the employment of French military instructors by the Laotian Government.

Article 6

The introduction into Laos of armaments, munitions and war material generally, except such quantities of conventional armaments as the Royal Government of Laos may consider necessary for the national defence of Laos, is prohibited.

Article 7

All foreign military persons and civilians captured or interned during the course of hostilities in Laos shall be released within thirty days after the entry into force of this Protocol and handed over by the Royal Government of Laos to the representatives of the Governments of the countries of which they are nationals in order that they may proceed to the destination of their choice.

Article 8

The Co-Chairmen shall periodically receive reports from the Commission. In addition the Commission shall immediately report to the Co-Chairmen any violations or threats of violations of this Protocol, all significant steps which it takes in pursuance of this Protocol, and also any other important information which may assist the Co-Chairmen in carrying out their functions. The Commission may at any time seek help from the Co-Chairmen in the performance of its duties, and the Co-Chairmen may at any time make recommendations to the Commission exercising general guidance.

The Co-Chairmen shall circulate the reports and any other important information from the Commission to the members of the Conference.

The Co-Chairmen shall exercise supervision over the observance of this Protocol and the Declaration on the Neutrality of Laos.

The Co-Chairmen will keep the members of the Conference constantly informed and when appropriate will consult with them.

Article 9

The Commission shall, with the concurrence of the Royal Government of Laos, supervise and control the cease-fire in Laos.

The Commission shall exercise these functions in full co-operation with the Royal Government of Laos and within the framework of the Cease-Fire Agreement or cease-fire arrangements made by the three political forces in Laos, or the Royal Government of Laos. It is understood that responsibility for the execution of the cease-fire shall rest with the three parties concerned and with the Royal Government of Laos after its formation.

Article 10

The Commission shall supervise and control the withdrawal of foreign regular and irregular troops, foreign para-military formations and foreign military personnel. Inspection teams sent by the Commission for these purposes shall be present for the period of the withdrawal at all points of withdrawal from Laos determined by the Royal Government of Laos in consultation with the Commission in accordance with Article 3 of this Protocol.

Article 11

The Commission shall investigate cases where there are reasonable grounds for considering that a violation of the provisions of Article 4 of this Protocol has occurred.

It is understood that in the exercise of this function the Commission is acting with the concurrence of the Royal Government of Laos. It shall carry out its investigations in full co-operation with the Royal Government of Laos and shall immediately inform the Co-Chairmen of any violations or threats of violations of Article 4, and also of all significant steps which it takes in pursuance of this Article in accordance with Article 8.

Article 12
The Commission shall assist the Royal Government of Laos in cases where the Royal Government of Laos considers that a violation of Article 6 of this Protocol may have taken place. This assistance will be rendered at the request of the Royal Government of Laos and in full co-operation with it.

Article 13
The Commission shall exercise its functions under this Protocol in close co-operation with the Royal Government of Laos. It is understood that the Royal Government of Laos at all levels will render the Commission all possible assistance in the performance by the Commission of these functions and also will take all necessary measures to ensure the security of the Commission and its inspection teams, during their activities in Laos.

Article 14
The Commission functions as a single organ of the International Conference for the Settlement of the Laotian Question, 1961–1962. The members of the Commission will work harmoniously and in co-operation with each other with the aim of solving all questions within the terms of reference of the Commission.

Decisions of the Commission on questions relating to violations of Articles 2, 3, 4 and 6 of this Protocol or of the cease-fire referred to in Article 9, conclusions on major questions sent to the Co-Chairmen and all recommendations by the Commission shall be adopted unanimously. On other questions, including procedural questions, and also questions relating to the initiation and carrying out of investigations (Article 15), decisions of the Commission shall be adopted by majority vote.

Article 15
In the exercise of its specific functions which are laid down in the relevant articles of this Protocol the Commission shall conduct investiga-

tions (directly or by sending inspection teams), when there are reasonable grounds for considering that a violation has occurred. These investigations shall be carried out at the request of the Royal Government of Laos or on the initiative of the Commission, which is acting with the concurrence of the Royal Government of Laos.

In the latter case decisions on initiating and carrying out such investigations shall be taken in the Commission by majority vote.

The Commission shall submit agreed reports on investigations in which differences which may emerge between members of the Commission on particular questions may be expressed.

The conclusions and recommendations of the Commission resulting from investigations shall be adopted unanimously.

Article 16

For the exercise of its functions the Commission shall, as necessary, set up inspection teams, on which the three member-States of the Commission shall be equally represented. Each member-State of the Commission shall ensure the presence of its own representatives both on the Commission and on the inspection teams, and shall promptly replace them in the event of their being unable to perform their duties.

It is understood that the dispatch of inspection teams to carry out various specific tasks takes place with the concurrence of the Royal Government of Laos. The points to which the Commission and its inspection teams go for the purposes of investigation and their length of stay at those points shall be determined in relation to the requirements of the particular investigation.

Article 17

The Commission shall have at its disposal the means of communication and transport required for the performance of its duties. These as a rule will be provided to the Commission by the Royal Government of Laos for payment on mutually acceptable terms, and those which the Royal Government of Laos cannot provide will be acquired by the Commission from other sources. It is understood that the means of communication and transport will be under the administrative control of the Commission.

Article 18

The costs of the operations of the Commission shall be borne by the members of the Conference in accordance with the provisions of this Article.

(a) The Governments of Canada, India and Poland shall pay the personal salaries and allowances of their nationals who are members of their delegations to the Commission and its subsidiary organs.

(b) The primary responsibility for the provision of accommodation for the Commission and its subsidiary organs shall rest with the Royal Government of Laos, which shall also provide such other local services as may be appropriate. The Commission shall charge to the Fund referred to in sub-paragraph (c) below any local expenses not borne by the Royal Government of Laos.

(c) All other capital or running expenses incurred by the Commission in the exercise of its functions shall be met from a Fund to which all the members of the Conference shall contribute in the following proportions:

The Governments of the People's Republic of China, France, the Union of Soviet Socialist Republics, the United Kingdom and the United States of America shall contribute 17.6 per cent each.

The Governments of Burma, Cambodia, the Democratic Republic of Viet Nam, Laos, the Republic of Viet Nam and Thailand shall contribute 1.5 per cent each.

The Governments of Canada, India and Poland as members of the Commission shall contribute 1 per cent each.

Article 19

The Co-Chairmen shall at any time, if the Royal Government of Laos so requests, and in any case not later than three years after the entry into force of this Protocol, present a report with appropriate recommendations on the question of the termination of the Commission to the members of the Conference for their consideration. Before making such a report the Co-Chairmen shall hold consultations with the Royal Government of Laos and the Commission.

Article 20

This Protocol shall enter into force on signature.

It shall be deposited in the archives of the Governments of the United Kingdom and the Union of Soviet Socialist Republics, which shall furnish certified copies thereof to the other signatory States and to all other States of the world.

In witness whereof, the undersigned Plenipotentiaries have signed this Protocol.

Done in two copies in Geneva this twenty-third day of July one thousand nine hundred and sixty-two in the English, Chinese, French, Laotian and Russian languages, each text being equally authoritative.

For the Union of Burma: U Thi Han
For the Kingdom of Cambodia: Nhiek Tioulong
For Canada: H. C. Green, Chester Ronning
For the People's Republic of China: Chen Yi
For the Democratic Republic of Viet-Nam: Ung-van-Khiem
For the Republic of France: M. Couve de Murville, Jacques Roux
For the Republic of India: V. K. Krishna Menon
For the Kingdom of Laos: Q. Pholsena
For the Polish People's Republic: A. Rapacki
For the Republic of Viet-Nam: Vu van Mau, Thanh
For the Kingdom of Thailand: Direck Jayanâma
For the Union of Soviet Socialist Republics: A. Gromyko
For the United Kingdom of Great Britain and Northern Ireland: Home, Malcolm Macdonald
For the United States of America: Dean Rusk, W. Averell Harriman

Source: United Nations, *Treaty Series,* No. 6564, pp. 324–29.

Appendix 3

MEMORANDUM FOR THE PRESIDENT

Note: This appendix is the complete declassified version of the sanitized memorandum that appears in *FRUS, 1961–1963, XXIV,* d. 477. The redacted portions of the *FRUS* document appear in bracketed, italicized type.

The root of the problem in Southeast Asia is the aggressive effort of the North Vietnamese to establish Communist control in Laos and South Viet-Nam as a stepping-stone to control all Southeast Asia. In response to this effort, we have pursued courses of action corresponding to the differing circumstances in Laos, South Viet-Nam and Thailand. US prestige is engaged in both Laos and South Viet-Nam. If we are to preserve the prospects for success in South Viet-Nam and keep our commitment to defend Thailand within manageable bounds, we must pursue our intention of preventing further expansion of Communist control in Laos.

Our efforts over the past year to obtain North Vietnamese withdrawal from Laos by international agreement have gained for us a great deal of political capital internationally. They should, therefore, not be abandoned lightly or before we have exhausted their possibilities completely. Since, however, the Communist effort is ambiguous, we require a program for graduated increases in US political and military pressure which, without setting into motion an irreversible pattern, will enable us to achieve, if not a truly neutral Laos under an effective Government of National Union, at least the facade of a neutralist government presiding over a stabilized <u>de facto</u> partition.

This memorandum outlines a program of action which the Secretaries of State and Defense recommend—not as a contingency response to Communist tactics—but as a method of influencing the over-all situation so that events will move in the direction of the stabilization we desire. It is fully recognized that if the Communists fail to respond to lesser pressures, the third phase of this program is such as to constitute the initiation of military action against North Vietnam which would logically call for a radically changed objective. The actions involved are included to demonstrate the sequential relationship of potential pressures in the event future circumstances dictate such a solution.

At this time, we recommend approval of this over-all concept in principle, and approval of Phase I and those Phase II actions not violating North Vietnamese sovereignty. When the effect of the initial actions can be evaluated, recommendations will be submitted with respect to necessity and timing of subsequent actions.

The Situation in Laos

Our continuing basic objective is to force a cessation of Communist encroachment in Southeast Asia in order to allow a peaceful development of the area. In Laos, Pathet Lao–Viet Minh forces, in violation of the Geneva Accords, are eliminating neutralist Kong Le positions piecemeal through military attacks and political pressures. The continuation of this Communist tactic, particularly in the Plain of Jars, will symbolize to Laotians, their Southeast Asian neighbors, and the Communists alike that force can be used to erode Free World positions without the risk of serious consequences. Moreover, so long as neither Moscow nor Peiping sees such consequences as imminent, their dispute over Communist strategy will encourage each to compete with the other in supporting Pathet Lao attacks.

To halt this process, we have considered ways of making the risk of serious consequences from further Communist incursions both credible and serious, especially for Hanoi on whom rests primary responsibility for Communist aggression in Laos and South Viet-Nam. We doubt that Communist plans in Laos include so gross and overt an act of aggression as to provide us with an obvious provocation which in itself would give reason for our intervention. Rather, their erosive tactics, successful in the past, will be employed in hope of steadily improving Communist positions without arousing Free World counteraction. However, we believe the situation sufficiently serious to require our seizing the initiative at a time of our choosing. Therefore our proposed moves are not linked to a future contingency but to the present and prospective situation. By so acting, we can halt North Vietnamese expansionist aggression in Laos and reduce its threat to peace in Southeast Asia.

We propose to achieve a stabilization of the situation either along the pattern of re-establishing the Government of National Union under the Geneva Agreements or through an informal but stabilized partition behind the facade of a neutralist government (i.e., without Pathet Lao participation). At the same time, we hope to retain our considerable political advantages by preserving the neutralist-conservative coalition under Souvanna Phouma.

The following is a phased program of action centering on Laos. However, in its final phase it will contribute toward a solution of the situation in South Viet-Nam. The three phases relate to a scale of escalation and objectives. The military measures include:

(1) the use of non-US forces which can be supported by stretching the Geneva Agreements,
(2) the non-combatant use of US forces, including certain violations of the Geneva Agreements, and
(3) the combat use of US forces.

We recommend these and associated steps in pursuit of the objective of (1) reconsition [sic] of the National Union Government under the Geneva framework, or (2) informal but stabilized partition under the facade of a neutralist government, growing out of a <u>de facto</u> cease-fire.

PHASE 1

<u>Objective</u>
Reconstitution of the National Union Government under Geneva Agreements. This would include:
1) Pathet Lao return to the cabinet in Vientiane.
2) Cease-fire.
3) Restoration of positions as of April 1, 1963.

4) Withdrawal of Viet Minh forces.

5) Agreement by the Communists to permit full freedom of action to ICC. Alternatively, we would settle for establishing an informal but stabilized partition under the facade of a neutralist government, this would include:

(1) Cease-fire.

(2) Full freedom for the ICC to supervise the cease-fire.

Rationale

We are not sanguine that this objective of reconstituting the Government of National Union will be achieved, but it is the proper starting point for a plan since it is politically advantageous to our side. Moreover, it establishes our moral position and provides a reasonable basis for the political and military actions planned for this phase.

The problem with an informal but stabilized partition is how to establish recognizable rules so that both sides would know when the arrangement was being respected and when violated. The minimum would appear to be (1) a cease-fire, and (2) full freedom for the ICC to supervise the cease-fire.

Political Actions

Discuss our plans generally with Souvanna Phouma to obtain his full cooperation at each stage. Utilize all available diplomatic, political, covert, and propaganda channels to generate additional pressure on the Communist side to meet the above objective. Convey the idea that our patience is growing short; if the Communists will not cooperate under the Geneva Agreements we must take other measures to protect Lao independence and regional peace. Stimulate supporting actions by friendly countries. Seek British cooperation, explaining that continued failure of the Communist side to cooperate would soon force us to take other measures. Brief SEATO and India and friendly Geneva signatories explaining that we are making a major effort to restore the Geneva Agreements to full operation before considering other courses.

Military Actions

1) Accept FAR and Kong Le forces at present levels, without further demobilization, and provide additional funds as necessary to support FAR and Kong Le forces through MAP and AID programs.

2) Step up flow of heavy weapons and replacement of worn-out equipment on a selective basis.

3) Establish direct US contact with neutralist forces and pro-Western tribal elements; encourage improved liaison, coordination, and military planning among these forces and the FAR.

4) Improve intelligence capabilities:

   (1) Increase intelligence reconnaissance and patrol activity in Southern Laos [*by South Vietnamese–led tribal teams*].

   (2) Provide additional [*third country*] intelligence and communications training with a view to increasing intelligence team activity in central Laos and the Bolovens area, and initiating such activity in northwest Laos.

5) Increase air re-supply of arms on a selective basis to Kong Le, pro-West tribal groups, and FAR outposts in Pathet Lao territory.

6) Expand tribal group program in non–Pathet Lao–held territory; intensify tribal group activity against Communist forces and supply lines in present areas of operation.

7) Augment Souvanna's airlift capabilities.

8) Encourage FAR forces to take positive action to gain firm control over areas not now controlled by the Pathet Lao. In addition, encourage FAR in eliminating Pathet Lao in areas now generally controlled by the FAR.

9) Provide T–28 aircraft and armament to FAR in Laos to conduct reprisal strikes.

10) Commence a combined social, political, and military effort through a strategic hamlet program in the Mekong Valley area.

11) Initiate aerial reconnaissance of Laos by ICC.

12) [*Expand the use of highly mobile South Vietnamese border patrols in Laos to interdict entry into South Viet-Nam and to gather intelligence.*]

Timing

Begin immediately.

PHASE 2

Objective

The objective remains the same as in Phase 1.

Rationale

A decidedly increased military effort in Laos, including some measures overtly outside the Geneva framework and coupled with a mobilization of US power outside of Laos, may accomplish our objectives.

Political Actions

Reiterate our support for the Geneva Agreements, but emphasize that, even though our objectives are limited, we will, in the face of Communist abandonment of the Agreements, take extraordinary measures to offset Communist expansionism. Gear all steps closely to the developing situation in Laos and to the willingness and ability of Souvanna Phouma to cooperate. Discuss with the British as a Co-Chairman, and with the French to obtain their support and cooperation. Brief our SEATO allies and the GVN on our estimate of the situation and intentions and ask the former to prepare to send contingents to Thailand. Continue close consultations with India and Canada and inform other friendly nations as appropriate.

If the Communists should propose a conference at this stage, we would insist that they first comply with the terms of the Agreements negotiated at the Geneva Conference. Maintain flexibility to take up any promising overtures.

Military Actions

1) Resume US aerial reconnaissance of Laos.

2) Expand US military advisory role to FAR and Kong Le forces.

3) Encourage selective offensive action by FAR/Kong Le forces.

4) Encourage selective offensive use of T–28's and T–6's.

5) Consider the retention in Thailand of US combat forces now there, for use in conjunction with other moves under this Phase.

6) [*Expand the use of PARUs (Police Aerial Reconnaissance Units) and other specialist teams (covert).*]

7) [*Expand the use of highly mobile South Vietnamese border patrols in Laos to conduct guerrilla operations in Laos Corridor.*]

8) Further enlarge pro-Western guerrilla units in Laos and expand operations in enemy-held territory.

9) [*Support third country Special Forces units in active operations against Pathet Lao, primarily SVN and Thai "volunteers." Encourage third country encadrement.*]

10) [*Provide sanitized combat aircraft and contract American or third country pilots to the Laotian forces and authorize their use against the Pathet Lao concentration and supply points.*]

11) [*Expand sabotage operations against Viet Minh bases, both in Laos and North Viet-Nam (covert).*]

12) Move US Air Force units into Thailand.

13) Move US naval carrier task force off South Viet-Nam.

14) Take selected Category II actions against North Viet-Nam. (Category II: Overflights, high and low altitude reconnaissance of Laos and North Viet-Nam; harassment of DRV shipping.)

15) Take preparatory measures for the implementation of CINCPAC OPPlan 32–63.

16) Request SEATO members to prepare to deploy forces to the area.

Timing

Begin upon determination that the objective under Phase 1 is unobtainable without further moves by us. Duration will depend on developments on the ground and our interpretation of Communist behavior and intentions. Continued Communist military pressures and political intransigence would force the conclusion that a new phase would have to be entered.

PHASE 3

Objective

In addition to the objectives in Phases 1 and 2, it may be desirable to agree to a Geneva Conference to establish a formal partition, in which case our objective would be to ensure non-Communist control of:

1) The Panhandle (to prevent DRV use to support subversion in South Viet-Nam).

2) The Mekong lowlands, Sayaboury Province, and southern Nam Tha Province (to protect the Thai frontier and control access to the River).

3) The Vientiane terrain compartment (to protect the base of the RLG).

4) If possible, a foothold in the Plain of Jars (for strategic and political reasons).

Rationale

At this stage, actions on the part of the United States should demonstrate unmistakenly US determination to achieve a stabilized Laos.

Political Actions

Seek an RLG request for, or approval of US and/or SEATO intervention. Once our forces have been introduced to points in Laos along the Mekong River, the extent to which they would advance and the extent of our operations against North Viet-Nam would depend on Communist behavior. If a formal partition subsequently seems desirable, announce that, since the PL/VM are dividing the country instead of cooperating to unify it under the Geneva Agreements, the only way to preserve the independence and neutrality of the non-Communist part against Communist aggression is to define the limitation of the Communist zone and establish an international force to patrol it. Seek the assistance of the British in negotiating the partition. Propose or accede to an international conference in accordance with our objectives. Present appropriate resolutions to the UN and inform it of our actions and our purposes, emphasizing that we are reacting only to the Communist violation of the Geneva Agreements. Remain flexible to take up and exploit any overtures which appeared promising in order to reach a stable arrangement as quickly as possible. Utilize appropriate channels to make it understood that our purposes are limited but our determination is not and that we will not be deterred by an attempted reprisals [sic] elsewhere in the world.

Military Actions

State Department Position	Defense Department Position
(a) Move US ground force units into Thailand.	(a) Move US ground force units into Thailand.
(b) Move token US forces into Laos occupying Vientiane, Savannakhet and Pakse.	(b) Implement selective Category III actions against North Viet-Nam (Category III: Intensified harassment of shipping; blockage of Haiphong or DRV; mining in the Gulf of Tonkin or Haiphong approaches; blocking river entrances or Haiphong Channel; bombing of selected targets in North Viet-Nam.)
(c) Simultaneously air strike against selected Pathet Lao/ Viet Minh targets in Laos.	(c) Simultaneously air strike against selected Pathet Lao/Viet Minh targets in Laos.

(d) Implement selective
Category III actions   (The above actions would be
against North Viet-Nam.   conducted concurrently.)
(Category III: Intensified
harassment of shipping;
blockade of Haiphong or
DRV; mining in the Gulf
of Tonkin or Haiphong
approaches; blocking river
entrances or Haiphong
channel; bombing of selected
targets in North Viet-Nam.)

(e) Commit US and allied   (d) Commit US and allied forces to
forces to North Viet-Nam   North Viet-Nam and Laos as
and Laos as appropriate to   appropriate to achieve the objective.*
achieve the objective.

* The Secretary of Defense and the
JCS would omit any separate course
of action introducing "token" US
forces into Laos, and the JCS would
prefer to designate Defense's (d) as a
separate Phase 4, to indicate that this
would be a major new element.

NOTE:

The commitment of US/Allied ground forces in Southeast Asia and air/naval action against North Viet-Nam would necessarily be preceded by preparatory and visible deployments. Actual commitment of forces would be phased as the situation required and would not necessarily require the full commitments contained in CINCPAC OPPlan 32–63.

Should earlier US political and military measures fail to accomplish the objectives, the plan culminates in major military action against North Viet-Nam.

Taking this final action will in itself enlarge our objective from that centered on Laos to the cessation of DRV subversive activity in the remainder of Southeast Asia.

Timing
To be carried out when it is determined Phase 2 has not succeeded and that direct utilization of US forces is essential.

June 17, 1963

Source: LOC, WAHP, box 483.

Notes

Abbreviations Used in the Notes and the Bibliography

AJBP	Andrew Jackson Boyle Papers
APP	American Presidency Project
ARMA	Army Attaché
ASFEA	Assistant Secretary for Far Eastern Affairs
BEA&PA	Bureau of East Asian and Pacific Affairs
BFEA	Bureau of Far Eastern Affairs
BIOA	Bureau of International Organization Affairs
CAS	Controlled American Source (CIA)
CDF	Central Decimal File
CFPF	Central Foreign Policy Files
CHMAAG	Chief, Military Assistance Advisory Group
CJCS	Chairman, Joint Chiefs of Staff
CREST	CIA Records Search Tool
"CSSECLC"	"Chronological Summary of Significant Events Concerning the Laotian Crisis"
CWYP	Charles W. Yost Papers
DA	Department of the Army
DDEL	Dwight D. Eisenhower Library
FAOHC	Foreign Affairs Oral History Collection
FRUS	*Foreign Relations of the United States*
GWBP	George W. Ball Papers
JFKL	John F. Kennedy Library
JFKLOHP	John F. Kennedy Library Oral History Program
KARC	Kennedy Assassination Records Collection
LBJL	Lyndon B. Johnson Library
LBJLOHP	Lyndon B. Johnson Library Oral History Program
LOC	Library of Congress
MACV	Military Assistance Command Vietnam
MFS	Microfiche Supplement
NARA	National Archives and Records Administration
NSAM	National Security Action Memorandum
NSF	National Security File

OCDL	Office of the Country Director for Laos
OCDLC	Office of the Country Director for Laos and Cambodia
OCI	Office of Current Intelligence
OSAA	Office of Southeast Asian Affairs
POF	President's Office Files
PPC	Policy Planning Council
RG 59	General Records of the Department of State
RG 84	Records of the Foreign Service Posts of the Department of State
RG 218	Records of the US Joint Chiefs of Staff
RG 330	Records of the Office of the Secretary of Defense
RG 472	Records of the US Forces in Southeast Asia, 1950–1976
RHP	Roger Hilsman Papers
USAMHI	US Army Military History Institute
USVR	*United States–Vietnam Relations, 1945–1967*
WAHP	W. Averell Harriman Papers

Introduction

1. Memorandum of conversation, April 21, 1963, *FRUS, XXIV,* d. 462.

2. Ibid.

3. Leonard Unger to State Dept., March 21, 1963, *FRUS, XXIV,* d. 446.

4. Memorandum of conversation, April 21, 1963.

5. W. Averell Harriman to McGeorge Bundy, January 11, 1962, *FRUS, XXIV,* d. 267; Harriman to Winthrop Brown, July 19, 1962, LOC, WAHP, box 530.

6. Harriman to State Dept., April 27, 1963, JFKL, NSF, Countries, box 137.

7. Memorandum, April 20, 1963, *FRUS, XXIV,* d. 459; JCS to Robert McNamara, April 23, 1963, *FRUS, XXIV,* MFS, no. 332.

8. "Memorandum for the President," June 17, 1963, LOC, WAHP, box 483. This is a complete version of the sanitized memorandum that appears in *FRUS, XXIV,* d. 477. The complete document, which discusses covert operations in Laos and North Vietnam, is reprinted in appendix 3.

9. Lucius D. Clay Jr., memorandum for the record, June 19, 1963, NARA, RG 218, CJCS-091 Laos, box 7; "Memorandum for the President," June 17, 1963.

10. Meeting with the president, July 30, 1963, JFKL, Presidential Recordings, tape 102.2.

11. State Dept. to Vientiane, November 7, 1963, JFKL, NSF, box 138A.

12. The 1962 "Geneva agreement" comprises three documents: a statement of neutrality by the Lao government; a declaration by the other thirteen conference participants that incorporates the statement of the Lao government; and a protocol for monitoring compliance with the provisions of the joint declaration. Throughout this book, the terms "Geneva agreement" and "Geneva accords" are used interchangeably to refer to the three documents. The Geneva declaration and protocol are reprinted in appendixes 1 and 2, respectively.

13. Rusk, *As I Saw It,* p. 429; meeting with the president, August 2, 1963, JFKL, Presidential Recordings, tape 103.

14. Meeting with the president, September 3, 1963, JFKL, Presidential Recordings, tape 108.3.

15. Hanyok, *Spartans in Darkness,* p. 94.

16. CIA, "North Vietnamese Support to the Viet Cong via Laos," January 23, 1963, NARA, CREST.

17. SNIE 14.3-69, "Capabilities of the Vietnamese Communists for Fighting in South Vietnam," July 17, 1969, estimated that "about 250,000" men infiltrated from North Vietnam into South Vietnam in 1968. According to "Appendix I," *Vietnam 1961–1968 as Interpreted in INR's Production* (Howells et al.), "some 215,000 NVA troops entered the pipeline in 1968 for deployment to South Vietnam."

18. Goscha, "Maritime Nature of the Wars for Vietnam," p. 78; "Notes on Visits to Thailand, Laos, Vietnam, and Okinawa," December 10, 1962, *FRUS, II,* d. 327.

19. Hilsman, "A Strategic Concept for South Vietnam," February 2, 1962, *FRUS, II,* d. 42.

20. Walt Rostow to Dean Rusk, November 28, 1962, NARA, RG 59, BFEA, ASFEA, Subject Files, 1960–1963, box 21.

21. Ibid.

22. Rostow, *Diffusion of Power,* p. 290.

23. On July 30, 1962, Kennedy said that many Pentagon officers shared the characteristics of his first chief of naval operations, Admiral Arleigh Burke: "admirable, nice figure, without any brains." Meeting on Europe and general diplomatic matters in Naftali, *Presidential Recordings: John F. Kennedy, I,* p. 49. (During that same conversation, Kennedy provided an equally harsh assessment of an "awful lot" of Foreign Service officers, "who don't seem to have *cojones.*") In his oral history for the Kennedy Library (March 1964), McGeorge Bundy said that Kennedy "had not much respect for brass hats."

24. M. Bundy to Kennedy, April 1, 1961, *FRUS, XXIV,* d. 47.

25. Memorandum for the record, April 18, 1963, NARA, KARC, RG 218, box 5.

26. Memorandum of conversation, July 17, 1963, NARA, RG 59, Lot File 70D328, State-JCS Meetings, 1959–1963, box 3.

27. NSAM 273, November 26, 1963, *FRUS, IV,* d. 331.

28. Memorandum, November 1, 1963, *FRUS, XXIV,* d. 490.

29. Michael Forrestal to M. Bundy, November 18, 1963, JFKL, NSF, box 320.

30. Meeting on Laos, August 15, 1962, in Naftali, *Presidential Recordings: John F. Kennedy, I,* p. 438.

31. Rust, *Before the Quagmire,* pp. 63–65. J. Graham Parsons, an American ambassador to Laos (1956–1958) and assistant secretary of state for far eastern affairs (1959–1961), called the civilian aid mission "probably the most unsatisfactory program in the entire world." Memorandum, May 29, 1958, NARA, RG 59, CF, Box 3365.

32. The Lao army was initially called the ANL (Armée Nationale de Laos). In

1959 the designation FAL (Forces Armées de Laos), which referred to all Laotian armed forces, came into use. In September 1961 both designations were replaced by FAR (Force Armée Royale). For the sake of reading ease, I only use the acronym FAR in this book.

33. Francois Queneau, memorandum, February 15, 1962, LOC, WAHP, box 259; Rust, *Before the Quagmire*, pp. 94–98, 151–54. Continuity and clarity in *A Piece of War* require the occasional reprise of material from *Before the Quagmire*.

34. CIA, "The Lao Communists," March 12, 1973, NARA, CREST.

35. CIA, "Counter-Insurgency Critical List," July 25, 1962, www.cia.foia.gov.

36. For a detailed discussion on the Kong Le coup and its aftermath, see Rust, *Before the Quagmire*, chapters 8–10.

37. Embassy-Army Attache-PEO-CAS to State Dept., undated (ca. December 31, 1960), DDEL, International File, box 11; memorandum of conversation, December 31, 1960, *FRUS, XVI,* d. 498; memorandum for the record, January 19, 1961, *FRUS, XXIV,* d. 8.

38. "Trip to the Middle East and Far East," November 14, 1951, JFKL, POF, Special Events through the Years.

39. "Remarks on Indochina," April 6, 1954, JFKL, Selected Speeches of John F. Kennedy.

40. "America's Stake in Vietnam," June 1, 1956, JFKL, POF, Special Events through the Years.

41. Kennedy, speech at the American Legion Convention, Miami Beach, FL, October 18, 1960, www.presidency.ucsb.edu.

42. Kennedy, memorandum, January 19, 1961, *FRUS, XXIV,* d. 7.

43. Mike Mansfield to Kennedy, January 21, 1961, JFKL, POF, Laos: General, 1961: January–March.

1. We Cannot Enforce What We Would Like

1. Memorandum of conversation, January 23, 1961, *FRUS, XXIV,* MFS, no. 93; Paul Nitze to McNamara, January 23, 1961, *FRUS, XXIV,* d. 10.

2. Memorandum of conversation, January 23, 1961.

3. "Report Prepared by the Inter-Agency Task Force on Laos," undated, attached to Nitze to McNamara, January 23, 1961.

4. Bissell, *Reflections of a Cold Warrior,* p. 147.

5. Ibid.; Rostow to Kennedy, February 28, 1961, *FRUS, XXIV,* d. 19.

6. George McGhee to Rusk, March 3, 1961, *FRUS, XXIV,* d. 22.

7. "Concept for the Recapture of the Plaine Des Jarres," March 9, 1961, NARA, KARC, RG 218, box 5.

8. Memorandum of conversation, March 9, 1961, *FRUS, XXIV,* d. 25.

9. Chester Clifton to Kennedy, March 10, 1961, *FRUS, XXIV,* d. 29.

10. Memorandum of conversation, March 9, 1961.

11. NSAM 29, March 9, 1961. (For a full discussion of the "dysfunctional" pro-

cess of declassifying this document, see Prados, "Last NSAM Standing.") JCS to CINCPAC, March 11, 1961, NARA, RG 218, CDF, 1961, box 172.

12. J. Graham Parsons to Rusk, March 17, 1961, NARA, RG 59, Records of Llewellyn E. Thompson, 1961–1970, box 6; Rostow to Kennedy, May 17, 1961, JFKL, POF, Staff Memos, box 64A.

13. Parsons to Rusk, March 17, 1961; memorandum of conversation, March 21, 1961, *FRUS, XXIV,* d. 36; State Dept. to Llewellyn Thompson, March 21, 1961, NARA, RG 59, CDF, 1960–1963, box 1760.

14. CINCPAC OPLAN 32-59 and OPLAN X-61, undated (ca. March 21, 1961), and Arleigh Burke to Harry Felt, March 21, 1961, both NARA, RG 218, CJCS-091 Laos, box 7.

15. Memorandum of conversation, March 21, 1961; Burke to CINCPAC, March 21, 1961; JCS, "CSSECLC," 2nd installment, p. 61.

16. Thomas Trapnell to Lyman Lemnitzer, March 23, 1961, NARA, RG 218, CJCS-091 Laos, box 7.

17. Press conference, March 23, 1961, APP.

18. Bailey, *Solitary Survivor,* pp. xvii–xix, 6.

19. Brown to State Dept., March 21, 1961, NARA, RG 59, CDF, 1960–1963, box 1760.

20. David Bruce to State Dept., March 24, 1961, Harold Macmillan to Kennedy, March 24, 1961, and State Dept. to Rusk, March 24, 1961, all NARA, RG 59, CDF, 1960–1963, box 1760.

21. Memorandum of conversation, March 26, 1961, NARA, RG 59, CDF, 1960–1963, box 1760.

22. Ibid.; Catterall, *Macmillan Diaries,* p. 369.

23. Memorandum of conversation, March 26, 1961, NARA, RG 59, CDF, 1960–1963, box 1760; Tarling, *Britain and the Neutralisation of Laos,* p. 119.

24. Kennedy to Rusk, March 27, 1961, NARA, RG 59, CDF, 1960–1963, box 1760.

25. Ibid.; memorandum of conversation, March 26, 1961, *FRUS, XXIV,* d. 40; Charles de Gaulle to Kennedy, March 26, 1961, NARA, RG 59, CDF, 1960–1963, box 1760.

26. De Gaulle to Kennedy, March 26, 1961.

27. Memorandum of conversation, March 26, 1961, *FRUS, XXIV,* d. 40.

28. State Dept. to Rusk, March 27, 1961, NARA, RG 59, CDF, 1960–1963, box 1760; Kennedy to Rusk, March 27, 1961, *FRUS, XXIV,* d. 43.

29. Huntington Sheldon to Allen Dulles, April 20, 1961, NARA, CREST; JCS, "CSSECLC," 3rd installment, p. 1.

30. Andrew Boyle to CINCPAC, April 16, 1961, State Department Circular, April 18, 1961, and London to Rusk, April 19, 1961, all "CSSECLC," 3rd installment, pp. 31–37.

31. Brown to State Dept., April 23, 1961, NARA, RG 59, CDF, 1960–1963, box 1762; Brown to State Dept., April 26, 1961, *FRUS, XXIV,* d. 60.

32. Watch Committee Report, April 26, 1961, JFKL, NSF, box 130A; Bowles to Kennedy, April 26, 1961, *FRUS, XXIV,* d. 61.

33. Memorandum of meeting, April 26, 1961, *FRUS, XXIV,* d. 62.

34. State Dept. to Brown, April 26, 1961, *FRUS, XXIV,* MFS, no. 133; JCS to CINCPAC, April 26, 1961, JCS, "CSSECLC," 3rd installment, p. 50.

35. State Dept. to Rusk, April 27, 1961, *FRUS, XXIV,* d. 65.

36. John Foster Dulles to W. Bedell Smith, May 12, 1954, *FRUS, XVI,* p. 788.

37. State Dept. to Rusk, May 9, 1961, and memorandum of conversation, May 31, 1961, both *FRUS, XXIV,* dd. 84 and 103, respectively.

38. Memorandum of conversation, May 31, 1961; memorandum of conversation, June 2, 1961, *FRUS, XIII,* d. 230.

39. Harriman to Rusk, May 24, 1961, *FRUS, XXIV,* d. 97.

40. Vientiane to State Dept., July 21, 1961, NARA, RG 59, CDF, 1960–1963, box 1764.

41. Gaddis, *Cold War,* p. 69.

42. Memoranda of conversation, June 3, 1961, and June 4, 1961, both *FRUS, XXIV,* dd. 107–108.

43. Memorandum of conversation, June 5, 1961, NARA, RG 59, Executive Secretariat, Conference Files, 1949–1963, box 254; Catterall, *Macmillan Diaries,* p. 390; record of conversation, June 5, 1961, *FRUS, XIV,* d. 34.

44. Macmillan, *Pointing the Way,* p. 357.

45. "Joint Communiqué of the Three Princes," June 22, 1961, NARA, RG 59, BIOA, Laos Conference, box 2.

46. Geneva to State Dept., June 27, 1961, *FRUS, XXIV,* d. 124; Brown to State Dept., June 28, 1961, *FRUS, XXIV,* MFS, no. 174.

47. Biographic profile, October 19, 1959, RG 59, and memorandum for the record, October 29, 1959, both BFEA, OSAA, Laos Files, 1954–1961, box 3; Brown to State Dept., January 21, 1961, *FRUS, XXIV,* MFS, no. 94.

48. Memorandum of conversation, September 9, 1960, *FRUS, XVI,* MFS.

49. Memorandum, June 28, 1961, *FRUS, XXIV,* d. 125.

50. Memorandum of conversation, June 29, 1961, *FRUS, XXIV,* d. 127.

51. Memorandum of conversation, June 30, 1961, *FRUS, XXIV,* d. 129.

52. Memorandum of conversation, June 29, 1961, *FRUS, XXIV,* d. 128.

53. Brown to State Dept., July 18, 1961, JFKL, NSF, box 131.

54. Lemnitzer to McNamara, July 12, 1961, *FRUS, XXIV,* d. 134.

55. Ibid.; Maxwell Taylor to Kennedy, July 26, 1961, *FRUS, I,* d. 104.

56. Thomas White to McNamara, May 2, 1961, *FRUS, XXIV,* MFS, no. 138.

57. Memorandum of conversation, April 29, 1961, *FRUS, XXIV,* d. 67.

58. Rostow, *Diffusion of Power,* pp. 664–65.

59. Brown to State Dept., June 4, 1961, *FRUS, XXIV,* d. 109.

60. Lemnitzer to JCS, March 28, 1961, NARA, RG 218, CJCS-091 Laos, box 7.

61. Brown to State Dept., June 23, 1961, *FRUS, XXIV,* d.118.

62. Memorandum of conversation, July 28, 1961, *FRUS, XXIV,* d. 148.

63. Ibid.
64. Ibid.
65. Ibid.
66. Ibid.

2. A Wide Measure of Discretion

1. Brown to State Dept., June 29, 1961, and Harriman to State Dept., August 1, 1961, both JFKL, NSF, box 131.

2. Felt to JCS, August 21, 1961, *FRUS, XXIV,* MFS, no. 200.

3. Biographic sketch, July 23, 1962, NARA, RG 59, BEA&PA, OCDLC, box 8.

4. Maurice Couve de Murville to Rusk, July 6, 1961, JFKL, NSF, box 131.

5. Memorandum of conversation, August 7, 1961, *FRUS, XXIV,* d. 153.

6. Bridle, "Canada and the International Commissions in Indochina," p. 441; Rusk to State Dept., August 7, 1961, *FRUS, XXIV,* d. 154.

7. Memorandum of conversation, August 7, 1961; Tarling, *Britain and the Neutralisation of Laos,* p. 262.

8. Tarling, *Britain and the Neutralisation of Laos,* p. 267; "Weekly Summary, Geneva Conference," September 8, 1961, and Robert Johnson, memorandum of conversation, August 29, 1961, both *FRUS, XXIV,* d. 177 and d. 172, respectively.

9. M. Bundy, memorandum of conversation, August 29, 1961, *FRUS, XXIV,* MFS, no. 208; R. Johnson, memorandum of conversation, August 29, 1961.

10. R. Johnson, memorandum of conversation, August 29, 1961; Rusk to Kennedy, August 29, 1961, *FRUS, XXIV,* d. 171.

11. R. Johnson, memorandum of conversation, August 29, 1961.

12. NSAM 80, August 29, 1961, *FRUS, XXIV,* d. 173; Walter McConaughy to U. A. Johnson, August 25, 1961, NARA, RG 59, BFEA/OSAA, Laos Files, 1954–1961, box 14; R. Johnson, memorandum of conversation, August 29, 1961.

13. Memorandum for files, August 29, 1961, LOC, WAHP, box 479.

14. Abramson, *Spanning the Century,* p. 576.

15. R. Johnson, memorandum of conversation, August 29, 1961.

16. Bruce to State Dept., September 8, 1961, NARA, RG 59, CDF, 1960–1963, box 1766.

17. Geneva to State Dept., September 9, 1961, NARA, RG 59, CDF, 1960–1963, box 1766.

18. Harriman to State Dept., September 15, 1961, *FRUS, XXIV,* MFS, no. 212.

19. Harriman to State Dept., September 15, 1961, *FRUS, XXIV,* MFS, no. 213.

20. Vientiane to Geneva, September 15, 1961, and Harriman to State Dept., July 28, 1961, both LOC, WAHP, box 528; Harriman to State Dept., September 17, 1961, *FRUS, XXIV,* MFS, no. 216.

21. Harriman to State Dept., 478, September 18, 1961, LOC, WAHP, box 528; Nolting to State Dept., September 18, 1961, *FRUS, I,* d. 133.

22. Harriman to State Dept., 478; Lall, *How Communist China Negotiates,* p. 77.

23. Harriman to State Dept., 478.

24. Harriman to Kennedy and Rusk, September 18, 1961, *FRUS, XXIV,* d. 184; Harriman to State Dept., 254, September 18, 1961, LOC, WAHP, box 528.

25. W. Averell Harriman, interview with Arthur M. Schlesinger Jr., January 17, 1965.

26. Brown to State Dept., September 20, 1961, *FRUS, XXIV,* d. 185.

27. Ibid.; CIA, "Cabinet Meeting of 20 September," LOC, WAHP, box 535.

28. JCS, "CSSECLC," 4th installment, pp. 223–25; Haydn Williams to McNamara, October 5, 1961, *FRUS, XXIV,* d. 196n.

29. Rostow to Kennedy, October 5, 1961, *FRUS, XXIV,* d. 195.

30. JCS to McNamara, October 9, 1961, *USVR, Part V-B4-Book I,* pp. 297–98.

31. JCS to McNamara, October 5, 1961, *USVR, Part V-B4-Book I,* pp. 295–96.

32. JCS to McNamara and draft State-Defense memorandum to the president, September 20, 1961, *USVR, Part V-B4-Book I,* pp. 249–57; draft State-Defense memorandum to the president, September 21, 1961, JFKL, NSF, box 131; JCS, "CSSECLC," 4th installment, p. 212.

33. JCS to McNamara, October 9, 1961.

34. M. D. Taylor, *Swords and Ploughshares,* p. 226.

35. Rusk to Kennedy, October 6, 1961, and State Dept. to Harriman, October 6, 1961, both *FRUS, XXIV,* d. 198 and d. 200, respectively.

36. Harriman to State Dept., September 13, 1961, *FRUS, XXIV,* d. 180.

37. State Dept. to Harriman, October 6, 1961.

38. Harriman to State Dept., October 10, 1961, *FRUS, XXIV,* d. 202.

39. Harriman to State Dept., October 15, 1961, *FRUS, XXIV,* d. 206.

40. "Secretary's Meeting with European Ambassadors," August 9, 1961, LOC, WAHP, box 499.

41. Harriman to Chester L. Cooper, October 18, 1961, LOC, WAHP, box 451.

42. Harriman to State Dept., October 10, 1961.

43. Urquhart, *Hammarskjold,* p. 460; Harriman to State Dept., October 12, 1961, NARA, RG 59, CDF, 1960–1963, box 1767.

44. Gaiduk, *Confronting Vietnam,* p. 157.

45. Thee, *Notes of a Witness,* p. 17.

46. Gaiduk, *Confronting Vietnam,* p. 154.

47. Zhai, *China and the Vietnam Wars,* p. 106.

48. Ibid., p. 104.

49. Goscha, "Vietnam and the World Outside," p. 183; "The Lao Communists," March 12, 1973, NARA, CREST.

50. Goscha, "Vietnam and the World Outside," p. 173; CIA, "The Growth and Current Deployment of the Laotian-Based 559th Transportation Group," February 1971, p. 3.

51. Brown and Zasloff, *Apprentice Revolutionaries,* p. 95; CHMAAG to CINCPAC, August 21, 1961, *FRUS, XXIV,* MFS, no. 202; Ang, *Vietnamese Communists' Relations with China,* p. 175.

52. A. A. Skoryukov-General Man, memorandum of conversation, May 13, 1961, in Gaiduk, *Confronting Vietnam*, p. 166.

53. Goscha, "Maritime Nature of the Wars for Vietnam," pp. 72–74.

54. Brown and Zasloff, *Apprentice Revolutionaries*, p. 28.

55. In *Before the Quagmire*, I mistakenly wrote that Nouhak was born in Savannakhet, across the Mekong from Mukdahan. I regret the error.

56. "The Sino-Soviet Dispute," February 20, 1961, www.foia.cia.gov.

57. SNIE 10-3-61, October 10, 1961, www.foia.cia.gov.

58. Frank N. Burnet, interview with Charles Stuart Kennedy, February 22, 1990, FAOHC.

3. Less Precise Language Than We Desire

1. Harriman to Kennedy and Rusk, October 26, 1961, *FRUS, XXIV,* d. 211.

2. Ibid.

3. Ibid., d. 212.

4. Harriman to Kennedy, September 26, 1961, *FRUS, XXIV,* d. 189.

5. Harriman to Kennedy and Rusk, October 26, 1961, d. 212.

6. State Dept. to Harriman, October 27, 1961, *FRUS, XXIV,* d. 213.

7. John Steeves to Chester Bowles, November 1, 1961, *FRUS, XXIV,* d. 214.

8. Carl Salans to Abram Chayes, November 1, 1961, JFKL, POF, Laos: Security, 1961.

9. Ibid.

10. Harriman to State Dept., October 30, 1961, and October 31, 1961, both NARA, RG 59, CDF, 1960–1963, box 1767.

11. Cross, *Born a Foreigner,* p. 139.

12. James C. Thomson, interview with Sheldon Stern, March 19, 1980, JFKLOHP.

13. Harriman to State Dept., October 30, 1961.

14. Notes of telephone conversation, November 1, 1961, *FRUS, XXIV,* d. 215.

15. Harriman to Kennedy, 809, and Harriman to Kennedy, 810, November 2, 1961, both *FRUS, XXIV,* dd. 218–19.

16. U. A. Johnson, *Right Hand of Power,* p. 301.

17. Ibid., pp. 325–26.

18. R. Johnson to Rostow, November 2, 1961, *FRUS, XXIV,* d. 220.

19. Harriman to State Dept., November 4, 1961, JFKL, POF, Laos: Security, 1961: July–December.

20. Asselin, *Hanoi's Road to the Vietnam War,* p. 2.

21. McNamara et al., *Argument without End,* pp. 131–34.

22. M. D. Taylor, *Uncertain Trumpet,* p. 6

23. M. D. Taylor, *Swords and Ploughshares,* p. 180.

24. McMasters, *Dereliction of Duty,* p. 15.

25. Maxwell D. Taylor, interview with Elspeth Rostow, April 26, 1964, JFKLOHP. In this oral history, Taylor observed that Kennedy "had the common civilian point of view that the senior people [in the military] are pretty stiff characters and not par-

ticularly catholic in their views of the world. I think eventually he got to recognize some of us as people, but he still had some doubts."

26. Taylor to Rusk, October 25, 1961, *FRUS, I,* d. 191.

27. Memorandum for the record, November 6, 1961, *FRUS, I,* d. 211.

28. Taylor to Kennedy, November 3, 1961, *FRUS, I,* d. 210.

29. Taylor to Kennedy, November 1, 1961, *USVR, Part V-B4-Book I,* p. 341.

30. Taylor to Kennedy, November 3, 1961; "Covert Annex," November 3, 1961, NARA, CREST.

31. Defense Dept., *USVR, Part IV-B-1,* p. 124; Rusk and McNamara to Kennedy, November 11, 1961, *USVR, Part V-B4-Book I,* p. 390.

32. M. Bundy, November 15, 1961, *FRUS, I,* d. 253.

33. Harriman to Kennedy, November 6, 1961, *FRUS, XXIV,* d. 221.

34. Memorandum of conversation, November 10, 1961, *FRUS, XXIV,* d. 223.

35. Brown to State Dept., November 12, 1961, *FRUS, XXIV,* d. 227n.

36. Brown to State Dept., November 7, 1961, *FRUS, XXIV,* d. 222.

37. Rusk to Brown, November 13, 1961, *FRUS, XXIV,* d. 227.

38. Brown to State Dept., November 14, 1961, NARA, RG 59, CDF, 1960–1963, box 1767; Brown to State Dept., November 15, 1961, *FRUS, XXIV,* d. 227n.

39. Brown to State Dept., November 16, 1961, *FRUS, XXIV,* d. 229.

40. State Dept. to Brown, November 19, 1961, *FRUS, XXIV,* d. 232; memorandum, "Background on Laos," April 13, 1961, JFKL, RHP, box 2; Brown to State Dept., November 24, 1961, NARA, RG 59, CDF, 1960–1963, box 1767. For a more complete discussion of the Hecksher-Smith conflict, see Rust, *Before the Quagmire,* pp. 132–46.

41. Harriman to State Dept., November 19, 1961, NARA, RG 59, CDF, 1960–1963, box 1767; Harriman to Brown, December 9, 1961, *FRUS, XXIV,* d. 241.

42. Brown to Harriman, December 10, 1961, *FRUS, XXIV,* d. 242.

43. Brown to State Dept., December 31, 1961, *FRUS, XXIV,* d. 252.

44. Memorandum of conversation, Phoumi, December 27, 1961, RG 59, CDF, 1960–1963, box 1768.

45. Memorandum of conversation, Boun Oum, December 27, 1961, RG 59, CDF, 1960–1963, box 1768.

46. Winthrop G. Brown, interview with Larry J. Hackman, February 1, 1968.

47. Brown to State Dept., December 26, 1961, NARA, RG 59, CDF, 1960–1963, box 1768.

48. Ibid.

49. Ibid.

50. Ibid.; Brown, interview, February 1, 1968.

51. Brown to State Dept., January 1, 1962, JCS, "CSSECLC," 5th installment, p. 5.

52. Ibid.

53. Brown to State Dept., January 5, 1962, JCS, "CSSECLC," 5th installment, pp. 12–13.

54. Taylor to M. Bundy, January 5, 1962, *FRUS, XXIV,* d. 259; memorandum to the "Special Group," January 5, 1962, JCS, "CSSECLC," 5th installment, pp. 18–19.

55. M. Bundy, memorandum for the record, January 6, 1962, *FRUS, XXIV,* d. 264.

56. John McCone, memorandum for the record, January 6, 1962, *FRUS, XXIV,* MFS, no. 246.

57. Ibid.

58. M. Bundy, memorandum for the record, January 6, 1962.

59. Ibid.; Rusk to Brown, January 5, 1962, NARA, RG 59, CDF, 1960–1963, box 1768.

60. McCone, memorandum for the record, January 6, 1962; JCSM 12–62, January 5, 1962, *FRUS, XXIV,* d. 269.

61. Memorandum of conversation with the president, December 4, 1961, NARA, KARC, RG 218, box 5. Lansdale, a controversial intelligence officer in the Pentagon and McNamara's assistant for special operations, had worked for the CIA in the Philippines and Vietnam. In November 1961 he was appointed chief of operations for Operation Mongoose, one of the numerous, ultimately futile efforts by the Kennedy administration to "get rid of" Fidel Castro. "Lansdale is characterized variously as a deeply knowledgeable student of Indochina and as a charlatan," Marine general Victor H. Krulak observed in an oral history for the Kennedy Library. Krulak added: "There are few individuals in my knowledge more damned and at the same time applauded." Central Intelligence director Richard Helms, in an oral history for the Johnson Library, offered a similarly ambivalent judgment about Lansdale: "Those who were working side by side with him and examining exactly what was going on did not think that he was the hot ticket that a lot of other people did. Lansdale was a very good promoter, and he was a very good promoter of Lansdale." One Lansdale characteristic that most officials seemed to agree on was his inability to function as a team player in the national security bureaucracy, a pattern of behavior enabled by high-level admirers such as Allen Dulles and Kennedy.

62. JCSM 12–62, January 5, 1962.

63. Ibid.

64. Ibid.

65. SNIE 58-2, January 11, 1961, www.foia.cia.gov.

66. Sherman Kent, "The Law and Custom of the National Intelligence Estimate," www.cia.gov. According to Kent, chief of ONE from 1952 to 1967, a "big paper" on such topics as Soviet military capabilities could take six months or more. Yet one "crash" estimate on Soviet intentions during the 1956 Suez crisis was produced in three hours. Referring to estimates written on an urgent basis, Kent wrote: "The penalties of rush procedures were obvious."

67. Harriman to Rusk, January 13, 1962, *FRUS, XXIV,* d. 269n.

68. Boyle to CINCPAC, January 25, 1962, *FRUS, XXIV,* MFS, no. 250; SNIE 58/1-62, January 31, 1962, www.foia.cia.gov. The earlier, January 11 estimate was

an embarrassment for the CIA, and "the President was angry about it," according to Forrestal. Memorandum of telephone conversation, April 14, 1962, JFKL, RHP, box 2.

4. A Disagreeable, Hard, and Dangerous Fact

1. In the FAR, a GM usually comprised three battalions. In the French army, a GM was a temporary unit formed for a specific operation. The FAR GMs were permanent units.

2. Boyle to CINCPAC, January 25, 1962, *FRUS, XXIV,* MFS, no. 250.

3. JCS, "CSSECLC," 5th installment, pp. 55–58.

4. Ibid., p. 34; White Star Mobile Training Team After-Action Report, in Wing et al., *Case Study of US Counterinsurgency Operations,* p. D46.

5. JCS, "CSSECLC," 5th installment, p. 58; CINCPAC to JCS, January 27, 1962, *FRUS, XXIV,* MFS, no. 251.

6. Fursenko and Naftali, *Khrushchev's Cold War,* p. 425.

7. Boyle to CINCPAC, January 25, 1962.

8. Charles Yost to State Dept., February 28, 1955, CWYP, box 13, folder 13.

9. Memorandum for the record, December 19, 1954, NARA, RG 84, US embassy, Vientiane, Classified General Records, box 1A.

10. Brown, "Narrative Study," September 1, 1958, USAMHI.

11. After-action report, March 1962, in Wing et al., *Case Study of US Counterinsurgency Operations,* p. D72.

12. Kraemer and Stewart, "Cross-Cultural Problems," p. 6.

13. Galbraith, *Ambassador's Journal,* p. 107.

14. Toye, *Laos,* p. 168.

15. Boyle to CINCPAC, January 25, 1962; Andrew J. Boyle, interview with Frank Walton, February 28 and March 27, 1971, USAMHI.

16. SNIE 58/1-62, January 31, 1962.

17. Hanyok, *Spartans in Darkness,* p. 105; Annex to SNIE 10-62, February 21, 1962, www.foia.cia.gov.

18. State Dept. to Brown, January 26, 1962, NARA, RG 59, CDF, 1960–1963, box 1769.

19. Memorandum of conversation, January 20, 1962, *FRUS, XXIV,* MFS, no. 249; Brown to State Dept., January 8, 1962, NARA, RG 59, CDF, 1960–1963, box 1768.

20. Brown to State Dept., January 8, 1962; State Dept. to Brown, January 26, 1962.

21. Brown to State Dept., 1051 and 1053, January 27, 1962, NARA, RG 59, CDF, 1960–1963, box 1769.

22. Memorandum of conversation, January 19, 1962, LOC, WAHP, box 529; Brown to State Dept., January 19, 1962, JCS, "CSSECLC," 5th installment, p. 50.

23. Tarling, *Britain and the Neutralisation of Laos,* p. 327.

24. Brown to State Dept., February 2, 1962, NARA, RG 59, CDF, 1960–1963, box 1769.

25. State Dept. to Brown, January 27, 1962, *FRUS, XXIV,* d. 279; memoranda of telephone conversations, January 25 and 27, 1962, LOC, WAHP, box 479.

26. Brown to State Dept., January 29, 1961, *FRUS, XXIV,* MFS, no. 252.

27. State Dept. to Brown, January 29, 1962, *FRUS, XXIV,* d. 282; Brown to State Dept., January 30, 1962, *FRUS, XXIV,* MFS, no. 253.

28. State Dept. to Brown, January 31, 1962, *FRUS, XXIV,* d. 285.

29. State Dept. to Brown, February 6, 1962, and memorandum for the record, February 6, 1962, both *FRUS, XXIV,* d. 290 and d. 289, respectively.

30. Brown to State Dept., 1146 and 1151, February 10, 1962, NARA, RG 59, CDF, 1960–1963, box 1769.

31. State Dept. to Brown, February 10, 1962, NARA, RG 59, CDF, 1960–1963, box 1769; *Central Intelligence Bulletin,* February 14, 1962, NARA, CREST.

32. Memorandum of conversation, February 21, 1962, *FRUS, XXIV,* d. 297.

33. Ibid.

34. Ibid.

35. Ibid.

36. Ibid.

37. Ibid.

38. Ibid.; memorandum of conversation, June 2, 1962, *FRUS, XXIV,* d. 384.

39. Brown to State Dept., February 25, 1962, JCS, "CSSECLC," 5th installment, pp. 121–23.

40. State Dept. to Brown, February 25, 1962, *FRUS, XXIV,* MFS, no. 261.

41. Brown to State Dept., February 26, 1962, *FRUS, XXIV,* d. 300.

42. Harriman to Brown, February 27, 1962, NARA, RG 59, CDF, 1960–1963, box 1770.

43. William H. Sullivan, interview with Dennis O'Brien, June 16, 1970, JFKLOHP; Brown, interview, February 1, 1968.

44. John M. Steeves, interview with Charles Stuart Kennedy and Thomas Stern, March 27, 1991, FAOHC.

45. Michael V. Forrestal, interview with Paige Mulhollan, November 3, 1969, LBJLOHP.

46. "Instructions Approved by President Kennedy," February 28, 1962, *FRUS, XXIV,* d. 301; "Harriman reactions," March 2, 1962, LOC, WAHP, box 259.

47. Brown to State Dept., March 5, 1962, NARA, RG 59, CDF, 1960–1963, box 1770; Brown to State Dept., March 10, 1962, *FRUS, XXIV,* d. 306.

48. Brown to State Dept., March 5 and 10, 1962.

49. U. A. Johnson to M. Bundy, March 6, 1962, *FRUS, XXIV,* d. 303.

50. Vientiane (CIA) to Washington, March 6, 1962, www.cia.foia.gov; State Dept. to Brown, January 27, 1962, *FRUS, XXIV,* d. 278.

51. White House to Vientiane (CIA), undated (ca. February 23, 1962), *FRUS, XXIV,* d. 298.

52. Vientiane to Washington, March 6, 1962, JCS, "CSSECLC," 5th installment, p. 139; Vientiane to Washington, March 6, 1962, www.cia.foia.gov.

53. Vientiane to Washington, March 6, 1962, www.cia.foia.gov; Richard Helms to M. Bundy, March 7, 1962, www.cia.foia.gov.

54. INR biographic sketch, May 1961, LOC, WAHP, box 527; memorandum of conversation, February 3, 1961, *FRUS, XXIV,* d. 13.

55. Vientiane to Washington, March 7, 1962, www.cia.foia.gov; JCS, "CSSE-CLC," 5th installment, pp. 141–42.

56. Vientiane to Washington, March 7, 1962.

5. A Severe Loss of Face

1. "Background Data on Thailand," January 22, 1962, NARA, RG 59, BFEA, OSAA, Thailand, 1960–1963, box 3.

2. SNIE 52-61, "Thailand's Security Problems and Prospects," December 13, 1961, www.foia.cia.gov; "Background Data on Thailand."

3. State Dept. to Bangkok, October 22, 1957, *FRUS, XXII,* d. 529; "Background Data on Thailand."

4. Bangkok to State Dept., January 16, 1962, JCS, "CSSECLC," p. 44.

5. "Comments by Prime Minister Sarit," February 26, 1962, *FRUS, XXIII,* d. 432 (emphasis in the original). Redacting the names of CIA officials is a common, though not universal, practice in *FRUS.* Given the sensitivity of the meeting's topic and the frank relationship between Jantzen and Sarit, the official was almost certainly the Bangkok chief of station.

6. M. Bundy to Kennedy, March 5, 1962, *FRUS, XXIII,* d. 434.

7. Memorandum of conversation, March 2, 1962, *FRUS, XXIII,* d. 433.

8. Ibid.; JCS, "CSSECLC," 5th installment, p. 113.

9. "The United States Commitment to Thailand," September 1970, NARA, RG 59, Executive Secretariat, Historical Office Research Projects, box 7.

10. Memorandum of conversation, March 2, 1962, and State Dept. to Brown, March 6, 1962, both NARA, RG 59, CDF, 1960–1963, box 1770.

11. Memorandum of conversation, March 5, 1962, *FRUS, XXIII,* d. 435.

12. Roger Hilsman, memorandum for the record, March 19, 1962, JFKL, RHP, box 5; Richard M. Nixon, speech at the American Legion Convention, October 18, 1960, www.presidency.ucsb.edu.

13. Hilsman, memorandum for the record, March 19, 1962.

14. Brown to State Dept., March 15, 1962, *FRUS, XXIV,* d. 307; memorandum of conversation, March 17, 1962, NARA, RG 59, CDF, 1960–1963, box 1771.

15. Brown to State Dept., March 19, 1962, NARA, RG 59, CDF, 1960–1963, box 1770.

16. State Dept. to Kenneth Young and Brown, March 19, 1962, NARA, RG 59, CDF, 1960–1963, box 1770.

17. Young to State Dept., March 20, 1962, NARA, RG 59, CDF, 1960–1963, box 1770.

18. Ibid.

19. Young to State Dept., March 21, 1962, NARA, RG 59, CDF, 1960–1963, box 1770.

20. Harriman to State Dept., March 20, 1962, JCS, "CSSECLC," 5th install-ment, pp. 163–64; State Dept. to Harriman, March 20, 1962, *FRUS, XXIV,* d. 310.

21. "Reactions to Certain US Courses in Laos," March 20, 1962, NARA, CREST; JCS, "CSSECLC," 5th installment, p. 167.

22. JCS, "CSSECLC," 5th installment, pp. 165–66. Also see memorandum for the record, March 21, 1962, *FRUS, XXIV,* d. 311.

23. State Dept. to Harriman, March 21, 1962, *FRUS, XXIV,* d. 312; memoran-dum of conversation, March 24, 1962, LOC, WAHP, box 259.

24. Memorandum of conversation, March 24, 1962.

25. Ibid.

26. Ibid.

27. Memorandum of conversation, March 25, 1962, LOC, WAHP, box 259.

28. Ibid.

29. Ibid.

30. Ibid.

31. Ibid.

32. Ibid.

33. Ibid.

34. Harriman to State Dept., March 26, 1962, *FRUS, XXIV,* d. 318; Sullivan, interview, June 16, 1970; Brown, *War in Shangri-La,* pp. 119–20.

35. Memorandum of conversation, March 28, 1962, and William Sullivan to State Dept., March 28, 1962, both NARA, RG 59, CDF, 1960–1963, boxes 1771 and 1770, respectively; ARMA Laos to DA, March 30, 1962, JCS, "CSSECLC," 5th installment, pp. 179–80.

36. Sullivan to State, April 1, 1962, *FRUS, XXIV,* d. 322.

37. Sullivan to State, March 27, 1962, NARA, RG 59, CDF, 1960–1963, box 1770; Sullivan to State, March 31, 1962, *FRUS, XXIV,* d. 321.

38. Sullivan to State, March 31, 1962, *FRUS, XXIV,* d. 320; memorandum of conversation, March 17, 1962.

39. State Dept. to Sullivan, Brown, and Young, March 30, 1962, NARA, RG 59, CDF, 1960–1963, box 1770.

40. Sullivan to Harriman, April 2, 1962, *FRUS, XXIV,* d. 321; Brown to Harri-man, April 4, 1962, *FRUS, XXIV,* MFS, no. 265.

41. Brown to Harriman, December 30, 1961, NARA, RG 59, CDF, 1960–1963, box 1768.

42. Brown, interview, February 1, 1968.

43. Ahern, *Undercover Armies,* p. 122.

44. Brown, interview, February 1, 1968.

45. Brown to Harriman, April 6, 1962, NARA, RG 59, CDF, 1960–1963, box 1771.

46. Forrestal to M. Bundy, April 6, 1962, *FRUS, XXIV,* d. 325.

47. SNIE 58-2-62, "Consequences of Certain US Courses in Laos," April 11, 1962, www.foia.cia.gov.

48. Ibid.

49. Thomas L. Hughes, interview with Charles Kennedy, July 7, 1999, FAOHC.

50. Hilsman to U. A. Johnson, November 4, 1961, JFKL, RHP, box 5.

51. Hilsman to Kennedy, January 12, 1962, JFKL, RHP, box 5; Hilsman, "A Strategic Concept for South Vietnam," February 2, 1962, *FRUS, II,* d. 42.

52. Hilsman to Hughes, February 28, 1962, JFKL, RHP, box 5.

53. Kent, "The Making of an NIE," www.cia.gov.

54. Brown to State Dept., April 17, 1962, JCS, "CSSECLC," 5th installment, p. 202; Joint State Dept./Defense Dept. message to Brown and Young, April 19, 1962, *FRUS, XXIV,* d. 331.

55. Young to State Dept., May 1, 1962, *FRUS, XXIV,* d. 337.

56. Brown to State Dept., April 30, 1962, *FRUS, XXIV,* MFS, no. 266.

57. Ibid.

58. State to Rusk, May 4, 1962, *FRUS, XXIV,* MFS, no. 270; State to Brown, May 3, 1962, NARA, RG 59, CDF, 1960–1963, box 1771; Forrestal to Kennedy, May 2, 1962, *FRUS, XXIV,* d. 338.

59. Boyle to William Yarborough, April 13, 1963, AJBP, USAMHI; JCS, "CSSE-CLC," p. 206.

60. State Dept. to Brown, April 30, 1962, and May 1, 1962, both NARA, RG 59, CDF, 1960–1963, box 1771; Boyle to Yarborough, April 13, 1963.

6. A Very Hazardous Course

1. Vientiane to State Dept., May 6, 1962, Vientiane to State Dept., May 7, 1962, MAAG to CINCPAC, May 7, 1962, all NARA, RG 59, CDF, 1960–1963, box 1771.

2. Vientiane to State Dept., May 6, 1962; Vientiane to State Dept., May 7, 1962; MAAG to CINCPAC, May 7, 1962.

3. Memorandum of telephone conversation, May 6, 1962, *FRUS, XXIV,* d. 343.

4. State Dept. to Rusk, May 6, 1962, NARA, RG 59, CDF, 1960–1963, box 1771.

5. Memorandum for the record, May 6, 1962, JFKL, RHP, box 2.

6. Ibid.; Michael V. Forrestal, interview with Joseph Kraft, July 28, 1964, JFKLOHP.

7. State Dept. to Rusk, May 6, 1962; Thompson to State Dept., May 8, 1962, *FRUS, XXIV,* MFS, no. 273.

8. Thee, *Notes of a Witness,* pp. 241–42.

9. Fursenko and Naftali, *Khrushchev's Cold War,* p. 425.

10. Ibid., p. 426.

11. Thee, *Notes of a Witness,* pp. 241–42.

12. Zhai, *China and the Vietnam Wars,* p. 106.

13. Johns, *Vietnam's Second Front,* p. 69.

14. Memorandum of telephone conversation, May 6, 1962, d. 344.

15. Press conference, May 9, 1962, APP.

16. SNIE 58-3-62, May 9, 1962, *FRUS, XXIV,* d. 350.

17. Hilsman, "Discussion Paper for White House Meeting, May 10, 1962," May 10, 1962, *FRUS, XXIV,* d. 351.

18. State Dept. to Brown, May 12, 1962, *FRUS, XXIV,* d. 361.

19. Memorandum for the record, May 10, 1962, *FRUS, XXIV,* d. 352.

20. Russell Baker, "Eisenhower Says Kennedy Seeks Too Much Power," *New York Times,* May 11, 1962.

21. McCone, memorandum for the record, May 10, 1962, and Forrestal, addendum, May 11, 1962, both www.foia.cia.gov.

22. Rust, *Before the Quagmire,* pp. 256–59.

23. Memorandum of conversation, January 2, 1961, *FRUS, XXIV,* MFS, no. 91.

24. Memorandum of telephone conversation, May 11, 1962, *FRUS, XXIV,* d. 355; memorandum of telephone conversation, May 10, 1962, *FRUS, XXIV,* MFS, no. 275.

25. JCS to McNamara, May 11, 1962, *FRUS, XXIV,* d. 356.

26. Ibid.; State–Joint Chiefs of Staff meeting, May 11, 1962, NARA, RG 59, Lot File 70D328, box 3.

27. Carter, memorandum for the record, May 13, 1962, www.foia.cia.gov.

28. Ibid.

29. Memorandum of telephone conversation, George Ball–James Greenfield, May 12, 1962, JFKL, GWBP, box 5; Max Frankel, "Accord Is Sought," *New York Times,* May 12, 1962.

30. Carter, memorandum for the record, May 13, 1962.

31. Memorandum of conversation, May 12, 1962, *FRUS, XXIV,* d. 357.

32. State Dept. to Brown, May 12, 1962, *FRUS, XXIV,* d. 361; JCS, "CSSE-CLC," p. 49.

33. State Dept. to Brown, May 12, 1962.

34. Memorandum of conversation, May 13, 1962, *FRUS, XXIV,* d. 363.

35. Memorandum of conversation, May 14, 1962, DDEL, DDE's Post-Presidential Papers, Augusta-Walter Reed Series, box 2.

36. Memorandum of conversation, May 15, 1962, *FRUS, XXIV,* d. 368.

37. State Dept. to Young, May 13, 1962, *FRUS, XXIII,* d. 441; State Dept. to Young, May 18, 1962, and May 15, 1962, both NARA, RG 59, CDF, 1960–1963, boxes 2142 and 2137, respectively.

38. Catterall, *Macmillan Diaries,* pp. 470–71; JCS, "CSSECLC," p. 94.

39. Memorandum of conversation, May 21, 1962, NARA, RG 59, BFEA, OSAA, Thailand, 1960–1963, box 4.

40. Young to State Dept., May 15 and 17, 1962, and State Dept. to Young, May 19, 1962, all NARA, RG 59, CDF, 1960–1963, boxes 1771, 2137, and 2142, respectively.

41. Forrestal, interview with Kraft, July 28, 1964; Forrestal to Kennedy, May 23, 1962, *FRUS, XXIV,* MFS, no. 285.

42. Brown to State Dept., May 13, 1962, *FRUS, XXIV,* MFS, box 1771.

43. J. M. Gavin, *On to Berlin*, p. 67; Reuben Tucker to CINCPAC, May 9, 1962, NARA, RG 59, CDF, 1960–1963, box 1771.

44. Brown to State Dept., May 13, 1962.

45. Ibid.

46. State Dept. to Brown, May 16, 1962, and Brown to State Dept., May 18, 1962, both NARA, RG 59, CDF, 1960–1963, box 1771.

47. Brown to State Dept., May 16, 1962, NARA, RG 59, CDF, 1960–1963, box 1771.

48. Brown to State Dept., May 10, 1962, NARA, RG 59, BEA&PA, OCDLC, Laos, 1955–1975, box 9; Brown to State Dept., May 18, 1962; James Gavin to State Dept., May 21, 1962, NARA, RG 59, CDF, 1960–1963, box 1771.

49. State Dept. to Brown, May 17, 1962, and State Dept. to London, May 22, 1962, both NARA, RG 59, CDF, 1960–1963, box 1771; Tarling, *Britain and the Neutralisation of Laos*, p. 413.

50. State Dept. to Brown, May 18, 1962, *FRUS, XXIV,* MFS, no. 283.

51. Forrestal to Kennedy, May 22, 1962, *FRUS, XXIV,* d. 374; State Dept. to Brown, May 20, 1962, NARA, RG 59, CDF, 1960–1963, box 1771.

52. Forrestal to Kennedy, May 22, 1962.

53. Forrestal to Kennedy, June 5, 1962, *FRUS, XXIV,* d. 387.

54. Memorandum for the record, June 4, 1962, JFKL, NSF, box 131; McNamara to Kennedy, June 4, 1962, *FRUS, XXIV,* d. 386.

55. Hilsman to Harriman, May 26, 1962, JFKL, RHP, box 2.

56. Hilsman to Rusk, June 5, 1962, *FRUS, XXIV,* MFS, no. 290.

57. Felt to McNamara, June 3, 1962, JFKL, RHP, box 2.

58. Memorandum of conversation, June 2, 1962, *FRUS, XXIV,* d. 384.

59. ONE, "Communist Reactions to Additional US Courses of Action in Laos and North Vietnam," June 6, 1962, NARA, CREST; INR, "Bloc Reactions to Contingent US Actions in Laos and North Viet-Nam," June 7, 1962, JFKL, RHP, box 2.

60. Sullivan to State Dept., December 15, 1965, *FRUS, XXVIII,* d. 211; State Dept. to Sullivan, December 27, 1965, LBJL, NSF, box 270.

61. Memorandum of conversation, May 26, 1962, *FRUS, XXIV,* d. 380; Rostow to Rusk, May 31, 1962, NARA, RG 59, PPC Subject Files, 1954–1962, box 271.

62. Rostow, "Guerrilla Warfare in the Underdeveloped Areas," *Department of State Bulletin,* August 7, 1961; McGeorge Bundy, interview with Richard Neustadt, March 1964, JFKLOHP.

7. A Colossal Booby Trap

1. Norris Smith to William Chadbourn, ca. June 11, 1962, NARA, RG 59, BEA&PA, OCDLC, Laos, 1955–1975, box 9.

2. Brown to State Dept., June 2 and June 4, 1962, NARA, RG 59, CDF, 1960–1963, box 1772.

3. Brown to State Dept., June 7, 1962, NARA, RG 59, CDF, 1960–1963, box 1772.

4. Biographic sketch, February 19, 1963, NARA, RG 59, BEA&PA, OCDLC, Laos, 1955–1975, box 9.

5. Brown to State Dept., June 8 and June 9, 1962, NARA, RG 59, BEA&PA, OCDLC, Laos, 1955–1975, box 9.

6. Memorandum of conversation, July 14, 1961, NARA, RG 59, CDF, 1960–1963, box 1764; biographic sketch, May 1961, LOC, WAHP, box 527.

7. Brown to State Dept., June 8, 1962, NARA, RG 59, CDF, 1960–1963, box 1772.

8. Brown to State Dept., June 10, 1962, NARA, RG 59, CDF, 1960–1963, box 1772.

9. State Dept. to Brown, June 9, 1962, and State Dept. to Young, June 13, 1962, both NARA, RG 59, CDF, 1960–1963, box 1772.

10. Memorandum of conversation, June 10, 1962, NARA, RG 59, CDF, 1960–1963, box 1773.

11. Brown to State Dept., June 11, 1962, and memorandum of conversation, June 11, 1962, both NARA, RG 59, CDF, 1960–1963, boxes 1772 and 1773, respectively.

12. Chadbourn to State Dept., June 18, 1962, NARA, RG 59, CDF, 1960–1963, box 1772.

13. Forrestal to M. Bundy, June 11, 1962, *FRUS, XXIV,* d. 394.

14. Jacques Nevard, "3-Man Executive to Govern Laos," *New York Times,* June 13, 1962.

15. Forrestal to M. Bundy, June 12, 1962, *FRUS, XXIV,* d. 395.

16. Ibid.

17. Memorandum of conversation, July 27, 1962, *FRUS, XXIV,* d. 412.

18. Memorandum for the record, June 13, 1962, www.foia.cia.gov; memorandum for the record, June 14, 1962, *FRUS, XXIV,* d. 398n.

19. Memorandum for the record, June 13, 1962.

20. Forrestal, interview with Kraft, July 28, 1964. James's appearance and behavior in Laos have been the source of many colorful stories, some of which are true and others perhaps apocryphal. Rufus Phillips, who served with him in Laos in the 1950s, recalled that James, at his own expense, imported cases of champagne from Paris for Christmas parties. And on one occasion, James arrived unannounced at the US mission in Saigon and decided to have a chat with the CIA chief of station, who assumed that James worked for the British Secret Intelligence Service. The CIA chief of station in Vientiane soon received a "rocket" from Saigon asking: "Who the hell is Campbell James? Why are we revealing all of our operations to him?" Rufus C. Phillips, interview with the author, October 21, 2009.

21. State to Brown, May 31, 1962, "CSSECLC," 6th installment, p. 134; Gavin to State Dept., June 25, 1962, NARA, RG 59, CDF, 1960–1963, box 1772.

22. Goscha, "Vietnam and the World Outside," p. 180; Asselin, *Hanoi's Road to the Vietnam War,* p. 120.

23. Forty years after the end of World War II, virtually every US government document related to that conflict had been declassified. For the events covered in

this book, most of which occurred more than fifty years ago, thousands of pages of State Department, Pentagon, and CIA documents remain classified.

24. CINCPAC to JCS, June 16, 1962, JCS, "CSSECLC," pp. 168–69.

25. CHMAAG to CINCPAC, October 3, 1962, in Wing et al., *Case Study of US Counterinsurgency Operations,* p. B-28.

26. Unger to State Dept., August 23, 1962, JFKL, NSF, box 136.

27. State Dept. to Unger, September 30, 1962, JFKL, NSF, box 136.

28. Memorandum of telephone conversation, October 5, 1962, *FRUS, XXIV,* d. 427.

29. State–Joint Chiefs of Staff meeting, June 15, 1962, NARA, RG 59, Lot File 70D328, box 3; CJCS to CINCPAC, June 13, 1962, NARA, RG 218, CJCS-091 Laos, box 7.

30. Richard Bissell to Allen Dulles, August 10, 1961, *FRUS, XXIV,* MFS, no. 194.

31. "CIA Support to Meo Tribesmen in Laos," April 8, 1963, NARA, CREST.

32. Ahern, *Undercover Armies,* p. 126.

33. Covert Annex, Status Report of the Task Force Southeast Asia, June 13–27, 1962, www.cia.foia.gov.

34. Hilsman to Rusk, June 5, 1962, *FRUS, XXIV,* MFS, no. 290.

35. EMB-USAID-MAAG-USIS to State, February 23, 1962, NARA, RG 59, CDF, 1960–1963, box 1770.

36. CIA, "Laos, the Divided Nation," LBJL, NSF, box 271.

37. State–Joint Chiefs of Staff meeting, June 15, 1962.

38. JCS, "CSSECLC," 6th installment, pp. 171–72.

39. Edward Lansdale to Taylor, ca. July 1961, in US Department of Defense, *Pentagon Papers,* vol. 2, p. 643; JCS, "CSSECLC," 6th installment, p. 173.

40. Sullivan to State Dept., June 24, 1962, NARA, RG 59, CDF, 1960–1963, box 1772.

41. Brown to State Dept., June 23, 1962, and State Dept. to Young, June 24, 1962, both NARA, RG 59, CDF, 1960–1963, box 1772.

42. *Robert Kennedy: In His Own Words,* p. 260.

43. Robert Kennedy to M. Bundy, July 11, 1962, *FRUS, XXIII,* d. 455. Kennedy's summary of his conversation with Bolshakov, which Bundy forwarded to Rusk, Ball, and Harriman, was written some three weeks after the meeting with the Soviet spy and the president's decision to make a token withdrawal of US troops from Thailand.

44. Ibid.

45. Memorandum of telephone conversation, Ball–M. Bundy, June 19, 1962, JFKL, GWBP, box 8.

46. Memorandum of telephone conversation, Ball-McNamara, June 25, 1962, JFKL, GWBP, box 8; Rusk to State Dept., June 28, 1962, NARA, RG 59, CDF, 1960–1963, box 2140.

47. Luther Heinz to Nitze, June 26, 1962, *FRUS, XXIII,* d. 454.

48. Young to State Dept., June 29, 1962, NARA, RG 59, CDF, 1960–1963, box 2140.

49. State Dept. to Young, June 27, 1962, NARA, RG 59, CDF, 1960–1963, box 2140.

50. Harriman to Rusk, June 26, 1962, NARA, RG 59, BEA&PA, OCDL, Laos, 1962–1966, box 1.

51. Ibid.

52. Ibid.

53. State Dept. to Geneva, July 6, 1962, NARA, RG 59, CDF, 1960–1963, box 1773.

54. A State Department legal adviser commenting on the meaning of Laotian "concurrence" later concluded that such "silence can be interpreted as representing agreement with our position or as merely a negotiating tactic." Salans to William Bundy, July 10, 1964, LOC, WAHP, box 483.

55. Harriman to State Dept., July 11, 1962, NARA, RG 59, CDF, 1960–1963, box 1773.

56. Ibid.

57. Gaiduk, *Confronting Vietnam,* pp. 160–61.

58. Sullivan, interview, June 16, 1970; Geneva to State Dept., August 25, 1961, NARA, RG 59, CDF, 1960–1963, box 1764.

59. JCS, "CSSECLC," 5th installment, p. 63; Lall, *How Communist China Negotiates,* p. 134.

60. JCS, "CSSECLC," 5th installment, p. 63; Sullivan, interview, June 16, 1970.

61. Ang, *Vietnamese Communists' Relations with China,* p. 233.

62. Zhai, *China and the Vietnam Wars,* pp. 109, 111.

63. President's Talking Paper, July 23, 1962, NARA, RG 59, BEA&PA, OCDLC, box 8.

64. Memorandum of conversation, July 22, 1962, NARA, RG 59, BFEA, ASFEA, Subject Files, 1960–1963, box 17.

65. Ibid.

66. Harriman to State Dept., July 5, 1962, NARA, RG 59, CDF, 1960–1963, box 1773.

67. Sullivan, *Obbligato,* pp. 176–78; memorandum of conversation, July 22, 1962, *FRUS, XXIV,* d. 410.

68. Memorandum of conversation, July 22, 1962, *FRUS, XXIV,* d. 410.

69. Ibid.

70. Memorandum of conversation, January 20, 1962, LOC, WAHP, box 534.

71. Memorandum of conversation, April 6, 1962, *FRUS, II,* d. 148.

72. Goldstein, *Lessons in Disaster,* pp. 138–39.

73. Young to State Dept., July 7, 1962, Frederick Nolting to State Dept., July 5, 1962, and Young to State Dept., July 13, 1962, all NARA, RG 59, CDF, 1960–1963, box 1773.

74. M. Bundy to Rusk, July 13, 1962, NARA, RG 59, CDF, 1960–1963, box

1773; Kennedy to Harriman, July 23, 1962, and Rusk to Harriman, July 13, 1962, both JFKL, NSF, box 135A.

75. Notes of meeting, April 9, 1968, *FRUS, VI,* d. 189; Stuart-Fox, *History of Laos,* p. 135.

76. Wehrle, "'Good, Bad Deal,'" p. 349.

8. We Do Not Have the Power of Decision

1. Max Frankel, "New Premier of Laos Is Welcomed to U.S. by Rusk," *New York Times,* July 27, 1962; Carroll Kilpatrick, "New Laotian Premier Greeted Here by Rusk," *Washington Post,* July 27, 1962.

2. Memorandum of conversation, July 27, 1962, NARA, RG 59, BFEA, OCDL, box 1.

3. Ibid.

4. Memorandum of conversation, July 27, 1962, *FRUS, XXIV,* MFS, no. 300.

5. Memorandum of conversation, July 28, 1962, *FRUS, XXIV,* d. 415.

6. Memorandum of meeting, July 27, 1962, *FRUS, XXIV,* d. 412; memorandum of conversation, July 28, 1962.

7. Memorandum of conversation, July 27, 1962, *FRUS, XXIV,* d. 413.

8. Ibid.

9. Ibid.

10. John Everton to State Dept., May 22, 1962, JCS, "CSSECLC," p. 103.

11. Press release, July 27, 1962, JFKL, POF, Laos: General, 1962.

12. "Status Report on Southeast Asia," August 8, 1962, JFKL, NSF, box 231A; Sullivan to Unger, August 17, 1962, NARA, RG 59, BFEA, OCDL, box 1.

13. Memorandum of conversation, July 27, 1962, *FRUS, XXIV,* MFS, no. 301.

14. JCS, Southeast Asia Situation Report, July 11, 1962, JFKL, NSF, Box 231A.

15. Forrestal to Kennedy, August 15, 1962, *FRUS, XXIV,* d. 418.

16. State Dept./AID to Vientiane, July 17, 1962, JFKL, NSF, box 135A.

17. State Department, "Lao Foreign Exchange Reserves," April 24, 1962, NARA, RG 59, BFEA, ASFEA, Subject Files, 1960–1963, box 11.

18. Meeting on Laos, August 15, 1962, in Naftali, *Presidential Recordings: John F. Kennedy, I,* p. 425.

19. Ibid., pp. 433–38.

20. "United States Operations in Laos and the Geneva Agreements," April 22, 1963, JFKL, NSF, box 132.

21. Bangkok to State Dept., August 14, 1962, NARA, RG 59, CDF, 1960–1963, box 1779; CINCPAC to JCS, August 16, 1962, JFKL, NSF, box 135A.

22. Vientiane to State Dept., August 15, 1962, NARA, RG 59, CDF, 1960–1963, box 1779.

23. Biographic sketch, February 4, 1963, NARA, RG 59, BFEA, ASFEA, Subject Files, 1960–1963, box 21.

24. Vientiane to State Dept., August 16, 1962, NARA, RG 59, CDF, 1960–1963, box 1779.

25. Harriman to U. A. Johnson, August 15, 1962, NARA, RG 59, ASFEA, Subject Files, 1960–1963, box 11; State Dept. to Vientiane, 190, August 16, 1962, NARA, RG 59, CDF, 1960–1963, box 1779.

26. State Dept. to Vientiane, 192, August 16, 1962, NARA, RG 59, CDF, 1960–1963, box 1779.

27. Vientiane to State Dept., August 19, 1962, NARA, RG 59, CDF, 1960–1963, box 1779.

28. Vientiane to State Dept., August 18, 1962, and State Dept. to Moscow, August 19, 1962, both JFKL, NSF, box 135A.

29. State Dept. to Moscow, August 19, 1962.

30. Hilsman to Harriman, September 24, 1962, *FRUS, XXIV,* d. 424.

31. State Dept. to Vientiane/Moscow, August 18, 1962, JFKL, NSF, box 135A.

32. Ibid.

33. Vientiane to State Dept., August 19, 1962, JFKL, NSF, box 135A.

34. Ibid.

35. State Dept. to Vientiane, August 20, 1962, JFKL, NSF, box 136.

36. Vientiane to State Dept., August 22, 1962, JFKL, NSF, box 136.

37. State Dept. to Vientiane/Moscow, August 18, 1962; State Dept. circular, August 21, 1962, JFKL, NSF, box 136.

38. London to State Dept., August 21, 1962, JFKL, NSF, box 136.

39. OCI, August 23, 1962, JFKL, NSF, box 132.

40. Vientiane to State Dept., August 24, 1962, JFKL, NSF, box 136.

41. Memorandum of conversation, August 24, 1962, NARA, RG 59, Lot File 70D328, State-JCS Meetings, 1959–1963, box 3.

42. Ibid.

43. Ibid.

44. Ibid.

45. Ibid.

46. Bailey, *Solitary Survivor,* p. 170.

47. Memorandum of conversation, August 24, 1962, NARA, RG 59, CDF, 1960–1963, box 1773.

48. Hilsman to Harriman, August 28, 1962, *FRUS, XXIV,* d. 421.

49. Memorandum of conversation, August 29, 1962, *FRUS, XXIV,* d. 422.

50. Hilsman to Rusk, July 16, 1962, FRUS, *II,* d. 243.

51. Memorandum of conversation, August 29, 1962, JFKL, NSF, box 136.

52. Ahern, *Undercover Armies,* p. 138.

53. Memorandum of conversation, August 29, 1962, *FRUS, XXIV,* d. 422.

54. Memorandum of conversation, July 28, 1962.

55. Memorandum of conversation, August 29, 1962, *FRUS, XXIV,* d. 422.

56. CHMAAG to CINCPAC, September 17, 1962, JFKL, NSF, box 136. Initially, there was some confusion within the US government over the exact withdrawal date prescribed by the formula in the Geneva agreement. October 7, rather than October 6, was the correct date.

57. Vientiane to State Dept., August 11, 1962, and Tucker to CINCPAC, August 17, 1962, both NARA, RG 59, CDF, 1960–1963, box 1773. According to a June 22, 1964, JCS memorandum, "116 Thai volunteer specialists in Laos (43 interpreters, 73 surgical specialists, x-ray technicians, code clerks, radio operators, T–6 pilots)" remained in Laos after the Geneva deadline. *FRUS, XXVII,* d. 278.

58. Worth Bagley to Taylor, January 5, 1962, *FRUS, XXIV,* d. 258.

59. CINCPAC to JCS, July 15, 1962, NARA, RG 59, CDF, 1960–1963, box 1773.

60. CHMAAG to CINCPAC, August 23, 1962, JFKL, NSF, box 136.

61. Paris to State Dept., July 19, 1962, NARA, RG 59, CDF, 1960–1963, box 1773; Vientiane to State Dept., September 6, 1962, JFKL, NSF, box 136.

62. Paris to State Dept., September 26, 1962, JFKL, NSF, box 136.

63. CIA, "Situation in Laos," January 23, 1963, and "The Military Situation in Laos," June 19, 1963, both NARA, CREST.

64. Naftali and Zelikow, *Presidential Recordings: John F. Kennedy, II,* p. 180.

65. Vientiane to State Dept., September 22, 1962, JFKL, NSF, box 136.

66. Vientiane to State Dept., July 31, 1962, NARA, RG 59, CDF, 1960–1963, box 1773.

67. NSAM No. 189, September 28, 1962, *FRUS, XXIV,* d. 426.

68. Harriman to W. Bundy, October 22, 1962, NARA, RG 59, BFEA, ASFEA, Subject Files, 1960–1963, box 14.

69. State Dept. to Vientiane, October 25, 1962, NARA, RG 59, CDF, 1960–1963, box 1774.

70. NSAM No. 189, September 28, 1962.

71. Young to State Dept., July 28, 1962, NARA, RG 59, CDF, 1960–1963, box 2137.

72. Forrestal to Kennedy, September 28, 1962, *FRUS, XXIII,* d. 466.

73. Memorandum of conversation, September 28, 1962, *FRUS, XXIII,* d. 467.

74. U. A. Johnson to Harriman, September 21, 1962, *FRUS, XXIV,* d. 423; Vientiane to State Dept., September 22, 1962, State Dept. to Vientiane, September 26, 1962, both JFKL, NSF, box 136.

75. Forrestal to Kennedy, September 28, 1962, *FRUS, XXIV,* d. 425; Tom Wicker, "Cuba Emerges as an Issue as Fall Campaign Begins to Roll throughout U.S.," *New York Times,* October 1, 1962.

76. Memorandum of conversation, October 4, 1962, *FRUS, XXIV,* d. 427.

9. Tenuous at Best

1. Vientiane to State Dept., November 11, 1962, NARA, RG 59, CFPF, 1963, box 3965.

2. Ibid.; Forrestal to M. Bundy, May 16, 1962, *FRUS, XXIV,* d. 372n; CINCPAC to JCS, January 13, 1963, JFKL, NSF, box 137; Vientiane to State Dept., November 18, 1962, NARA, RG 59, CFPF, 1963, box 3965.

3. Vientiane to State Dept., November 2, 1962, and November 9, 1962, both

NARA, RG 59, CFPF, 1963, box 3965; Vientiane to State Dept., August 11, 1962, NARA, RG 59, CDF, 1960–1963, box 1773.

4. "Laotian Premier Says He May Quit," *New York Times*, November 8, 1962; Vientiane to State Dept., November 8, 1962, NARA, RG 59, CFPF, 1963, box 3965.

5. Talking Paper, November 8, 1962, *FRUS, XXIV*, d. 432.

6. State Dept. to Vientiane, November 9, 1962, *FRUS, XXIV*, d. 433; Forrestal to Harriman, November 9, 1962, LOC, WAHP, box 479.

7. Vientiane to State Dept., February 18, 1963, JFKL, NSF, box 137; Vientiane to State Dept., November 14, 1962, NARA, RG 59, CFPF, 1963, box 3965.

8. NSC Briefing, August 18, 1960, NARA, CREST.

9. Annex to SNIE 10-62, February 21, 1962, www.foia.cia.gov.

10. Vientiane to State Dept., October 5, 1962, JFKL, NSF, box 136.

11. Memorandum of conversation, October 29, 1962, NARA, RG 59, BFEA, OCDL, box 1.

12. Vientiane to State Dept., November 11, 1962.

13. Forrestal to Harriman, November 9, 1962; State Dept. to Vientiane, November 15, 1962, NARA, RG 59, CFPF, 1963, box 3965.

14. In remote Phong Saly, General Khamouane Boupha led a smaller, independent neutralist force that the US government unsuccessfully sought to align with the FAR.

15. Vientiane to State Dept., November 17, 1962, *FRUS, XXIV*, d. 436; Vientiane to State Dept., November 20, 1962, NARA, RG 59, CFPF, 1963, box 3965.

16. Vientiane to State Dept., November 17, 1962, NARA, RG 59, CFPF, 1963, box 3965; Bagley to Taylor, November 14, 1962, *FRUS, XXIV*, d. 435.

17. Naftali and Zelikow, *Presidential Recordings: John F. Kennedy, II*, pp. 450–58.

18. Telephone conversation, November 15, 1962, *FRUS, XI*, d. 182.

19. Fursenko and Naftali, *Khrushchev's Cold War*, p. 496; Zubok, *Failed Empire*, pp. 193–94.

20. Memorandum of conversation, November 29, 1962, *FRUS, XXIV*, d. 438.

21. Ibid.

22. Memorandum of conversation, November 29, 1962, *FRUS, XI*, d. 219.

23. Memorandum of conversation, November 29, 1962, *FRUS, XXIV*, d. 438.

24. William Leary, "Air America Chronology: 1962," p. 31, Eugene McDermott Library, University of Texas, Dallas; Vientiane to State Dept., November 27, 1962, NARA, RG 59, CFPF, 1963, box 3965.

25. Forrestal to Kennedy, November 28, 1962, JFKL, NSF, box 137A; Vientiane to State Dept., November 27, 1962.

26. Vientiane to State Dept., 823, November 29, 1962, NARA, RG 59, CFPF, 1963, box 3965.

27. Vientiane to State Dept., November 13, 1962, NARA, RG 59, CFPF, 1963, box 3965; Vientiane to State Dept., 824, November 29, 1962, NARA, RG 59, CDF, 1960–1963, box 1775.

28. Vientiane to State Dept., November 30, 1962, NARA, RG 59, CFPF, 1963, box 3965.

29. Ibid.

30. "Notes on Visits to Thailand, Laos, Vietnam, and Okinawa," December 10, 1962, LOC, WAHP, box 477.

31. Ibid.

32. Memorandum of conversation with Souphanouvong, December 5, 1962, JFKL, NSF, box 137.

33. Memorandum of conversation with Ngon, December 5, 1962, JFKL, NSF, box 137; "Notes on Visits to Thailand, Laos, Vietnam, and Okinawa."

34. Memorandum of conversation with Souvanna, December 5, 1962, JFKL, NSF, box 137.

35. Vientiane to State Dept., December 16, 1962, JFKL, NSF, box 137.

36. Bridle, "Canada and the International Commissions in Indochina," pp. 444–46; State Dept. to Ottawa, February 22, 1963, JFKL, NSF, box 137.

37. Bridle, "Canada and the International Commissions in Indochina," p. 441; Forrestal, "Report on Laos," undated (ca. January 15, 1963), FRUS, XXIV, d. 440.

38. Unger to State Dept., January 11, 1963; CINCPAC to JCS, January 13, 1963; Forrestal, "Report on Laos."

39. "CIA Support to Meo Tribesmen in Laos," April 8, 1963, NARA, CREST.

40. Forrestal, "Report on Laos."

41. Vientiane to State Dept., October 1, 1962, JFKL, NSF, box 136; Forrestal, "Report on Laos."

42. Forrestal and Hilsman, memorandum, January 25, 1963, FRUS, III, d. 19.

43. Ibid.

44. Rostow to Rusk, November 28, 1962, NARA, RG 59, BFEA, ASFEA, Subject Files, 1960–1963, box 21.

45. Forrestal and Hilsman, memorandum, January 25, 1963; Rostow to Rusk, November 28, 1962.

46. William Jorden to Harriman, March 20, 1963, FRUS, III, d. 64.

47. NSAM 124, January 18, 1962, USVR, Part V-B4-Book II, p. 442; "Notes on Visits to Thailand, Laos, Vietnam, and Okinawa"; Lyman Kirkpatrick to Ray Cline, January 18, 1963, NARA, CREST.

48. "North Vietnamese Support to the Viet Cong via Laos," January 23, 1963, NARA, CREST.

49. Ibid.

50. Ibid.

51. Ibid.

52. Ibid.

53. Holm, Craft We Chose, p. 126.

54. Frederick Nolting to State Dept., September 13, 1961, NARA, RG 59, BFEA, Laos, 1954–1961, box 15. See also Horace Smith to State Dept., December 30, 1959, CDF, 1955–1959, box 3369.

55. Forrestal and Hilsman, memorandum, January 25, 1963.

56. Memorandum of conversation, September 10, 1962, *FRUS, II*, d. 277.

57. "JCS Team Report on South Vietnam," January 1963, *FRUS, III*, d. 26.

58. Ibid.

59. CIA, "Situation in Laos," January 23, 1963, NARA, CREST.

60. Ibid.

61. State Dept. to Vientiane, February 5, 1963, NARA, RG 59, CFPF, 1963, box 3965.

62. State Dept. to Vientiane, February 7, 1963, no. 781 and no. 784, JFKL, NSF, box 137.

63. State Dept. to Ottawa and New Delhi, February 10, 1963, JFKL, NSF, box 137.

64. "Comments on Other Delegations," October 19, 1962, LOC, WAHP, box 530.

65. State Dept. to Ottawa and New Delhi, February 10, 1963.

66. Ottawa to State Dept., February 12, 1963, JFKL, NSF, box 137.

67. State Dept. to Ottawa and New Delhi, February 10, 1963; State Dept. to Vientiane, February 7, 1963, no. 781.

68. State Dept. to Ottawa and New Delhi, February 11, 1963, JFKL, POF, Laos: Security, 1963: January–May.

69. Bridle, "Canada and the International Commissions in Indochina," p. 407.

70. Biographic sketch, February 18, 1963, NARA, RG 59, BEA&PA, OCDLC, 1955–1975, Laos, box 9.

71. Memorandum of conversation, February 25, 1963, memorandum of conversation, February 27, 1963, and Vientiane to State Dept., March 21, 1963, all *FRUS, XXIV*, dd. 444–46.

72. Memorandum of conversation, February 25, 1963.

73. Ibid.

74. "Lao Internal Problems," February 19, 1963, NARA, RG 59, BEA&PA, OCDLC, Laos, 1955–1975, box 9; memorandum of conversation, February 27, 1963.

75. State Dept. to Moscow, February 14, 1963, *FRUS, XXIV*, d. 442.

76. "Attitudes of the Principal Members of the King's Party," February 19, 1963, NARA, RG 59, BEA&PA, OCDLC, 1955–1975, Laos, box 9.

77. Memorandum of conversation, February 26, 1963, NARA, RG 59, BEA&PA, OCDLC, 1955–1975, Laos, box 9.

78. Ibid.

79. State Dept. to Vientiane, March 15, 1963, JFKL, NSF, box 137.

80. Ibid.

81. Vientiane to State Dept., March 21, 1963.

82. CINCPAC to JCS, March 27, 1963, JFKL, NSF, box 137.

10. A Piece of War

1. Hughes to Rusk, April 4, 1963, JFKL, RHP, box 2; CIA information report, April 2, 1963, www.foia.cia.gov.

2. NSC Meeting, April 10, 1963, JFKL, Presidential Recordings, tape 80.

3. Ibid.; Vientiane to State Dept., April 6, 1963, NARA, RG 59, CFPF, 1963, box 3967.

4. State Dept. to Vientiane, March 15, 1963, JFKL, NSF, box 137; Vientiane to State Dept., April 8, 1963, no. 1402, NARA, RG 59, CFPF, 1963, box 3967; NSC Meeting, April 10, 1963.

5. NSC meeting, April 10, 1963.

6. Vientiane to State Dept., February 18, 1963, NARA, RG 59, CFPF, 1963, box 3965; NSC meeting, April 10, 1963.

7. Telephone conversation, Kennedy-Harriman, April 10, 1963 [*sic*], JFKL, Presidential Recordings, Dictabelt F. This phone call was also summarized in a written memorandum of conversation, dated April 19, 1963, in *FRUS, XXIV.* Based on the substance of the conversation, April 19 is the correct date for the call.

8. Ibid.; telephone conversation, Harriman–M. Bundy, April 19, 1963, *FRUS, XXIV,* d. 455n.

9. Forrestal to Kennedy, April 19, 1963, *FRUS, XXIV,* d. 456; Hughes to Rusk, April 20, 1963, NARA, RG 59, NSC Meetings and Policy Reports, 1959–1966, box 2.

10. Meeting with the president, April 19, 1963, JFKL, Presidential Recordings, tape 82.1.

11. Hilsman to Rusk, June 8, 1962, JFKL, RHP, box 2.

12. Memorandum for the record, April 18, 1963, NARA, KARC, RG 218, box 5; US Department of Defense, "CINCPAC Command History 1963," April 27, 1964, Nautilus Institute, www.nautilus.org.

13. Meeting with the president, April 19, 1963.

14. Ibid. Perennially dissatisfied with the Cuban situation as long as Fidel Castro ruled the country, Kennedy was referring here to the continuing presence of Soviet troops on the island.

15. NSC Meeting, April 20, 1963, JFKL, Presidential Recordings, tape 82.1.

16. Ibid.

17. Ibid.

18. Ibid.

19. Colby to McCone, undated, *FRUS, XXIV,* d. 460; NSC Action 2465, April 20, 1963, JFKL, POF, Laos: Security, 1963: January–May.

20. Memorandum of conversation, April 21, 1963, *FRUS, XXIV,* d. 462.

21. Colby to M. Bundy, April 22, 1963, and OCI, "Resupply Efforts for Kong Le and Meo Forces in Plaines des Jarres Area," May 2, 1963, JFKL, both NSF, box 132; Vientiane to State Dept., April 25, 1963, NARA, RG 59, CFPF, 1963, box 3965.

22. Vientiane to State Dept., April 21, 1963, NARA, RG 59, CFPF, 1963, box 3967.

23. Ibid.

24. Ibid.

25. Vientiane to State Dept., April 11, 1963, and April 19, 1963, both NARA, RG 59, CFPF, 1963, box 3965.

26. Vientiane to State Dept., April 25, 1963; Vientiane to State Dept., April 22, 1963, NARA, RG 59, CFPF, 1963, box 3730.

27. NSC Meeting, April 22, 1963, JFKL, Presidential Recordings, tape 82.2.

28. Ibid.; "United States Operations in Laos and the Geneva Agreements," April 22, 1963, JFKL, NSF, box 132.

29. NSC Meeting, April 22, 1963.

30. Ibid.; Joint Staff, "Daily Report to Secretary of Defense," April 22, 1963, JFKL, NSF, box 132.

31. NSC Meeting, April 22, 1963; Tad Szulc, "National Security Council to Meet Today on Plan for Fleet Maneuvers," *New York Times*, April 22, 1963.

32. JCS to McNamara, April 23, 1963, *FRUS, XXIV,* MFS, no. 322.

33. Stephen Loftus to Nitze, April 20, 1963, NARA, RG 59, BFEA, ASFEA, Subject Files, 1960–1963, box 21.

34. L. D. Clay, memorandum of conversation, April 18, 1963, NARA, KARC, RG 218, box 5.

35. Loftus to Nitze, April 20, 1963.

36. London to State Dept., April 25, 1963, NARA, RG 59, CFPF, 1963, box 3967; London to State Dept., April 23, 1963, *FRUS, XXIV,* MFS, no. 321.

37. London to State Dept., April 25, 1963, and memorandum of conversation with Gromyko, April 26, 1963, both NARA, RG 59, CFPF, 1963, box 3967.

38. Memorandum of conversation with Gromyko, April 26, 1963. More than four years later, after the "secret war" in Laos had escalated significantly, Gromyko still appeared disturbed by Quinim's assassination. Denouncing "false stories" about the foreign minister's involvement in Colonel Ketsana's murder, Gromyko told Dean Rusk that Quinim's assassination had "complicated the situation" in Laos. Memorandum of conversation, March 21, 1967, *FRUS, XXVIII,* d. 293.

39. Memorandum of conversation with Gromyko, April 26, 1963; Sullivan, *Obbligato,* p. 184.

40. Memorandum of conversation with Gromyko, April 26, 1963.

41. Moscow to State Dept., April 27, 1963, JFKL, NSF, box 137A.

42. State Dept. to Moscow, 2273, April 23, 1963, *FRUS, VI,* d. 97.

43. Memorandum of conversation with Khrushchev, April 26, 1963, *FRUS, XXIV,* MFS, no. 326.

44. Ibid.

45. Ibid; Sullivan, interview, June 16, 1970; memorandum for the record, April 30, 1963, *FRUS, XXIV,* d. 467.

46. Moscow to State Dept., April 27, 1963; memorandum of conversation, April 29, 1963, LOC, WAHP, box 538.

47. Hughes to Rusk, May 16, 1963, LOC, WAHP, box 483.

48. Harriman to Hilsman, May 30, 1963, LOC, WAHP, box 483.

49. Vientiane to State Dept., May 9, 1963, NARA, RG 59, CFPF, 1963, box 3965.

50. "Talking Points on Laos," undated (ca. May 5, 1963), NARA, RG 59, BFEA, ASFEA, Subject Files, 1960–1963, box 21.

51. Harriman to M. Bundy, May 7, 1963, *FRUS, XXIV*, d. 469.

52. CINCPAC, "Record of the Secretary of Defense Conference," May 8, 1963, NARA, KARC, RG 218, box 5.

53. Ibid. In a conversation with Marine Major General Victor H. Krulak, the JCS special assistant for counterinsurgency and special operations, McCone said that he "favored making the war more costly for the North Vietnamese," but "he was not optimistic about receiving high-level [presidential] approval for such a program." Krulak to Taylor, June 6, 1963, NARA, KARC, Taylor Papers, box 7.

54. CINCPAC, "Record of the Secretary of Defense Conference," May 8, 1963.

55. Kennedy-McNamara meeting, May 7, 1963, JFKL, Presidential Recordings, tape 85.2; memorandum, R. C. Forbes, March 4, 1963, NARA, KARC, RG 218, box 3.

56. Kennedy-McNamara meeting, May 7, 1963. McNamara had been making plans to "phase out of major US combat, advisory and logistics support activities" since July 1962. "Record of the Sixth Secretary of Defense Conference," July 23, 1962, *FRUS, II*, d. 248. The proposal for withdrawing one thousand US advisers by the end of 1963 was first suggested by R. G. K. Thompson, the British counterinsurgency expert. Memorandum of conversation, April 1, 1963, *FRUS, III*, d. 73.

11. We're Going to Have to Take Some Action

1. Unger to State Dept., May 18, 1963, NARA, RG 59, CFPF, 1963, box 3967.

2. State Dept. to Unger, May 24, 1963, *FRUS, XXIV*, d. 472.

3. Ahern, *Undercover Armies*, p. 157.

4. Bromley Smith, June 7, 1963, *FRUS, XXIV*, d. 475n.

5. "Memorandum for the President," June 17, 1963. A sanitized version of this memorandum is printed in *FRUS, XXIV*, d. 477. The complete version of this document, available at the LOC, WAHP, box 483, is reprinted in appendix 3.

6. Ibid.

7. Ibid.

8. SNIE, "Communist Reactions to US Actions Taken with Regard to Laos," June 18, 1963, www.foia.cia.gov.

9. Ibid.; "Memorandum for the President," June 17, 1963.

10. Forrestal to Kennedy, June 18, 1963, *FRUS, XXIV*, d. 477.

11. Clay, memorandum for the record, June 19, 1963, NARA, RG 218, CJCS-091 Laos, box 7; William Colby, memorandum for the record, undated, *FRUS, XXIV*, d. 479.

12. Colby, memorandum for the record, undated.

13. Clay, memorandum for the record, June 19, 1963; Felt to JCS, June 19, 1963, JFKL, NSF, box 138.

14. Colby, memorandum for the record, undated; Forrestal, memorandum for the record, June 19, 1963, *FRUS, XXIV*, d. 478; Clay, memorandum for the record, June 19, 1963.

15. NSAM 249, June 25, 1963, *USVR, Part V-B4-Book II*, p. 525; Clay, memorandum for the record, June 19, 1963.

16. Unger to Hilsman, June 20, 1962, NARA, RG 59, BFEA, ASFEA, Subject Files, 1960–1963, box 19.

17. Sturdevant et al., "Examination of the Viet Cong Reaction," p. v.; Vientiane to State Dept., June 22, 1963, NARA, RG 59, CFPF, 1963, box 3967.

18. Vientiane to State Dept., June 20, 1963, NARA, RG 59, CFPF, 1963, box 3967.

19. Bruce to State Dept., June 20, 1963, JFKL, NSF, box 138; memorandum of conversation, June 21, 1963, NARA, RG 59, CFPF, 1963, box 3965.

20. Memorandum of telephone conversation, Forrestal and Harriman, June 24, 1963, LOC, WAHP, box 581; memorandum of telephone conversation, Ball–Carl Kaysen, June 24, 1963, JFKL, GWBP, box 5.

21. Memorandum of conversation, June 24, 1963, NARA, RG 59, CFPF, 1963, box 3967.

22. Ibid.

23. State Dept. to Rusk, June 26, 1963, JFKL, NSF, box 138; State Dept. to Vientiane, June 28, 1963, NARA, RG 59, CFPF, 1963, box 3967.

24. Meeting with the president, July 4, 1963, JFKL, Presidential Recordings, tape 96.

25. Ibid.

26. Harriman to Kennedy, November 12, 1961, *FRUS, I*, d. 239; meeting with the president, July 4, 1963.

27. Krulak Report, undated (ca. July 2, 1963), *FRUS, III*, d. 207

28. Chadbourn to State Dept., 26, July 4, 1963, JFKL, NSF, box 138.

29. Ibid.

30. Chadbourn to State Dept., 25, July 4, 1963, JFKL, NSF, box 138.

31. Memorandum for the record, July 9, 1963, NARA, RG 218, CJCS-091 Laos, box 7; memorandum of conversation, July 18, 1963, *FRUS, XXIV*, d. 480

32. SNIE 14.3-63, June 26, 1963, *FRUS, III*, d. 188; memorandum of conversation, July 18, 1963.

33. Memorandum for the record, July 10, 1963, *FRUS, VII*, d. 320; Moscow to State Dept., July 31, 1963, *FRUS, V*, d. 341.

34. Meeting with the president, August 2, 1963, JFKL, Presidential Recordings, tape 103.2.

35. "Memorandum for the President," undated (ca. July 29, 1963). A sanitized version of this memorandum is printed in *FRUS, XXIV*, d. 481. An unexpurgated version of the document is available at NARA, RG 59, BFEA, ASFEA, Subject Files, 1960–1963, box 21.

36. Meeting with the president, July 30, 1963, JFKL, Presidential Recordings, tape 102.2.

37. Ibid. It is difficult to believe that there remains a valid national security reason for this excision.

38. Chadbourn to Hilsman, August 4, 1963, NARA, RG 59, BEA&PA, OCDL, Laos, 1955–1975, box 10; State Dept. to Vientiane, July 30, 1963, NARA, RG 59, CFPF, 1963, box 3730.

39. "Memorandum for the President," undated (ca. July 29, 1963).

40. CINCPAC Conference, July 12, 1963, NARA, RG 472, MACV, Historians Background Material, box 1; CINCPAC OPLAN 34-63, November 20, 1963, Honolulu Briefing Book, JFKL, NSF, box 204.

41. Meeting with the president, July 30, 1963.

42. Ibid.

43. Ibid.

44. Ibid.

45. Memorandum of conversation, August 30, 1963, *FRUS, IV,* d. 28.

46. M. Bundy to Kennedy, September 1, 1963, *FRUS, IV,* d. 43.

47. Meeting with the president, September 3, 1963, JFKL, Presidential Recordings, tape 108.3.

48. Meeting with the president, August 29, 1963, JFKL, Presidential Recordings, tape 108.3.

49. Memorandum of conversation, September 23, 1963, *FRUS, XXIV,* d. 489. In an October 7 conversation with French foreign minister Couve de Murville, Kennedy said: "General de Gaulle's statement on Vietnam had been unhelpful, particularly with regard to its timing." Reflecting the optimistic military views of McNamara and Taylor, who had just returned from South Vietnam, Kennedy told Couve that the situation there "was being made to appear worse than it is." *FRUS, XIII,* d. 275.

50. Memorandum of conversation, September 23, 1963.

51. Memorandum of conversation, August 9, 1963, *FRUS, XXIV,* d. 484.

52. Meeting with the president, August 26, 1963, JFKL, Presidential Recordings, tape 107.1.

53. Ibid.

54. Memorandum of conversation, August 26, 1963, *FRUS, V,* d. 350. Because of my own limitations in transcribing Dobrynin's accented English, I have relied on this document, drafted by Llewellyn Thompson, for the Soviet diplomat's response.

55. Foy Kohler to State Dept., September 10, 1963, *FRUS, V,* d. 354.

56. Meeting with the president, October 10, 1963, JFKL, Presidential Recordings, tape 115.3.

57. "Laos Weekly Situation Report," October 29, 1963, NARA, CREST.

58. "Status Report on the Laos Program and Plans," October 12, 1963, and George Barbis to Joseph Neubert, October 15, 1963, both NARA, RG 59, BFEA, ASFEA, Subject Files, 1960–1963, box 21; CIA Saigon 2441, November 14, NARA, KARC, RG 218, box 4.

59. Forrestal to Barbis, October 15, 1963, LOC, WAHP, box 483.

60. State Dept. to Unger, October 26, 1963, JFKL, NSF, box 138A.

61. Loftus to W. Bundy, October 29, 1963, NARA, RG 330, Country Files, 1963, box 27.

62. "The Situation in Laos," November 1, 1963, *FRUS, XXIV,* d. 490.

63. Kennedy, November 4, 1963, JFKL, Telephone Recordings: Dictation Belt 52.1.

64. Rostow to Rusk, November 1, 1963, NARA, RG 59, BFEA, ASFEA, Subject Files, 1960–1963, box 21.

65. CIA to State Dept., November 19, 1963, *FRUS, IV,* d. 320; William Trueheart to State Dept., November 26, 1963, NARA, RG 59, CFPF, 1963, box 3969.

66. NSAM 273, November 26, 1963, *FRUS, IV,* d. 331.

67. Henry Koren, "Pressure on North Vietnam," December 4, 1963, NARA, RG 59, BFEA, ASFEA, Subject Files, 1960–1963, box 21. Also see the attached, unsigned document on the phased program of pressure in Laos and the role of cross-border operations.

68. Unger to State Dept., December 13, 1963, LBJL, NSF, box 265.

69. McNamara to Lyndon Johnson, December 21, 1963, *FRUS, IV,* d. 374.

Epilogue

1. Hilsman to Rusk, November 23, 1963, NARA, RG 59, BFEA, ASFEA, Subject Files, 1960–1963, box 21.

2. Herbert D. Riley to Taylor, January 30, 1964, NARA, RG 218, CJCS-091 Laos, box 7.

3. SNIE 50-64, "Short-Term Prospects in Southeast Asia," February 12, 1964, www.foia.cia.gov.

4. Hilsman to Rusk, February 25, 1964, *FRUS, XXVIII,* d. 6.

5. JCS to McNamara, January 22, 1964, in US Department of Defense, *Pentagon Papers,* vol. 3, p. 496; Peter Solbert to McNamara, undated (ca. February 26, 1964), *FRUS, XXVIII,* d. 7.

6. Unger to State, March 1, 1964, *FRUS, XXVIII,* d. 11.

7. Ibid.

8. L. B. Johnson to Lodge, March 17, 1964, *FRUS, I,* d. 85.

9. George Ball, interview with Paige Mulhollan, July 8, 1971, LBJLOHP.

10. Abramson, *Spanning the Century,* p. 632. Harriman's protégé, Michael Forrestal, also switched jobs. Transferred from the White House to the State Department in July 1964, Forrestal served briefly as Dean Rusk's special assistant for Vietnamese affairs before leaving government altogether in early 1965 to resume his career as an international lawyer.

11. Unger to State Dept., April 17, 1964, LBJL, NSF, box 266.

12. Thomas Hughes to Rusk, April 2, 1964, LBJL, NSF, box 265; Vientiane to State Dept., April 9, 1964, NARA, RG 59, CFPF, 1964–1966, box 2417.

13. Chadbourn to State Dept., April 18, 1964, NARA, RG 59, CFPF, 1964–1966, box 2420.

14. "Background of the 19 April Rightist Coup in Laos," April 22, 1964, *FRUS, XXVIII,* d. 33; ARMA Vientiane to DA, May 2, 1964, LBJL, NSF, box 266.

15. Memorandum for the record, April 19, 1964, *FRUS, XXVIII,* d. 23.

16. Transcript of teletype conference, April 19, 1964, *FRUS, XXVIII,* d. 27.

17. Unger to State Dept., April 20, 1964, LBJL, NSF, box 266; Zasloff and Unger, *Laos: Beyond the Revolution,* p. 280.

18. Unger to State Dept., April 22, 1964, LBJL, NSF, box 266.

19. Unger to State Dept., April 26, 1964, LJBL, NSF, box 266.

20. Vientiane to DA, May 2, 1964; Unger to State Dept., May 3, 1964, LBJL, NSF, box 266.

21. Hong Kong to State Dept., April 9, 1964, *FRUS, XXVIII,* d. 20.

22. "Summary Record of the 528th Meeting of the National Security Council," April 22, 1964, *FRUS, XXVIII,* d. 35.

23. Unger to State Dept., May 4, 1964, LBJL, NSF, box 266.

24. Vientiane to State Dept., April 30, 1964, and May 7, 1964, both NARA, RG 59, CFPF, 1964–1966, box 2417; Unger to State Dept., May 3, 1964.

25. "Watch Report of the United States Intelligence Board," April 29, 1964, LBJ, NSF, NSC Meetings File, box 1; "Summary Record of the 529th Meeting of the National Security Council," April 29, 1964, *FRUS, I,* d. 131.

26. Unger to State Dept., May 22, 1964, no. 1398, LBJL, NSF, box 267.

27. Unger to State Dept., May 19 and May 20, 1964, LBJL, NSF, box 266.

28. Memorandum of conversation, May 19, 1964, NARA, RG 59, CFPF, 1964–1966, box 2423.

29. Unger to State Dept., May 22, 1964, no. 1395, *FRUS, XXVIII,* d. 56.

30. Unger to State Dept., May 20, 1964, no. 1368 and no. 1370, LBJL, NSF, box 266; Unger to State Dept., May 24, 1964, *FRUS, XXVIII,* d. 59.

31. W. Bundy to the executive committee of the National Security Council, May 24, 1964, *FRUS, XXVIII,* d. 60.

32. M. Bundy to L. B. Johnson, May 25, 1964, *FRUS, I,* d. 173.

33. Telephone conversation, L. B. Johnson–Adlai Stevenson, May 27, 1964, in McKee, *Presidential Recordings: Lyndon B. Johnson, VI,* p. 869.

34. Telephone conversation, L. B. Johnson–Richard Russell, May 27, 1964, in McKee, *Presidential Recordings: Lyndon B. Johnson, VI,* pp. 878–84.

35. Ibid.

36. Telephone conversation, L. B. Johnson–M. Bundy, May 27, 1964, in McKee, *Presidential Recordings: Lyndon B. Johnson, VI,* pp. 887–88.

37. Ibid.

Bibliography

Archival Sources

The American Presidency Project, University of California, Santa Barbara,
www.presidency.ucsb.edu

Central Intelligence Agency, FOIA Electronic Reading Room, www
.foia.cia.gov

Dwight D. Eisenhower Presidential Library, Abilene, KS

Foreign Affairs Oral History Collection (FAOHC) of the Association for
Diplomatic Studies and Training, Library of Congress, http://memory.loc.gov/
ammem/collections/diplomacy/index.html

Georgetown University Library, Special Collections Division, Washington, DC
J. Graham Parsons Papers

Lyndon Baines Johnson Presidential Library (LBJL), Austin, TX
LBJL Oral History Program (LBJLOHP)
National Security Files (NSF)

John F. Kennedy Presidential Library (JFKL), Boston, MA
George W. Ball Papers
Roger Hilsman Papers
JFKL Oral History Program (JFKLOHP)
National Security Files
Presidential Office Files
Presidential Recordings

Library of Congress (LOC), Washington, DC
W. Averell Harriman Papers (WAHP)

Miller Center, University of Virginia, www.millercenter.org

National Security Archive, George Washington University, www.gwu
.edu/~nsarchiv

Princeton University, Seeley G. Mudd Manuscript Library, Princeton, NJ
Charles W. Yost Papers

US Army Military History Institute (USAMHI), Carlisle Barracks, PA
Andrew Jackson Boyle Papers

US Department of Defense, Office of the Secretary of Defense and Joint Staff Reading Room, www.dod.mil/pubs/foi

US Department of State, Office of the Historian, http://history.state.gov/ historicaldocuments

US National Archives and Records Administration (NARA), College Park, MD
CIA Records Search Tool (CREST)
Kennedy Assassination Records Collection (KARC)
RG 59, General Records of the Department of State
RG 84, Records of the Foreign Service Posts of the Department of State
RG 218, Records of the US Joint Chiefs of Staff
RG 330, Records of the Office of the Secretary of Defense
RG 469, Records of US Foreign Assistance Agencies
RG 472, Records of the US Forces in Southeast Asia, 1950–1976

Vietnam Center and Archive, Texas Tech University, www.vietnam.ttu .edu.

US Government Documentary Sources and Histories

Ahern, Thomas L., Jr. *The Way We Do Things: Black Entry Operations into North Vietnam, 1961–1964.* Washington, DC: Central Intelligence Agency, 2005.
———. *Undercover Armies: CIA and Surrogate Warfare in Laos, 1961–1973.* Washington, DC: Central Intelligence Agency, 2006.
Anthony, Victor B., and Richard R. Sexton. *The United States Air Force in Southeast Asia: The War in Northern Laos.* Washington, DC: Center for Air Force History, 1993.
Birtle, Andrew J. *US Army Counterinsurgency and Contingency Operations Doctrine, 1942–1976.* Washington, DC: US Army, Center of Military History, 2006.
Central Intelligence Agency. "Draft History: John A. McCone, the Sixth Director of Central Intelligence." 1987. NARA, KARC, CIA histories.
———. "The Growth and Current Deployment of the Laotian-Based 559th Transportation Group." February 1971. NARA, CREST.
———. "The Lao Communists." March 1973. NARA, CREST.
———. "Laos, the Divided Nation." June 1967. LBJL, NSF, box 271.
Hanyok, Robert J. *Spartans in Darkness: American SIGINT and the Indochina War, 1945–1975.* Center for Cryptologic History, National Security Agency, 2002, www.gwu.edu/~nsarchiv.
Howells, W. Dean, Dorothy Avery, and Fred Greene. *Vietnam 1961–1968 as Interpreted in INR's Production.* US Department of State, 1969, www.gwu .edu/~nsarchiv.

National Intelligence Council. "Estimative Products on Vietnam, 1948–1975." Washington, DC: Government Printing Office, 2005.

Poole, Walter S. *The Joint Chiefs of Staff and National Policy. Volume VIII, 1961–1964.* Washington, DC: Government Printing Office, 2011.

Schulimson, Jack. *The Joint Chiefs of Staff and the War in Vietnam, 1960–1968, Part 1.* Washington, DC: Office of Joint History, Office of the Chairman of the Joint Chiefs of Staff, 2011.

US Department of Defense. "Chronological Summary of Significant Events Concerning the Laotian Crisis." 2nd installment, February 1 to March 31, 1961. Historical Division, Joint Secretariat, Joint Chiefs of Staff, 1961. www.dod.mil/pubs/foi.

———. "Chronological Summary of Significant Events Concerning the Laotian Crisis." 3rd installment, April 1 to May 31, 1961. Historical Division, Joint Secretariat, Joint Chiefs of Staff, 1961. www.dod.mil/pubs/foi.

———. "Chronological Summary of Significant Events Concerning the Laotian Crisis." 4th installment, June 1 to December 31, 1961. Historical Division, Joint Secretariat, Joint Chiefs of Staff, 1962. www.dod.mil/pubs/foi.

———. "Chronological Summary of Significant Events Concerning the Laotian Crisis." 5th installment, January 1 to April 30, 1962. Historical Division, Joint Secretariat, Joint Chiefs of Staff, 1962. www.dod.mil/pubs/foi.

———. "Chronological Summary of Significant Events Concerning the Laotian Crisis." 6th installment, May 1 to July 31, 1962. Historical Division, Joint Secretariat, Joint Chiefs of Staff, 1962. www.dod.mil/pubs/foi.

———. "CINCPAC Command History 1963." 1964. Nautilus Institute. www.nautilus.org.

———. "Historical Analysis of the Lao Incident, August 1960 to May 1961, Part II." Weapons Systems Evaluation Group, October 1, 1963. www.dod.mil/pubs/foi.

———. *History of the Office of the Secretary of Defense: The McNamara Ascendancy, 1961–1965.* Washington, DC: Government Printing Office, 2006.

———. "Laos Staff Study." 1965. NARA, RG 472, MACV, Historians Background Material, box 4.

———. *The Pentagon Papers: The Defense Department History of United States Decisionmaking on Vietnam.* Gravel Edition. Boston: Beacon Press, 1971.

———. *United States–Vietnam Relations, 1945–1967.* 1969. www.archives.gov.

US Department of State. *American Foreign Policy: Current Documents 1961.* Washington, DC: Government Printing Office, 1965.

———. *American Foreign Policy: Current Documents 1962.* Washington, DC: Government Printing Office, 1966.

———. "Comments on Other Delegations to the International Conference on the Settlement of the Laotian Question and Secret Memoranda and Other Classified Papers Relating to the Conference." October 1962. LOC, WAHP, box 530.

———. *Foreign Relations of the United States, 1961–1963. Volume I, Vietnam.* Washington, DC: Government Printing Office, 1988.

————. *Foreign Relations of the United States, 1961–1963. Volume II, Vietnam.* Washington, DC: Government Printing Office, 1990.

————. *Foreign Relations of the United States, 1961–1963. Volume III, Vietnam.* Washington, DC: Government Printing Office, 1991.

————. *Foreign Relations of the United States, 1961–1963. Volume IV, Vietnam.* Washington, DC: Government Printing Office, 1991.

————. *Foreign Relations of the United States, 1961–1963. Volume V, Soviet Union.* Washington, DC: Government Printing Office, 1998.

————. *Foreign Relations of the United States, 1961–1963. Volume VII, Arms Control and Disarmament.* Washington, DC: Government Printing Office, 1995.

————. *Foreign Relations of the United States, 1961–1963. Volume XIII, Western Europe and Canada.* Washington, DC: Government Printing Office, 1994.

————. *Foreign Relations of the United States, 1961–1963. Volume XIV, Berlin Crisis, 1961–1962.* Washington, DC: Government Printing Office, 1993.

————. *Foreign Relations of the United States, 1961–1963. Volume XXIII, Southeast Asia.* Washington, DC: Government Printing Office, 1994.

————. *Foreign Relations of the United States, 1961–1963. Volume XXIV, Laos Crisis.* Washington, DC: Government Printing Office, 1994.

————. *Foreign Relations of the United States, 1961–1963. Volumes XXII–XXIV, Northeast Asia; Laos.* Microfiche Supplement. Washington, DC: Government Printing Office, 1997.

————. *Foreign Relations of the United States, 1964–1968. Volume XXVII, Mainland Southeast Asia; Regional Affairs.* Washington, DC: Government Printing Office, 2000.

————. *Foreign Relations of the United States, 1964–1968. Volume XXVIII, Laos.* Washington, DC: Government Printing Office, 1998.

————. "The Laos Story." May 1962. JFKL, NSF, box 131.

————. "The United States Commitment to Thailand: Background, Formulation, and Differing Initial U.S. and Thai Interpretations of the Rusk-Thanat Communiqué of 1962." September 1970. NARA, RG 59, Executive Secretariat, Historical Office Research Projects, box 7.

US Senate, Select Committee to Study Governmental Operations. *Alleged Assassination Plots Involving Foreign Leaders.* Washington, DC: Government Printing Office, 1975.

Oral Histories and Interviews

Amory, Robert, Jr. Interview with Joseph E. O'Connor. February 9 and 17, 1966. JFKLOHP.

Ball, George. Interview with Paige E. Mulhollan. July 8, 1971. LBJLOHP.

Barbis, George M. Interview with Raymond C. Ewing. October 8, 1996. FAOHC.

Bissell, Richard. Interview with Joseph E. O'Connor. April 25, 1967. JFKLOHP.

Boyle, Andrew J. Interview with Frank Walton. February 28 and March 27, 1971. USAMHI.

Brown, Winthrop G. Interview with Larry J. Hackman. February 1, 1968. JFKLOHP.
Bundy, McGeorge. Interview with Richard Neustadt. March 1964. JFKLOHP.
Bundy, William P. Interview with Elspeth Rostow. November 12, 1964. JFKLOHP.
———. Interview with William W. Moss. April 25, 1972. JFKLOHP.
Burke, Arleigh A. Interview with Joseph E. O'Connor. January 20, 1967. JFKLOHP.
Burnet, Frank N. Interview with Charles Stuart Kennedy. February 22, 1990. FAOHC.
Cross, Charles T. Interview with Charles Stuart Kennedy. November 19, 1997. FAOHC.
Decker, George H. Interview with Larry J. Hackman. September 18, 1968. JFKLOHP.
Forrestal, Michael V. Interview with Joseph Kraft. April 8 and July 28, 1964. JFKLOHP.
———. Interview with Paige E. Mulhollan. November 3, 1969. LBJLOHP.
———. Interview with William J. Rust. September 2, 1981.
Gilpatric, Roswell L. Interview with Ted Gittinger. November 2, 1982. LBJLOHP.
Harriman, W. Averell. Interview with Arthur M. Schlesinger Jr. January 17, 1965. JFKLOHP.
Heinz, Luther C. Interview with William W. Moss. July 20 and July 27, 1970. JFKLOHP.
Helms, Richard. Interview with Ted Gittinger. September 16, 1981. LBJLOHP.
Hilsman, Roger. Interview with Paige Mulhollan. May 15, 1969. LBJLOHP.
Hughes, Thomas L. Interview with Charles Stuart Kennedy. July 7, 1999. FAOHC.
Johnson, U. Alexis. Interview with William Brubeck. June 18, 1964. JFKLOHP.
Krulak, Victor H. Interview with William W. Moss. November 19, 1970. JFKLOHP.
Kuhn, Ernest C. Interview with Arthur J. Dommen. March 25, 1995. FAOHC.
Lair, Bill. Interview with Steve Maxner. December 11–13, 2001. Vietnam Center and Archive, Texas Tech University.
Lemnitzer, Lyman L. Interview with Ted Gittinger. March 3, 1982. LBJLOHP.
Lilley, James R. Interview with Charles Stuart Kennedy. May 21, 1998. FAOHC.
Phillips, Rufus C. Interview with William J. Rust. October 21, 2009.
Pratt, Mark S. Interview with Charles Stuart Kennedy. October 21, 1999. FAOHC.
Rusk, Dean. Interview with Paige Mulhollan. July 28 and September 26, 1969, January 2 and March 8, 1970. LBJOHP.
Steeves, John M. Interview with Dennis J. O'Brien. September 5, 1969. JFKLOHP.
———. Interview with Charles Stuart Kennedy and Thomas Stern. March 27, 1991. FAOHC.
Sullivan, William H. Interview with Dennis O'Brien. June 16, 1970. JFKLOHP.
Taylor, Maxwell D. Interview with Elspeth Rostow. April 12, April 26, and June 21, 1964. JFKLOHP.
Thomson, James C. Interview with Sheldon Stern. March 19, 1980. JFKLOHP.
Unger, Leonard. Interview with Charles Stuart Kennedy. May 10, 1989. FAOHC.
Wheeler, Earle G. Interview with Chester V. Clifton. July 11, 1964. JFKLOHP.

Yarborough, William P. Interview with John R. Meese and Houston P. Houser III. March 28, 1975. USAMHI.

Memoirs

Bailey, Lawrence R., Jr., with Ron Martz. *Solitary Survivor: The First American POW in Southeast Asia.* Washington, DC: Brassey's, 1995.

Ball, George W. *The Past Has Another Pattern.* New York: W. W. Norton, 1982.

Bissell, Richard M. *Reflections of a Cold Warrior: From Yalta to the Bay of Pigs.* New Haven, CT: Yale University Press, 1996.

Bridle, Paul. "Canada and the International Commissions in Indochina." In *Conflict and Stability in Southeast Asia,* edited by Mark W. Zacher and R. Stephen Milne. Garden City, NY: Anchor Books, 1974.

Brown, Mervyn. *War in Shangri-La: A Memoir of Civil War in Laos.* London: Radcliffe Press, 2001.

Bundy, William P. Unpublished Vietnam War manuscript. LBJL.

Colby, William E. *Honorable Men: My Life in the CIA.* New York: Simon and Schuster, 1978.

Cooper, Chester L. *In the Shadows of History: 50 Years behind the Scenes of Cold War Diplomacy.* Amherst, NY: Prometheus Books, 2005.

———. *The Lost Crusade: America in Vietnam.* New York: Dodd, Mead & Company, 1970.

Cross, Charles T. *Born a Foreigner: A Memoir of the American Presence in Asia.* Lanham, MD: Roman & Littlefield, 1999.

Galbraith, John Kenneth. *Ambassador's Journal: A Personal Account of the Kennedy Years.* New York: Houghton Mifflin, 1969.

Helms, Richard. *A Look over My Shoulder: A Life in the Central Intelligence Agency.* New York: Random House, 2003.

Hilsman, Roger. *American Guerrilla: My War behind Japanese Lines.* Washington, DC: Potomac Books, 2005.

———. *To Move a Nation: The Politics of Foreign Policy in the Administration of John F. Kennedy.* Garden City, NY: Doubleday, 1967.

Holm, Richard L. *The Craft We Chose: My Life in the CIA.* Mountain Lake Park, MD: Mountain Lake Press, 2011.

Hughes, Thomas H. "Experiencing McNamara." *Foreign Policy* (Autumn 1995).

Johnson, U. Alexis. *The Right Hand of Power: The Memoirs of an American Diplomat.* Englewood Cliffs, NJ: Prentice-Hall, 1984.

Kennedy, Robert F. *Robert Kennedy in His Own Words: The Unpublished Recollections of the Kennedy Years.* Edited by Edwin O. Guthman and Jeffrey Shulman. New York: Bantam Press, 1988.

Lair, Bill. "The Thai PARU and the War in Laos." October 21, 2006. Vietnam Center and Archive.

Lall, Arthur. *How Communist China Negotiates.* New York: Columbia University Press, 1968.

Lilley, James, with Jeffrey Lilley. *China Hands: Nine Decades of Adventure, Espionage, and Diplomacy in Asia.* New York: Public Affairs, 2004.
Macmillan, Harold. *At the End of the Day, 1961–1963.* New York: Harper & Row, 1973.
———. *Pointing the Way, 1959–1961.* New York: Harper & Row, 1972.
McNamara, Robert S. *In Retrospect: The Tragedy and Lessons of Vietnam.* New York: Times Books, 1995.
Parsons, J. Graham. Unpublished manuscript. J. Graham Parsons Papers, Georgetown University, Washington, DC.
Rostow, Walt W. *The Diffusion of Power: An Essay in Recent History.* New York: Macmillan, 1973.
Rusk, Dean. *As I Saw It.* New York: W. W. Norton, 1990.
Sananikone, Oudone. *The Royal Lao Army and U.S. Army Advice and Support.* Washington, DC: Department of the Army, Office of Chief of Military History, 1978.
Sorensen, Ted. *Counsellor: A Life at the Edge of History.* New York: Harper, 2008.
Sullivan, William H. *Obbligato: Notes on a Foreign Service Career.* New York: W. W. Norton & Company, 1984.
Taylor, Maxwell D. *Swords and Ploughshares.* New York: W. W. Norton & Company, 1972.
Thee, Marek. *Notes of a Witness: Laos and the Second Indochinese War.* New York: Random House, 1973.

Books, Articles, and Other Secondary Sources

Abramson, Rudy. *Spanning the Century: The Life of W. Averell Harriman, 1891–1986.* New York: William Morrow and Company, 1992.
Ang, Cheng Guan. *Vietnamese Communists' Relations with China and the Second Indochina Conflict, 1956–1962.* Jefferson, NC: McFarland & Company, 1997.
———. "The Vietnam War, 1962–1964: The Vietnamese Communist Perspective." *Journal of Contemporary History* 35, no. 4 (October 2000).
Asselin, Pierre. *Hanoi's Road to the Vietnam War, 1954–1965.* Berkeley: University of California Press, 2013.
Binder, L. James. *Lemnitzer: A Soldier for His Time.* Washington, DC: Brassey's, 1997.
Blaufarb, Douglas S. *The Counterinsurgency Era: U.S. Doctrine and Performance, 1950 to the Present.* New York: Free Press, 1977.
Brinkley, Alan. *John F. Kennedy.* New York: Times Books, 2012.
Brown, MacAlister, and Joseph J. Zasloff. *Apprentice Revolutionaries: The Communist Movement in Laos, 1930–1985.* Stanford, CA: Hoover Institution Press, 1986.
Castle, Timothy N. *At War in the Shadow of Vietnam: U.S. Military Aid to the Royal Government, 1955–1975.* New York: Columbia University Press, 1993.
Catterall, Peter, editor. *The Macmillan Diaries, Vol. II, Prime Minister and After, 1957–1966.* London: Pan Books, 2012.
Conboy, Kenneth. *Shadow War: The CIA's Secret War in Laos.* Boulder, CO: Paladin Press, 1995.

Dallek, Robert. *An Unfinished Life: John F. Kennedy, 1917–1963.* New York: Little Brown and Company, 2003.

Dommen, Arthur J. *The Indochinese Experience of the French and the Americans: Nationalism and Communism in Cambodia, Laos, and Vietnam.* Bloomington: Indiana University Press, 2001.

Duiker, William J. *The Communist Road to Power in Vietnam.* 2nd ed. Boulder, CO: Westview Press, 1996.

Evans, Grant. *The Last Century of Lao Royalty: A Documentary History.* Chiang Mai, Thailand: Silkworm Books, 2009.

Fineman, Daniel. *A Special Relationship: The United States and Military Government in Thailand, 1947–1958.* Honolulu: University of Hawaii Press, 1997.

Finlayson, Kenn. "Operation White Star: Prelude to Vietnam." *Special Warfare* (June 2002).

Freedman, Lawrence. *Kennedy's Wars: Berlin, Cuba, Laos, and Vietnam.* New York: Oxford University Press, 2000.

Fursenko, Aleksandr, and Timothy Naftali. *Khrushchev's Cold War: The Inside Story of an American Adversary.* New York: W. W. Norton & Company, 2007.

Gaddis, John Lewis. *The Cold War: A New History.* New York: Penguin Press, 2005.

———. *Strategies of Containment: A Critical Appraisal of Postwar American National Security Policy.* Revised and expanded ed. New York: Oxford University Press, 2005.

Gaiduk, Ilya V. *Confronting Vietnam: Soviet Policy toward the Indochina Conflict, 1954–1963.* Washington, DC: Woodrow Wilson Center Press, 2003.

Gavin, Francis J. "The Gold Battles within the Cold War: American Monetary Policy and the Defense of Europe, 1960–1963." *Diplomatic History* 26, no. 1 (Winter 2002).

Gavin, James M. *On to Berlin: Battles of an Airborne Commander, 1943–1946.* New York: Viking Press, 1978.

Gilbert, Marc Jason, editor. *Why the North Won the Vietnam War.* New York: Palgrave, 2002.

Goldstein, Gordon M. *Lessons in Disaster: McGeorge Bundy and the Path to War in Vietnam.* New York: Henry Holt and Company, 2008.

Goscha, Christopher E. "The Maritime Nature of the Wars for Vietnam (1945–1975): A Geo-Historical Reflection." *War & Society* 24, no. 2 (November 2005).

———. "Vietnam and the World Outside: The Case of Vietnamese Communist Advisers in Laos (1948–62)." *South East Asia Research* 12, no. 2 (July 2004).

Hannah, Norman B. *The Key to Failure: Laos and the Vietnam War.* Lanham, MD: Madison Books, 1987.

Herring, George. *America's Longest War: The United States and Vietnam, 1950–1975.* 4th ed. Boston: McGraw Hill, 2002.

Jacobs, Seth. *The Universe Unraveling: American Foreign Policy in Cold War Laos.* Ithaca, NY: Cornell University Press, 2012.

Johns, Andrew L. *Vietnam's Second Front: Domestic Politics, the Republican Party, and the War.* Lexington: University Press of Kentucky, 2010.

Johnson, Robert David, and Kent B. Germany, editors. *The Presidential Recordings: Lyndon B. Johnson. Volume IV, Toward the Great Society, February 1, 1964–March 8, 1964.* New York: W. W. Norton & Company, 2007.

Johnson, Robert David, and David Shreve, editors. *The Presidential Recordings: Lyndon B. Johnson. Volume II, The Kennedy Assassination and the Transfer of Power, November 1963–January 1964.* New York: W. W. Norton & Company, 2007.

Kaiser, David. *American Tragedy: Kennedy, Johnson, and the Origins of the Vietnam War.* Cambridge: Belknap/Harvard, 2000.

Kempe, Frederick. *Berlin 1961: Kennedy, Khrushchev, and the Most Dangerous Place on Earth.* New York: G. P. Putnam's Sons, 2011.

Kislenko, Arne. "A Not So Silent Partner: Thailand's Role in Covert Operations, Counter-Insurgency, and the Wars in Indochina." *Journal of Conflict Studies* (Summer 2004): http://journals.hil.unb.ca.

Kraemer, Alfred J., and Edward C. Stewart. "Cross-Cultural Problems of U.S. Army Personnel in Laos and Their Implications for Area Training." September 1964. George Washington University Human Resources Research Office.

Langer, Paul F. "The Soviet Union, China, and the Pathet Lao: Analysis and Chronology." RAND Corporation, 1972.

Langer, Paul F., and Joseph J. Zasloff. *North Vietnam and the Pathet Lao: Partners in the Struggle for Laos.* Cambridge: Harvard University Press, 1970.

Leary, William M. "CIA Air Operations in Laos, 1955–1974." Center for the Study of Intelligence, *Studies in Intelligence* (Winter 1999–2000). www.foia.cia.gov.

Logevall, Fredrik. *Choosing War: The Lost Chance for Peace and the Escalation of War in Vietnam.* Berkeley: University of California Press, 1999.

———. *Embers of War: The Fall of an Empire and the Making of America's Vietnam.* New York: Random House, 2012.

McKee, Guian A. *The Presidential Recordings: Lyndon B. Johnson. Volume VI, Toward the Great Society, April 14, 1964–May 31, 1964.* New York: W. W. Norton & Company, 2007.

McMasters, H. R. *Dereliction of Duty: Lyndon Johnson, Robert McNamara, the Joint Chiefs of Staff, and the Lies That Led to Vietnam.* New York: HarperCollins Publishers, 1997.

McNamara, Robert S., James G. Blight, and Robert Brigham. *Argument without End: In Search of Answers to the Vietnam Tragedy.* New York: Public Affairs, 1999.

Moise, Edwin E. "JFK and the Myth of Withdrawal." In *A Companion to the Vietnam War,* edited by Marilyn B. Young and Robert Buzzanco. Oxford: Blackwell Publishers, 2002.

Naftali, Timothy, editor. *The Presidential Recordings: John F. Kennedy, The Great Crises. Volume I.* New York: W. W. Norton & Company, 2001.

Naftali, Timothy, and Philip Zelikow, editors. *The Presidential Recordings: John F. Kennedy, Volume II, The Great Crises.* New York: W. W. Norton & Company, 2001.

Nguyen, Lien-Hang T. *Hanoi's War: An International History of the War for Peace in Vietnam*. Chapel Hill: University of North Carolina Press, 2012.

Oberdorfer, Don. *Senator Mansfield: The Extraordinary Life of a Great American Statesman and Diplomat*. Washington, DC: Smithsonian Books, 2003.

Ostermann, Christian F., editor. "Inside China's Cold War." *Cold War International History Project Bulletin* (Fall 2007–Winter 2008).

Palmer, Bruce, Jr. "US Intelligence and Vietnam." *Studies in Intelligence* (1984). www.foia.cia.gov.

Pelz, Stephen E. "When Do I Have Time to Think?" *Diplomatic History* (April 1979).

Prados, John. *The Blood Road: The Ho Chi Minh Trail and the Vietnam War*. New York: John Wiley & Sons, 1998.

———. "Laos: The Geneva Protocol and the Not-So-Secret War." *VVA Veteran* (January–February 2007). www.vva.org.

———. "The Last NSAM Standing." National Security Archive, April 21, 2011. www.gwu.edu/~nsarchiv/.

———. *Lost Crusader: The Secret Wars of CIA Director William Colby*. Oxford: Oxford University Press, 2003.

Reeves, Richard. *President Kennedy: Profile of Power*. New York: Simon & Schuster, 1994.

Rusk, Dean. "The President." *Foreign Affairs* (April 1960).

Rust, William J. *Before the Quagmire: American Intervention in Laos, 1954–1961*. Lexington: University Press of Kentucky, 2012.

———. *Kennedy in Vietnam*. New York: Charles Scribner's Sons, 1985.

Schlesinger, Arthur M., Jr. *A Thousand Days: John F. Kennedy in the White House*. New York: Houghton Mifflin, 1965.

Sherman, Stephen. *Who's Who from HOTFOOT/WHITESTAR*. Houston: RADIX Press, 2004.

Sorensen, Theodore C. *Kennedy*. New York: Harper and Row, 1965.

Stanton, Shelby L. *Green Berets at War: US Forces in Southeast Asia, 1956–1975*. Novato, CA: Presidio Press, 1985.

Stuart-Fox, Martin. *A History of Laos*. New York: Cambridge University Press, 1997.

Sturdevant, C. V., J. M. Carrier, and J. L. Edelman. "An Examination of the Viet Cong Reaction to the Vietnamese Strategic Hamlet Program." Santa Monica, CA: RAND Corporation, 1964.

Tarling, Nicholas. *Britain and the Neutralisation of Laos*. Singapore: NUS Press, 2011.

Taubman, William. *Khrushchev: The Man and His Era*. New York: W. W. Norton & Company, 2003.

Taylor, John M. *General Maxwell Taylor: The Sword and the Pen*. New York: Doubleday, 1989.

Taylor, Maxwell D. *The Uncertain Trumpet*. New York: Harper and Brothers, 1960.

Thomas, Evan. *Robert Kennedy: His Life*. New York: Simon & Schuster, 2000.

Thorpe, D. R. *Supermac: The Life of Harold Macmillan.* London: Chatto & Windus, 2010.

Toye, Hugh. *Laos: Buffer State or Battleground.* London: Oxford University Press, 1968.

United Nations. "Declaration on the Neutrality of Laos." *Treaty Series,* no. 6564. New York: United Nations, 1963. www.un.org.

———. "Report of the Security Council Sub-Committee under Resolution of 7 September 1959." November 5, 1959. S/4236. www.un.org.

Urquhart, Brian. *Hammarskjold.* New York: W. W. Norton, 1972.

Usowski, Peter S. "Intelligence Estimates and US Policy toward Laos." *Intelligence and National Security* 6, no. 1 (April 1991).

Verrone, Richard Burks. "Behind the Wall of Geneva: Lao Politics, American Counterinsurgency, and Why the U.S. Lost in Laos, 1961–1965." PhD dissertation, Texas Tech University, 2001.

Warner, Roger. *Shooting at the Moon: The Story of America's Clandestine War in Laos.* South Royalton, VT: Steerforth Press, 1996.

Wehrle, Edmund F. "'A Good, Bad Deal': John F Kennedy, W. Averell Harriman, and the Neutralization of Laos, 1961–1962." *Pacific Historical Review* 67, no. 3 (August 1998).

Wing, Roswell B., et al. *Case Study of US Counterinsurgency Operations in Laos, 1955–1962.* McLean, VA: Research Analysis Corporation, 1964.

Zasloff, Joseph J. *The Pathet Lao: Leadership and Organization.* Lexington, MA: Lexington Books, 1973.

Zasloff, Joseph J., and Leonard Unger, editors. *Laos: Beyond the Revolution.* New York: St. Martin's Press, 1991.

Zeiler, Thomas W. *Dean Rusk: Defending the American Mission Abroad.* Wilmington, DE: SR Books, 2000.

Zelikow, Philip, and Ernest May, editors. *The Presidential Recordings: John F. Kennedy, Volume III, The Great Crises.* New York: W. W. Norton & Company, 2001.

Zhai, Qiang. *China and the Vietnam Wars, 1950–1975.* Chapel Hill: University of North Carolina Press, 2000.

Zhang, Xiaoming. "China's Involvement in Laos during the Vietnam War, 1963–1975." *Journal of Military History* (October 2002).

Zubok, Vladislav M. *A Failed Empire: The Soviet Union in the Cold War from Stalin to Gorbachev.* Chapel Hill: University of North Carolina Press, 2007.

Index

CPSIA information can be obtained at www.ICGtesting.com
Printed in the USA
BVOW05*1653030414

349584BV00003B/4/P